WITHDRAWN
UTSA LIBRARIES

B·E·Y·O·N·D
REGULATION

B·E·Y·O·N·D
REGULATION

The Informal Economy in Latin America

A study prepared for the International Labour Office within the framework of the World Employment Programme

edited by
Víctor E. Tokman

Lynne Rienner Publishers ▪ Boulder & London

The designations employed in International Labour Office (ILO) publications, which are in conformity with United Nations practice, and the presentation of material therein do not imply the expression of any opinion whatsoever on the part of the ILO concerning the legal status of any country, area, or territory, or of its authorities, or concerning the delimitation of its frontiers.

The responsibility for opinions expressed in studies and other contributions rests solely with their authors, and publication does not constitute an endorsement by the ILO of the opinions expressed in them.

Reference to names of firms and commercial products and processes does not imply their endorsement by the ILO, and any failure to mention a particular firm, commercial product, or process is not a sign of disapproval.

This book is based on *Más allá de la regulacion: El sector informal en América Latina*, published by PREALC, Santiago.

Published in the United States of America in 1992 by
Lynne Rienner Publishers, Inc.
1800 30th Street, Boulder, Colorado 80301

and in the United Kingdom by
Lynne Rienner Publishers, Inc.
3 Henrietta Street, Covent Garden, London WC2E 8LU

©1992 by International Labour Organisation. All rights reserved by the publisher

Library of Congress Cataloging-in-Publication Data
Beyond regulation : the informal economy in Latin America / edited by Víctor E. Tokman.
Includes bibliographical references and index.
ISBN 1-55587-318-9
1. Informal sector (Economics)—Latin America. 2. Informal sector (Economics)—Law and legislation—Latin America. I. Tokman, Víctor E. II. Title.
HD2346.L38M3713   1992
330—dc20   92-14361
                                                                                       CIP

British Cataloguing in Publication Data
A Cataloguing in Publication record for this book
is available from the British Library.

Printed and bound in the United States of America

The paper used in this publication meets the requirements
of the American National Standard for Permanence of Paper
for Printed Library Materials Z39.48-1984.

Contents

Preface vii

PART 1   SYNTHESIS AND CONCLUSIONS

1   The Informal Sector in Latin America:
    From Underground to Legality, *Víctor E. Tokman*   3

PART 2   INFORMALITY AND ILLEGALITY

2   Informality and Illegality, A False Identity:
    The Case of Bolivia, *Roberto Casanovas*   23

3   Illegality in the Urban Informal Sector of
    Mexico City, *Néstor Elizondo*   55

PART 3   THE COST OF LEGALITY

4   Barriers to Legality and Their Costs for the
    Informal Sector, *Ricardo A. Lagos*   87

5   Real Versus Ideal and the Brazilian *Jeitinho*:
    A Study of Microenterprise Registry Under the New
    Microenterprise Statute, *Johanna W. Looye*   109

6   The Costs of Becoming Legal for Informal Firms:
    The Case of Venezuela, *Vanessa Cartaya*   141

PART 4 REGULATION AND INFORMALITY

7 Protection for the Informal Sector in Latin America
   and the Caribbean by Social Security or
   Alternative Means, *Carmelo Mesa-Lago*   169

8 The Taxi Market in Chile: Regulation and
   Liberalization Policies, 1978–1987, *Mariana Schkolnik*   207

9 Consequences of the Legal and Regulatory Framework in
   Peru's Taxi Market, *Eliana Chávez*   247

Bibliography   277
Index   287
About the Book and the Editor   295

Preface

In 1987, we started a regional study of policies to support the urban informal sector at the International Labour Office (ILO) Regional Employment Programme for Latin America and the Caribbean (PREALC). Activities were carried out in Bolivia, Brazil, Colombia, Chile, Ecuador, El Salvador, Guatemala, Honduras, Mexico, Panama, Peru, the Dominican Republic, Uruguay, and Venezuela. The project was financially supported by the United Nations Development Programme.

The study searched for the effects of three policy areas on employment and incomes in the informal sector. First, it dealt with administrative and legal rules that frame the functioning of informal units. Different institutional settings were identified in several countries. A second focus concerned the linkages between expenditures, both public and private, and sales, incomes, and employment in the informal sector. Finally, the project evaluated the experience in managing credit programs for the informal sector.*

This book contains the results achieved in the first area of analysis. The subject of regulations for the informal sector in Latin America has attracted great interest in recent years, given its economic, social, and political importance. At the same time, it has served to provoke other discussions, somewhat different but closely linked to this issue, such as the importance of the underground economy, the role of the state in economic regulation, and even the role of private initiative in capitalist development in peripheral countries. Despite two decades of studies of the informal sector, only recently have policies to deal with it become a matter of general concern. Academics, government officials, politicians, nongovernmental organizations, and the common citizen, for many reasons, are now taking positions and decisions

---

*As a result, three books were published in Spanish: *Más allá de la regulación: El sector informal en América Latina* (Santiago, PREALC, 1991); *Ventas informales: Relaciones con el sector moderno* (Santiago, PREALC, 1990); and *Lecciones sobre crédito al sector informal* (Santiago, PREALC, 1990).

about this central problem in the Latin American development process.

This book starts with a summary and main conclusions prepared by the coordinator of the project and editor of this book, Víctor E. Tokman. It is then divided into three parts. The first addresses the relation between informality and illegality. These two concepts are increasingly considered identical, but as the chapters sustain, they are in fact entirely different.

The second part of the book presents a series of case studies about administrative and legal costs confronted by informal units that aspire to become legal. The importance of these costs as barriers for informal growth has become a major policy and ideological issue. The chapters in this section contribute to weighing, with evidence, the effective importance of such costs and the potential impact of action in this field. Perhaps the main conclusion suggested here is that regulatory barriers are indeed important, but they are not the cause of informality, nor do they constitute a policy area that, by itself, will ensure economic development.

In the third and final part of the book, two issues are analyzed that relate to the ever-present dilemma of whether to formalize the informal units, or to informalize the formal ones, as prescriptions for policy action. The first refers to the need for and possibilities of giving social protection to those working in the informal sector. It is shown that the answer here depends on the size of the informal sector and on the health of the social security system. In some cases "formalization" can be achieved; in others there is need for major reforms, not only to improve the present system, but also to introduce new, generally private, ways to provide social protection. The latter refers to deregulation as a proposition applied to a specific market, that of taxi services. A comparative analysis shows that there are matters of public interest that supersede short-run private benefits, and these must be considered when deregulation is examined. Deregulation in this context can result in economic and social inefficiencies.

* * *

PREALC and I, as the coordinator of the project, would like to express our gratitude to all the people and institutions that made this book possible. Most of the authors are identified in their respective chapters. Following an editorial suggestion, six contributions are summarized in Chapter 4; the authors who undertook the case studies are acknowledged in that chapter. Given time and space constraints, the original versions of the chapters have been edited and, in some cases, shortened without final approval of the respective authors; any responsibility for inappropriate changes is mine. Finally, the collaboration of Ricardo A. Lagos during the editing of the book, of Emilio Klein during the coordination of the project, and of Gabriela Nathan, who went through the painful task of correcting and putting all the manuscripts into a common format, is gratefully recognized.

Víctor E. Tokman

PART 1
SYNTHESIS AND CONCLUSIONS

1

The Informal Sector in Latin America: From Underground to Legality

Víctor E. Tokman

The idea that the informal sector operated in unregulated markets and constituted a clandestine activity, mostly performed outside the law and in some cases even against it, was one of the main factors considered in the pioneering work on the sector in Kenya back in 1972. This factor, although recognized, was not allocated much significance because the focus of the analytical innovation was to study the working poor, defined as those performing low-productivity activities. In fact, the many studies undertaken after 1972 mostly followed this form of production approach, distancing themselves somewhat from the initial mix between illegality and informality.

During the 1980s the situation changed. Today regulation in general, and legality in particular, have become key conceptual tools to analyze and to prescribe solutions for the informal economy. Two different approaches have contributed to this change.

The first approach conceptualizes the informal sector as an outcome of the decentralization and reorganization of the production and work processes at the global level. The existence of the informal sector is perceived as the result of the search for flexibility and the need to reduce labor costs, which forces it to operate outside the regulatory framework. This allows the bypassing of laws and regulations, which are expensive in terms of financial costs and rigidities. Internally, the decentralization of production and its effect on work arrangements provides a functional response to the need to increase profit margins by diminishing or avoiding trade union power and by allowing the transfer of the cost of demand fluctuations outside the firm. New technologies make this process technically feasible (Piore and Sabel, 1987; Gordon, Edwards, and Reich, 1983).

At the same time, increased international competition and the rapid penetration by the newly industrialized countries of world markets heightened the emphasis on the reduction of costs, particularly labor costs, in order to retain both domestic and international markets (Portes, Castells, and Benton,

1989). As a result, the informal sector, defined as comprising all activities performed beyond government regulation, became a universal feature of increasing dimensions in developing, as well as developed, countries.

The second approach follows a neoliberal concept and is founded on the observation that informal activities are performed beyond the law in developing countries. This, in turn, is the result of inadequate legislation, excessive red tape, and inefficient bureaucracy. Both approaches recognize that informality and illegality became similar concepts, but this approach differs from the previous one in that it purports that this merging is generated by the impossibility of complying with the existing regulatory apparatus and not by the need to lower costs or to increase flexibility. Laws, procedures, and government are then targeted as being responsible for the existence of a large and increasing share of employment in low productivity and badly remunerated jobs. It is further argued that regulations constitute a barrier preventing the development of informal activities because access to resources and more dynamic markets can be gained only through the existing legal and institutional machinery (De Soto, 1986).

Our conceptualization of the informal sector in Latin America is closer to the first interpretation. In part, the informal sector is being generated as a result of economic restructuring, which has led to production decentralization. But these processes take place in a different structural context, the main characteristic of which is the existence of labor surplus. The result is a different informal sector. Decentralization ensures, by its functionality, a more dynamic insertion in terms of links with markets, technological change, and resource availability. This might well result in increased remuneration at the cost of reduced protection and stability in relation to waged working arrangements. In developing countries, the competitive pressure of excess labor in the quest for survival pushes down incomes and generates subsistence activities that are not dynamically linked to expanding modern sectors but cater to low-income markets, which lack access to capital, skills, and technology. Average incomes are low and the informal sector becomes more heterogeneous, as it contains segments with different possibilities of expansion (Tokman, 1978, 1989b).

In spite of different interpretations, the three approaches share the belief that informal activities are performed beyond regulation because of functional requirements alone or mixed with survival strategies, or simply because of an inadequate regulatory system. The observation could be common, but the diagnosis and hence the prescriptions differ. This opens a broad area for analysis. However, the objectives of this chapter are to concentrate on the common points in an attempt to test the validity of the conceptual distinction that identifies informality with illegality, and to examine the importance of the barrier presented by the regulatory framework in becoming legal and in operating within it. This chapter will end with some general conclusions about regulations and working arrangements in the informal sector.

This chapter is based on part of a cooperative research project coordinated by the author in Latin America. Sources will be duly identified in each case. In general, they refer to three types of analysis. One type is at a more aggregate level, undertaken in Bolivia and Mexico, in studies that explore the relations between informality and illegality. Another type is based on case studies of Bolivia, Brazil, Chile, Ecuador, Guatemala, Mexico, Uruguay, and Venezuela, which analyze the effect of existing barriers in terms of monetary costs and time. The third type is found in a study made of the feasibility of providing social security coverage for all those working in the informal sector. Although the conclusions are founded on this collective research base, they are not necessarily shared by the authors of each respective contribution, as they represent any author's personal reading of the results.

Illegality and Informality: The Predominance of Gray Areas

If to be legal means to comply with all existing regulations, one must consider whether the informal sector operates beyond legality. For that purpose, it is necessary to differentiate at least two stages of legality. One is legal recognition, which allows any business, firm, or individual to become a full part of the regulated economy, and usually entails registration with local and national authorities. A second stage honors legality during the actual operation of the business activity, complying with all established obligations.

Three types of legality can be distinguished according to prevailing systems. The first refers to legal recognition as a business activity, usually requiring registration and, in some cases, health and security inspections. A second sphere of legality is that relating to taxes, which implies registration for the purposes of identification as a potential contributor, but also generates a permanent commitment to pay the different taxes according to national legislation. Finally, a third aspect of legality refers to labor matters. This varies from registration as an employer and giving contracts to employees, to ensuring nonwage benefits such as annual leave, to such matters as working hours and social security contributions.

The main assumption derived from the conceptual discussion in its several variants suggests that informal activities are performed illegally, as opposed to formal ventures, which comply with existing legal requirements. At the extreme, this should imply underground economic units. Reality, however, is different. Cases at either end of the continuum running from legality to illegality do not constitute the majority; most cases are found in the middle of the continuum. To sustain this conclusion we will review the available evidence.

First, the study for Mexico by Néstor Elizondo (Chapter 3) shows that only 27 percent of the cases studied are unregistered, and at the other extreme only 18 percent can be considered fully legal, having fulfilled all registration requirements and permanently honoring commitments. Intermediate situations constitute the majority—nearly 55 percent; the most prevalent case consists of economic units that had made all the necessary registrations but had not paid all their legal obligations (see Table 1.1). In addition, it is interesting that unregistered informal units were found only in the industrial sector, mainly in home-based activities. Informal commercial activities are always located in the gray area between underground and legality.

A second source of information is provided by Roberto Casanovas (Chapter 2) for Bolivia. He reports that 49 percent of the informal units of the country were registered in the taxpayer registry (*Registro Unico de Contribuyentes*). As in the case of Mexico, higher registration (around 95 percent) is found in commerce, whereas only 18 and 15 percent of informal units in services and manufacturing, respectively, comply with this obligation. It is interesting to note that registration is even higher at the local level. In the city of La Paz, about 65 percent of all informal activities operate under a municipal license. Legality shows an important reduction when effective tax contributions are examined. Only 19 percent of those registered are paying. As in Mexico, the informal sector of Bolivia is, in terms of legal status, in an intermediate position. This should not, however, lead to an underestimation of the fiscal contribution made by the informal sector. Even street sellers, usually considered as underground par excellence, have around a 35 percent registration in La Paz and contribute US$536,000 per year to the municipal budget.

Information from case studies confirms the predominance of an intermediate status and allows the identification of distortions in what might

Table 1.1 Mexico: Enterprises by Legality Status (percentages)

Legality status	Underground	Restricted illegality	Restricted legality	Legal	Total
Number of enterprises	27.3	18.2	36.4	18.2	100.0
Sector of activity					
Manufacturing industry	46.1	23.1	7.7	23.1	59.1
Commerce	—	25.0	75.0	—	18.2
Services	—	—	80.0	20.0	22.7
Location					
Shop	9.1	27.3	36.4	27.3	50.0
Home	55.6	11.1	22.2	11.1	40.9
Without fixed location	—	—	100.0	—	9.1

Source: Elizondo (1990).

Note: Underground refers to enterprises with no registration; restricted illegality refers to enterprises with some registration at no cost or requiring only a once-for-all payment; restricted legality refers to enterprises with all required registrations but not contributing to some of them; and legal refers to enterprises with all requirements of inscription and contributions met.

appear to be legal situations. An interesting illustration, for example, is provided by Vanessa Cartaya (Chapter 6) in her study of Venezuela. A business producing and selling cosmetics (depilation wax) is underground on the production side but legal on the marketing side. This latter part of the business is split between the owner's home, where he keeps a small stock by which he justifies legal sales, and well-established premises that he rents in downtown Caracas for three hours a week. There he receives his clients and uses a business card with telephone numbers, telex, and even the fax number of the firm from which he rents. This office also provides the informal operator with secretarial help and message recording. At home, the commercial activity is legal; but in a backroom, in fact, he produces the product. Legalizing this part of his business requires many licenses because the handling of chemical inputs is subject to a variety of controls. Although his intention is to become fully legal and he has taken some steps in that direction, he meanwhile keeps a false license, lent by a friend, just in case his operation is detected by the inspectors.

This example, rather than constituting an exception, is found systematically in most developing countries. In some, such as Brazil, these situations have even become institutionalized. According to a study by Johanna W. Looye (Chapter 5), a popular way to move in the real world of Brazilian legality is with a system by which the firm registers, but then uses different sorts of arrangements (*jeitinhos*) to diminish the cost of legality. These arrangements are diverse, including, for example, underdeclaration of initial capital or declaration that the business is a new venture rather than an ongoing one (both make the business eligible to receive subsidies); registration of only some of the activities, as in the previous example of Venezuela; use of legal bills only for part of the sales; underdeclaration of incomes; use of probationary contracts to avoid being the subject of labor law obligations; and underdeclaration of the number of workers and/or wages for social security purposes. Indeed, the use of some of these *jeitinhos* is made not only by informal units; rather they are a resource also used by economic units outside the informal sector. Illegality in this broader context then becomes a criterion that cannot be used to distinguish different segments of the economy.

The main question concerns why the most common activities operate in the gray area between underground and legality. It seems that such status offers a higher probability of obtaining average incomes. In the case of Mexico, underground activities can be found at both extremes of the income distribution, whereas legal firms tend to be concentrated in the above average income bracket (more than three minimum wages). The highest frequency of enterprises with average incomes between one and three minimum wages operates under restricted legality. This arrangement allows the informal enterprise to have access to benefits, to minimize risks, and to reduce costs, particularly operational costs.

This arrangement also allows access to benefits because in most cases it is sufficient to be registered to enable the business to start operations legally. This is a requirement that generally takes a short time and does not involve high costs, particularly when in most cases it is not necessary to complete all registrations. The first registration generally gives access to organized markets because the informal shop can become visible and is entitled to give legal bills for its sales. In addition, registration potentially permits a business to request credits. This, however, has not emerged as a determining factor in the cases studied because collaterals constitute the main requirement.

Risks of sanctions are also minimized by partially legalizing activities. That is why businesses that are more exposed show a higher level of registration. Commerce activities, which need to be visible to attract their clientele, record proportionally more registration than industries that do not depend so heavily on direct sales to the public. The risk is also associated with the inspection capacity of government, which tends to be greater at the local level. This explains why in La Paz registration at that level is the highest.

Being in the gray area also allows for cost reductions by paying less taxes and/or diminishing labor costs. This is also the case for formal firms. The difference is perhaps one of degree, particularly in relation to labor costs. Informal units have a different arrangement of the work process, which is mostly organized on a family basis with fluctuating hours and high turnover and hence, in most cases, not being subject to labor protection laws. The point is that this form of production is the result of survival strategies and production decentralization in an economic environment characterized by limited resources and insufficient job creation in modern sectors. In some cases more control of existing laws could enforce labor protection, but in the majority it is not economically feasible, either because the organization of work is beyond the normative framework or simply because the surplus generated by the economic unit is insufficient to absorb additional costs. This calls for new forms of regulation to be considered.

Barriers to Becoming Legal

In spite of the difficulties of defining what is underground or legal, it is important to estimate the cost of becoming legal. This requires a series of registrations, which involve costs in terms of money and time. The time required is the result of the degree of complexity of the existing normative framework and of the efficiency of public agencies to process the applications or to undertake inspections when needed. The data available from the case studies, which are presented in Table 1.2, present three interesting pieces of information.

The first refers to the time involved in filling all the registration

Table 1.2 Costs of Entry to Legality

Country	Economic Sector	Time (Number of working days)[a]	Financial Costs			
			Without Modifications		Required Modifications	
			Amount (US$)	Percentage of Annual Profits	Amount (US$)	Percentage of Annual Profits
Bolivia	Commerce	15–30	14	2.8		
	Industry	15–30	13	0.25–1.6		
	Services	15–30	16	0.25–1.6		
Brazil	Commerce	31–60	44	3.5–7.5[b]		
	Industry	44	84	17.7[b]		
	Services	31	99	—		
Chile	Commerce	12	110	—	5,308	128.3
	Industry	65	222	2.8–5.4	11,135	147.8
Ecuador	Commerce	60–75	32	15.5	70	33.8
	Industry	180–240	239	23.4	70	6.8
Guatemala	Commerce	179	216	4.2		
	Industry	525	894	8.6		
Mexico	Commerce	83–240	210–368	—		
	Industry	83–240	210–368	—		
	Services	83–240	210–368	—		
Uruguay	Industry	75–90	337	159.5	613	290.5
	Services	75–90	405	6.1–13	613–675	19.7–10.2
Venezuela	Commerce	170–310		5.7		21.5
	Industry	170–310		23.5		181.5

Sources: Bolivia: Escobar de Pabón (1990); Brazil: Looye (see Chapter 5); Chile: Velásquez (1990); Ecuador: Placencia (1990); Guatemala: Sáenz (1990); Uruguay: Quijano and Antía (1990); and Venezuela: Cartaya (see Chapter 6).

[a] For Bolivia, Mexico, and Venezuela, this refers to calendar days. The time required was the effective time spent in Bolivia, Brazil, and Uruguay. The rest were estimated on the basis of time required for each specific legalization step.

[b] As a percentage of invested capital.

requirements. This is highly variable between countries and even within countries. The range of time involved is from one month to one year, with the exception of Guatemala where it is close to two years. The upper limit coincides with the results reported by De Soto (1986) about the time required to initiate activities in the clothing industry to be located in Lima (289 days). However, this is not the case in all countries. In some countries—for example, Ecuador, Guatemala, Mexico, and Venezuela—the time seems to be close to the upper limit, but in Bolivia, Brazil, Chile, and Uruguay the time spent in the process varies between one and three months.

The second piece of information available is that financial costs of entry are also highly variable. They can vary from US$1 paid by a street seller in

La Paz to be able to operate legally, to US$1,080 paid by a small car repair shop in Uruguay. The proportion of costs in relation to annual profits of the surveyed informal units varies from less than 2 percent to almost 160 percent (see Table 1.2).

The third piece of evidence suggests that in most cases it is more costly to legalize activities in manufacturing than in commerce.

The dates and the histories of the cases studied also allows us to make two additional comments. The first is that a key factor in determining both the time and cost involved in entry to legality is whether the unit requesting registration needs to introduce changes in its premises. These can constitute requirements relating to health, security, or other matters; final approval of registration is usually conditional on fulfilling such requirements. The increased cost can be seen in Table 1.2 to usually exceed the normal costs of legalization by a considerable margin. The issue is then whether these additional requirements constitute unjustified constraints or whether they should be enforced to protect the more general interests of the population. Three of the cases studied are illustrative of the conflict between the interests of the informal operator and those of other private and public concerns. The additional request made by labor authorities in the case of an establishment in Ecuador was to build sanitary facilities on the premises, given that three permanent workers were usually working for the firm. The cost of this construction amounted to 34 percent of the annual profits and the total costs of legalization increased to 50 percent of annual profits. In spite of the additional cost, the regulation in this case is meant to protect the workers' rights to a minimum standard of working conditions, which should be beyond discussion in any civilized society.

A second example refers to the establishment in Uruguay of an enterprise to produce sandwiches. As this is a food-producing industry, there are construction requirements to ensure proper production conditions. In this case, the requirements were the installation of protection nets on the windows to keep out insects, a spring attached to the washroom door to ensure that it closed automatically, and ceramic tiles on the floor and walls up to a height of 1.80 meters. The additional cost amounted to US$500, making it impossible for the informal entrepreneur to comply with regulations due to lack of funds. The issue here, as in the previous example, is not that this is reason enough to deregulate, because in this particular instance the norm has been introduced to protect minimum health standards to avoid risks for the consumers. The financial inability of the informal producer cannot in this case be solved at the cost of endangering consumers' health.

Finally, a third example in which there are conflicts between private and public interests can be illustrated by the situation in taxi markets. A comparative analysis made for Lima, Peru (see Chapter 9), and Santiago, Chile (see Chapter 8), shows the importance of regulations. In Lima, regulations are not observed, nor is there any will or capacity on the part of the authorities to enforce them. As a result, the taxi service is performed in very poor conditions. No meters are required, so fares are bargained each time. Car inspections and insurance are not compulsory, so the security of neither the passenger nor the public in general is protected. In addition, as the entry to the market is open, competition generated by an excess labor supply pushes down tariffs and hence net incomes are low, affecting the renewal and maintenance of cars. The case of Santiago, however, illustrates the opposite situation. Consistent with the general policies followed in the country in recent years, deregulation was also applied to the taxi market. There, however, all regulations to ensure that a public service (although performed by the private sector) maintains its standard were retained. Flexibility was introduced into the requirements for entry and tariffs. The superiority of results in terms of the service available is evident to any visitor to these two cities. The general point is that norms and regulations generally protect legitimate interests of other private groups or of the public in general. The proposals for deregulation, even if justifiable in view of the private costs that regulations entail for informal producers, cannot be socially sustained.

Another observation that can be made on the basis of the information available is that country situations differ. A typology could be made including, at one end, those countries in which the case study analyses show that legalization is not a costly process in terms of time or money. This is the case in Bolivia, Brazil, and Chile. There is also an intermediate group, in which the financial costs involved are not too high but legalization is time consuming. At the other extreme, one can group countries such as Ecuador, Guatemala, and Peru, where the process of becoming legal involves high financial costs and takes a long time.

Such classification leads to the question of causes. The first, obvious factor is the combination of regulation inadequacy and bureaucratic inefficiency—a factor that applies to most countries, and particularly to the latter group. Table 1.3 shows that countries in the most time-consuming category also require the most administrative steps. However, the correlation is not high because, although Bolivia requires the fewest administrative requirements, this is not the case for Brazil and Chile, which are similar to the countries in the intermediate group. The situation is different for a country that is highly centralized than for one in which there is decentralization. This, in turn, is also related to the administrative organization of the country. It is also linked to the efficiency of government in general, not only in processing registration permits. Chile has a traditionally efficient public administration, and hence registration can be accomplished in a shorter period.

An additional factor is the adequacy of promotional regimes, which can either help to ease the process or constitute barriers that worsen the situation. Examples of the former can be found in Bolivia and Brazil, both of which are in our first group. A major tax reform was introduced in Bolivia in 1987 to

Table 1.3 Administrative Steps Required for Registration

Country	Initial Registration	Location	Health and Security	Taxes	Labor	Total
Bolivia	4	—	—	1	—	5
Brazil	6	3	3	10	—	22
Chile	4	10	4	5	—	23
Ecuador	39[a]	—	5	6	9	60
Guatemala	4	—	10	12	5	31
Mexico	16	2	1	2	—	21
Uruguay	5	2	2	3	4	16
Venezuela	13	1	5	4	5	28

Sources: See sources for Table 1.2.
[a]Includes thirty-four steps required by promotion laws for classification.

simplify and consolidate the numerous taxes. This reform allowed for an automatic and inexpensive registration process, which, as we have seen, resulted in almost half of the informal units being registered. In Brazil, a new statute for microenterprises was introduced, accompanied by a system to help the informal producers in their registration process. This also resulted in increased legality. The opposite situation can be seen in Ecuador, where the incentives law is old and the understanding of the prevailing regulatory framework is further complicated by the sanctioning of a new law, which did not completely replace the previous one and in some cases overlapped with it. As Table 1.3 shows, Ecuador requires sixty administrative steps, of which thirty-four are related to a cumbersome process of classification and skill recognition related to the promotion law.

This shows the importance of placing the discussion in the appropriate perspective: the richness of information at the microlevel should not be allowed to mislead those responsible for the diagnosis and the proposed solutions, but should contribute to raising specific issues in a context of what should be a more general discussion. Regulations should not be seen merely as obstacles to informal entrepreneurship development, but be analyzed rather as instruments resulting from state organization and policies, incentive systems, and governmental responsibility to protect different groups and society as a whole.

The Costs of Being Legal

To the costs of entering into legality must be added those involved in complying with legal requirements during the operation of the enterprise, which relate mostly to tax and labor obligations. The information available raises several issues of policy significance.

First, the costs of remaining legal permanently mainly affect those informal units with hired workers. They do not significantly affect the self-employed or those using only unpaid family labor because they are not subject to most of the legal obligations. Second, as in the case of entry costs, the situation varies according to country, with the costs of remaining legal ranging from 17 to 70 percent of annual profits. The incidence is, however, high in all cases as they more than duplicate registration costs. In addition, there are cases similar to that in Bolivia in which—although as a result of the tax reform the permanent costs are around 13 percent of annual profits—taxes, if paid, would create a reduction of around one-third of family incomes.

Third, labor costs are the highest component of permanency costs. Taxes do not have a heavy incidence because income taxes and profits are insignificant at the prevailing level of profits in these units. Value-added tax, which is the most significant cost in most countries, greatly diminishes its impact if properly calculated. Labor costs account for the largest share, ranging from 64 percent of total costs of permanency to 90–93 percent in the cases of Bolivia and Colombia (Caro and Acevedo, 1986). This would imply an increase in labor costs of around 20 percent, absorbing what is estimated as average profit ratios for informal units (Tokman, 1988). The additional labor costs are divided more or less equally between two main components: benefits, such as vacations and thirteen-month indemnities, and contributions to social security.

Why is it that most informal units only partially observed these obligations? A first explanation is that they are unable to absorb the increased costs involved. This, in turn, is the result of the way in which the informal sector operates. Lack of access to resources and markets, in conjunction with surplus labor unable to find well-remunerated jobs, lead to heavy competition at low levels of surplus. The inability is not then a matter of insufficient funds or inadequate regulations; it is a structural constraint. A second explanation is that the work process is organized in a different manner within the informal units: labor relations are not subject to contracts, working hours and remuneration are flexible, and ad hoc payment arrangements exist.

The studies also suggest two additional observations. The first, based on an analysis of the conditions for success in Bolivia (Larrazabal, 1989), is that the growth of the informal firm brings a progressive improvement in the observance of labor obligations. Three-quarters of the successful firms studied show that as they expanded they recognized vacations and thirteen-month payments. Part of the increased benefits is then distributed to the workers through this mechanism. However, none of the successful firms was making contributions to social security. This suggests that the subject of social security goes beyond the microlevel discussion, and should be dealt with by a systemic approach.

The other observation is that this semilegal way of operation constitutes a nonconflictual working agreement. This arrangement is far removed from the class conflict environment, which historically has resulted in increased labor protection and social security. In some cases, paternalistic working relations tend to be developed in a context in which family ties, apprenticeship relations, and direct personal involvement of the owner of the informal unit prevail. No unions exist in such small-sized enterprises. In addition, the high instability associated with the sector leads workers to envisage these jobs as transitory employment. No career development is foreseen and hence the basis for contributing to social security, particularly in relation to potential retirement benefits, does not exist. This, together with the previous observation, indicates that if the incorporation of the informal units into the social security system is an objective, the process will not occur automatically because the basic assumptions upon which most of the systems are based are not relevant for this form of production.

Formalizing the Informal: The Case of Social Security

If those working in the informal sector cannot have access to social security coverage, given the characteristics of the sector, the question that should be asked is whether it is possible to ensure social security coverage by going in the opposite direction: Should the social security system be able to reach informal workers? This question has been analyzed in depth for four Latin American countries by Carmelo Mesa-Lago (see Chapter 7), who arrives at the conclusion that there is no single answer because each country constitutes a special case.

There are several key parameters that determine the feasibility of reaching universal social security. The size of the informal sector is an important factor—the larger the employment share of the sector, the more difficult the task. Feasibility also depends on the prevailing system, particularly in relation to its present coverage, the type of benefits, and its financial situation—characteristics that vary from country to country. In some countries, such as Jamaica, coverage is compulsory for all workers, including self-employed and domestic servants. In Peru, domestic servants are also supposed to be insured on a compulsory basis, but for the self-employed it is optional. The same happens for both categories of informal workers in Mexico and Costa Rica. There are also differences according to the coverage by type of benefits. Health is universally covered in most cases, whether outside the social security system through a national health service, as in Jamaica, or because the system guarantees access to hospitals, medical care, and maternity benefits for the whole population, as in Costa Rica. Finally, there are differences regarding pensions: in some cases special support is envisaged for the most impoverished, whereas in others there is a requirement of previous contributions independent of the insured person's income level.

As health coverage is high in Latin America, the main issue is basically to analyze why only between 2 and 5 percent of the self-employed, who are the largest group within the informal sector, have access to social security. Four factors help to explain this situation. First, the cost of the contribution is high. Required contributions of the self-employed are usually two to four times those of wage-workers. In relation to incomes, however, the differences are smaller because in some of the prevailing systems it is possible to contribute on the basis of a fraction of total income. The second factor is of an administrative nature, concerning problems of identification, registration, and control of social security in general, but particularly in small units. The current levels of arrears and evasion are high. The third explanation is that pensions have deteriorated in real terms and hence incentives to join the system voluntarily are low. In Jamaica, for example, average pensions are one-fifth of per capita income, being clearly insufficient to ensure an adequate level of living. Finally, access to social security does not constitute a high priority for those working in the informal sector, mostly because of their uncertain occupational career. Political pressure from the potential beneficiaries is low or nonexistent and this, as history has shown, has been one of the main factors behind increased social security coverage.

Possibilities of reaching those working in the informal sector differ according to country situations. In Chapter 7, Mesa-Lago analyzes the cases of Costa Rica, Jamaica, Mexico, and Peru. In Costa Rica it is feasible to cover all informal workers with the present system. Present coverage is already high, the informal sector is relatively small, and the financial position is sound, because operating surpluses are registered in both health and pensions. The aspect that requires attention is the high cost involved for the self-employed; perhaps a differential pension, lower than the minimum, could be introduced so a reduced contribution would be required. The answer seems to be positive also in the case of Jamaica. In spite of a large informal sector, the system presents the advantage of being limited to pensions and being of fairly recent origin. The ratio of pensioners to contributors is still very low and the expansion of the system can be absorbed given its favorable financial situation. Hence, both cases illustrate that universalization from the system to the informal units is feasible.

The situation is different in the case of Mexico. Present coverage is low and the system registers operating deficits in both health and pensions. An expansion of the system cannot be absorbed financially under these conditions. There are, however, some proposals under consideration to enlarge the coverage by state participation in the contributions of the self-employed (providing one-third of the contributions) and to offer a reduced package of services. The answer in Mexico seems to be a search for differentiation within the system.

The last country examined, Peru, clearly illustrates that the task is unfeasible. Low coverage is accompanied by an undercapitalized system with significant operational deficits, low quality of health services, and insufficient pensions. If all the informal units were covered, the Peruvian Institute of Social Security would have to expand its coverage by 180 percent and its health expenditure would have to increase by 88 percent. This requires answers outside the system. The existing system needs to be drastically reformed to cover those already incorporated adequately. Protection for those outside the system can be improved by other solidarity arrangements on a private basis. Some interesting experiences of this type are already under way in Peru.

The answer provided by a systemic approach is not uniform. In some countries, such as Costa Rica and Jamaica, it is feasible to provide universal protection, in which case what is required is to find ways to ensure that the cost involved is consistent with the absorptive capacity of those working in the informal sector. This is not just a financial problem because working arrangements and job instability also constitute strong disincentives to join the system. Cost reduction measures would probably have to be accompanied by other changes to ensure portability of contributions or to shift from benefit-defined to contribution-defined systems. There are intermediate cases such as that in Mexico, where it seems feasible to explore solutions within the system. This could imply differential benefits, but compared to the existing situation it could still result in increased equity. Finally, there are cases in which the feasible way to improve protection of informal workers can be solidarity arrangements outside the state system. These arrangements can help to mitigate the situation, but do not constitute long-term alternatives to the necessary reform of the prevailing system.

Formalizing the Informals: The Case of Taxis

An alternative to the suggested policy to allow for the productive development of the informals is to abolish the regulating barriers that protect the informal activity. It is argued that this could result in greater income possibilities for the informals and in gains for the consumers. To analyze this option in depth, the case of the taxis in Santiago, Chile (see Chapter 8), and in Lima, Peru (see Chapter 9), were selected. This activity presents the advantages of being a relatively homogeneous service and of having been subject to different degrees of regulation, both in a given country through time as well as between countries.

Given that the taxi activity is performed under conditions of regulation of access, of tariffs, and of functioning norms, the outcome is the creation of a protected market, which results in a quasi-rent for the "privileged" taxi operators. The social cost that this situation generates is shared by the users who have to pay a higher tariff and by those excluded from this activity, who have to resort to less profitable activities. The prescription is, then, to deregulate. This policy was followed in Chile, where since 1978, all requirements to operate a taxi were eliminated and tariffs previously fixed by the government were left open. In Peru, the policy is applied de facto because the number of vehicles that perform the taxi service has increased under government tolerance, and this has resulted, in fact, in free entry, flexible tariff, and no regulation of operating conditions.

A comparison of the cases studied, however, denotes a first difference in relation to the coverage of liberalization. In Chile, the norms geared to protect the taxi users and the public in general were not deregulated. These refer to the condition of the vehicle (technical revisions such as measures of the level of pollutants emitted by the engine) to compulsory car insurance, to the driver's ability (special driving license), and to working hours and itinerary. In Peru, on the contrary, these types of rules were also deregulated. The result in terms of the quality and reliability of the service offered is clear. In Chile, the quality, security, and tariff transparency is generally ensured, whereas in Peru these conditions are not met and the tariff is a matter of bargaining on a case-by-case basis. External diseconomies such as environmental damage and traffic jams in certain parts of the city are partly the result of insufficient regulation. This denotes that the norms and rules geared to protect consumers or the public in general can hardly be abolished to generate an eventual benefit to the informals who would perform as new taxi operators or to the users of the taxi service.

The effects of liberalization in access and tariff were a significant increase in the number of vehicles working as taxis and tariffs smaller than those of other means of public transport. These, in principle, were the desired effects because the quality of the service improves, the waiting time is shorter, and the cost is smaller in relative terms. There are, however, other effects that need to be considered and that condition the previous advantages. First, the increase in the number of vehicles brings about environmental external diseconomies, and in economic terms means an inefficient use of capital due to the increase in the time that the vehicles remain unused. In addition, the adjustment is achieved at decreasing net income levels because the decreased tariff is not enough to finance the increase of input prices (fuel and tires). This results in sacrificing maintenance and replacement. The situation deteriorates due to the fact that a large part of the new taxi operators take loans in foreign exchange to buy a vehicle, and hence the changes in both the rate of exchange and the rate of interest absorb an increasing proportion of operating incomes. The net result is that the improvement in the service constitutes only a short-term gain that cannot be maintained in the long run.

The inconsistency between the short and long run suggests that the balance achieved with liberalization is more apparent than real. On the one hand, the peculiar characteristics of the taxi market, even though it looks like a competitive market, is subject to a problem of geographical desynchronization of information (see Chapter 8). In this context, the tariff is relatively inelastic to the changes in the number of vehicles. The market adjusts more by quantity than by price. On the other hand, the effects depend on how general the liberalization policy is because, in general, the policy experience is framed in a context of parallel decisions to increase other key prices such as fuel, tires, rate of exchange, and rate of interest, which results in a profit squeeze of the deregulated sector.

Finally, there is a need to place the analysis of the liberalization policy in the relevant macroeconomic framework. The two case studies show the importance of the level of unemployment, of real wages, and of other variables to determine the effect of the same policy measure. For example, a greater increase of vehicles occurs when the policy of easing access is adopted when unemployment is higher, input tariffs are low, and credit is easily available. The same happens when wages deteriorate, particularly in the public sector. This generates the need for secondary employment, which does not necessarily follow the same logic of a competitive market, as there are persons who would accept an income level lower than that required to keep the taxi service running on the longer term.

There is also a need to consider the distributive changes generated by liberalization. In general, given the average income levels of taxi operators before the policy and of the beneficiaries, whether by increased access to the previously protected market or by the short-run gains for the users, there will most likely be a redistribution of middle-income groups. In the best scenario, if the new entrants were previously unemployed, there would be a progressive redistribution from the middle to the poor groups.

Conclusions

This analysis leads us to four main conclusions. First, the informal sector operates between underground and legality. In doing so, the informal producer obtains access to what he or she evaluates as important while minimizing the risks associated with illegality. Nonobservance of regulations—a common feature attributed to informality according to all interpretations—becomes a relative matter.

Second, regulations in the context of the informal sector discussion have a much longer history than the present policy of diminishing government intervention in economic activity. These rules and procedures were introduced to protect the general interest of society or to safeguard the absolute needs of those more vulnerable groups. When placed in this perspective, some of today's common prescriptions to promote the development of informal sector entrepreneurs are clearly unacceptable. There is, however, room for improvement. The studies show that a case in point involves the special promotion laws, often well intentioned but usually ill conceived; the same is true of tax systems that are the result of hundreds of modifications adding new taxes or creating special cases that result in widespread evasion. Simple and semiautomatic promotional laws and tax structures have proved to be more efficient, and they can promote the regularization of the informal sector in particular. In addition, they diminish bureaucratic interference, reducing the time and costs involved in becoming legal.

Third, there is the issue of labor legality. On this there are several comments that should be made. Although in this chapter we have defined the informal sector from the point of view of the productive unit, confusion arises between this concept and informal labor. The latter refers to nonpermanent forms of labor use, which have sometimes evolved with small productive units, implying some overlap with the former definition. Although these new arrangements can be promoted voluntarily by members of the labor force searching for work flexibility, the main impulse probably comes from the firm, both to reduce costs and to increase flexibility. This calls for new forms of regulation because the existing standards, devised for permanent workers, become inapplicable. The boundaries for part-time or decentralized arrangements should include those small enterprises created exclusively for that purpose and dependent on the parent firm for their survival. New or existing norms require additional enforcement capacity in this case.

Furthermore, many of those in the prevailing informal units are self-employed. In such units, the issue of labor standards becomes entangled with the subjective issue of self-exploitation. However, from a macrolevel perspective, access to social security becomes an important area for policy reform because the costs and incentives of the prevailing systems discriminate against the self-employed. For wage-workers in informal units, estimated at between 10 and 20 percent of total informal employment, the whole range of labor standards should in principle be applicable.

It could be useful to distinguish the type of labor regulations according to objectives, as some of them try to ensure current income and working conditions (minimum wage, vacations, working hours), whereas others are meant to protect employment security (hiring and firing regulations), and still others cover loss of income due to accident or illness or retirement (social security). From the preceding analysis, it seems that the enforcement of the first set of standards improves with the growth of the informal unit. The second is generally not applicable because of the prevailing working arrangements, and the third is not considered because of financial incapacity and even lack of interest on the part of the would-be beneficiaries.

One tactical approach could be to regulate the application of standards in order to increase the likelihood of enforcement. This could be done by diminishing the requirements or by allowing for progressive implementation. Partial solutions tend to be difficult to enforce, to perpetuate differences, and to lower the standards of those already protected because there is a downward pressure for equalization. In this sense, if the needs are so strong, the preference should be for a systemic reform rather than ad hoc adaptation.

As we have seen, the answers in relation to social security will vary, depending on the country concerned. In some countries, only a few mitigating measures outside the system can be envisaged. In others, the problems of cost of entry must be confronted, preferably avoiding increased differentiation if the prevailing system is benefit defined. This would require government contributions or very efficient management of the system, which might allow a more ambitious income redistribution. If this is not feasible, as is the case in many countries, it might be advisable to reconsider the whole system by, for instance, introducing a contribution-defined system accompanied by a minimum guaranteed income. This would introduce differentiation, but would also ensure basic coverage for all members of the labor force. The reform in this case, although probably solving the problem of access of the informal workers to social security, would surely have to be based on an evaluation of the situation of those already within the system.

The issue of hiring and firing regulations should also be approached systematically. If present regulations introduce excessive rigidities, the problem would involve modifying the general norm without taking the prevailing flexibility in the informal sector as a benchmark. The main objective should be, as in the case of social security, to improve the overall efficiency of regulation and, as a by-product, to facilitate its enforcement in the informal sector. That would be preferable to introducing special treatment, which would almost certainly result in lower labor standards for all.

Finally, although this chapter has concentrated on regulations, this should not lead to the conclusion that they are the cause of informality. As argued in the introduction to this book and elsewhere (Tokman, 1989a), operating beyond regulations represents a way to produce goods and services in a structural environment characterized by lack of well-remunerated job opportunities and by excess labor. For this reason, a policy encouraging regulation would help, but cannot constitute by itself a sound policy for supporting the informal sector.

Part 2

Informality and Illegality

2

Informality and Illegality, a False Identity: The Case of Bolivia

Roberto Casanovas

The main objective of this chapter is to provide a general analysis of the conditions of legality or illegality that prevail in the informal sector in Bolivia. The specific objectives are: (1) to quantify the extent of the informal sector in Bolivia; (2) to establish reference points to be used as the bases for determining the degree of "illegality" of the informal sector, and its significance and importance in terms of the real cover of national and municipal legal provisions; and (3) to quantify the cost of legality, as well as the advantages and disadvantages for informal activities of operating illegally, taking into account the present situation in Bolivia.

This chapter is divided into three parts. The first part contains a brief analysis of the changes caused by the employment crisis during the past decade, with special emphasis on the impact of the New Economic Policy (NPE, Nueva Política Económica), begun in August 1985, on the functioning and magnitude of the informal sector. The second part attempts to quantify the "real," or "effective," coverage of the different registers, taxes, and other types of obligation—whether national, local, or municipal—in order to establish the level of compliance and the importance of the phenomenon of illegality in the informal sector. The last part analyzes the advantages and disadvantages for informal workers of operating outside the law and the extent to which their behavior can be explained by the state's inability to verify fulfillment of obligations.

The Urban Informal Sector in Bolivia: The Global Situation

The Economic Crisis and Changes in the Employment Situation

The economic crisis that has affected Bolivia since the beginning of the 1980s has resulted in a permanent deterioration of the employment situation, which is expressed in three ways. First, there is a drastic increase in the rate of open unemployment, which has reached unprecedented levels as a direct result of the decrease in economic activity. Second, the crisis is causing reorganization of production, and its impact on the employment structure can be seen in the constant growth and expansion of jobs with low productivity, which constitute a refuge against unemployment. Third, there has been a reduction in salaries and incomes in real terms as a result of the application of neoliberal adjustment measures. To varying degrees and in line with each country's specificities, the effects of the economic crisis on the employment situation are being felt in almost all countries in the region, as can be seen from recent studies (PREALC, 1985, 1987).

Open unemployment

During the 1970s, the Bolivian economy had low levels of unemployment, generally around 6 percent. From the 1980s, notably following the emergence of the crisis and hyperinflation (1983–1985), unemployment increased to reach a level of 20 percent, which means that around 1986 one in five of the active population did not have a job (ECLAC, 1986a).

This phenomenon is closely linked to the general diminution in production, which has led to a drastic decrease in the rate of job creation, particularly in some branches of economic activity such as construction, specific manufacturing sectors, and public services, which were characterized by a high level of job creation in the 1970s. In the period 1980–1985, the gross domestic product (GDP) showed negative rates of growth, around 2.4 percent, which clearly show the level of stagnation of the economy. This situation has not changed to any significant extent to the present.

The dramatic increase in open unemployment has been accompanied as well by important changes in the characteristics of the unemployed. In the 1970s, the sectors most affected by unemployment were mostly young people, women who were not heads of the household and the highly qualified, whereas now those most affected are people formerly employed rather than newcomers to the labor market, heads of households at the most active age, and people with low qualifications. These important changes in the profile of the unemployed show that the crisis is increasingly affecting the primary population and consequently the principal wage earners of the poorest families in urban areas.

New composition of the sectoral structure of the labor force

Another effect that will undoubtedly continue beyond the short term and medium term concerns the changes in the production structure and the sectoral composition of employment caused by the economic crisis. The general orientation of economic policy during the 1980s, especially the adjustment measures that form part of the New Economic Policy in force since 1985, was directed at encouraging and promoting development of the tertiary sector (mainly commerce and banking) to the detriment of other production sectors. This is demonstrated by the positive increases in the commercial GDP of 3.9 percent and 6.5 percent, respectively in 1985 and 1986, whereas manufacturing showed rates of -9.3 percent for 1985 and 2.1 percent for 1986 (Morales, 1987).

The form in which the labor force is integrated in the urban production sector reveals three aspects: an increased trend toward the tertiary sector in the labor force, a constant reduction of salaried employment within the total employment sector, and a sustained increase in jobs in the urban informal sector. Obviously these three aspects are closely related and ultimately correspond to the changes that are taking place regarding the role and predominance of the public and private sectors in the economy.

During the period 1967–1987, far-reaching changes took place in the sectoral structure of employment in the principal cities of the departments (La Paz, Oruro, Cochabamba, Potosí, Sucre, Tarija, and Santa Cruz). Although the main branches of the tertiary sector (commerce, services, and finance) increased their share of total employment from 60 percent to 67 percent, there were variations among the different branches (see Table 2.1).

Although employment in the services sector shows a clear downward trend in its share of the overall employment percentage, commerce and finance show an upward trend. For the same period, there was a high rate of increase in employment in commerce, which paralleled the annual cumulative increase in people employed.

Moreover, manufacturing, but above all the construction industry, showed a noticeable decrease in their share of the total employment figure. The trends shown during this period were accentuated after 1985 with the adoption of the New Economic Policy, which consolidated and encouraged the trend toward the tertiary sector to the detriment of production sectors. The

Table 2.1 Breakdown of Urban EAP by Branch of Activity, 1976–1987 (percentages)

	1976	1987
Agriculture	2.7	1.7
Commerce	15.1	25.9
Construction	10.9	6.5
Electricity, gas, and water	0.3	0.3
Finance	2.5	3.9
Manufacturing	16.2	14.4
Mining	3.0	2.2
Services	42.0	37.3
Transport	7.3	7.8
Total urban, economically active population (numbers)	462,449	848,125

Source: INE (1976, 1987).

indiscriminate opening to foreign trade, the liberalization of all goods and services, the wage freeze, the free hiring of labor, and the policy of "relocating" employees in the public sector all constituted a favorable background for accentuation of this process.

Another effect of the crisis on employment concerns the form in which workers are integrated in the urban economic structure. One way of approaching this study is through an analysis of the employment structure by job category, which shows indirectly the extension of salaries as a form of remuneration for work. It also shows the growing importance of other ways of organizing production in which wages are not the main form of remuneration. Table 2.2 illustrates these changes for the period 1976–1987.

A noticeable reduction in the percentage of wage earners in the overall employment structure can be seen in Table 2.2 (68.2 percent to 54.5 percent), and, as a counterpart, an increase in jobs for one-person economic units and family work units. In the former case, this is due to reductions in the number of workers (as a result of the crisis in the manufacturing industry and the opening of the market to foreign trade) and of domestic employees (which can be explained by the lower salaries and incomes of the middle classes, who have had to give up this service), which has affected mainly women's employment. In the latter case, the increase in the percentages of self-employed, unpaid family members, and employers is consistent with the growth of employment in the informal sector, particularly in activities with low productivity and profitability in the commerce and services sectors and, to a lesser extent, in manufacturing. Independently of the economic and social implications of the phenomenon of growth in employment in family and small-scale enterprises, almost half of Bolivia's urban workers do not have access to social security nor to other social benefits provided for in the General Labor Law.

The foregoing analysis would be incomplete without consideration of the employment structure related to the various forms of organization of

Table 2.2 Breakdown of Urban EAP by Job Category, 1976–1987 (percentages)

	1976	1987
Employees	68.2	54.5
Workers	16.8	11.0
Employees	40.3	38.6
Domestic employees	11.1	4.9
Nonemployees	31.8	45.5
Employers	1.7	4.5
Independent professionals	1.6	1.4
Self-employed	27.6	35.3
Unpaid family workers	0.9	4.3

Source: INE (1976, 1987).

production that coexist in the urban economic structure. This analytical perspective allows the identification of more homogeneous forms of work organization from the point of view of dominant labor relations (Casanovas, Escobar de Pabón, and Ormachea, 1982).

It has thus been possible to identify the state, enterprise, semienterprise, family, and domestic service sectors, which differ according to the dominant labor relations within each business, the various forms of ownership of the means of production, and the degree of participation by owners in the processes of production, exchange, or supply of services. These five sectors show differing patterns of relationships among themselves, and their ability to create jobs varies according to the economic situation at any given time.

For the purposes of this study, the semienterprise sector means the sector composed of small enterprises whose economic activities and organization do not differ substantially from economic units in the family sector, although the amount of capital invested and the scale of the enterprise's operations necessitate the recruitment of permanent salaried workers. Unlike capitalist enterprises, the owner, in addition to looking after the organization and administration of the enterprise, participates directly and actively in the production process. The division of labor—generally not highly developed—and the criteria governing recruitment of workers are directly related to increases in the means of production. Given the small scale of operations and the strong fluctuations in demand affecting such enterprises, the employees are subject to a high level of employment instability. Moreover, the economic organization of enterprises in the family sector is based on ownership of the means of production and work carried out personally by the producer himself. Members of a self-employed worker's family group may participate in the enterprise's activities as unpaid family workers. Organization of production therefore basically centers on the family labor force with some participation by apprentices and/or possibly salaried workers. The small size of this type of business does not allow for a better division of labor. In any event, manual labor predominates over mechanized production. Minimum technology is used in the production process, consistent with the simplicity of the processes employed. In many cases, workers in this sector habitually use consumer durables as capital assets; for example, they use their homes as production and sales outlets. The relative "ease of entry" into this sector makes it possible for a large number of women to participate in self-employed activities.

During the period under review, important changes took place in the capacity of the aforementioned sectors to absorb employment (see Table 2.3). To make the definitions used in this book compatible with those of PREALC, employment in the state and enterprise sectors will be termed the "formal sector," and that related to semienterprises and family units will be termed the "informal sector."

At the global level, between 1976 and 1987, the formal sector's share of

Table 2.3 Distribution of Urban EAP by Sector, 1976–1987 (percentages)

	1976	1987
Formal sector	44.2	41.2
State	33.9	23.4
Enterprises	10.3	17.8
Informal sector	44.5	54.6
Semienterprises	16.1	18.1
Family units	28.4	36.5
Domestic service	11.2	4.2

Source: INE (1976, 1987).

total employment decreased from 44.2 percent to 41.2 percent. The reduction in the relative importance of the formal sector in overall employment can be explained by the drastic reduction in employment in the public sector, mainly due to low salaries, wage freezes, and the policy of mass layoffs implemented by the government beginning in August 1985. This trend contrasted with the increase in the percentage share of the private enterprise sector, from 10.3 percent to 17.8 percent for the same period, which shows that some branches of activity benefited from the NPE and demonstrated a dynamic capacity to create jobs.

Furthermore, the impact of the economic crisis on income levels in medium-income sectors led to a dramatic fall in demand for domestic services and resulted in a drop in this sector's percentage share of total employment from 11.2 percent in 1976 to 4.2 percent in 1987.

In contrast, toward 1987, family units and semienterprises in the informal sector showed a clear trend toward an increase in employment, amounting to almost 55 percent of total urban employment—a situation that underlines the true magnitude of the employment problem in Bolivia.

The New Economic Policy and the Growth of the Informal Sector in Bolivia

The economic measures contained in Supreme Decree No. 21.060, adopted on August 29, 1985, gave rise to the New Economic Policy, whose implementation proved extremely costly for low-income social sectors and particularly for workers in the informal sector. The NPE basically had two objectives: to reduce hyperinflation by stabilizing the economy and to reestablish "the State's authority over the public administrative and production apparatus through the restructuring and decentralization of public enterprises." However, the implicit objectives of this series of economic policy measures—in the medium and long term—were not only to transform the structure and functioning of the Bolivian economy but also the role of the public and private sectors, giving the latter pride of place in economic policy and future development plans. This is the significance of "letting market forces" define the fundamental orientation of the economy, including the role and scope of the public sector, especially public enterprises (Casanovas, 1986).

Within the framework of the NPE, the following provisions have a direct or indirect effect on the informal sector:

- Liberalization of foreign trade, mainly the free import of goods;
- Liberalization of the prices of all goods and services, elimination of subsidies on the principal products in the family shopping basket, and fixing of "real charges" for essential collective consumer services (e.g., electricity and water);
- Decentralization of the major revenue-earning enterprises in the public sector and shutting down of some enterprises in the mineral-metallurgical sector;
- Free recruitment of staff in both the public and private sectors and "relocation";
- Consolidation of all bonuses additional to basic salaries and freezing of wages.

Freedom of recruitment, provided for in Supreme Decree No. 21.060, together with the policy of mass dismissal (relocation) in both the public and private sectors, led to an unprecedented increase in the rate of open unemployment from 1985. The Bolivian Workers' Union (*Central Obrera Boliviana*) estimates that during the first two years of implementation of the New Economic Policy around 50,000 workers in the public sector, half of whom worked in nationalized mining companies, lost their jobs. According to official sources, in 1987 the unemployment rate reached 21.5 percent. Although there is justified doubt concerning the reliability of official information on the employment situation, unemployment has become one of the most critical social problems faced by the present government.

Because of the very limited possibility of finding a job in the public or private enterprise sectors, a large number of the unemployed have turned to the informal sector, especially to activities such as commerce and services, which do not require high levels of qualification and can be started with very small amounts of capital. This rapid increase in employment in the informal sector has led to increased competition among informal units in a market that is not favorable to expansion in the short term.

To the constant increase in urban unemployment must be added the ongoing deterioration in workers' salaries and wages. According to the review *Coyuntura Económica Andina (Andean Economic Situation)*, workers have suffered an initial reduction of 37 percent in purchasing power as a result of the stabilization plan. The incorporation of bonuses in the basic salary, the abolition of subsidized shops in large enterprises, and the liberalization of prices of all goods and services have resulted in a substantial reduction of incomes in real terms for wage-earners, who represent approximately 55 percent of the urban labor force. This reduction in purchasing power has had a direct negative effect on demand for the goods and services supplied by the informal sector.

In addition, the policy of unrestricted access of foreign goods and the increase in smuggled goods from neighboring countries have resulted in the collapse of the manufacturing industry, faced with the impossibility of competing with goods from outside. The current cost structure in small-scale manufacturing industries makes it virtually impossible to compete with products imported legally or illegally, and this situation has also directly affected crafts workshops. Integration of this vast contingent of new informal workers, taking into account the constant decrease in demand, can therefore be effected only by lowering present income levels still further.

One interesting aspect that has emerged as a result of the economic crisis is the rate of increase of employment and the size and present structure of the informal sector. This analysis will subsequently serve as a basic reference for the following chapters. During the last eleven years, total employment has grown at a rate of 5.6 percent annually, whereas employment in the informal sector has risen at an annual average rate of 7.6 percent. The result of this trend has been that, up to 1987, 55 percent of total employment in Bolivia's major cities (equivalent to 451,106 workers) has been related to informal activities—37 percent in family units and 18 percent in semienterprises. Taking as a basis the average number of workers in each business in the various sectors of activity, it is possible to estimate the approximate number of informal enterprises existing in the major cities, as shown in Table 2.4.

Table 2.4 Breakdown of Informal Enterprises by Branch of Activity, According to Sector, 1987 (percentages)

	Informal sector	Family sector	Semi-enterprise sector
Manufacturing	16.0	14.6	21.0
Construction	7.2	6.1	11.0
Commerce	44.8	50.3	24.9
Transport	8.0	8.2	7.2
Finance	2.9	2.1	5.5
Services	21.2	18.6	30.4
Informal enterprises (numbers)	335,239	262,750	72,489

Source: Calculated on the basis of information from INE (1987).
Note: The total number of enterprises refers only to those identified by branches and do not coincide with the tables following, which refer to regional breakdown and national aggregates.

The economic crisis has led to considerable focusing of the informal sector's economic activity on commerce (44.8 percent), mainly in the form of family units. In second place are services and manufacturing, which together account for 37.2 percent of informal enterprises. Attention should be drawn to the importance of these two branches of activity in the semienterprise sector, where together they account for 51.4 percent of enterprises permanently employing salaried workers, although on a small scale. Despite the crisis and economic policies that do not encourage development and consolidation of production sectors, within the informal sector some specific branches of manufacturing and production-support services are capable of future growth and expansion.

Levels of Coverage and the Cost of Legality

Main National and Municipal Registers

Single National Register of Taxpayers

To define overall requirements in the light of the specificities of each of the taxes fixed under the Tax Reform Law (LRT, *Ley de Reforma Tributaria*) and to replace the taxpayers' certification and certificate of registration with the General Directorate of Inland Revenue (DGRI, *Dirección General de la Renta Interna*), the government adopted Supreme Decree No. 21.520. This decree provided for the continuation of the Single National Register of Taxpayers (RUC, *Registro Nacional Unico de Contribuyentes*) established by Decree Law No. 13.622 on June 3, 1976, under the responsibility of the DGRI.

This supreme decree, enacted on February 13, 1987, prescribes that all natural persons or legal entities subject to value-added tax, the value-added tax complementary regime, taxes on transactions, the presumptive income of enterprises, and specified consumer goods, as well as those empowered to collect such taxes, must be registered in the RUC.

For the purposes of compiling the list of taxpayers, the regulations of the Single National Register of Taxpayers, contained in Administrative Decision No. 05-53-87 of February 20, 1987, differentiate between the General Regime (RG, Régimen General), basically directed at the modern sector of the economy; the Simplified Tax Regime (RTS, *Régimen Tributario Simplificado*), which mainly concerns the urban informal sector; and the Integrated Tax System (STI, *Sistema Tributario Integrado*) for carriers, and make it obligatory to submit forms F.3014 in the first case, F.3027 in the second, and F.3115 in the third.

Supreme Decree No. 21.521 of February 13, 1987, established the Simplified Tax Regime, which harmonizes taxes on the value-added transactions, the presumptive income of enterprises, and the value-added tax complementary regime. The objective was to broaden the tax basis by incorporating retailers, stallholders, and craftsmen through a simplified flexible system for the payment of their tax obligations.

The RTS originally established four categories of taxpayer according to their levels of income from sales and services and their estimated capital, equivalent to 20 percent of the total annual income from sales or services. The previous scale fixed an annual tax of Bs 250 (US$128) payable every two months in six installments for the first category, corresponding to the lowest level of taxpayer, and Bs 2,400 (US$1,129) for the fourth category, corresponding to the highest level.

This classification of taxpayers under the RTS was rejected by the principal national and provincial organizations of trade unions, retailers, and craftsmen because its implementation would have a significant effect on already reduced levels of income in the sector. For three months the sector carried on an intense campaign against the measure, accompanied by negotiations between the leaders of the National Confederation of Trade Unions, Retailers, and Craftsmen (*Confederación Nacional de Gremiales, Comerciantes Minoristas y Artesanos*), the Confederation of Bolivian Craftsmen's Trade Unions (*Confederación Sindical de Trabajadores Artesanos de Bolivia*), and the Ministry of Revenue. As a result of this process, on May 28, 1987, the government issued Supreme Decree No. 21.612, which added two further categories (A and B) "with the object of facilitating compliance with the aforementioned obligations on the part of the retail sector." Taxpayers under the RTS are therefore subject to the scale of taxes shown in Table 2.5.

On April 11, 1988, the Single Register of Taxpayers, with its three established systems (General Regime, Simplified Tax Regime, and Integrated Tax System) had a national coverage of 274,219 potential taxpayers as a result of the registration carried out by the twenty-six local offices of the General Directorate of Inland Revenue. Details of this registration are shown in Table 2.6.

Table 2.5 Simplified Tax Regime: Annual Tax and Bimonthly Installment by Category (in Bs)

Category	Annual Income	Estimated Capital	Annual Tax	Bimonthly Installment
A	under 1,500	300	75	13
B	1,501–3,000	600	150	25
1	3,001–5,000	1,000	250	42
2	5,001–10,000	2,000	500	83
3	10,001–24,000	4,800	1,200	200
4	24,001–48,000	9,600	2,400	400

Source: Supreme Decree No. 21.612 of May 28, 1987.

Table 2.6 Total Number Registered in the RUC by Type of Regime (April 4, 1988)

Type of Regime	Total Number Registered	Percentage of Total
General regime (RG)	94,804	34.6
Legal entities	7,759	
Natural persons	86,729	
Undivided succession	316	
Simplified Tax Regime (RTS)	177,557	64.8
Integrated Tax System (STI)	1,858	0.6
Total	274,219	100.0

Source: Calculated on the basis of information from the General Directorate of Inland Revenue, 1988.

It is significant, but not surprising, that around two-thirds of those registered in the RUC come under the Simplified Tax Regime, which mainly covers economic units in the informal sector. The low number of those under the Integrated Tax System is noteworthy in view of the fact that up to 1987 the number of public service vehicles registered with the Bolivian Police's National Registration Department amounted to 50,840. It should be pointed out that a large proportion of these do not belong to public transport enterprises and therefore do not come within the scope of application of the General Regime, and even less the Integrated Tax System.

The statistical information available shows that up to the first months of 1988 the RUC achieved a good level of coverage of activities in the informal sector, despite the enormous difficulties involved in registering these activities, which take place on a small scale. Of the estimated total of 338,638 informal economic units in all the departmental capitals except Trinidad (Beni) and Cobija (Pando), 166,591 were registered in the RUC under the Simplified Tax Regime, showing that until April 1988 total coverage of potential taxpayers in the urban informal sector had reached 49 percent (see Table 2.7).

However, an analysis of registration by city indicates that levels of coverage vary. The cities with the highest rates of coverage are Oruro (71.6 percent) and La Paz (58.6 percent), and those with the lowest rates are Tarija (27.1 percent) and Santa Cruz (28.4 percent). In the other cities (Cochabamba, Potosí, and Sucre), the RUC coverage is close to the national average.

An analysis of the situation by sector or branch of activity also shows that there are significant variations in the level of coverage. Whereas in commerce, 95.1 percent of the estimated number of informal units are registered in the RUC, in the services sector and manufacturing (crafts), coverage was only 18.3 percent and 15.0 percent, respectively (see Table 2.8). In the other

Table 2.7 RUC Coverage Under the Simplified Tax Regime by City

City	Number of Informal Economic Units	Number Registered in the RUC	Coverage (in percent)
Cochabamba	43,398	22,785	52.5
La Paz	154,188	90,352	58.6
Oruro	21,401	15,315	71.6
Potosí	10,673	5,434	50.9
Santa Cruz	87,945	25,018	28.4
Sucre	9,974	4,685	47.0
Tarija	11,059	3,002	27.1
Total	338,638	166,591	49.2

Sources: The number of informal economic units are calculated on the basis of information from the INE (1987). The number registered in the RUC are calculated on the basis of information from the General Directorate of Inland Revenue, April 1988.

Table 2.8 RUC Coverage Under the Simplified Tax Regime by Branch of Activity

Branch of Activity	Number of Informal Economic Units	Number Registered in the RUC	Coverage (in percent)
Manufacturing	53,646	8,030	15.0
Construction	24,064	1,049	4.4
Commerce	150,216	142,829	95.1
Transport	26,721	3,001	11.2
Finance	9,606	805	8.4
Services	70,986	13,023	18.3
Total	335,239	168,737	50.3

Sources: Same as Table 2.7.

branches of activity, where the presence of the informal sector is not very important, levels of coverage are still lower, varying between 4.4 percent and 11.2 percent. This situation, with slight variations, can be found in practically all of Bolivia's major cities.

Available information shows a high concentration of potential taxpayers in the lowest categories of the scale: almost 75 percent are to be found in category A (annual income below Bs 1,500 and estimated capital of approximately Bs 300). Combining categories A and B, 88 percent of those registered under the RTS declare annual incomes below Bs 3,000 and an estimated capital of up to Bs 600 (see Table 2.9). These figures are true for nearly all of Bolivia's main cities except Santa Cruz, which has a higher proportion in the intermediate categories.

A second aspect that should be highlighted is the determining influence of the cities of the La Paz–Cochabamba–Santa Cruz axis in relation to the total registered. Just over three-quarters of those registered come from these three cities, particularly La Paz, which has 50 percent of the total. And another significant fact is that, of the 90,352 registered in La Paz, 26,270 (29 percent) are in the city of El Alto, which thus has more contributors registered than either Santa Cruz or Cochabamba.

A third feature is that the information shows that the breakdown of potential contributors by branch of economic activity does not correspond to the sectoral breakdown by informal economic unit. Out of the total registered in the RUC, 84.8 percent have an economic activity related to commerce, whereas in the sectoral breakdown, informal activities in the commerce sector account for only 44.8 percent (see Table 2.10).

Important differences can also be seen in the case of services and manufacturing (crafts). One possible explanation for this phenomenon of

Table 2.9 Number of Those Registered in the RUC Under the Simplified Tax Regime by City and Category

City	Total	Category					
		A	B	1	2	3	4
Cochabamba	22,785	16,018	3,625	2,533	489	100	20
La Paz	90,352	73,206	9,234	6,146	1,389	296	81
Oruro	15,315	12,727	1,414	1,029	116	22	7
Potosí	5,434	4,408	649	315	50	10	2
Santa Cruz	25,018	13,303	5,370	4,580	1,415	293	57
Sucre	4,685	3,618	826	170	51	16	4
Tarija	3,002	2,201	461	247	72	13	8
Other	10,966	6,930	1,861	1,650	393	109	23
Total	177,557	132,411	23,440	16,670	3,975	859	202

Source: General Directorate of Inland Revenue Tax.

Table 2.10 Informal Economic Units and Registration in the RUC by Branch of Activity (in percentages of total)

Branch of Activity	Informal Economic Unit	Registered in the RUC
Manufacturing	16.0	4.7
Construction	7.2	0.6
Commerce	44.8	84.8
Transport	8.0	1.8
Finance	2.9	0.4
Services	21.2	7.7

Sources: Informal economic unit percentages are calculated on the basis of information from the INE (1987). Percentages for total RUC registrants are calculated on the basis of information from the General Directorate of Inland Revenue, 1987.

excessive concentration of registered activities in commerce is that the latter is a "visible" activity and is therefore subject to greater control and inspection mechanisms than is the case for crafts workshops and services.

Another factor that explains this situation is the degree of development of retail trade unions, which in many cases have played an important role in persuading their members to register in several registers, including the RUC. Finally, it is possible that in some branches the level of income of retail traders is higher than that of craftsmen and other service workers. From this point of view, those in retail trade are in a better economic position to fulfill their tax obligations.

Concerning the amount of capital and the number of employees, information could be obtained only for La Paz. This shows that, on average, the capital of economic units registered under the RTS is Bs 278 (US$116). These data are related to the structure of the sector, which is highly concentrated in commerce and in category A, which includes enterprises with capital up to Bs 300. A study of self-employed workers in La Paz showed that 65 percent declared capital lower than $b 50,000 (US$100) (Casanovas and Escobar de Pabón, 1984). For those registered under the RTS, 74 percent declared the total capital of their economic units to be less than Bs 240 (US$100).

In parallel with the above, almost all (99.2 percent) those registered under the RTS declared that they were self-employed, situating themselves unequivocally in the family unit sector of the urban economy, in which there are no permanent employees. The few businesses that declared dependent salaried workers have a maximum of six employees. This information suggests that some owners of enterprises that are registered under the RTS do not declare the employment of dependent workers because of all the implications of fulfilling legal provisions under labor and social security legislation.

National Register of Commerce

The scope of application of the National Register of Commerce (RNC, *Registro Nacional de Comercio*) makes it compulsory to register all commercial activities in the widest sense including manufacturing, services, and all economic activities in the market sector, in addition to commerce. However, Article 8.3 of the Code of Commerce excludes economic activities in the family sector of the economy from this obligation, stating that "(3) manual work and services by craftsmen, workers and others who do not have the status of enterprises and whose income depends on such products . . . are not commercial acts."

The obligation to register in the RNC therefore concerns only semi-enterprises that work in the informal sector and, of course, all those belonging to the private enterprise sector. Nevertheless, the special way in which many semienterprises are organized makes it impossible for them to fulfill some of the requirements for registration in the RNC. For example, many cannot submit balance sheets because they do not keep proper accounts. Another fact that supports this conclusion is that, out of a total of 74,301 businesses in La Paz registered in the RUC as being under the RTS, only 104 (about 0.1 percent) declare that they are registered in the RNC.

Table 2.11 shows an estimate of the number of businesses in 1987 at the national level, by sector or organizational structure, and the number of registrations in the RNC. The table shows that the RNC has a global coverage of only about 19 percent of the estimated total of businesses in the private enterprise and semienterprise sectors. On the assumption that 100 percent of the enterprise sector fulfills this legal obligation, only approximately 10 percent of semienterprises (undoubtedly those with the most capital) are registered in the RNC.

National Register of Small-Scale and Crafts Industries

One of the functions and duties of the National Register of Small-Scale and Crafts Industries (INBOPIA, *Registro Nacional de Pequeña Industria y Artesanía*), defined in paragraphs 13 and 14 of Article 7 of its statutes, is the creation of the National Crafts Register (RNA, *Registro Nacional Artesanal*). The purpose of the RNA is to keep an up-to-date statistical record of small-scale industries (utilitarian, services, artistic, folk art) to be used as the basis for formulating and implementing policies to promote and develop crafts in Bolivia.

Faced with a variety of criteria at governmental and private levels for classifying activities as "crafts industries," the Ministry of Industry and

Table 2.11 Distribution of Businesses by Sector and Number of Registrations in the RNC, 1987

Sector	Total Number of Businesses	Number Registered in the RNC	Coverage (percentage of total)
Private enterprise sector	8,340	8,340	100.0
Informal sector	338,638		
Semienterprises	74,750	7,337	9.8
Family units	263,888		
Total	346,978	15,677	

Sources: Number of private enterprise sector businesses calculated on the basis of information from the INE (1983); number of informal sector businesses calculated on the basis of information from the INE (1987); total number of businesses registered in the RNC calculated on the basis of information from the General Directorate of the Register of Commerce and Joint Stock Companies, 1988; and an estimate of the number of private enterprise sector businesses registered in the RNC is based on the assumption that all businesses in the private enterprise sector fulfill this requirement.

Commerce decided to classify as "crafts workshops" all those whose fixed assets did not exceed US$8,000. In addition, although not officially, another criterion used is the number of workers in enterprises for the purpose of differentiating microenterprises, small-scale and medium-scale industrial enterprises, and large-scale industry. In accordance with this criterion, economic units that employ up to four workers, and possibly up to nine, are deemed to be microenterprises in the manufacturing (crafts) sector (Sánchez and Pereyra, 1988).

Although the concept of the operational criteria adopted by INBOPIA and the analytical categories used in this study are not fully compatible, it can be assumed that a large proportion of the economic units that comprise the semienterprise and family sectors of manufacturing have the same general characteristics as those used at the official level to define crafts workshops. In this sense, all the family and semienterprise businesses in manufacturing and some special branches of personal and repair services constitute crafts workshops subject to the obligation to register in the RNA. Table 2.12 shows the "real" cover of the RNA in relation to the total estimated number of crafts economic units at the national level in the city of La Paz.

There are fundamentally three reasons for the low coverage of the RNA. First, compliance with the RNA provision is not of any direct benefit to the craftsman. For various reasons, since its creation in 1974, INBOPIA has not been capable of elaborating and implementing promotion and technical assistance programs aimed at improving the operating conditions of small-scale activities and overcoming their lack of success in integrating the market. Second, the few promotion efforts made in the last few years have not had any noticeable social or economic impact and have not helped to

Table 2.12 Crafts Enterprises and Number of Registrations in the RNA

	Number of Crafts Enterprises		Number of Registrations	Coverage (percentage of total)	
	National	La Paz		National	La Paz
Semienterprise sector	36,001	16,699			
Manufacturing	15,196	8,424			
Services	20,805	8,275			
Family sector	84,633	42,515			
Manufacturing	38,450	17,817			
Services	46,183	24,698			
Total	120,634	59,214	2,591	2.1	4.4

Sources: Number of crafts enterprises are calculated on the basis of information from the INE (1987). Number of registrations from INBOPIA, 1987.

solve the basic problems in this sector—access to production resources, training, and access to larger markets. Third, the crafts sector is one of those most affected by the New Economic Policy and the increase in smuggling. As a result, it is one of the sectors of the economy that has the lowest income levels and consequently the greatest difficulty in paying its tax obligations and in registering because this implies financial outlay.

Municipal Register of Taxpayers

In Resolution No. 149/87 of March 19, 1987, the senate approved the Ordinance on the Municipal Tax System for Licenses and Taxes for the 1987 fiscal year, which states, "all natural persons or legal entities with or without a fixed establishment that carry on an economic activity . . . are obliged to register in the Municipal Register of Taxpayers [*Padrón Municipal de Contribuyentes*, PMC] before commencing their activities in order to obtain an operating license, which legalizes and guarantees exercise of the economic activity." Although this obligation forms part of the series of legal requirements to be fulfilled by businesses in order to be legally recognized, the basic premise of this provision is to compile a register of economic activities for tax purposes.

The operating license is an annual tax paid monthly and it represents a contribution to the economic activity carried out within the scope of municipal jurisdiction. In addition to this register, municipal authorities have established charges for the use of public and/or municipal property under the name of "rental contracts." Furthermore, in the case of small-scale economic activities that do not occupy property or have permanent premises for the purpose of carrying on their activities (for example, street vendors), a daily tax called the *sentaje* or *sitiaje*, has been established and is paid to the municipal authority for the use of predetermined sites or spaces for possible and/or itinerant activities.

Table 2.13 summarizes the number of operating licenses granted and in use in La Paz. Unfortunately, the municipal authority kept a systematic register of all licenses granted only until 1982; since then there has been no up-to-date information on this aspect. As a result, estimates of the total number of potential holders of operating licenses is based on figures for 1983, whereas the statistics on operating licenses are for 1982.

Table 2.13 shows that operating licenses cover a large percentage of economic activity in La Paz. On the premise that all enterprises in the private enterprise sector fulfill this provision, available information shows that 64.8 percent of informal sector activities are registered with the municipal authority through the operating license system. Nevertheless, information on total economic activity in La Paz is based on data from the National Business Directorate of the INE, which lists only "visible" economic activity and not activity that takes place within homes, generally

Table 2.13 Total Economic Units and Operating Licenses Granted by the Municipal Authority of La Paz

	Total Economic Units	Number of Operating Licenses Granted	Number of Operating Licenses in Use	Coverage (percentage of total)
Enterprise sector	3,074		3,074	100.0
Informal sector	61,350		39,756	64.8
Permanent premises	25,018			
Permanent stall	11,532			
Mobile stall	24,800			
Total	64,424	53,538	42,830	66.5

Sources: Total economic units calculated on the basis of information from the INE (1983). Number of operating licenses granted from municipal authority of La Paz. It is estimated that approximately 20 percent of the businesses registered ceased activity before 1983.

self-employed activity. It is therefore probable that some activities, such as domestic crafts and personal services, have been underestimated and that the real coverage of operating licenses is lower.

National and Municipal Tax Coverage

Number of taxpayers and rate of payment under the Simplified Tax Regime

Notwithstanding the fact that Article 17 of Supreme Decree No. 21.521 fixes July 10, 1987, as the date for first payment of taxes for the May-June two-month period under the RTS, the General Directorate of Inland Revenue Tax has figures on the number of taxpayers and the rate of payment only from the month of October 1987. The following information therefore covers only the period October 1987–March 1988.

For this period, the number of taxpayers remained more or less stable both at the national level and in the major cities. On average, at the national level, 19,858 businesses that were registered under the RTS paid taxes monthly. The variations in the number of taxpayers at the national level mainly correspond to the dates of payment of tax obligations, which are paid every two months. The months showing a larger number of taxpayers should correspond to the dates fixed in Supreme Decree No. 21.521, namely, the tenth of the months of March, May, July, September, and November, and January of the following year. In most cities, it can be seen that January is the month with the largest number of taxpayers during this period (see Table 2.14), undoubtedly because it is one of the most profitable months for

Table 2.14 Trend in the Number of Taxpayers Under the Simplified Tax Regime by City, October 1987–March 1988

Period and Month	Total	Cocha-bamba	La Paz	Oruro	Potosí	Santa Cruz	Sucre	Tarija	Other
Period 1	36,516	3,733	14,321	3,580	1,582	3,140	1,132	3,706	5,322
October 1987	19,180	2,221	7,073	1,210	789	478	469	3,213	3,727
November 1987	17,336	1,512	7,248	2,370	793	2,662	663	493	1,595
Period 2	48,440	5,047	24,823	4,014	3,332	5,379	1,149	793	3,903
December 1987	20,053	2,035	11,476	1,633	807	2,297	380	262	1,163
January 1988	28,387	3,012	13,347	2,381	2,525	3,082	769	531	2,740
Period 3	34,291	3,578	18,029	2,985	1,227	3,940	978	986	2,568
February 1988	12,637	1,577	5,170	1,050	437	1,835	355	402	1,811
March 1988	21,654	2,001	12,859	1,935	790	2,105	623	584	757

Source: General Directorate of Inland Revenue, 1988.

commerce as a result of the higher level of economic activity during end-of-year festivities.

As in the situation of registration in the RUC, there is a high concentration of taxpayers in the major cities and in the lowest categories of the tax schedule. More than two-thirds of the taxpayers are situated in the cities of La Paz, El Alto, Cochabamba, and Santa Cruz. Furthermore, more than three-quarters of the taxpayers are in category A (the lowest in the schedule), corresponding to payment of an amount equivalent to Bs 13 every two months. If taxpayers in categories B and 1 of the schedule are included, the proportion rises to 98 percent.

Regarding the rate of payment of taxes under the RTS, the aforementioned trends can also be seen. The average monthly tax revenue under this system amounts to Bs 392,759 (US$163,650) (see Table 2.15).

Taxpayers under the RTS therefore contribute an average of Bs 20 every two months to the General Directorate of Inland Revenue, and this is borne out by the high concentration in categories A and B of the tax schedule, which corresponds to payments of Bs 13 and Bs 25, respectively.

To summarize, Table 2.16 shows the degree of effective fulfillment of tax obligations under the RTS by the informal sector. This table also shows the high proportion of informal economic units registered in the RUC. During the first ten months in which this provision was in force almost half of Bolivia's informal businesses fulfilled their obligation to register for tax purposes. This shows a political will on the part of the informal sector to

Table 2.15 Trend in the Number of Taxpayers and the Rate of Payment Under the RTS, October 1987–March 1988

Period and Month	Number of Taxpayers	Rate of Payment (Bs)	Bimonthly Contribution by Taxpayer (Bs)
Period 1	36,516	719,732	19.7
October 1987	19,180	355,381	
November 1987	17,336	364,351	
Period 2	48,440	952,519	19.6
December 1987	20,053	381,196	
January 1988	28,387	571,323	
Period 3	34,291	684,302	19.9
February 1988	12,637	269,895	
March 1988	21,654	414,407	
Total		2,356,553	

Source: Calculated on the basis of information from the General Directorate of Inland Revenue, 1988.

Table 2.16 Informal Businesses Registered in the RUC and Number of Taxpayers by City

	Total	Cocha-bamba	La Paz	Oruro	Potosí	Santa Cruz	Sucre	Tarija
Number of informal businesses	338,638	43,328	154,188	21,401	10,673	87,945	9,974	11,059
Number registered in the RUC	166,591	22,785	90,352	15,315	5,434	25,018	4,685	3,002
Number of taxpayers	31,723	3,578	18,029	2,985	1,227	3,940	978	986
Percentage of total informal businesses registered in the RUC	49.19	52.50	58.60	71.56	50.91	28.45	46.97	27.1
Percentage of registered businesses that are taxpayers	19.04	15.70	19.95	19.49	22.58	15.75	20.88	32.8
Percentage of total informal businesses that are taxpayers	9.37	8.24	11.69	13.95	11.50	4.48	9.81	8.9

Source: Calculated on the basis of information from the INE (1987) and the General Directorate of Inland Revenue.

comply with the legal regulations in force, and this fact should be emphasized. It should also be noted that in the cities of Oruro and Potosí, where the effects of the economic crisis were most keenly felt due to the mining crisis, RUC coverage reaches levels that overall are above the national average.

Despite this initial determination, only 19.04 percent of all those registered in the RUC paid their taxes in the last two-month period under review, and this proportion reaches only 9.37 percent when compared to the number of taxpayers in the estimated total of informal businesses in the major cities.

From a global perspective, since the Tax Reform Law came into force, the informal sector has contributed Bs 2,356,553 (just under US$1 million) to the National Treasury (see Table 2.15). However, when one compares the rate of payment under the RTS with the total inland revenue receipts from all taxes under the general regime, it can be seen that the direct fiscal contribution by the informal sector through the RTS is much more modest. During the period October 1987–March 1988, the share of RTS taxes in the global tax revenue fluctuated between 1 and 1.5 percent.

Municipal taxes

Article 89 of the Tax Reform Law lays down a series of regulations for the policy governing sharing of tax revenue, stating that "the revenue from the collection of taxes established under this Law and the Customs Revenue shall be divided between the Central Government, the Departments, the Municipalities and the Universities in the following manner: 75 percent to the Central Government, ten percent to the Municipalities, five percent to the Universities, and ten percent to the Departments." Furthermore, Article 90 of the Law prescribes that division of the revenue from taxes "shall be effected locally according to the actual collection in each jurisdiction of the different beneficiaries."

As a result of the foregoing provisions, the Tax Reform Law expressly limits the responsibilities of the municipal authorities in connection with the fixing and collection of specific taxes when it states: "not including taxes and/or contributions fixed by Municipalities whose tax obligations are analogous to the taxes fixed under Chapters I to VII of this Law, with the exception of municipal taxes mentioned in Articles 63 and 68" (concerning taxes on property, cars, motorboats, and airplanes). Article 95 also specifies that "in future, Municipalities shall not fix taxes whose obligations are analogous to those created under this Law and which are the subject of co-sharing, with the aforementioned exception."

The Tax Reform Law therefore repeals and amends certain articles of the Organic Law on Municipalities of January 10, 1985, relating to tax matters.

For example, the new text of Article 95 (amended) provides that "in accordance with the Political Constitution of the State, Municipal Authorities shall be empowered to impose, within their jurisdiction, license fees, municipal public service taxes, charges for municipal public works and taxes for taxable elements not subject to taxes established by the Central Government, subject to approval of the Fees and Taxes Ordinance by the Senate."

This has led to a sort of "conflict of authority" between the central government and municipal authorities following the new tax provisions that entered into force with the enactment of Law No. 843 of May 20, 1986, which again raised the issue of political and administrative decentralization as a major subject for discussion.

On March 19, 1987, the senate approved the Ordinance on the Municipal Tax System for Fees and Taxes for the 1987 fiscal year, laying down general regulations for the registration of taxpayers in the Municipal Register of Taxpayers, the payment of taxes on property and cars, and the settlement and form of payment of operating licenses. According to article 113 of the ordinance, an operating license "constitutes a direct tax on economic, industrial, and commercial activity and services in general when carried out within the Municipality's jurisdiction," and is defined as an annual tax to be paid monthly, although municipalities may collect it every two or three months. The ordinance, approved by the senate, fixes the charges in accordance with certain scales, which are in turn predetermined in accordance with the extent, frequency, and location of economic activities. In short, these are municipal fees and taxes imposed in the form of charges fixed by the central government through the Tax Reform Law.

This background information serves to illustrate what subsequently would become the focus of conflict among the central government, municipal authorities, and taxpayers' organizations, which emphatically rejected any idea of double taxation. In this connection, informal workers, gathered together in their national, departmental, and local unions, were the most tenacious in rejecting new taxes on their already impoverished economies.

From the time of enactment of the Municipal Ordinance in March 1987 until September 1987, there were widespread demonstrations and protests by retail traders, craftsmen, and workers in the service sector, which ended with the adoption of Senate Resolution No. 032/87 of September 2, 1987, which suspended paragraphs one and three of article 111 of the Municipal Ordinance. One month later this was extended to practically all economic activities. This positive measure was extended until April 1988, when the senate, in another decision, transferred discussion of the tax issue to those directly involved, namely, the municipal authorities and trade and crafts unions.

During May, June, and July 1988, various negotiations took place among the different sectors with the participation of the Bolivian Workers' Union (COB). These negotiations concluded on July 21, 1988, with an agreement signed by the COB; the National Confederation of Trade Unions,

Retailers, Craftsmen and Stallholders; the Confederation of Bolivian Craftsmen's Trade Unions; the La Paz Retailers' Departmental Federation; the Taxpayers' Defense Committee; and the La Paz Municipal Authority. The salient provisions of this agreement are: (a) recognition of the existence of double taxation (fiscal and municipal) on the same taxable event, and (b) a commitment by the mayor of La Paz to "request the Municipal Council at an opportune moment to review the draft Ordinance on Municipal Fees and Taxes, exempt from payment of Operating Licenses those sectors indicated which are registered under the Simplified Tax Regime and, exceptionally, those trade unionists who, in accordance with its requirements and conditions, should be included under the Simplified Tax Regime but who for operational or work reasons are at present registered under the General Tax Regime."

Undeniably, the political circumstances—the eve of elections programmed for 1989—played a vital role in the success of the negotiations, even though until 1988 they had been confined to the local level and had no impact at the national level.

As a result of the aforementioned agreement, economic activities registered under the Simplified Tax Regime and some activities under the General Regime were exempted from payment of fees and operating licenses and were subject only to payment of charges related to rental under the "occupation of municipal public sites and locations" (rental contracts) and *sentaje*, or *sitiaje* in places and sites set aside for possible and/or itinerant activities.

Rental contracts. A rental contract involves payment of a monthly rent by a tenant for occupying a physical space belonging to the municipality, rather than payment of a tax. This special form of economic activity includes stalls (e.g., kiosks, stands, or barrows) both within and outside markets. The Municipal Property Division is responsible for drawing up and controlling the provisions of such contracts, which stipulate the special areas of the city where such operations can take place, the economic activities that can be carried on in this form, the monthly rent, the duration of the contract, and so forth.

Rental of a physical space for a specified period, usually one year, is subject to payment of a fixed amount per square meter, which varies by zone between Bs 10 and Bs 7 a month according to proximity to the city center.

According to the results of research carried out in La Paz on the self-employed sector (Casanovas and Escobar de Pabón, 1984), approximately half of all economic activity takes place in the street or in private homes. Taking these findings as a reference point, it is possible to calculate for 1987 the breakdown of workers in the family sector according to the type of premises, taking as a basis information in the INE's Permanent Household Survey. It is then possible to estimate the total number of economic activities in the family sector that are carried on in an establishment (permanent premises), have a permanent stall in the street, or are itinerant (see Table 2.17).

Table 2.17 La Paz: Family Sector, Type of Premises by Branch of Activity, Rental Contracts and *Sentaje*, 1987

	Total	Establishment-Type Premises	Permanent Stall	Mobile Stall	Rental Contract	*Sentaje*
Family sector	85,071	42,548	18,522	24,001	1,950	8,283
Manufacturing	13,825	12,954	373	498		
Commerce	51,021	19,643	16,531	14,847		
Services	20,225	9,951	1,618	8,656		

Source: Calculated on the basis of information from the INE (1987).

Of the total number of self-employed workers in manufacturing, commerce, and services, one-half have some form of premises for carrying on their activities, whether these premises are also used as a home, exclusively for economic activity, or are outside the home. Of the other half working in the street, 21.8 percent have a permanent stall and 22.2 percent constitute part of itinerant commerce and services. The information given in Table 2.17 shows significant differences among the various branches of activity. Manufacturing shows a marked tendency to use the home for production, and commerce and services show large numbers of workers who carry on their activities in the street.

The total estimated number of permanent stalls in La Paz up to 1987 was 18,522, of which around 90 percent had activities in the commerce sector. Of this total, only 1,950 (11 percent) were registered with the Municipal Property Division of the municipal authority and the majority of these were kiosks (48 percent), stands (31 percent), and stalls for selling various types of products (21 percent). This low level of coverage under rental contracts can mainly be explained by the widespread dissemination of permanent stalls in the various zones of the city, a factor that limits the capacity of the municipal authority to control them. Another no less important reason is the high cost of rental for sites set aside by the municipal authority for installing stalls. For example, a stand that occupies three square meters must pay an average monthly rent of approximately Bs 24 (US$10) a month.

Sentaje. Sentaje, or *sitiaje,* forms part of the municipality's legal provisions on occupation of public sites and spaces. It is a daily tax collected by the municipal authority police for use of a site in designated areas of the city. Despite the fact that the 1987 Municipal Ordinance lays down a scale that varies from Bs 0.50 to Bs 6 a day, depending on the type of economic activity, the average amount collected daily by the municipal authority under this provision amounts to only Bs 0.50 per person.

An estimate of the number of persons paying *sentaje* daily was made taking as a reference point one week in May 1988. During that week, the La Paz Municipal Authority had eighteen persons responsible for collecting this tax, each of whom covered a specific area of the city. The total amount collected during the week was Bs 24,850 over six working days. If it is assumed that, on average, each mobile or itinerant stall pays Bs 0.50 a day, during the week the number of taxpayers amounted to 49,700, or an average of 8,283 taxpayers per day. If this figure is compared with the estimated number of mobile stalls in La Paz, which was 24,000 (see Table 2.17), the effective cover of *sentaje*, or *sitiaje*, was equivalent to 35 percent of potential taxpayers. Moreover, the bimonthly payments incumbent on street vendors are higher than the payments under the Simplified Tax Regime. For example, traders and workers in the services sector with mobile stalls have to pay approximately Bs 26 (US$11) every two months, whereas those registered under the Simplified Tax Regime pay an average of Bs 20 every two months, even though their capital and annual sales are much higher than those of street vendors.

Furthermore, annual collection of *sentaje* by the municipal authority represents a considerable amount. Taking a stable number of 8,300 street vendors who pay Bs 0.50 daily, six days per week, the total amount is Bs 1,292,200 (US$536,183).

The Cost of Legality

It has been established that, in order to operate legally, informal economic units have to comply with a series of legal rules and provisions in the constitutional, fiscal, and labor fields whose scope of application (national or municipal) is clearly defined. Moreover, this series of provisions lays down a number of different obligations according to the form of organization of production and the type of labor relations that predominate within the business or economic unit. In this connection, informal businesses have to pay different charges for carrying out their economic activities according to whether production takes place in family units or semienterprises.

The view generally expressed is that the cost of fulfilling legal obligations plays an important role in the decisions of the persons concerned to situate themselves within the prevailing legality or to remain outside. The number of bureaucratic procedures that have to be followed by the owner of a small economic unit and the time and money spent in fulfilling obligations could incite a large proportion of these small enterprises to decide to carry on their activities outside the law. This manner of envisaging the issue of legality-illegality implies that a person has the possibility and opportunity to chose one or the other situation after analyzing the "cost-benefit" ratio and that person also has all the necessary information to justify the final decision. In our view, a number of structural factors—such as the characteristics of the economic structure in Bolivia's cities, the rate of increase in the surplus labor force, the degree of development and consolidation of the public and private enterprise sectors, and the size of markets, among other factors—govern the possibilities of integration of individuals in a specific economic structure, as well as the form of their relations with the state and the type of strategy used to generate income and utilize their labor and that of their families. Therefore, simply not complying with a certain type of legal regulation is a consequence of carrying on economic activity in the informal sector rather than one of the causes.

The following is a summary of the main costs payable by an informal economic unit in order to operate legally, drawing an initial distinction among costs involved in setting up an economic activity legally, taxes, and—in the case of semienterprises in which worker-employer relationships come into play—labor costs.

Cost of legal constitution

Taking into account the heterogeneous nature of the informal sector, Table 2.18 differentiates among the costs of legally constituting family businesses and semienterprises in the fields of commerce, manufacturing, and services. Within commerce, a further distinction is drawn among itinerant commerce, permanent stalls, typical market stalls, and the local permanent shops or establishments.

Table 2.18 Cost of Legally Constituting an Informal Economic Unit According to the Type of Establishment (in Bs)

Register	Commerce				Manufacturing		Services		Number of Days to Complete Process
	ITI	PS	MS	LSE	Family Business	Semi-enterprise	Family Business	Semi-enterprise	
RUC	2	2	2	2	2	2	2	2	0.5
RNC	—	—	—	50	—	50	—	50	10
RNA appl.	—	—	—	—	8	10	8	8	2
reg.	—	—	—	—	20	70	20	20	3
PMC	—	—	—	—	—	—	—	—	6
Op. lic.	—	34	44	165	30	30	38	38	9
Ren. con.	—	—	—	—	—	—	—	—	3
Total	2	36	46	217	60	162	68	118	33.5

Source: Calculated on the basis of information from the General Directorate of Inland Revenue, the National Register of Commerce, and the Municipal Register of Taxpayers.

ITI = itinerant commerce
PS = permanent stalls
MS = typical market stalls
LSE = local permanent shops or establishments

Table 2.18 shows the important differences in the direct costs to be paid by individuals for the legal constitution of a business in order to obtain the right to carry out any economic activity legally. The highest costs clearly relate to established businesses, which must pay around Bs 217 (US$90) to legalize their situation. In the case of manufacturing and services, semienterprises must pay between Bs 118 and Bs 162 to comply with registration requirements contained in the different legal provisions. For any of the three types of business mentioned above, which are obliged to fulfill all the registration requirements (with the exception of rental contracts), the approximate time needed to complete the formalities and procedures is 30 days; taking as a basis the minimum national wage, this is equivalent to spending approximately an additional Bs 90 (Bs 60 over 1.5 months).

Note that the largest sum in the total cost to be paid by those in the informal sector for legal recognition concerns the National Register of Commerce (RNC), which does not have any real and effective purpose for the informal sector and does not comprise any political measures that are of direct benefit to activities in this sector.

Taxes and operating costs

The second component of legally running a business relates to the periodic costs of operation and pursuance of economic activity, mainly the result of tax obligations and other types of charges that the informal sector must pay for the use of physical spaces belonging to the municipality. Following recognition of the existence of double taxation in the 1987 Municipal Ordinance, the only taxes currently in force are those under the Tax Reform Act, which have national scope and are basically restricted to the Simplified Tax Regime.

Table 2.19 shows that monthly tax obligations vary between Bs 7 and Bs 27 (between US$3 and US$11), mainly depending on the category of registration under the Simplified Tax Regime and whether physical spaces belonging to the public or municipal authorities are used. What is surprising is the heavy tax burden on street vendors in the commerce and service sectors, who have to pay a daily tax (*sentaje*) equivalent to Bs 0.50 for use of the public highways. In the case of street vendors and workers in commerce who have permanent stalls, nontax costs for the use of spaces that are public property represent the heaviest charge in the overall structure of costs for carrying on and pursuing an economic activity.

Labor and social security costs

The scope of application of labor provisions is limited solely to those businesses in which there is a worker-employer relationship; it therefore applies only to semienterprises that employ a limited number of wage-earners.

There can be no doubt that social security costs represent the heaviest burden on employers, not only in the semienterprise sector but also in public and private enterprise sectors. For an employer in the semienterprise sector, labor costs paid under the provisions of the General Labor Law and the Code of Social Security amount on average to around 42 percent of wages. Table 2.20 shows the percentage of wages for each of the benefits laid down in the various legal provisions in force in the labor and social security fields. For the purpose of calculating the benefits, a basis of twelve months wages equal to 100 was used.

Table 2.20 shows that the real cost of wages amounting, for example, to Bs 180 (three minimum national wages) for an employer in the semi-enterprise sector is equivalent to approximately Bs 256 if he fulfills all of the

Table 2.19 Monthly Taxes for an Informal Economic Unit by Type of Establishment (in Bs)

	Commerce				Manufacturing		Services	
	ITI	PS	MS	LSE	Family Business	Semi-enterprise	Family Business	Semi-enterprise
Category A	7	7	7	—	7	—	7	—
Category B	—	—	—	13	—	—	—	—
Category 1	—	—	—	—	—	21	—	21
Municipal rent control	—	20	—	—	—	—	—	—
Sentaje	12	—	—	—	—	—	—	—
Total	19	27	7	13	7	21	7	21

Source: Calculated on the basis of information from the General Directorate of Inland Revenue and the Municipal Authority.
ITI = itinerant commerce
PS = permanent stalls
MS = typical market stalls
LSE = local permanent shops or establishments
Note: Monthly taxes include national taxes and RTS charges.

Table 2.20 Monthly Labor Costs for a Semienterprise (percentages)

Wages	100.0
Health insurance contributions	10.0
Bonus	8.3
Compensation	8.3
Holidays	5.8
Pension fund contributions	5.0
Other benefits	3.0
FOMO contributions	1.0
FONVI contributions	1.0
Total	142.4

obligations prescribed by the law. This means that, in practice, small informal enterprises adopt one of the following three positions when faced with such high labor costs: (1) they avoid recruiting permanent workers and prefer to recruit temporary labor when necessary; (2) they do not fulfill all of their obligations following verbal agreement with their workers; or (3) they institute other mechanisms for dealing with labor relations, such as paying different forms of collateral benefits, which permit flexibility with regard to some of the costs (adjusting working hours, carrying out some of the work at home, lending tools and equipment for work, and so on). It can be assumed that the semienterprise sector has evolved a very special sort of legal-labor framework in order to deal with the problem of the high costs involved in recruiting salaried workers, combining elements from all three of the above-mentioned alternatives.

Advantages and Disadvantages of Operating Illegally: A Global View

The data analyzed in the previous sections have given an approximate picture of the real levels of compliance with the legal provisions in force on the part of informal businesses and the nominal costs incumbent upon different types of informal economic units in order to operate legally. In general, requirements on legal constitution, which require the fulfillment of a number of administrative registration procedures, are not many, and compliance with them does not require an excessive amount of time or money.

Tax obligations do not in general involve large amounts that cannot be paid by those carrying on informal activities, with the exception, perhaps, of taxes paid by traders with permanent stalls in the form of rent for the use of sites that are public or municipal property or payment of the daily *sentaje* by street vendors. Labor and social security costs, on the other hand, do involve large sums for each employee in an economic unit and are therefore one of the legal provisions that presents the greatest difficulties due to the considerable implications their fulfillment has for any informal activity.

In this connection, it is interesting to study how operating outside the law affects informal units, what are the advantages and disadvantages of operating illegally, and what is the effective capacity of the state to ensure compliance with the legislation in force in view of the widespread restrictions in the public sector as a result of the adjustment measures implemented by the government in 1985, 1986, and 1987. This analysis will provide some explanation of why those in the informal sector do not fulfill many of the laws and obligations contained in the three aforementioned municipal orders.

Advantages of Operating Illegally

The acute economic crisis affecting Bolivia since approximately 1983 has had a direct negative impact on the series of activities that take place within the informal sector, affecting, in particular, the already low levels of income in this sector. This phenomenon has meant that those in the informal sector have deployed a number of strategies aimed at guaranteeing a minimum subsistence wage that allows them to cover in part the needs of the family. From this point of view, it is logical to assume that small informal enterprises give priority in their cost structure to the maintenance of a certain minimum level of income and remuneration of their labor force over operating costs such as the payment of taxes and other obligations.

In this context, the generalized economic crisis has led to a genuine inability on the part of the informal sector to fulfill their legal obligations. Nevertheless, this behavior corresponds to a strategy for limiting the operating costs of the business and does not necessarily imply a deliberate act of evasion of all legal and tax obligations. Rather, the definition of priorities of the informal sector allows compliance with only some of these legal and tax provisions. This explains, for example, why almost half of all informal economic units have fulfilled the obligation to register in the Single Taxpayers' Register, because it does not involve payment but allows the pursuance of an economic activity and is a basic requirement for fulfilling other registration requirements, such as the National Register of Commerce, the National Crafts Register, and the Municipal Register of Taxpayers. It should be noted, however, that these requirements imply expenditure and this is one of the reasons why the level of coverage of some of the registers, especially the RNC and the RNA, is fairly limited.

In addition, the government's "fiscal austerity" measures have had a direct effect on the capacity of the institutions responsible for registration to carry out inspections because many of the employees who had inspection and supervisory responsibilities and verified compliance with the provisions have been dismissed. It should also be noted that the public institutions responsible for keeping these registers are unable to assimilate and process the information collected as a result of such obligations and are likewise unable to use it in order to formulate policies, plans, and projects.

A similar situation exists as far as tax obligations are concerned. Despite the fact that enactment of the Tax Reform Law represents a significant step forward by establishing different regimes for large and small taxpayers and by simplifying bureaucratic procedures for paying taxes, tax evasion by the informal sector is widespread. It is estimated that only 10 percent of all potential taxpayers in the informal sector comply with their tax obligations.

The reasons for this situation are the same as those regarding registration for the purposes of legal constitution and are related to the cost of fulfilling these obligations and the priorities defined by those in the informal sector. In the first instance, taxes for small-scale activities are relatively high, even taking into account the decision to suspend payment of municipal permits and operating licenses for reasons of double taxation. For example, a street vendor with a monthly income of two minimum wages (Bs 120) must set aside Bs 13, or 11 percent of his monthly income, solely to cover payment of the daily *sentaje*.

Furthermore, it can be assumed that those in the informal sector have decided to pay local or municipal taxes rather than national taxes on their economic activity. This can be explained by the greater degree of control exercised by municipal authorities over street vendors and other activities that take place on the streets. This is the only explanation why 35 percent of street vendors in La Paz pay the *sentaje* daily.

Finally, the information available shows that labor costs under the General Labor Law and the Code of Social Security are the most difficult to bear for the informal sector. Social charges and benefits represent around 42 percent of the average cost of salaries and so small enterprises have little incentive to recruit labor. The result is that informal units employ only the indispensable number of permanent salaried workers under terms and conditions previously agreed between the parties, the majority of which are outside the provisions of the General Labor Law.

Nevertheless, informal enterprises are small not because of a strategy to avoid being discovered by the authorities, as stated by some authors, but because of the structural limitations on access to production resources and the size of the market, which are determining factors for most branches of activity. It should also be emphasized that one factor that makes it possible or permissible to fail to comply with labor regulations is the incapacity of the Ministry of Labor to control and ensure fulfillment with labor legislation. For example, in 1988 the ministry had eleven inspectors for the whole of La Paz, and they received a monthly salary of Bs 100, equivalent to 1.6 minimum salaries.

To summarize, evasion of tax or any other type of obligation allows informal economic units to reduce substantially their production costs and thereby guarantee a certain level of competitiveness in the market.

Disadvantages of Illegality

Undoubtedly, operating illegally has a number of tangible and intangible consequences. Not having an operating license, not paying taxes, or not fulfilling registration requirements imposes on those in the informal sector a number of limitations on carrying on their economic activities, which need to be analyzed. One of the main limitations is the impossibility of access to certain public and private enterprise markets. For example, informal units are de facto excluded from tendering in the public sector by the requirements laid down in some of the registers, which are not adapted to their form of operation.

Second, failure to fulfill many of the provisions of the Labor Law results in a high degree of instability in informal businesses, which, in turn, is expressed in indirect costs for the economic unit. The investment in training made by an informal employer does not fully benefit the business due to the high turnover of staff.

An often-cited disadvantage of operating outside the law is the difficulty of obtaining credit. However, this limitation is only an apparent difficulty because the main obstacle to obtaining credit is the lack of security rather than the legal situation of the business. A brief survey of six banks in La Paz revealed that documentation guaranteeing the legal constitution of an economic unit was usually a secondary factor in assessing an application for credit. A mortgage or the client's creditworthiness played a much more important role.

Another factor that is an obvious disadvantage is the impossibility for many informal units of advertising in various ways the products or services they arrange, sell, or provide, for fear of being discovered by the authorities. This mechanism is usually an important factor in attracting customers, particularly where the physical location of the business is not favorable and generally far from the principal markets.

Finally, more than a disadvantage, the payments and bribes that those in the informal sector have to pay in order not to be harassed by the authorities are additional costs that in some cases represent fixed sums that have a significant impact on the structure of regular costs to be paid by those in the informal sector.

Note

The author is grateful for the collaboration received from Gary Montaño, research assistant, and for comments by Silvia Escobar de Pabón, Hernando de Larrazabal and Antonio Pérez, research workers with CEDLA, La Paz, Bolivia.

3

Illegality in the Urban Informal Sector of Mexico City

Néstor Elizondo

In early studies by the International Labour Office (ILO), consideration of illegality was directly linked to definition of the informal sector, using as a basic indicator the fact that enterprises in the informal sector, independently of their activities, operate outside state regulation.[1] Illegality, however, became important in another way as a result of the varying emphases given in relevant studies to the enterprise-state relationship. For structuralists, the main problem resided in the asymmetrical but functional relationship between the state and informal enterprises, which subordinates the state's role to protecting the functional nature of informal enterprises compared to the formal sector of the economy. In this way, the motor for expansion of the informal sector is basically to be found in economic dynamism or, for neomarxists, in the accumulation pattern.[2]

For neoliberals, the heart of the matter is the regulatory and interventionist function given to the state so that it becomes the focus for all decisionmaking and consequently for the informal-illegal momentum; for this current of thought, agents of the state encourage illegality because of its "mercantile" nature. It follows that this view of the state reveals an agent that is not modern and does not encourage modernization but whose function is rather to hinder social modernization.[3] On the other hand, the neomarxists consider the state agent to be a modernizer due to its regulatory function in the formal-informal relationship.

In both cases, the problem of illegality has been situated in a context of exclusiveness, whether in the form of the state or the process of economic formalization of enterprises. In the first case, a state-illegality opposition prevents access to legality, whereas in the second case, the functioning of the formal-informal sector relationship, although intermittent, makes it improbable that illegal informal enterprises will become formal and legal.

Another feature of the studies, although not discussed with the same empirical conviction as the previous one, is the logic of the internal organization of enterprises. It is curious to note that this is the bastion for justification based on the principal paradigms, which, logically, proclaim the unprofitable nature of such units, the low levels of mobility, the low rate of reinvestment—in short, the economic irrationality of such enterprises. This is to say that irrationality is associated with the "entrepreneurial tradition" that characterizes owners of microenterprises. Even when another more "responsible" image of traditionalism—the state—is evoked, both images assume a logic specific to the enterprise or imposed from outside, which ultimately implies a situation of backwardness of the small-scale economy.

The causal structure that links the behavior of the microeconomic variables is not, in fact, so simple. Strictly speaking, neomarxists consider, for example, that price fixing mechanisms do not affect the small-scale, marketplace, or family economy, or in the worst case, the precapitalist economy. It is considered that the incapacity of microenterprises to confront market influences is seen in the scope of the market, as well as in the money or work. In all three cases it is suggested, although not always proved, that such logic makes it necessary to transfer the output of microenterprises to medium-scale and large-scale industry because of the inevitable shortcomings of productivity in the former and/or a backward system of production.

Another feature of this theory is that microenterprises could accelerate the process of association with the rest of the formal market through one of the three markets or all of them, showing increased flexibility in contracting commercial relations with formal financial networks, marketing structures, and formal recruitment mechanisms. According to this theory, the process could be accelerated if it is not hindered by state regulation; in other words, the internal momentum of enterprises is causally hampered by such regulation. Nevertheless, whichever hypothesis is adopted at the outset, it is necessary to consider the momentum of internal variables in enterprises, especially the way in which each of them is linked to the outside.

One important aspect of these studies is the difference between the macrosocial or macroeconomic scale and the microsocial field. This study shows only the internal situation in enterprises. However, in this context it should be noted that, although the scope of the study of enterprises does not permit consideration of matters such as the development process or the relationship between social elaboration of prices and the individual practices of entrepreneurs, it can make a decisive contribution to what modern sociology and anthropology call the entrepreneur's decisionmaking process within the context of a particular legal, fiscal, and labor system. It should be emphasized, however, that the results of this research show that the problem of legality-illegality in the urban informal sector, seen in terms of a diametrical opposition at the macrosocial level, is not sufficient to explain the genuine dynamism of such enterprises inasmuch as they are characterized by a high degree of heterogeneity, numerous ways of adapting themselves to the situation in the various sectors, different types of labor employed, and varying levels of productivity, among other factors, which imply differing possibilities for resourcefulness in administrative management, despite all being under the same legal regime.[4]

Research Methodology

Originally, it was decided to carry out the research in the field study by selecting a number of enterprises in each sector—industry, commerce, and services—according to the relative importance of the informal sector in each of these branches. It was also decided that, of the eighteen enterprises to be studied, twelve should be illegal and six legal. The selection gave rise to a number of difficulties, the most important of which was to identify the exact number of enterprises in the informal sector that met these preconditions.

Failure to register the enterprise with the Trade and Industrial Promotion Secretariat (*Secretaría de Comercio y Fomento Industrial*) was chosen as a basis for defining illegality, on the assumption that registration with this governmental body conditioned commencement of operations for the units to be studied. It was therefore necessary first of all to undertake preliminary research to identify enterprises that met this criterion and then to obtain from them information that would enable the study to be carried out. However, as will be seen later, this criterion was amended so as better to circumscribe the various forms of association of such enterprises with the legal-administrative-governmental framework.

Penetration of informal enterprises, particularly those deemed to be illegal, was almost impossible precisely because of their clandestine situation. Moreover, although at no time was any attempt made to ensure sample representativeness of the sector studied, it was decided that there should be functional representativeness, so the case studies were selected in the first instance according to their numbers and the persons employed in the three sectors of the informal economy—industry, commerce, and services. This initial indicator was assumed to reveal significant similarities and differences concerning the relationship of the enterprises chosen with market circuits and, ultimately, to show the varying degrees of fulfillment or nonfulfillment of legal requirements and therefore have considerable implications for their functioning.

Finally, it was decided to distribute a questionnaire to units that, in addition to the criteria already fixed, fulfilled that of scale of production.[5] The basis used was the typology elaborated by Francisco Giner de los Ríos for industrial enterprises in the informal sector, focusing on those that employed up to five workers—a scale that was consistent with the characteristics of informality, such as low productivity, little division of labor, little fixed capital, and low income.[6]

Consideration of the case studies selected raised another problem, namely, how to make sure that the information was minimally comparable in each case. This was solved by using a series of general questions in the questionnaire, and although their classification was complex it also gave considerable opportunities for analysis. Information was obtained on approximately 120 variables divided into seven sections: general characteristics of the enterprise, production, material inputs, composition of the labor force, credit, growth of the enterprise, and procedures vis-à-vis government bodies.

Information was collected on the basis of estimates by the head of the enterprise or the employer regarding the volume, type, and other parameters of operation of his unit. Nevertheless, when classifying variables that necessitated a measure of quantification for the purposes of comparison, it was decided to make a reasonable estimate that limited to the maximum possible extent the margin of error in the replies received. The way the questionnaire was worded was aimed at quantifying the means of production, salaries, inputs, and so forth. The main problem, however, lay in the fact that entrepreneurs do not systematically calculate their receipts and expenditures and their estimates of assets are subjective. Therefore, there exists a danger that the information may be biased.[7]

The need to make comparisons among individual enterprises meant that research could be carried out in areas that other studies had not been able to estimate quantitatively. Classic anthropological case studies progressed in qualitative terms, but they cannot be strictly compared. On the other hand, quantitative studies usually only focused on the macroeconomic aspects, which do not take into account the anthropocentric element. The questionnaire enabled a synchronic comparison of several cases to be made over and above the ad hoc causality. The consistency of the information obtained allowed considerable progress to be made in illustrating the degree of complexity of the overall informal sector, but especially regarding "illegal" enterprises in the sector. The questionnaire sought to combine sociological and anthropological aspects, thus combining quantification and an analysis of case studies. Finally, it should be emphasized that, although it cannot be assumed that the survey is representative, at least in terms of statistical representativeness, it provides systematic information on the functional situation of illegality within the informal sector. The study can perhaps serve as a point of departure for a statistical analysis of the question in the course of subsequent research.

Characteristics of the Enterprises Studied

Sectoral Location and Periods of Operation

The first characteristic of these enterprises is their physical location. The illegal subsector within the informal enterprises studied is not concentrated in recently created urban zones, although it can be situated in districts of Mexico

City that correspond to the socioeconomic strata of the population (Schteingart and Garza, 1984). Enterprises are frequently set up and disappear in low-income zones, and certain zones are traditionally occupied by specific strata of producers and retailers. In the northeast, there are long-established groups of shoemakers, as well as new processing industries. In the southeast, in the satellite cities, there are specific groups of small-scale agricultural enterprises and new crafts industries. In the oldest part of the city, there are small shops, such as those in the well-known La Lagunilla and La Merced districts, as well as clandestine trade, for example, the Tepito Market. To ensure representativeness of the various zones in the city, it was decided to select enterprises located in these areas.

The original proposal was for the enterprises to be divided equally among the three economic sectors. However, a preliminary survey showed that, although the proportion of the informal sector population working in commerce was greater than in industry, in absolute terms the latter represented a more significant number of enterprises, as well as people working informally and not complying with tax and labor regulations. For this reason, and due to the relative difficulty of access to enterprises, twenty-two enterprises were selected, distributed as shown in Table 3.1.

Of the total number of enterprises selected for the survey, those in commerce account for 18.2 percent. These are small shops, which mainly sell basic necessities—for example, food, footwear, and general supplies—to the working classes.

The thirteen microindustries are basically involved in the production of finished consumer goods, with the exception of one, which manufactures manual tools. The bulk of production concerns leather goods, clothing, furniture, food processing, footwear, and chemical products. They are small-scale producers directly and necessarily linked to other formal enterprises but whose advantage is that their operating costs are so low that they can offer products at very competitive prices. Unlike small-scale commerce, these microindustries are linked to the market through certain intermediate mechanisms so that regulations can more easily be evaded.

In the case of microenterprises in the service sector, which represent 22.7 percent of the survey, those chosen basically depend on the final consumer,

Table 3.1 Enterprises Selected by Sector of Activity

Sector	Number of Enterprises Selected	Percentage of Total
Commerce	4	18.2
Industry	13	59.1
Services	5	22.7
Total	22	100.0

for example, car repair and electrical installation services. Their occasional relations with enterprises in the formal sector, however, exert considerable pressure on these microenterprises to regularize their operations so as to be able to invoice the sale of their services.

Despite the fact that some enterprises in this sector have existed for more than fifteen years, the majority have been created only recently. Table 3.2 shows that half of the enterprises studied commenced their activities during the past four years. This is due to a number of factors, among them the fact that the economic crisis has been most acute during this period and so the population in general has been seeking different alternatives in order to generate income.

Another aspect is that owners of such enterprises are heads of growing families; more than one-third require another source of income, usually the main income, although this is not sufficient. Family expenditure is almost exclusively covered by the head of the family, only occasionally assisted by a wife's income, so the situation is difficult, particularly because dependents are still of school age.

Legality and Illegality: Problems of Identification

As mentioned previously, in practice it was extremely difficult to put into operation the legality-illegality criteria. The concepts of total legality or total illegality simply express an ideal structure that occurs only exceptionally in the cases studied because the network of relationships in which these enterprises are integrated is fairly heterogeneous, from the points of view of both integration in economic activity and legal-administrative relations. The information contained in Table 3.3 highlights the variety of situations existing among the cases studied with regard to procedures at various governmental and private offices.

One possible definition of the status of these enterprises distinguishes

Table 3.2 Commencement of Operations According to Availability of Another Job

Date of Commencement of Operations	Other Job? Yes	No	Total	Percentage of Total
Before 1965	—	2	2	9.1
1965–1974	1	2	3	13.6
1975–1984	1	5	6	27.3
1985–1988	5	6	11	50.0
Total	7	15	22	100.0
Percentage of total	31.8	68.2	100.0	

Table 3.3 Public and Private Entities Visited by Type of Enterprise

Branch of Activity of Enterprise Visited	Sector	Office Visited
1. Manufacture of kitchens	Industry	SHCP, SS
2. Manufacture of clothing	Industry	Private bank, SHCP, trade unions, IMSS, DDF Treasury
3. Footwear	Commerce	SHCP, DDF Treasury
4. General supplies	Commerce	SHCP, SS, Fire Department
5. Car repairs	Service	Public bank, SHCP, accountants' office
6. Electrical installations	Service	SHCP, SECOFI, CFE, DDF Treasury
7. Plumbing	Service	SHCP, IMSS
8. Car repairs	Service	SHCP, SS, DDF Treasury
9. Manufacture of chemical products	Industry	
10. Manufacture of footwear	Industry	SHCP
11. Printing of wearing apparel	Industry	
12. Food processing	Industry	
13. Food processing	Industry	Private bank, CFE, SHCP, SS, INFONAVIT, DDF, IMSS
14. Retail trade	Commerce	DDF, DDF Treasury
15. Retail trade	Commerce	SPV
16. Car repairs	Service	SHCP, DDF, Firemen
17. Food processing	Industry	SHCP, SS, DDF, SECOFI, DIFOCOST
18. Food processing	Industry	
19. Leather goods	Industry	
20. Manufacture of footwear	Industry	
21. Manufacture of tools	Industry	
22. Furniture	Industry	

Note: The acronyms correspond to the following governmental departments or bodies:
CFE, Comisión Federal de Electricidad (Federal Electricity Commission)
DDF, Departamento del Distrito Federal (Federal District Department)
DIFOCOST, Dirección General de Fomento Cooperativo y Organización Social para el Trabajo (General Directorate of Cooperative Promotion and Social Work Organization)
IMSS, Instituto Mexicano del Seguro Social (Mexican Social Security Institute)
INFONAVIT, Instituto del Fondo Nacional de Vivienda para los Trabajadores (Institute of the National Workers' Housing Fund)
SECOFI, Secretaría de Comercio y Fomento Industrial (Trade and Industrial Promotion Secretariat)
SHCP, Secretaría de Hacienda y Crédito Público (Finance and Public Credit Secretariat)
SPV, Secretaría de Protección y Vialidad (Protection and Highways Secretariat)
SS, Secretaría de Salud (Health Secretariat)

the different degrees of legality or illegality in accordance with three criteria: (1) formalization of legal status (registration with the Trade and Industrial Promotion Secretariat [SECOFI] and the Federal District Department [DDF]); (2) fulfillment of fiscal obligations (Finance and Public Credit Secretariat [SHCP], Treasury, and DDF); and (3) fulfillment of labor obligations (Mexican Social Security Institute [IMSS] and Institute of the National Workers' Housing Fund [INFONAVIT]). The information given in Table 3.3 indicates that enterprises establish an order of priorities regarding their legal, fiscal, and labor obligations that does not necessarily depend on the amount, complexity, or relative length of time of the formalities, but rather on the economic burden represented by legalization or the likelihood of being "caught." In the cases studied, the enterprises considered the determinant element of "legal" functioning to be a minimum of registration for tax purposes, even though this does not mean that they fulfill their obligations. It is frequently noted that enterprises, whether or not registered with the finance authorities, do not see the need for any other form of registration or license.

In some cases, particularly for commerce and some services, enterprises are registered with the respective local government office of the DDF, which seems to be the result of the recent administrative decentralization of the DDF—control over the right to occupy sites having become a local responsibility, the capacity to ensure that taxes are paid is therefore greater. This is undoubtedly also true for registration with the Fire Department and the Health Secretariat (SS), whose local inspectors carry out periodic visits. This is a relatively simple procedure, although if health, safety, or fire requirements are not met, bribery is common.[8]

Labor obligations are those least frequently complied with by the enterprises studied, which is paradoxical inasmuch as Mexico—which is often deemed to be "interventionist" as far as the economy is concerned, partly due to its role in controlling labor relations—tolerates to a significant extent evasion of labor legislation. In practice, the controlling state hands over responsibility for monitoring these laws to the trade unions or relies on the good faith of the employers.

However, such a mechanism is extremely difficult to operate effectively. First of all, labor relations have more to do with economic relations than with trade or employer relations; and second, membership of trade unions is highly unlikely in the enterprises studied due to their instability and the high turnover of labor or simply due to the impossibility of employing the minimum number of workers to obtain registration with the Social Security and Labor Secretariat.

Taking into account the above, as well as the order of priority that enterprises establish regarding the minimum or maximum legal requirements to be complied with or their decision to evade all or some of them, it is possible to establish a sequence of degrees of legality-illegality based on the importance attached to each of the registers.[9]

In Table 3.4, the lowest value corresponds to a situation of total illegality and the highest value corresponds to the total legality. The categories were defined according to the following criteria: generalized illegality signifies that the enterprise is not registered anywhere and does not have a license; restricted illegality includes enterprises with minimum registration and a single financial obligation, payable when commencing operations, or no financial obligation at all; generalized legality includes enterprises listed in the maximum number of registers, including the tax and labor registers, that systematically fulfill their obligations; and

Table 3.4 Number of Enterprises by Degree of Legality

Category	Value	Number of Enterprises	Percentage of Total Enterprises	Cumulative Percentage
Generalized illegality	0.0	6	27.3	27.3
Restricted illegality	1.0	4	18.2	45.5
Restricted legality	2.0	8	36.3	81.8
Generalized legality	3.0	4	18.2	100.0

Table 3.5 Breakdown of Enterprises by Degree of Legality and Sector of Activity

Category	Commerce	Industry	Services
Generalized illegality		6	
Restricted illegality	1	3	
Restricted legality	3	1	4
Generalized legality		3	1
Total	4	13	5

restricted legality signifies enterprises that are registered in the aforementioned registers but do not fulfill the obligations these entail. Table 3.4 shows that most enterprises are to be found in this latter category.

As will be seen below, the significance of this classification scheme resides in the fact that, on the basis of the sample chosen, we can make a more systematic and precise comparison among the enterprises and perceive a pattern of behavior that is closely linked to legal status.

Using the criteria cited, it is possible to analyze the breakdown of these legal-illegal categories according to sectors of economic activity. Table 3.5 shows that of the microenterprises studied, those in the industrial sector are the only ones in the generalized illegality category. At the same time, other enterprises in the industrial sector are totally legal. Many enterprises in the commerce and services sector function with the minimum requirements prescribed by the law and show varying degrees of compliance with regulations.

It can be stated that illegality has different levels and cannot necessarily be restricted to the exclusive duality of fulfillment or nonfulfillment of legal, tax, and labor regulations. The variety of situations shown is the result of the characteristics of the enterprise and its integration in the market, as well as of the regulations and obligations applicable in each case, together with the state's capacity to control or tolerate failure to comply with the law when dealing with this type of activity.

Furthermore, this classification scheme allows identification of the economic areas in which state regulation is practically absent or evasion is easier. The macroeconomic theory that the maximum number of illegal enterprises is to be found in the industrial sector is confirmed in Table 3.6, which shows that enterprises that are totally illegal are usually located in premises that serve as both homes and work premises, whereas this situation tends to disappear as one moves further toward legality. This is undoubtedly due to the fact that in situations of total illegality, enterprises are obliged to work clandestinely within homes; in situations involving contact with customers or selling in public places, as is the case for commerce and services, it is necessary to have some form of registration, even though it does not necessarily have to be the most costly (tax). Conversely, the more legal businesses—whether or not they fulfill their obligations—are usually located in workshops solely used for production. In both cases, the reasons are different. Whereas in the first instance it can be assumed that the decision on location is the result of the clandestine activity, allowing the enterprise to avoid paying rent and to evade tax, in the second case, the enterprise's activity makes it subject to control because it is carried on in premises that cannot easily be hidden away. The branch of activity, legality, and type of premises are therefore linked in different ways in the situations described. The logic of entrepreneurial management in respect of the degree of legality is thus separate from decisions regarding the calculation of maximum profit alone.[10]

Orientation of Informal Entrepreneurs

For the aforementioned reasons, decisionmaking by small-scale entrepreneurs is limited in its capacity to catalyze their activities. However, the management of enterprises, with the exception of capitalist employers up to a certain point, has its own rationale. Table 3.7 shows the major expenditures by owners under the various headings. The figures illustrate extremely well the entrepreneurial logic that underlies such enterprises. The item that predominates among the costs paid by the enterprise is expenditure

Table 3.6 Breakdown of Enterprises by Type of Premises and Degree of Legality

Category	Type of Premises			Total Enterprises
	Workshop	Home	None	
Generalized illegality	1	5		6
Restricted illegality	3	1		4
Restricted legality	4	2	2	8
Generalized legality	3	1		4
Total	11	9	2	22
Percentage of total	50.0	40.9	9.1	100.0

Table 3.7 Percentage Breakdown of Enterprises by Allocation of Resources According to Major Costs

Percentage of Resources Spent in Category	Inputs	Family Costs	Administrative Costs	Wages	Reinvestment
Less than 10%	4.5	9.1	18.2	0.0	27.3
11–25%	22.7	13.6	9.1	9.1	22.7
26–50%	22.7	27.3	18.2	4.5	0.9
More than 50%	31.8	18.2	0.0	4.5	0.0
Not recorded	18.2	31.8	54.5	81.6	50.0

Note: The percentages correspond to the number of enterprises whose costs are situated in each category divided by the total number of enterprises.

on inputs; almost one-third of the enterprises surveyed stated that their main financial expenditure was on inputs. Regarding wages, 81.6 percent of the enterprises do not have a special heading for wages. This is not due to lack of information. In fact, it signifies that these enterprises do not place any market value on the hours per worker investment in their activities, precisely because a large number of these enterprises utilize family members. In contrast, the entrepreneur-capitalist calculation gives a large place to wages. For such enterprises, payment of wage or labor benefits is not necessary and therefore compliance with labor legislation is frequently evaded.

Under the heading of administrative costs, just over half the enterprises do not make any allocation for payment of electricity, rent, or administrative costs such as accounts. If we add the 18.2 percent who spend only 10 percent of their resources on such expenditure, almost two-thirds of the sample consider this type of expenditure to be marginal. On the other hand, 18.2 percent of enterprises allocate up to 50 percent of their resources for administrative costs, and these are to a large extent enterprises in the generalized legality category.

As shown on Table 3.6, 40.9 percent of those questioned declared that they work in the same place where they live, which explains the low proportion of expenditures on administrative costs (rent, electricity, water, and so on) attributable to their activity, but at the same time it reaffirms the view that, if activities are carried out in separate premises, the administrative costs can be excessively high, thus placing these units in a very unstable economic situation.

Under the heading of reinvestment, half of the enterprises do not consider this item to be an immediate expenditure and 27.3 percent allocate up to 10 percent for the purchase of assets or the extension of their business. This might imply that there is an involuted trend, which will render these enterprises more vulnerable in the long term, although it does not prevent them from continuing to operate in a precarious way.

The microenterprises themselves have their own views on the reasons that incite them to remain outside the law. The reasons are the result of a combination of objective and subjective factors. Although microenterprises possess a degree of entrepreneurial initiative, they also lack adequate qualifications to make precise calculations of the degree of risk incurred with regard to the possibility of earning a living. For these entrepreneurs, for example, capital investment in any case depends on their own resources and the vicious circle of no access to credit → absence of registration → no access to credit is marginal for them. This is because they have the alternative of access to monetary resources from other activities or reliance on family loans, but also because, if they had recourse to a formal credit source, the risk to which they would expose themselves, given the volume and type of production and the uncertainty of the market, would not be reasonable from any point of view. The reasonable attitude for them is to assume the risk themselves, thereby ensuring that eventual failure, which is a distinct possibility in times of crisis, will not mean total exposure to creditors. This perhaps helps to explain their failure to break free of the vicious circle microactivity → instability → illegality → microactivity.

The Effects of Legality/Illegality on the Functioning and Performance of Enterprises

Personnel Employed

The relation between the enterprises in the informal sector studied and the degree of legality in which they function results in an impulsion that is heterogeneous but also relatively consistent as far as integration in the macrosocial framework is concerned. Studies of this sector have advanced the hypothesis that the composition of the labor force in these enterprises is mainly of a family nature. Furthermore, in view of the category chosen (in general, microenterprises not employing more than five workers), the units are characterized by a low degree of division of labor, low wages, and low profitability. As can be seen in Table 3.8, half of the cases studied employed up to two full-time workers at the time of the survey.

The information obtained shows that the smallest enterprises tend to be concentrated in the generalized illegality category, although two of them are in the generalized legality category. On the other hand, enterprises that employ up to five workers are mainly situated in the restricted legality category, and generalized legality is the common feature of the two enterprises that employ up to fifteen workers.

Although the correlation between the degree of legality and the number of workers is not significant, there is nevertheless a positive correlation. This might suggest that employing a greater number of workers exerts pressure on an enterprise to comply with all or some of the labor and tax regulations.

Volume of Profits

The options that combine structural imperatives and the development of each unit generally result in a certain surplus, which can be measured in multiples of the minimum wage. This can been seen in Table 3.9, which shows the breakdown of enterprises by volume of gross profits according to degrees of legality. Enterprises whose gross profits are equivalent to between one and three minimum wages constitute 45.5 percent of the sample, and there are equal numbers of enterprises with higher and lower profits. In principle, there is no clear direct correlation between legal status and levels of gross profit. For example, the information shows that although enterprises of relatively low profitability tend to be found in the illegal categories, there are also five enterprises in the same category that earn profits equivalent to three or more times the minimum wage. Moreover, it is clear that fulfilling at least the

Table 3.8 Breakdown of Enterprises by Personnel Employed and Degree of Legality

Category	Full-time Personnel Employed			Total
	Up to 2	Up to 5	Up to 15	
Generalized illegality	4	2		6
Restricted illegality	2	2		4
Restricted legality	3	5		8
Generalized legality	2		2	4
Total	11	9	2	22
Percentage of total	50.0	40.9	9.1	100.0

Table 3.9 Breakdown of Enterprises by Volume of Profits and Degree of Legality

Category	Volume of Gross Profits[a]			Total Enterprises
	Up to 1 Minimum Wage	Up to 3 Minimum Wages	More than 3 Minimum Wages	
Generalized illegality	3	1	2	6
Restricted illegality	2	1	1	4
Restricted legality	1	7		8
Generalized legality		1	3	4
Total	6	10	6	22
Percentage of total	27.3	45.5	27.3	100.0

Note: The monthly minimum wage in force in the metropolitan area of Mexico City at the time of the study was 240,000 pesos (US$105).
[a]Gross profits were calculated by subtracting from earnings for total annual sales the amount of inputs, wages, and other costs related to the activity.

formal requirements without strictly complying with the law—restricted legality—makes it highly likely that owners will have earnings up to three times the minimum wage. This is the case for more than one-third of the enterprises. These figures suggest that there exists not only a wide variety of profit levels in the informal sector but also within the subsector generally termed illegal. It will be shown below how legalization of these enterprises would affect them differently, albeit within the same categories of legality.

Alternative Employment

For the reasons cited in relation to Table 3.9, the traditional concept of low profitability and productivity in illegal enterprises is extremely difficult to uphold. This subject will be discussed in more detail when referring to estimates of productivity levels. But there is also another common belief: enterprises in the informal sector should in theory be enterprises whose functioning is unstable due to the low levels of productivity and earnings; therefore, their owners should be obliged to seek alternative employment as a vital necessity. However, the majority of owners of the enterprises surveyed did not have any additional jobs. Table 3.10 shows the relation between degrees of legality and alternative employment.

As can be seen in the table, the owners of fifteen of the twenty-two enterprises do not have another job, whereas seven find it necessary. It appears fairly clear that the more illegal an enterprise, the more the owner is likely to have another job, depending on his level of income, whereas owners of enterprises in the generalized legality category do not have other jobs, which can be explained by their greater capacity to generate income from one single activity. In the intermediate legal and illegal categories, the majority of owners of enterprises do not have any other source of income. Therefore, there is a clear direct link between a greater degree of legality and economic independence. The foregoing suggests that those who have a second job to

Table 3.10 Breakdown of Enterprises by Degree of Legality and Alternative Employment

Category	Other Job	
	Yes	No
Generalized illegality	3	3
Restricted illegality	1	3
Restricted legality	3	5
Generalized legality		4
Total	7	15
Percentage of total	32.0	68.0

supplement their income consider that it is only temporary, experimental, or that their economic success is highly uncertain and they do not wish to formalize their business for the time being. On the other hand, if in the long term the second job provides sufficient income, there will be a greater incentive to legalize, although, as will be seen later, other factors affect this decision.

The Capacity to Absorb Tax and Labor Obligations

Data on the cost of legalizing an enterprise indicate that the establishment and installation of microenterprises such as those studied does not involve high monetary costs (between 2 and 3.5 times the current minimum monthly wage), even if a trading company is set up. For example, in the case of microindustries that decide to adopt the tax regime of natural persons in order to save expenditure on constituting a legal entity—authorization, registration of the statutes with a public attorney, and inclusion in the public property register—the cost would be almost nothing.

Nevertheless, whatever tax regime is decided upon, there are eleven procedures that must be followed when setting up a business: ten authorities are involved, thirteen forms have to be filled out, and between 83 and 240 days are needed to complete the formalities. These figures are taken from the procedural rules of the governmental authorities involved and do not take into account the issue of any permits such as those for building or use of gas and authorizations to process food, which require more complicated and lengthy procedures. The real time needed to complete these formalities is considerably longer.

The following analysis focuses only on the objective effect on gross profits if enterprises respect all their tax obligations and the minimum legal payment of contributions resulting from the employment of workers.[11] It is thus possible to estimate their relative capacity to absorb such costs.

The application of tax and labor laws involves different criteria in each case, and the total tax and labor costs borne by individual units have different effects. Table 3.11 shows the percentage of gross profits represented by tax and labor costs on the assumption that enterprises fulfill all their obligations; in other words, it shows what Hernando de Soto called the costs of remaining legal. The results show that almost one-third of these enterprises, which do not employ salaried personnel or only occasionally employ family members, are legally exempt from any payment of tax. On the other hand, it also shows that a total of ten microenterprises that scrupulously fulfill their obligations are faced with total costs that vary between 28 and 50 percent of their profits. This means that a large number of enterprises are in very precarious circumstances for the continuation of their activities, mainly those that generate profits equivalent to between one and three minimum wages. It

Table 3.11 Total Fiscal and Labor Costs by Enterprise as a Percentage of Gross Profits

Cost as Percentage of Profits	Number of Enterprises	Percentage of Enterprises[a]	Cumulative Percentage[a]
0.00	6	27.3	27.3
0.00	1	4.5	31.8
0.12	1	4.5	36.4
0.16	2	9.0	45.5
0.18	2	9.0	54.5
0.28	1	4.5	59.1
0.29	1	4.5	63.6
0.37	1	4.5	68.2
0.38	1	4.5	72.7
0.39	1	4.5	77.3
0.43	2	9.0	86.4
0.44	1	4.5	90.9
0.50	2	9.0	100.0
Total	22	100.0	

[a]Columns do not total 100 due to rounding.

should be pointed out that the scale of tax and labor charges varies between 0 and 50 percent for the category of enterprises commonly identified on the basis of their small scale. Although this might be considered inequitable as such, it also illustrates the range of productivity prevailing in the sector surveyed.

To assess the different effects of the costs of remaining legal, one must analyze the separate implications of tax and labor charges with respect to the profits of the enterprises. Table 3.12 shows the percentage of costs to be paid by these enterprises to comply with their tax commitments, mainly those related to profits tax. Table 3.13 shows the percentage of labor costs that officially have to be paid on payrolls and wages, as well as compulsory benefits such as employers' contributions to social security and the workers' housing fund and the annual sharing of profits.

Comparison of Tables 3.12 and 3.13 shows that, in spite of the fact that a larger number of enterprises are obliged to pay taxes, these represent a much lower average cost (13.4 percent) than would be the case if all the benefits legally due to workers were paid (24.3 percent).[12] The burden of these charges on already limited profits is one of the reasons why these enterprises commonly use unpaid labor and are reluctant to employ more workers, as is borne out by the fact that 50 percent of the cases studied do not wish to employ additional labor.

The effect of total fiscal and labor costs by category of legality also varies. A more precise assessment of the potential effects of legalizing

Table 3.12 Fiscal Costs by Enterprise as a Percentage of Gross Profits

Cost as Percentage of Profits	Number of Valid Enterprises	Percentage of All Enterprises	Percentage of Valid Enterprises[a]	Cumulative Percentage[a]
0.00	3	13.6	18.8	18.8
0.04	1	4.5	6.3	25.0
0.08	2	9.0	12.5	37.5
0.09	1	4.5	6.3	43.8
0.12	2	9.0	12.5	56.3
0.13	1	4.5	6.3	62.5
0.16	1	4.5	6.3	68.8
0.18	2	9.0	12.5	81.3
0.21	1	4.5	6.3	87.5
0.38	2	9.0	12.5	100.0
Total	16	72.7	100.0	
Not valid	6	27.3		

[a]Columns do not total 100 due to rounding.

Table 3.13 Labor Costs by Enterprise as a Percentage of Gross Profits

Cost as Percentage of Profits	Number of Valid Enterprises	Percentage of All Enterprises[a]	Cumulative Percentage
0.06	1	4.5	9.1
0.12	1	4.5	18.2
0.16	1	4.5	27.3
0.17	1	4.5	36.4
0.22	1	4.5	45.5
0.25	1	4.5	54.6
0.27	1	4.5	63.7
0.30	1	4.5	72.8
0.31	1	4.5	81.9
0.40	1	4.5	91.0
0.41	1	4.5	100.0
Total	11	50.0	
Not valid	11	50.0	

[a]Columns do not total 100 due to rounding.

enterprises on their economic results can be made on the basis of the information given in Table 3.14. The relationship between the degree of legality and the range of total fiscal and labor costs does not show any clear trend in the cases studied. In the case of enterprises in the generalized illegality category, even though they are usually in the lower tax range because the majority are exempt from taxes, one case is situated in the 11–30 percent of tax on

Table 3.14 Breakdown of Enterprises by Degree of Legality and Range of Total Fiscal and Labor Costs

Category	0–10% of Profits	11–30% of Profits	31–50% of Profits	Total
Generalized illegality	4	1	1	6
Restricted illegality	1	2	1	4
Restricted legality	1	2	5	8
Generalized legality	1	2	1	4
Total	7	7	8	22
Percentage of total	31.8	31.8	36.4	100.0

profits category and one in the maximum charges category. In these cases, it can be assumed that illegality is an effect of the negative assessment by employers of the potential costs because they are prepared to run the risk of being discovered. The same could be said of enterprises in the restricted illegality sector; in other words, the breakdown by category is relatively homogeneous. On the other hand, in the restricted legality category, the majority of enterprises are in the maximum range of total charges. This could be due to a number of factors, such as high earnings or intensive use of salaried employees. Whatever the reason, according to the entrepreneur's logic, the burden is excessive and, at least in theory, is a reason to evade obligations, even when the necessary registration and licenses are obtained, even though the obligations are not strictly fulfilled.[13] This suggests that it is, in fact, the law that to a certain extent encourages evasion.

The main problem for these enterprises is their period of exposure to the market, their greater scale of production, and the need to issue and receive invoices for sales and purchases, which obliges them to fulfill at least formally their legal obligations. This means that, although the risk of control increases, their relatively high earnings, partly due to evasion of tax and labor costs, allow them to absorb the fines and penalties.

Lastly, the breakdown of enterprises within the generalized legality category is relatively homogeneous with regard to the different ranges of total fiscal and labor costs, expenditures that are presumably absorbed by them. If one compares these figures with the information given in Table 3.9, it can also be seen that these enterprises do not bear an excessive tax burden even though they generate relatively high earnings. This might indicate that their legalization has allowed them to have access to certain fiscal exemptions from which other relatively illegal enterprises cannot benefit.

Table 3.15 shows the effect of current tax obligations on enterprises, taking into account their degree of legality and the period when they commenced functioning. For the two enterprises that have been in existence longest, the tax burden is the highest, as their legal situation is situated

Table 3.15 Breakdown of Enterprises by Degree of Legality, Total Fiscal and Labor Costs, and Period of Commencement of Activities

Category and Period Activities Commenced	Total Fiscal and Labor Costs			Total	Percentage of Total Enterprises
	0–10%	11–30%	31–50%		
Generalized illegality					
Before 1965			1	1	4.5
1965–1974					
1975–1982	1			1	4.5
1983–1988	3	1		4	18.2
Restricted illegality					
Before 1965			1	1	4.5
1965–1974					
1975–1982	1			1	4.5
1983–1988		2		2	9.0
Restricted legality					
Before 1965					
1965–1974	1			1	4.5
1975–1982			3	3	13.6
1983–1988		2	2	4	18.2
Generalized legality					
Before 1965					
1965–1974		1	1	2	9.0
1975–1982		1		1	4.5
1983–1988	1			1	4.5

between totally illegal enterprises and those that have complied with some registration requirements but evade the heavy fiscal and labor charges they should pay in theory. In other words, their stability and growth is partly due to tax evasion.

The three enterprises established between 1965 and 1974 are concentrated in the legal categories, mainly in the generalized legality category, and they are to be found in the three ranges of fiscal and labor costs. The ability to remain in the market is due to economic consolidation over a certain period, which has allowed them to fulfill their legal obligations. These examples show that, despite far-reaching changes in fiscal and labor regulations, which have led to important increases in taxes since 1965, these enterprises have been able to absorb the fiscal and labor burden without opting for illegality. It should be emphasized that this has so far been the period of greatest economic development, which undoubtedly meant that these enterprises' profit levels were such that they were not obliged to transgress fiscal and labor regulations.

During the period 1975–1982, which corresponds to the period of commencement and consolidation of the economic crisis, six enterprises within the restricted legality category commenced activities. In this category, the heaviest fiscal and labor costs affect these enterprises. This clearly indicates that, although the commencement of activities is closely linked to the macrosocial situation, continued existence—relative stability—is possible only to the extent that these enterprises took the most appropriate solution, namely, to remain outside the law and not fulfill their obligations. This means that, under the same regulatory framework, administrative procedures, and tax burden, variations in macroeconomic activity are also a determining factor in inciting entrepreneurs to remain outside the law.

Finally, of the eleven enterprises (50 percent of those studied) that commenced activities at the most acute stage of the crisis affecting the Mexican economy, 1983–1988, five of them are subject to intermediate levels of taxes. It should also be emphasized that the majority (six enterprises) are situated in the generalized illegality and restricted legality categories, which serves to confirm the statement made above.

The enterprise deemed to be completely legal was able to commence activities only because it found in existing provisions a framework that allowed it to have the maximum legality and at the same time totally evade taxes. This is the case for cooperative enterprises, which give workers the opportunity to reach a *modus vivendi* in response to the reduction in formal labor markets and provide an example of legal possibilities for exemption from taxes. The difficult conditions governing the creation of private enterprises can be overcome only if the risks are reduced to the minimum. It should also be noted that all these workers had lost their previous jobs, and their political experience allowed them to join together and obtain support in the form of credit from an international foundation. The casuistic situation of this unit nevertheless shows how exceptional it is for an enterprise to fulfill all the fiscal requirements and still be in a position to function under adverse macroeconomic conditions.

For the above-mentioned reasons, it can be concluded that the majority of enterprises in the informal sector that are in the categories of illegality or restricted legality are of recent creation and their situation outside the law can be explained by the heavy fiscal and labor costs legality would entail in respect of gross profits in an unfavorable macroeconomic context. The rationale of the enterprise is not to develop production as an alternative in order to increase net earnings in absolute terms, but rather the negative assessment of the percentage to be paid for legalization.

Before the 1970s, control of the functioning of enterprises in Mexico City, including the metropolitan zone, was highly centralized. The opposite became the case when enterprises were created in the 1980s and the government adopted a plan for simplifying official administrative procedures, which meant that those related to the creation and installation of an enterprise could be carried out relatively easily and promptly. However, an analysis of recently created enterprises shows how fiscal and labor costs, despite official incentives, still tend to be a determining factor in the decision to be illegal, even though the importance of this factor basically depends on the prevailing macroeconomic situation. In other words, with relevant reservations, the figures tend to support the following hypothesis: in periods of relative economic stagnation, the legal, fiscal, and labor framework applicable to enterprises becomes "excessive" and therefore increases the propensity for evasion. On the other hand, in times of relative economic prosperity, the institutional framework appears "reasonable" and thereby increases the propensity for enterprises to fulfill their legal obligations.

Consideration will now be given to the impact of overall fiscal and labor costs according to the type of activity of the enterprises studied. Table 3.16 shows important differences in this regard. In the case of enterprises in the commerce sector, there is a relation, albeit slight, between greater legality and higher fiscal and labor charges, these enterprises being situated in the intermediate tax range. As already mentioned, this is due to the fact that there is a greater need for retailers to carry on their work in public, and this makes it more likely that they will fulfill their legal obligations, at least formally.

In contrast to the foregoing, in the industrial sector the distribution of

Table 3.16 Breakdown of Enterprises by Degree of Legality, Total Fiscal and Labor Costs, and Sector of Economic Activity

Category and Type of Activities	Total Fiscal and Labor Costs			Total	Percentage of Total Enterprises
	0–10%	11–30%	31–50%		
Generalized illegality					
Commerce					
Industry	4	1	1	6	27.3
Services					
Restricted illegality					
Commerce					
Industry	2	1	1	4	18.2
Services					
Restricted legality					
Commerce	1	2		3	13.6
Industry			1	1	4.5
Services			4	4	18.2
Generalized legality					
Commerce		1		1	4.5
Industry		1	1	2	9.0
Services		1		1	4.5
Total	7	7	8	22	
Percentage of total enterprises	31.8	31.8	36.4	100.0	

ranges of fiscal and labor costs is homogeneous, but enterprises tend to be in the illegal category due to the fact that relations with markets are carried out through intermediaries. Despite the fact that their low scale of production and earnings would make them exempt, it is likely that their illegality is also the result of their recent creation or the lack of information on registration formalities that would not involve significant expenditure. It could also reflect a form of protection against unstable markets.

Service enterprises are located in the middle levels of legality, probably due to their direct contact with the public and the high fiscal and labor costs they would have to bear. As it would be very costly for them to become fully legal, they prefer to run the risk of being "caught"—a risk that is not very high because, according to those interviewed, control by government officials is infrequent and inspectors almost never visit their workshops.

To further approximate the impact of the probable costs for the enterprises studied, an indicator of productivity in terms of value added by worker was calculated. In principle, the results show that informal enterprises should not necessarily be considered as having low productivity. In addition, although it is not possible to state that the generalized legality or illegality has a positive or negative effect on productivity levels, there are in fact important links, which will be described below.

The information given in Table 3.17 shows that, in the generalized illegality category, there are enterprises with low, medium, and high levels of productivity that are positively related, in general terms, to the three ranges of fiscal and labor charges. This implies that higher productivity means higher fiscal and labor charges, thereby showing a certain progressiveness and, up to a certain point, fairness in the distribution of costs in accordance with an enterprise's capacity to generate value added. Nevertheless, it should be noted that some enterprises with similar levels of productivity have to bear very different charges, which can have a very regressive impact.

Second, the three levels of productivity are also represented in the restricted legality category, although enterprises tend to be concentrated in the medium levels of productivity. Unlike the situation in the generalized illegality category, in this category all the enterprises pay the maximum fiscal and labor charges. It is also blatantly unfair to impose the same charges on enterprises with different levels of productivity.

Finally, it is important to note that there are elements that indicate that, first, even though the average level of productivity in the enterprises studied is low in comparison with enterprises in the formal sector, there are important differences among them. Second, there is a positive correlation between the degree of legality and the level of productivity; in other words, the move from generalized illegality to generalized legality is directly linked to progress from lower to higher levels of productivity. Although the sample size in this analysis is small, it is nevertheless possible to suggest that an increase in the average level of productivity in informal enterprises, as well

Table 3.17 Breakdown of Enterprises by Category of Legality, Total Fiscal and Labor Charges, and Levels of Productivity

Category and Level of Productivity[a]	Total Fiscal and Labor Costs			Total	Percentage of Total
	0–10%	11–30%	31–50%		
Generalized illegality					
Low	2	1		3	21.4
Medium		1	1	2	14.3
High			1	1	7.1
Restricted illegality					
Low		1		1	7.1
Medium					
High					
Restricted legality					
Low			1	1	7.1
Medium			3	3	21.4
High			1	1	7.1
Generalized legality					
Low					
Medium					
High		1	1	2	14.3
Total				14[b]	

[a] Low productivity = two times the legal minimum wage (US$210/month); medium productivity = four times the legal minimum wage (US$420/month); high productivity = five or more times the legal minimum wage (US$630/month).
[b] This does not include enterprises that are exempt from payment of tax and/or do not employ labor.

as a decrease in the average tax and labor costs or their more equitable distribution, would incite a larger number of enterprises to legalize their activities.

Summary and Evaluation of the Results

One of the objectives of this study was to analyze the functioning and economic performance of a number of informal production units that operate under varying conditions of legality and illegality. In addition, on the basis of a statistical study of the enterprises selected, as well as the regulations in force regarding formalities for creation, installation, and functioning that are applicable to the enterprises selected, estimates were made of the cost in time and money of legalizing these enterprises, as well as their relative capacity to absorb such costs.

Twenty-two enterprises situated in different areas of Mexico City, representing illegal market sectors, were chosen. These were disseminated among the three economic subsectors: four enterprises in the commerce sector (foodstuffs, footwear, and general supplies), thirteen in industry (leather goods, clothing, furniture, food processing, footwear, chemical products, and manufacture of manual tools), and five in services (car repairs and electrical installation). The great majority of the enterprises studied did not employ more than five workers, whether unpaid members of the family or salaried workers, and eleven of them started functioning during the last four years. In general, owners were heads of families whose spouses helped in the work and whose children were of school age.

Information concerning the formalities fulfilled by owners vis-à-vis various public bodies for obtaining registration, permits, and other legal obligations for their activities showed that there was a wide variety of legal situations and circumstances among the enterprises. The owners accorded greater importance to fiscal registration—registration for the collection and payment of value-added tax and profits tax—considered as the minimum indispensable for carrying on their activities. On the other hand, fulfillment of legal formalities required by trade and industrial promotion authorities and local government authorities for the purpose of authorization to use urban areas, as well as registration with the labor authorities, were the least frequent. Even where there is some type of registration, the degree of compliance with legal provisions is also very different. The casuistic explanation is the result of a number of different factors such as trade links with other formal enterprises, direct contact with the public or through intermediaries, the number of salaried workers employed, the level of macroeconomic activity, the owners' belief that their activity is temporary or very unstable or that full-scale legalization would be too costly, as well as the relative ease with which the authorities can be deceived or bribed if one is found out.

The foregoing showed that the distinction between "legal" and "illegal" enterprises was not realistic, and it was decided to establish degrees of legality/illegality in accordance with the hierarchical order followed by the owners themselves in defining the minimum or maximum requirements to be fulfilled or the total or partial evasion of fiscal or labor costs. Six of the twenty-two enterprises that had no form of registration or license and transgressed all the fiscal and labor laws were situated in the generalized illegality category; the restricted illegality category contained four enterprises that were at least formally registered with the finance authorities or had a local government authorization but had only a single financial obligation or paid nothing; the restricted legality category included eight enterprises that had the greatest number of registrations, permits, and the like in the legal, fiscal, and labor spheres but whose fulfillment of the implicit legal provisions was partial or nonexistent; finally, only four enterprises comprised the generalized legality category on the basis of their declaration of strict compliance with all the regulations, tax obligations, and benefits for their employees.

The results show that industrial enterprises are found in all the categories but tend to be situated in the illegal categories, whereas commercial and service enterprises are concentrated in the restricted legality category. This is because industrial activities take place independently and have links with other enterprises through intermediaries, whereas commerce and service enterprises are obliged to have greater public contact with their customers and are thus more easily detectable by local and federal inspectors. This view is reinforced when one considers that activities that take place in premises that serve as both homes and places of work—as is the case for industrial workshops—tend to be situated in the generalized illegality category. In contrast, enterprises specializing in services to the public are obliged, at least formally, to comply with the regulations in force and thus are found in the legal categories. It is therefore possible to affirm that the type of activity and the form of relationship to markets are determinant factors in the tendency to remain outside the law.

It should be noted that, independent of the legal status of the microenterprises studied, there are similarities among them. For example, 82 percent of the enterprises do not include under expenditure any payment for labor because most of them use family members and, in general, the salaried workers do not receive the remuneration prescribed by the law. Those questioned stated that this was due to high turnover and lack of reliability among workers. Two-thirds of the enterprises do not allocate expenditure for administrative costs, and the majority of the enterprises do not use credit sources—nor do they wish to because they consider credit to be expensive and very risky given the uncertainty of the market. They are not used to keeping reserves for reinvestment and contingencies, either. The above clearly reflects the absence of capitalist orientation in the activities of these enterprises. The rationale of their entrepreneurial activity is rather to guarantee the minimum indispensable income for family needs, and not accumulation of wealth as such. This is why they do not see the need to formalize their activities properly or do so only partially, particularly when the activity constitutes a second source of income.

In spite of the similarities among the enterprises, there are specific differences according to legal situation. There is a clear correlation between the number of workers employed and the degree of legality. Enterprises employing up to two workers tend to be in the generalized illegality category, whereas those with three to five workers are in the restricted legality category; only four of the enterprises (two with up to fifteen employees) stated that they fulfilled all their obligations, which clearly indicates that the number of personnel employed decisively influences decisions on compliance with legislation.

Although there is no clear correlation between the volume of gross profits and the degree of legality—highly profitable or unprofitable enterprises can be either legal or illegal—almost half of these enterprises have profits equivalent to between one and three times the minimum wage and are usually found in the restricted legality category. There is a wide variety within this sector of enterprises, but even more important is the fact that a high degree of legality does not guarantee higher levels of income, nor does functioning in a totally illegal situation mean low incomes. What does appear true, however, is the likelihood of having medium levels of profits when one functions in the restricted legality category. It would appear that the most advantageous and least risky situation is to combine formal legality with partial compliance or noncompliance with legislation, which is the case for seven of the twenty-two enterprises selected.

Another important indicator of the extreme heterogeneity of enterprises on a similar scale is the varying impact of the cost of maintaining legal status, in other words, the fiscal and labor costs, although it must be recognized that the initial financial expenditure resulting from the formalities to be fulfilled when creating an enterprise are not costly and can be met by all the enterprises. One-third of the enterprises studied were exempt from payment of taxes and labor benefits, although for eleven enterprises total deductions represented between 28 and 50 percent of their gross profits, an excessive amount if one considers that average levels of profits are from one to three times the current minimum wage, and they are therefore difficult to absorb. Although the weighted average of overall fiscal and labor costs is 30 percent, the range of the cost—between 0 and 50 percent—applicable to units with very similar levels of earnings, employees, and sales is highly inequitable. Moreover, when the overall cost is divided into its fiscal and labor components, it can be seen that although the fiscal cost affects a larger number of enterprises, its impact on gross profits (13.4 percent on average) is much lower than that of labor costs (24.3 percent). This underlines the existence of an implicit tax penalty for employing labor and therefore hinders the creation of jobs in this type of unit or, at least, results in a greater tendency toward evading labor costs rather than taxes.

Enterprises in the restricted legality category bear the greatest burden of overall fiscal and labor costs, whereas those in the generalized legality category, which is one of the most profitable, show a homogeneous distribution among the three ranges of costs. This might indicate, although there is not sufficient proof, that legalization provides the opportunity for enterprises to obtain fiscal exemptions that allow them to reduce considerably the impact of tax on their profits and consequently on their capacity to develop. Nevertheless, the majority of enterprises in the illegal and restricted legality categories commenced their activities during the past decade, which was characterized by a recession in macroeconomic activity and instability, whereas totally legal enterprises were created in the previous years of relative prosperity. It is therefore easy to understand that the uncertainty of the economic situation incites entrepreneurs to be more reluctant to comply with the legislation in force, which they consider to be excessive, compared to the high degree of risk implicit in their activities. These enterprises have been able to continue, and some of them to grow, in terms of earnings and sales, only by evading taxes and labor obligations.

With the help of a simple indicator of levels of worker productivity:

$$\frac{\text{salaries + gross profits}}{\text{persons employed}}$$

it is possible first of all to see that there is a great disparity between the various levels of productivity, which vary between the equivalent of US$210 and US$630 per month for enterprises on a fairly similar scale. Second, although in the generalized illegality category there is a positive correlation between the three levels of productivity and the three ranges of overall fiscal and labor costs, there are also cases in which the same level of productivity entails different costs and vice versa. In the restricted legality category, the cost is equivalent to between 30 and 50 percent of gross profits for enterprises with different levels of productivity, and this underlines the high degree of regression implicit in the fiscal and labor legislation.

To summarize, although the cases studied are not statistically representative of the informal enterprise sector as a whole, which is generically designated illegal, they do show the high degree of heterogeneity prevalent in the sector, in terms of both economic performance and relative capacity to absorb the costs implicit in possible legalization because the same fiscal and labor regulations have a very different and inequitable effect on enterprises on a similar scale. It has also been shown that decisions by owners with regard to the degree of "legality" or "illegality" they deem necessary or sufficient is the result of a number of factors such as family structure, type of activity, market exposure, alternative employment, the capacity of government authorities to control such enterprises, and the possibility of bribing authorities. It is therefore not only the consequence of the excessive and burdensome regulations in force, as some authors have suggested.

The simplification or modification of regulations implied by economic incentives for such enterprises, together with more equitable sharing of the tax and labor costs, is necessary, but it will not be sufficient to slow down expansion of this sector, particularly during a period of economic recession.

This research does not provide an exhaustive analysis of the problems characterizing this sector in its microsocial scope in the institutional framework, nor does it aim to put forward a possible field of action to remedy the situation. But it does highlight the complexity of the subject and the need to undertake more detailed analyses. The aim should be to define the causality and interaction among the factors that determine the origin and development of illegality in the urban informal sector. More rigorous systematic studies that go into greater detail and have wider scope than the present study, methodologically relating the microsocial and macrosocial spheres, will make it possible to suggest alternative policies for a possible solution that will be both viable and equitable. This study represents a modest contribution to that process.

Notes

1. The pioneer work on this subject by Keith Hart (1972) Africa was published by the ILO.
2. In this connection, see Tokman (1979).
3. The prime exponent of this view is Hernando de Soto (1986), whose research was carried out in Peru in 1984.
4. The significance of this statement will be explained in the course of this study. In any event, it will be seen how the fragmentation of the overall sector studied is sufficiently complex to permit a global explanation of the problem.
5. The total number of enterprises and their final distribution depended on the available list of enterprises that were probably outside the law, according to the criteria selected, but permitted more reliable control of the margin of probable error regarding their legal status.
6. See Giner de los Ríos (1986). This study lists three strata of microenterprises; the only indicator used to define microenterprises is a limit of fifteen workers, and the variants used are the number of salaried and nonsalaried workers. According to the author, the strata are defined as simple, transitional, and capitalist.
7. This problem was dealt with in two ways: by recording the costs of the previous week, month, or day according to information supplied by the owner and by analyzing these figures. In addition, in order to verify this information, the respondent was asked to give earnings as a percentage in accordance with the various headings under expenditures. Nevertheless, it cannot be unequivocally stated that in all cases the results of analysis of the data are sufficiently consistent.
8. Decisions resulting from tax inspection by the SHCP or the DDF Treasury do not depend upon the inspectors because their visits are generally governed by an established order. In the case of inspection by the SS or the Fire Department, the inspector himself decides whether or not the regulation requirements have been met.
9. This calculation was made by giving the maximum weight to registers that imply systematic expenditure for enterprises and the least weight to those that are necessary only in order to start functioning.
10. Regarding the subject of clandestine operations, see Bromley (1980).
11. Gross profits were calculated by deducting from earnings for total annual sales the amount of inputs, wages, and other costs related to the activity. Further details analyzing tax and accounts in each of the twenty-two cases studied has been discussed earlier in this chapter. As this analysis shows, the concepts of operating profits and net profits involve, among other things, deductions for profits tax and employers' contributions to social security, as well as various costs. The cost in time and money of making calculations, filling in forms, and dealing with the tax, labor, and regulatory authorities has not been taken into account.
12. Calculation of the labor costs was made solely taking into account the minimum fixed benefits laid down in the Federal Labour Law on the basis of the minimum integrated wage, independently of whether or not the workers in these

enterprises were paid less than this; the labor costs shown are therefore underestimated.

13. As was seen previously, the major concentration of enterprises in the restricted legality sector by range of gross profits is to be found among those corresponding to one to three minimum wages. Imposing taxes equivalent to 50 percent of their profits would virtually ensure the disappearance of these enterprises.

Part 3

The Cost of Legality

4

Barriers to Legality and Their Costs for the Informal Sector

Ricardo A. Lagos

To set up a microenterprise, minimum requirements in terms of investment, technology, experience, and legal procedures have to be met. One aspect of this that has been much discussed in recent years relates to the obstacles posed by the institutional and legal framework to the possibility of "formalizing" the informal sector. In fact, it has been strongly maintained that government intervention through disproportionate regulation and bureaucracy imposes high financial costs and is excessively time consuming—a circumstance that would explain the ever-growing trend toward unregulated activities.[1]

That argument is partially correct. It is true that for an informal unit to become and stay legal it needs to comply with different legal requirements, which involve financial costs as well as time. Financial costs include a series of initial registration fees, as well as payments of tax and labor obligations during the functioning of the unit. Time costs depend on the degree of intricacy of the registration procedure and the degree of efficiency of state institutions involved in the registration process.

What is not correct, however, is the statement that time and financial costs are always excessive due to disproportionate regulations. Case studies of eight Latin American countries show that both time and financial costs vary widely among countries, and that the number of informal activities exceeds that purported by the institutional-and-legal-obstacle argument.

Based on those case studies, this topic is analyzed in this chapter, and an attempt is made to identify how important the costs imposed by the regulatory framework are to the informal sector. In the next section, the prominent legal barriers to becoming and staying legal are identified and the main conclusions drawn from the case studies in terms of time and financial costs are highlighted, emphasizing the general patterns found and pointing to country differences. Finally, some concluding remarks are presented.

The research focused on eight Latin American countries: Bolivia, Brazil, Chile, Ecuador, Guatemala, Mexico, Uruguay, and Venezuela.[2] The studies were carried out in 1988–1989 by independent researchers who worked under the general guidance of Víctor Tokman, director of PREALC. In broad terms the aim of the case studies was to determine the procedures and costs (expressed in time and resources) for legally constituting and consolidating urban informal units or microenterprises. Specifically, the objective was to determine the time it takes to register firms and the bureaucratic steps required; the financial resources devoted to the payments of registration, permits, fees, taxes, and so forth; and the burden associated with the operational costs (taxes and labor obligations). The research was based on interviews with informal units that had undergone or were in the process of formalization. The number of microenterprises studied in each country varied from two to twenty-two. The total number of enterprises studied was sixty, of which thirty-one operate in manufacturing activities, fifteen in the service sector, and fourteen in the trade sector. The number and type of microenterprises studied is shown in Table 4.1. An effort was made to select those informal units that seem to illustrate best the typical microenterprise in each respective field or activity.

Legal Barriers and Their Costs

The case studies show that in general the process of formalization (legalization) of a microenterprise consists of two related but differentiated aspects: (a) entry to legality, and (b) staying legal.

Entry to Legality

Basically, entry to legality for a microenterprise means the possibility of becoming part of the regulated or formal economy. In all the cases studied, to achieve legal recognition, it is necessary to comply with several registrations in public offices at both the local and national levels. The purpose of the registrations is to acknowledge the legal existence of the microenterprise at different levels: as an economic unit authorized to operate in determined activities (e.g., trade, production, or services); as an economic unit subject to tax obligations; and as an economic unit that belongs to certain associations of producers, traders, and so forth. Furthermore, and as important, the purpose of registration is, in principle, to ensure that certain minimum standards are met in terms of health standards or product quality (e.g., activities related with food handling, chemical products, or security at work).

The barriers

According to the country studies, the procedure for legally establishing a microenterprise can involve up to five different sets of requirements: (1) the

Table 4.1 Microenterprises Studied by Country and Economic Activity

	Commerce	No.	Manufacture	No.	Services	No.
Bolivia		4		11		7
	vegetable store	2	clothing factory	5	car repair	2
	sweets store	1	wood products factory	2	shoe repair	2
	fruit store	1	steel products factory	3	radio & TV repair	1
			shoe production	1	snacks-cafeteria	1
					hairdresser	1
Brazil		2		1		1
	cosmetics retailer	1	clothing factory	1	telephone installation	1
	used furniture marketing	1				
Chile		1		2		
	grocery store	1	clothing factory	1		
			food processing factory	1		
Ecuador		1		1		
	grocery store	1	locksmith	1		
Guatemala		1		1		
	curtain shop	1	soap production factory	1		
Mexico		4		13		5
	shoe marketing	1	production of kitchens	1	car repair	3
	grocery store	1	clothing factory	1	electrical fittings	1
	retailer shop	2	chemical production	1	plumber	1
			shoe production	2		
			stamp clothing factory	1		
			food processing	4		
			harness-maker	1		
			tool production	1		
			wood production	1		
Uruguay				1		2
			food processing	1	shoe repair	1
					laundry	1
Venezuela		1		1		
	cosmetics retailer	1	plastic products factory	1		
Total		14		31		15

Sources: Bolivia: Escobar de Pabón (1990); Brazil: Looye (see Chapter 5); Chile: Velásquez (1990): Ecuador: Placencia (1990); Guatemala: Sáenz (1990); Mexico: Elizondo (1990); Uruguay: Quijano and Antía (1990); and Venezuela: Cartaya (see Chapter 6).

initial registration process, (2) procedures concerning the location of the microenterprise, (3) procedures related to health and safety standards, (4) registrations concerning taxes, and (5) rules related to labor.

Initial registration. The initial registration process refers to a number of registrations with the sole objective of obtaining legal existence as an economic unit. The actual initial registration process is similar in all the cases studied. It requires, most of the time, the physical presence of the applicant in different institutions or public offices, basic documentation, and specific forms filled in. Basically, initial registrations are carried out mainly at three levels: municipal councils (this is the case in all the countries), commercial registries (in Bolivia, Brazil, Guatemala, Uruguay, and Venezuela), and public promotional institutions that deal specifically with the interests of determined sectors (in Bolivia, Ecuador, and Mexico), as shown in Table 4.2.

The procedures that take place at municipal councils relate mainly to obtaining licenses and permits that will enable informal units to carry out commercial or productive activities. The registration process is rather simple and basically consists of filling out forms and attaching some documentation. The documentation requested by municipalities varies from case to case, but generally it requires the presentation of identification documents, proof of the constitution of the individual firm or company (where demanded), previous municipal tax receipts, and the payment of an enrollment fee.

In most cases the working license is granted on a temporary basis under the assumption that the applicants will comply with all the other requirements in due time (whether at the same municipality or other governmental offices). The case studies showed that access to a temporary license constitutes one of the main incentives toward registration at this level—a circumstance that might explain the high rate of compliance compared to the registration rate of microenterprises with commercial registries and even public promotional institutions.[3] Two other elements that explain the tendency to register at the municipal level are the low level of complexity of the procedures and the control and pressure exercised by municipal inspectors on informal units.

In contrast, the inscriptions at commercial registers (e.g., Register of Companies) show different levels of complexity, compliance, and effects for the informal units. In Bolivia, the registration is mandatory, but in practice it can be avoided because it is always possible to acquire some degree of legality without registration. In fact, there was no compliance with this registration step by the Bolivian units surveyed. Explanations for this vary from the degree of complexity of the procedure (one must understand accountancy methods and present balance sheets) to the perception that the registration is not required for small firms. However, in both Brazil and Venezuela the registration before the Register of Companies (*Junta Comercial*, in the case of Brazil) is widely observed by informal units because it is essential for obtaining at least a temporary license. In fact, the system is structured upon the basis that without this registration microenterprises are prevented from taking any other step toward legality. Furthermore, the regulations established for registering the firms are simple and straightforward. This is specially so in the case of Brazil, in which the registration before the *Junta Comercial* has been conceived to be of easy

Table 4.2 Initial Registration Procedures

Bolivia
- Registration with the Register of Companies (*Registro de Comercio*) (2 steps)
- Registration with the National Register of Small-Scale and Craft Industries (*Registro Nacional de Pequeña Industria y Artesanía*) (1 step)
- Registration in the Municipal Roll of Taxpayers (*Padrón Municipal de Contribuyentes*) (1 step)

Brazil
- Constitution of an individual firm or partnership and specification of the amount of capital invested (1 step)
- Registration before the *Junta Comercial* (3 steps)
- Obtaining an operating permit from the municipal government (2 steps)

Chile
- Approval by the Committee of Local Residents (*Junta de Vecinos*) of the neighborhood where the unit will operate (2 steps)
- Obtaining a working license from the competent municipality (2 steps)

Ecuador
- Registration at the competent municipality (2 steps)
- Inspection of the microenterprise by the Ministry of Finance to check declared amount of working capital and assets (1 step)
- Obtaining a working license from the competent municipality (2 steps)
- Skill recognition (*calificación*) and classification of the informal unit (34 steps)

Guatemala
- Registration of the owner of the unit in the Register of Companies (*Registro Mercantil*) as an individual trader or merchant (6 steps)
- Registration of the microenterprise with the Register of Companies (4 steps)

Mexico
- Constitution of a company before a public notary (*notario público*) (3 steps)
- Setting-up the informal unit (9 steps)
- Registration with the Commerce and Industrial Chambers (*Cámaras de Comercio e Industriales*) (1 step)
- Authorization to operate given by the Federal District and the Municipal Council (1 step)
- Securing a construction license (2 steps)

Uruguay
- Constitution of an individual firm or company before a public notary (*notario público*) (3 steps)
- Obtaining a commercial license given by the Public and General Register of Commerce (*Registro Público y General de Comercio*) (1 step)
- Registration with the National Economic Census (*Censo Económico Nacional*) (1 step)

Venezuela
- Registration in the Register of Companies (*Registro Mercantil*) (8 steps)
- Obtaining permit from the Ministry of Promotion (*Ministerio de Fomento*)—applicable only to industries (2 steps)
- Obtaining the industrial and commercial license at the competent municipal council (2 steps)
- Tax clearance certificate from the Municipal Urban Sanitation Institute (*Instituto Municipal de Aseo Urbano*) (1 step)

Sources: Bolivia: Escobar de Pabón (1990); Brazil: Looye (see Chapter 5); Chile: Velásquez (1990): Ecuador: Placencia (1990); Guatemala: Sáenz (1990); Mexico: Elizondo (1990); Uruguay: Quijano and Antía (1990); and Venezuela: Cartaya (see Chapter 6).

Note: Number in parentheses represents the number of steps required to carry out the procedure.

access to informal units. In the case of Guatemala, the registration before the Register of Companies is not difficult in itself, but the applicant must attach to the application a number of authenticated documents confirming the type of firm and its capital, certified by a public notary and previously approved by an accountant.

The case studies showed that the mandatory registration of informal units with public promotional institutions varies among countries. In both Bolivia and Mexico, the process is fairly easy and not expensive. However, in the case of Ecuador, the registration process is long and complex. An interesting aspect that arose from the studies in Bolivia and Ecuador is that the rate of compliance of the registrations, although compulsory in both cases, differ significantly. In Bolivia, in spite of having a simpler procedure, the registration is widely unobserved. In fact, only two of the twenty-two microenterprises studied were registered with the National Register of Small-Scale and Craft Industries (*Registro Nacional de Pequeña Industria y Artesanía*). On the other hand, in Ecuador, where the registration procedure is extremely complicated, an estimated 12 percent of the urban informal units were registered with one of the two institutions that deal with the promotion of microenterprises.[4]

It seems that what explains this difference is the importance of registration for carrying out further procedures and the perception, by the informal units seeking legalization, of the potential benefits such registration might imply. In fact, in Bolivia the surveyed units maintain that it was rather easy to operate without registration to the extent that many public offices, which in theory were forced to demand proof of registration before granting permits or even credit, did not bother to request it. Furthermore, another element that reinforces the low interest in registering in Bolivia is the belief that the National Register of Small-Scale and Craft Industries does not have a coherent promotion policy toward small-scale units, in spite of being created with that sole objective, and as a consequence it is not perceived as providing any significant benefits. In Ecuador, instead, the procedures that deal with the promotional regime, besides being extremely complicated due to an overlap of two different sets of laws that regulate the formalization of microenterprises, is unavoidable if a certain degree of legality is to be achieved. In fact, the process of classification and skill recognition (*calificación*) of informal units, which is done, respectively, by the Board for the Protection of Craftsmen or the Under Secretary of Small-Scale and Craft Industries, is the cornerstone of the whole formalization process.

Four countries (Brazil, Mexico, Uruguay, and Venezuela) require that in advance of the registration itself the informal unit must be constituted as an individual firm or a company or mercantile enterprise. The formalities differ according to the type of company (e.g., limited liability company, sole proprietor, and so on). Because most of the legislation has no specific designation for microenterprises,[5] the usual procedure is to constitute it either as an individual firm or as a limited liability company (*sociedad de responsabilidad limitada*). In Venezuela, the constitution of a company is acquired by registering the informal unit with the Register of Companies. A similar step takes place in Brazil, where the firm owners determine the type of firm they will adopt, and then they fill out a special form in the case of individual firms or prepare a partnership contract in the case of limited liability companies, for which a standard model contract is provided. In addition, they also register the firm or company with the local *Junta Comercial*. On the contrary, in Mexico and Uruguay, the constitution of a firm must be acquired through formal documents and before a public notary (equivalent to a solicitor). The services provided by the public notary are private and therefore constitute another expense. The exhibition of the documents certifying the constitution of the company or enterprise is an essential requisite of the registration process, to the extent that the legalization of an informal unit cannot be granted even under provisional terms without it.

Finally, in both Brazil and Chile, the initial procedures include obtaining the approval of the location where the unit intends to operate. In Brazil, approval is given by municipal authorities after an official inspection. In Chile, besides municipal approval, approval by the committee of local residents (*junta de vecinos*) of the neighborhood where the unit will operate is also required. Although these requirements form part of the initial steps toward formalization, its nature, particularly in the Chilean case, is related more to general requirements concerning urban regulations, as is shown next.

Location of the unit. The procedures concerning the location of microenterprises refer to the authorization given by local and residential authorities about the placement and the quality of the shop itself. Requirements of this type were found in the case of informal units in Brazil, Chile, Mexico, Uruguay, and Venezuela (see Table 4.3). The objectives behind these authorizations are to test the adequacy of the locale in terms of regulatory and environmental aspects. However, a study is also made of the property rights of the land where the unit will be placed. The authorization by local authorities consists of checking the locale where the informal unit will perform its activities against regulatory urban city plans concerning the location of industries and business.

The regulatory elements involved in the authorization of the unit's location are particularly severe in Mexico, Venezuela, and Chile. The authorities' main concern is related to the overpopulation of urban areas, particularly in Mexico and Venezuela. In fact, in Venezuela, there is complete prohibition for installation of any new industry in the Caracas metropolitan area; only informal units engaged in commercial activities can apply for installation permits. The study of Venezuela sustained that even in the latter case, only under exceptional circumstances is such a permit granted, and it is

Table 4.3 Administrative Steps Concerning the Location of Informal Units

Brazil
- Approval of the place where the firm intends to locate given by the Municipal Government. Two documents are required: the application itself and an authenticated copy of the last bill paid for local taxes. Afterwards, the municipal inspection takes place. (3 steps)

Chile
- Approval of both the place where the firm will be located and the quality of the construction by the Municipality's Public Works Service (*Servicio Municipal de Obras Públicas*). One must consult with the municipality regarding information about the site where the firm intends to be established, apply for approval of the location if it is possible to use the land for commercial or productive purposes, and register with the water and electricity company and ask them to inspect the water and electrical installations of the locale. (10 steps)

Mexico
- Authorization of conformity of use given by the Federal District and the Municipal Council. (1 step)
- Authorization of the locale's license given by the Urban Development Secretary (*Secretaría de Desarrollo Urbano*). (1 step)

Uruguay
- Approval of the locale by the Municipal Council. The approval requires a certificate from the fire brigade approving the locale's space and the firm's building plans signed by an architect. (2 steps)

Venezuela
- Authorization of conformity of use given by the Municipal Engineering Department (*Dirección de Ingeniería Municipal*). The application specifying the location of the unit is checked against the urban regulatory plans. (1 step)

Sources: Brazil: Looye (see Chapter 5); Chile: Velásquez (1990): Mexico: Elizondo (1990); Uruguay: Quijano and Antía (1990); and Venezuela: Cartaya (see Chapter 6).
Note: Number in parentheses represents the number of steps required to carry out the procedure.

expensive and still not completely legal. The situation for Chilean informal units highlighted a similar situation concerning the limitations for establishing small industries. In Chile, besides the municipal council permit, the approval of the committee of local residents (*junta de vecinos*) of the neighborhood where the microenterprise will operate is required. The requirement for a location permit approved by the local residents has been introduced to protect residential areas. Although the council permit in principle also shares this objective, the desire by local authorities to increase the business sector in their communities tends to conflict with the environmental aspects and the interests of residential area inhabitants.

The case studies (e.g., Uruguay and Venezuela) showed that when informal units were confronted with the impossibility of obtaining the approval of their locale, the actual solution was to conceal their activity and remain illegal or to establish a commercial activity with all its permits and to illegally run an industrial activity in the backyard of the site.

Health and safety. Health and safety requirements are demanded by national and local authorities with the objective of ensuring reasonable safe and healthy working environments as well as output (whether it be a product or a service), which comply with minimum quality standards. Health and safety requirements were mandatory in all the cases studied, although differences among countries were found in the procedures followed. Basically, there is an inspection by local authorities (e.g., engineers and architects from local councils and firemen) to verify whether the economic activity and the number of people working are compatible with the size, construction materials, water supplies, and other conditions of the plant and if the firm complies with safety regulations concerning machinery and clothing.[6] If the building does not meet the required standards, the informal unit is forced to carry out specific adjustments before continuing with the formalization process.

In all the cases studied the regulations were more stringent for manufacturing industry activities (especially in Brazil, Ecuador, Guatemala, and Venezuela), particularly those that involve food (especially in Chile and Uruguay), than for trade activities.

Tax registrations. The tax registrations—demanded by all legislations to all firms—are carried out at the national and local levels. At the national level, the informal unit must be registered with the Finance Ministry and/or the Inland Revenue Service. Besides the obvious purpose of taxing the microenterprises—although in many cases they are exempted because of their low level of earnings—the aim of registrations at the level of ministries and/or revenue services is to ensure an adequate identification system for tax purposes. Moreover, registration with the revenue services is essential to apply for credits, whether to the public or private sectors, and to deal with public services. Nevertheless, many of the registrations observed concerning taxes were carried out at the local level (i.e., municipalities). Most taxes deal with securing licenses (industrial or commercial) and with a wide set of permits regarding the use of sites and public services.

The structure of the tax registration process is basically similar in all countries studied. The differences concern the amount of paperwork, the complexity of the registration procedure, and the adequacy of the tax legislation to fit the economic features of the informal units. In most cases studied, the process has been simplified in recent years, but until the end of the 1970s, many of the procedures were difficult to follow and expensive.

The studies show that tax reforms carried out in Bolivia, Chile, and Brazil have simplified the process for microenterprises, substantially reducing the number of times the applicant must go to the tax institutions, the amount of paperwork, and the degree of complexity. In Bolivia, for example, tax registration is virtually free, the applicant defines to which tax category he/she is subject, and the procedure involves few administrative requirements.[7] In Chile, the tax registration process is also free (including the sealing of commercial receipts and account books) and simple. The process is carried out in only two institutions: the municipal council and the Inland Revenue Service, a circumstance that greatly reduces the registration time. In Brazil, the tax registration procedures are also concentrated in two institutions: the *Junta Comercial* and the State Internal Revenue Office. However, several documents are required (e.g., a copy of the certificate of constitution of an individual firm or partnership, proof of previous fees, and certified declarations, among others), and every registration requires a fee. In Uruguay, although the registration process is not free, it is simple, quick, and takes place in only one institution.

In other countries, such as Ecuador and Guatemala, the process still tends to be complicated or time-consuming. In some countries, registrations carried out at the level of the Ministry of Finance or the Inland Revenue Service were free (or nearly so), but those carried out at the municipal level required the payment of fees, as was the case in Mexico and Venezuela.

In spite of the tendency toward more simple tax systems, the main problem for microenterprises seems to be that the tax registration structure is designed to suit the features of formal firms and thus it contains a number of requirements that sometimes exceed the needs of small microenterprises (the case of Guatemala is illustrative in this respect). The introduction of legislation designed to cope with the economic structure of smaller units has proven to be effective in Mexico, with the sanctioning in 1988 of the Special Statute for the Promotion of Microenterprises (*Régimen Especial de Fomento de la Microindustria*), and in Brazil, with the Microenterprise Statute adopted in 1985.

Labor registration requirements. The registrations related to labor apply only to those informal firms that employ paid labor. The requirements basically involve recording the names and number of workers with the ministries of labor and/or labor inspectorates and with health and social security institutions. The main purpose for these registrations is to protect and guarantee labor rights of employees in terms of payments, working conditions, access to social security, and possible unemployment benefits.

The cases where information was available show that compliance with these regulations by informal units, although in some cases this may involve several steps or procedures, is simple and not expensive. In Guatemala, Uruguay, and Venezuela, registration is free; in Ecuador, it is inexpensive. Nevertheless, in Ecuador, registration entails indirect costs as a consequence of the employer's legal obligation to adjust wages to a determined legal minimum. Because in most cases the level of wages in informal units is below the legal minimum wage, this wage increase became a substantial burden.[8] Indirect costs are also present in Guatemala because after registration the owner is forced by law to contribute the equivalent of 10 percent of the payroll to the Guatemalan Social Security Institute.

The costs

The costs of fulfilling the different legal requirements mentioned above were measured in terms of the number of procedures or steps needed, the time (in days) involved, and the financial resources required.

Procedures. The case studies show that in most of the cases between 20 and 30 steps are required to register an economic activity. There were two extreme cases, Bolivia and Ecuador, in which the number of steps were five and fifty-nine, respectively (see Table 1.3 in Chapter 1, which presents a summary of the information contained in Tables 4.2 to 4.6). Most registration steps deal with two types of requirements: initial registration and procedures related to taxes. This situation is probably the consequence of the need of the government to regulate the type and number of economic activities carried out (in the case of initial registration requirements) and to control tax evasion.

Moreover, initial registration procedures and tax inscriptions were the requirements that most informal units complied with in the cases of Bolivia, Chile, Ecuador, Uruguay, and Venezuela because they give access to provisional legal existence and allowed operations to start.

Time costs. The time involved in the registration process greatly varies between countries, and even within countries. As is shown in Table 1.2, the time it takes to fulfill the registration requirements generally varies, in broad terms, from fifteen to thirty working days to a year. In some countries, such as Ecuador, Mexico, and Venezuela, the process takes around a year, and in the exceptional case of Guatemala, almost two years. In others, such as Bolivia, Brazil, Chile, and Uruguay, the time involved is between one and three months.

The data on procedures and time costs suggest two observations. First, the number of steps is not always related to the time it takes to perform them. In fact, in those countries in which the number of steps required to register a firm is high, the time it takes to comply with those steps is not necessarily high. The number of steps required to register a firm in Chile or Brazil, for example, is similar to the number required in Mexico or Venezuela, but in the latter countries the process is much more time consuming than in the former. This information suggests that the time it takes to legalize informal units is less related to the number of steps—although perhaps some or many of the requirements may be an excessive burden—than to the time it takes for the bureaucracy to process the applications.

The obstacles presented by the bureaucracy, expressed in the delay in processing registrations, are, in turn, the result of the degree of centralization/decentralization of a particular country, the type of administrative organization, and the complexity of the required procedures. In

Table 4.4 Administrative Steps Concerning Health and Security

Brazil
- Authorization by the Municipal Health Department (*Departamento de Salud Municipal*) (in the case of firms that work with food). The applicant must attach three documents: a petition for the firm to be inspected, an application to be enrolled in the health register, and a copy of the registration with the Inland Revenue Service (3 steps)

Chile
- Authorization by the Ministry of Health. The applicant must report to the Environment Health Service of the Health Ministry to determine whether the firm's economic activity involves a toxic or dangerous process and what the basic health requirement is. The applicant must submit the locale's floor plans for approval and apply for the health resolution. After these requirements are fulfilled, the health inspection takes place (4 steps)

Ecuador
- Authorization by the Municipal Sanitary Office (*Dirección de Higiene Municipal*). The applicant must apply for the sanitary permit and for an inspection of the informal unit; after the municipal inspection, it is necessary to go back to the Sanitary Office to obtain the permit (5 steps)

Guatemala[a]
- Authorization from the Ministry of Health. The applicant is required to obtain a license to run a laboratory to produce the product, to register the brand of the product with the Register of Intellectual Property, and to register the formula used to produce the product. The formula should be certified by a chemist and it should be patented (10 steps)

Mexico
- Obtaining a sanitary license from the Secretary of Health (1 step)

Uruguay
- Authorization given by the Bromathologic Institute (*Instituto Bromatológico*). The applicant is required to exhibit a certificate by the fire brigade and an inspection and qualification of the locale by the Bromathologic Institute (2 steps)

Venezuela
- Approval of the locale by the Fire Department (2 steps)
- Obtaining permit from the Ministry of Health (2 steps)
- Obtaining health certificates of owner and employees of informal unit (1 step)

Sources: Brazil: Looye (see Chapter 5); Chile: Velásquez (1990); Ecuador: Placencia (1990); Mexico: Elizondo (1990); Uruguay: Quijano and Antía (1990); and Venezuela: Cartaya (see Chapter 6).

Note: Number in parentheses represents the number of steps required to carry out the procedure.

[a]The procedures described are those required for the formalization of a small unit that produces soap—a circumstance which adds a number of extra procedures than those normally demanded in the case of productive activities.

Chile and Brazil, the registration process is highly decentralized, a circumstance that significantly increases the time in which permits are processed. In Bolivia, although the registration process has not undergone a significant decentralization, the number and, as important, the complexity of the registration process has been reduced.

The issue of the degree of intricacy of some requirements affects the registration process on the side of the informal unit as well as on the side of

Table 4.5 Administrative Steps Concerning Taxes

Bolivia
- Registration with the Single National Register of Taxpayers (*Registro Nacional Unico de Contribuyentes*). The applicant is only required to provide the name of the firm, to fill out a couple of applications, and to pay a very small fee (1 step)

Brazil
- Registration with the Internal Revenue Service at the *Junta Comercial* (1 step)
- Registration with the State Internal Revenue Office (*Coletoria Estadual da Fazenda* or *Coletoria Estadual*) (3 steps)
- Printing of official receipts, which enable them to carry out commercial transactions (2 steps)

Chile
- Obtaining the Single Tax Register (*Rol Unico Tributario*) (1 step)
- Declaration before the Inland Revenue Service of the initiation of economic activities (3 steps)
- Sealing of documents (account books and official receipts forms) (1 step)

Ecuador
- Registration with the Single National Register of Taxpayers (*Registro Unico de Contribuyentes*) at the Ministry of Finance (5 steps)
- Procurement of a seal with the number of the Single National Register of Taxpayers (1 step)

Guatemala
- Registration with the Unified Tax Register (*Registro Tributario Unificado*) at the Ministry of Finance. This requires a certificate of residence certified by a public notary (4 steps)
- Registration as a taxpayer of income tax at the Ministry of Finance. This requires a certificate of residence certified by a public notary; specification of the type of system used to value inventories and the name and number of the accountant responsible for keeping the firm's books; and indication, through a notarized certificate, of whether the owner has dependents and insurances (4 steps)
- Registration as a taxpayer of the value-added tax (2 steps)
- Sealing of and authorization to use account books (six different account books) by the Register of Companies and the Inland Revenue Service (2 steps)

Mexico
- Registration with the Federal Register of Taxpayers (*Registro Federal de Contribuyentes*) (1 step)
- Registration as a Value-Added Tax taxpayer with the local municipal treasury (*Ayuntamiento*) (1 step)

Uruguay
- Registration with the General Tax Office (*Dirección General Impositiva*). This requires previous registration with the Bank of Social Prevision (*Banco de Previsión Social*) and the certification of the applicant's signature by a public notary (3 steps)

Venezuela
- Registration with the Register of Tax Information (*Registro de Información Fiscal*) (2 steps)
- Obtaining a Tax Clearance Certificate (*Solvencia de Derecho de Frente*) (property tax) (2 steps)

Sources: Bolivia: Escobar de Pabón (1990); Brazil: Looye (see Chapter 5); Chile: Velásquez (1990); Ecuador: Placencia (1990); Guatemala: Sáenz (1990); Mexico: Elizondo (1990); Uruguay: Quijano and Antía (1990); and Venezuela: Cartaya (see Chapter 6).

Note: Number in parentheses represents the number of steps required to carry out the procedure.

Table 4.6 Administrative Steps Concerning Labor Registrations

Ecuador
- Registration of the owner and employees at the Ecuadorian Social Security Institute (IESS, *Instituto Ecuatoriano de Seguridad Social*). The registration process involves two inspections at the firm's locale by different services of the IESS, the exhibition of documents certifying the classification or skill recognition (*calificación*) of the owner, and the elaboration and approval of the payroll forms (9 steps)

Guatemala
- Handing over of labor contracts between owner and employees to the General Labor Inspectorate (*Inspección General del Trabajo*) (1 step)
- Registration of the owner as a "patrono" (employer) with the Guatemalan Social Security Institute (IGSS, *Instituto Guatemalteco de Seguridad Social*). This is applicable only to those firms with three or more employees. Besides some basic documentation (e.g. copy of the registration with the Register of Companies and of the certificate of residence) the firm undergoes an inspection to verify if the required legal conditions in terms of hygiene and security are met (4 steps)

Uruguay
- Registration with the Bank of Social Welfare (*Banco de Previsión Social*) (2 steps)
- Registration of the firm's payroll at the Ministry of Labor (1 step)
- Insurance of the firm's employees with the Insurance State Bank (*Banco de Seguros del Estado*) (1 step)

Venezuela
- Statistical Register at the Ministry of Labor (1 step)
- Registration in compliance with labor requirements. This registration involves two types of registrations: with the Labor Inspectorate and fulfillment of safety and industrial hygiene standards (2 steps)
- Registration with the Venezuelan Social Security Institute (*Instituto Venezolano de Seguros Sociales*) (2 steps)

Sources: Ecuador: Placencia (1990); Guatemala: Sáenz (1990); Uruguay: Quijano and Antía (1990); and Venezuela: Cartaya (see Chapter 6).
Note: Number in parentheses represents the number of steps required to carry out the procedure.

the public administration, as complex procedures may put an "excessive burden" on low-skilled civil servants. Based on this point, it could be maintained that when dealing with the issue of the time spent in the legalization process, the restructuring of the services that deal with the registration process should be examined, in addition to the number of steps required.

The second element refers to the fact that there are a larger number of steps and more time is spent to legalize economic activities engaged in manufacture than in commerce (see Table 1.2). This is because regulation concerning productive activities are stricter in terms of safety and health measures. There are more requisites to fulfill in terms of permits from labor and health authorities and more modifications to the locale than in the case of units involved in commercial activities.

The modifications concerning the locale are the ones that take most of the time because the law can be very rigorous. For example, for a Venezuelan microenterprise involved in the processing of plastic products to comply with the law for microenterprises would have involved checking and amending surface walls, the slope of the floors, the existence of toilet facilities, satisfactory ventilation, proper lighting, and so on.

Financial costs. The financial costs for becoming legal also show significant variations among countries. On the one hand, in countries such as Bolivia, Brazil, and Chile, financial costs of microenterprises fluctuate between less than 1 percent and 5 percent of annual profits (see Table 1.2). On the other hand, the financial costs in Ecuador, Uruguay, and Venezuela are significantly high, exceeding 20 percent of annual profits.

Also, the number of procedures or steps, and particularly the financial costs toward legalization, vary attending to whether or not the informal unit seeking legalization will be asked to introduce modifications in its locale. In fact, the case studies show that the financial costs involved in the modification of the outlet substantially increased the legalization costs in Chile, Ecuador, Uruguay, and Venezuela (see Table 4.7).

Basically, two aspects will determine the need to introduce such modifications: whether the informal unit will utilize labor and what type of activity the unit will pursue. For those microenterprises that use labor, all the legislations contemplate strict norms regarding the locale's conditions. Concerning the economic activity, there is a distinction among units that operate in production, trade, or services. Usually, those firms involved in trade are less exposed to the need to carry out modifications. In the case of economic units involved in goods, and particularly for those that require

Table 4.7 Financial Costs of Locale's Modifications

Country	Economic Branch	Cost (US$)	Monthly Profit (US$)	Ratio Between Cost and Monthly Profit	Annual Profit (US$)	Costs as Percentage of Annual Profit
Chile	commerce	5,308	345	15.4	4,135	128.3
	industry	11,135	650	17.1	7,798	147.8
Ecuador	commerce	70	17	4.1	207	33.8
	industry	70	85	0.8	1,020	6.8
Uruguay	industry	613	18	34.8	211	290.5
	services	613–675	258–550	2.4–1.2	3,099–6,600	19.7–10.2
Venezuela[a]	commerce	27,000	10,427	2.6	125,120	21.5
	industry	186,361	8,553	21.8	102,636	181.5

Sources: Chile: Velásquez (1990); Ecuador: Placencia (1990); Uruguay: Quijano and Antía (1990); Venezuela: Cartaya (see Chapter 6).
[a]costs and profits in Bs.

handling of harmful and toxic products, the number of steps is higher, as it is for those microunits involved in services that could eventually affect the health or safety of consumers.

In brief, because very few of the informal units seeking legalization operate in sites that possess all of the characteristics demanded by law, the number of modifications to be done are substantial. The latter is not surprising because informal units involved in manufacturing almost by definition operate in poor conditions regarding not only technology and resources, but also in terms of the actual structure of the building and safety and hygienic standards.

Staying Legal

As was mentioned previously, the process of turning legal or formalizing an informal unit embraces not only the aspects related to the entry to legality, but also implies the fulfillment of legal requirements during the actual operation of the unit. For an informal unit to be thoroughly formal is not enough to comply with the set of requirements regarding its legal existence—it must also comply with those requirements that enable the unit to stay legal.

As a legally established economic unit, a microenterprise is subject to a series of regulations that—unlike those concerning the entry to legality—will take place continuously as long as the microenterprise exists. Although in general the fulfillment of these operational or permanent costs are not as time consuming as the procedures for entry to legality, they are nonetheless considerable.

The barriers

The structural procedure for fulfilling the requirements for staying legal is quite different from the procedure for entry to legality. As was seen above, the procedure concerning the entry to legality entails many administrative steps such as carrying out specific registrations, going to state offices to fill out different sets of papers, or complying with specific regulations concerning the locale.

Instead, in order to stay legal, the main requirements are related to the fulfillment of obligations that are automatically due as the microenterprise starts operating legally. According to the case studies, the main operational costs confronted by informal units are related to two types of obligations: tax and labor obligations.

Tax obligations. Tax obligations entail the declaration and payment of two main types of taxes: income taxes and the value-added tax. In all the cases studied, the informal unit that wanted to stay legal had to observe laws that taxed income and profits. Although the low level of economic activity of legalized firms means that these latter taxes have small effective incidence, the firms are still required to keep accountancy books and to present an annual declaration of profits for the previous year.

The value-added tax is applied in all countries studied. It is interesting to point out that the obligation to contribute the value-added tax was considered as a cost by many of the microenterprises studied, when technically it is not. In fact, the whole objective of the value-added tax is that it is the consumer who pays, because the tax is transferred to the final price of the good. However, due to the lack of knowledge on how the tax should be calculated, microenterprises absorb more than they would if they properly transferred the authorized proportion to the price.

Nevertheless, there are two other significant reasons that also explain the difficulty of transferring the value-added tax to the price of goods. Some microenterprises cannot include the value-added tax in their prices because they may reduce their competitiveness. In some other cases, the links with illegal units for the supply of inputs or for their sales makes it impossible for the firm to transfer the tax to the price.

In addition, there are a number of other taxes that have a small incidence, such as the renewal of municipal licenses and permits for using public sites.

Labor obligations. By definition, the permanence costs that arise from labor obligations affect only those microenterprises that utilize labor, and thus informal units that rely only on unpaid family labor or are self-employed are exempted from this obligation.

In most cases, labor obligations include the usual aspects demanded by laws regarding labor contracts: the payment of legal minimum salaries and the fulfillment of a number of labor benefits and social security obligations. In particular, benefits include extra payments for working overtime and on holidays, payments for holidays and end of the year bonuses (thirteen-month salary), and contributions to social security.

There are different steps for tax obligations according to the volume of operations and size or level of annual profits. Hence, the tax burden is flexible according to the size of the business. In the case of labor obligations, however, due to the particular nature of labor contracts, such legal flexibility does not exist. Microenterprises hiring paid labor must comply with all the requirements fixed by law the same as any other company.

The costs

Three aspects should be mentioned regarding tax and labor costs. First, there is not a single or regular pattern of entry costs among countries; situations differ from country to country. In countries such as Chile, the permanence costs range between 17 and 30 percent of annual profits. In Mexico and Venezuela, these costs range between 50 and 60 percent of annual profits. In Bolivia, the cost of staying legal for microenterprises is between 9.2 and 26.2 percent of their production costs, and in Guatemala, these costs are 50 and 60 percent of their production costs.

A second aspect that is worth noting concerning permanence costs is that although there are wide country differences, these costs in all the cases studied more than doubled the costs of entry to legality. This may explain the higher compliance of microenterprises in this stage of the legalization process as compared to the stage of registration.

The third aspect suggested by the case studies is that the contribution to the costs for staying legal are not the same for tax and labor obligations. The bulk of the costs for staying legal are the consequence of labor obligations; for example, they account for 64 percent of the permanence cost in Bolivia. This can be explained by the fact that, as noted above, tax obligations are not significant due to the low level of profits registered by informal units; in many cases, informal units are exempted from paying taxes at all. But labor obligations constitute a fixed cost, independent of size and economic performance. Given the high costs represented by labor obligations, it could be useful to explore the possibility of defining new contractual relationships at the microenterprise level. This certainly is a conflictive issue because it could mean a way of diminishing overall labor protection. However, some adaptation can be introduced into the current legislation to allow microenterprises to comply because labor standards are settled for formal economic units. Alternatively, if the labor standards cannot be modified, a selective compliance of those of a more basic nature combined with higher administrative tolerance could be envisaged.

Conclusions

As it was seen, for informal units the process of becoming legal entails two different aspects: the entry to legality and the permanence in legality. Achieving legality in both aspects implies costs in terms of time and financial resources. The objective of the studies summarized here has been to point out the procedures and costs involved in the process of formalizing informal units to determine how important these costs are.

A caveat must first be made. The results presented are not conclusive, nor do they pretend to be so. They could be questioned on many grounds (e.g., lack of representation of the units chosen or small number of microenterprises studied). However the same criticism can be made about other studies, particularly De Soto (1986), which was based on a single case of an administrative lawyer and four assistants who needed 289 days to comply with the requirements to set up a small workshop with two sewing machines on the outskirts of Lima. In spite of this, DeSoto's study has inspired policy recommendations in many Latin American countries. Certainly, the study contributed to highlighting the obstacles confronted by informal units. The same can be argued in relation to the case studies presented in this work. They might not be fully representative, but they do show that country diversity is a strong finding.

The main conclusion is that the situation in relation to legalization costs is highly variable among countries. In fact, the results make it possible to attempt a typology of three groups of countries. The first group is composed of countries such as Bolivia, Brazil, and Chile, in which the time and financial costs involved are relatively low. At the other extreme is a group of countries such as Ecuador, Guatemala, and Venezuela, in which the process entails higher costs and where administrative barriers are significant. Finally, there are countries in an intermediate situation, such as Mexico and Uruguay.

This typology suggests several observations. The first is that the ordering of countries according to the significance of administrative and regulatory barriers bears no relation to the size of the informal sector in each country. According to the information compiled by PREALC, the largest informal sector (measured as percentage of nonagricultural labor force) can be found in Bolivia and Guatemala. In the previous ranking they are exactly in the opposite groups. The same can be shown with countries like Chile and Venezuela, which register the smaller share of informal employment and are also very different in terms of legalization costs. The intermediate group also reflects this difference: Mexico has a large informal sector and Uruguay has a small one.

There is, then, no causal relation between administrative and regulatory barriers and informality. Other factors are related better to informality. The level of development, measured by income per person, degree of urbanization, and population dynamics, is closely related to the size of the informal sector. Structure and economics are more important than law and administration in understanding informality.

The second observation is that a combination of administration and law presents a major barrier, but the most important in terms of cost is the law, particularly labor legislation. As mentioned, labor costs are the most important part of permanence costs. To soften this cost requires more than a simple answer. These costs are at the core of social functioning of the system because ensuring minimum standards for the entire population is the main characteristic of development. There are some basic labor standards that are considered human rights and hence cannot be sacrificed for the sake of employment. But employment is also a basic social need and, very often in the past, a right. Labor standards that are not basic can be revised in light of the economic capacity of the firm. This could imply trade-offs between protection and employment or between protection for organized labor and for informal workers. In addition, although labor costs are significant and legally compulsory when the informal firm uses hired labor, equally important is unprotected independent labor. Such labor is not illegal, and legislation does not represent a growth constraint, but from a social angle independent labor can constitute a most vulnerable group, which should be a matter of policy concern (see Chapter 7).

The third observation refers to the administrative barrier. As mentioned before, no strong correlation was found between the number of steps and time involved to become legal. Administrative costs are then related to bureaucratic processes, and procedures are only one component. But bureaucratic performance is, again, a complex issue. In a broader sense, it is a result of the nature of the state. It is not surprising that those countries that have a long tradition of good governance and a strong national state, such as Chile and Bolivia, are also those more efficient in handling microenterprise procedures. The opposite is true in Guatemala, Ecuador, and Peru, where national states have been historically weak and governance subject to many constraints. These countries are also found in the group of countries where administrative barriers are the most important. The conclusion is not necessarily that nothing can be done unless the state changes. It only denotes the real possibilities of administrative reforms, which according to the case studies have proven to be effective in Bolivia, Chile, and Brazil. The real challenge for these reforms is to work in an unfavorable general government context such as that found in the other countries included in the analysis.

A fourth and final observation is the difficulty of evaluating how important the costs are in hindering informal growth. The costs as percentages of profits are not high except in a few cases, but they could still be unaffordable for many informal producers and they could constitute a constraint to grow. This, however, does not seem to be the case because the informal sector has been growing in all countries considered. This probably has been the result of government tolerance and employment needs. Yet, can they expand more without administrative and regulatory barriers? The answer is likely to be yes. There will be costs involved, mainly outside the informal activity. The rules of competition will also be changed because regulatory changes, if not introduced as special treatment, affect not only informal units but also those organized under the present legislation.

To sum up, the studies analyzed suggest that there is room for improvement in the administrative and regulatory fields. But they also show that the prescriptions are not simple, nor are they unique, and that the potential effects will depend on other country characteristics.

Notes

1. The best known study supporting this thesis is De Soto (1986).
2. The sources for the case studies for the countries mentioned are: Bolivia: Escobar de Pabón (1990); Brazil: Looye (see Chapter 5); Chile: Velásquez (1990);

Ecuador: Placencia (1990); Guatemala: Sáenz (1990); Mexico: Elizondo (1990); Uruguay: Quijano and Antía (1990); and Venezuela: Cartaya (see Chapter 6). These case studies have been published in a slightly reduced version in Spanish by PREALC (PREALC, 1990).

3. This is the case in Bolivia, where 90 percent of the microenterprises surveyed had carried out the registration at the municipal level; in Ecuador, where the majority of the informal workshops comply with the initial registration steps; and in Uruguay. In the case of Venezuela, registration rates are higher with the Register of Companies, which is the institution that grants the temporary permits.

4. In 1985, 10 percent of the informal units were registered with the Board for the Protection of Craftsmen (*Junta de Defensa del Artesano*). The percentage of informal units registered with the Under Secretary of Small-Scale and Craft Industries (*Subsecretaría de la Pequeña Industria y Artesanía*) did not reach 2 percent of the total units.

5. The cases of Brazil and Mexico constitute an exception to this because in the mid-1980s a series of laws were passed that specifically deal with the legalization and functioning of microenterprises.

6. Not infrequently, the inspection ends up in a fine to the microenterprise seeking legalization for carrying out economic activities without legal permits. For this reason, informal units seeking legalization either stop their activities until after the municipal inspection, hide the machinery and working equipment, or add ex ante the amount of the fine to the costs of formalization. This was the case in Brazil, Ecuador, and Venezuela.

7. In Bolivia after the tax reform that took place in 1987, which was characterized by a drastic simplification of the tax system, 90 percent of the microenterprises studied registered under the General Tax System or the Simplified Tax System.

8. According to Placencia (1990), this situation seems to explain, to a great extent, the low level of compliance with this registration. According to figures from the economic census of 1981–1982, only 40,000 craftsmen out of 1,500,000 (3 percent) were registered with the Ecuadorian Social Security Institute.

5

Real Versus Ideal and the Brazilian *Jeitinho:* A Study of Microenterprise Registry Under the New Microenterprise Statute

Johanna W. Looye

The research reported in this chapter relates the experience of four microenterprises that recently went through the process of registering their activities legally in the city of Fortaleza, Ceará, in the northeast of Brazil. Five central questions were considered in the case studies presented. First, how much time was necessary for a firm to become legally registered and what bureaucratic procedures were followed? Second, what expenses were incurred in terms of registrations, municipal permits, operating licenses, and other fees or taxes necessary to initiate the legalized operation of the firm? Third, what was spent on the modifications (e.g., safety, health, labor contacts, minimum salaries) necessary to obtain the actual legalization? Fourth, how do these costs in time and registration and modification expenses compare with the benefits resulting from the legalization? Fifth, and finally, what is an estimate of the costs of illegal operation?

Before recounting the individual experiences, this chapter presents the background of the Microenterprise Statute that governs the process that the firms underwent and an outline of the official procedure for firm registration. Next, the obligations and rights of a registered microenterprise in carrying out its business operations are enumerated. Following this overview of the official procedures is a description of the registration assistance provided by the local Center of Small Business Assistance of the State of Ceará (CEAG, *Centro de Apoio à Pequena e Média Empresa do Estado do Ceará*). An account of the actual experiences of four firms as they went through registration and the initiation of their legalized operations comes next. The chapter concludes with a description of how the Microenterprise Statute really works. This discussion brings into consideration the way in which the Brazilian institutions of the *jeitinho* and the *despachante*[1] have been overlaid upon the new legislation and points out the limitations that the implantation of a microenterprise statute based on the Brazilian model might have where the *jeitinho* or the *despachante* are not the norm.

Background of the Microenterprise Statute

In 1984 and 1985, at the instigation of the since-defunct Ministry of Debureaucratization, a series of laws were passed in Brazil creating special conditions for the operation of small-scale businesses. The perceived problem was that complicated bureaucratic procedures and heavy tax and social welfare obligations were discouraging small firms from registering legally. This operation "on the margin" of the economy made the day-to-day existence of the firms difficult because they were subject to inspectors' pressures at any moment. At the same time, the governments suffered because the firms neither paid taxes nor generated indirect tax revenues through their purchases with official receipts (fiscal notes). The new legislation created simplified and preferential treatment for registered microenterprises in the effort to address the above-mentioned problems.

Exemptions and Incentives for Registered Microenterprises

In brief, a microenterprise is defined by the new legislation as any commercial, industrial, or service-delivering firm, whether owned by an individual or by partners, that does not surpass the legally established limits at the different governmental levels.[2] At the federal level, the limit is 10,000 OTN,[3] whereas the limit varies among states and municipalities, where it is set locally. For the State of Ceará, the limit is 4,000 OTN, and for Fortaleza it is 1,200 OTN. In bureaucratic terms, legal registration is a separate procedure from qualification as a microenterprise. Only individual enterprises or partnerships (limited liability companies) registered legally (at the State Commercial Registration Office, or *Junta Comercial*[4]) are eligible to qualify for microenterprise status (and thereby exemptions), with this status depending upon the limits at each level of government. For example, if a firm had sales totaling 5,000 OTN, it would be exempt from federal income taxes because it is under the 10,000 OTN limit, but it would still have to pay tax on commercial transactions, such as ICM (*Imposto sobre Circulação de Mercadoría*) because it surpassed the state-set-limit of 4,000 OTN.

According to the legislation, benefits granted at the federal level include simplified and free registration; special lines of credit, such as tax exemptions (income tax, financial operations, transport and communications services, extraction of minerals); exemption from paying the PIS and FINSOCIAL fees;[5] payment of the minimum rate for social security or IAPAS (*Instituto de Administração Financeira de Previdência e Assistência Social*) and elimination of several labor norms.

In Ceará, the benefits granted by the state legislation include simplified registration; special lines of credit; exemption from the tax on commercial transactions (ICM); exemption from certain state fees; and the elimination of the use of fiscal books,[6] official receipts, reports for value added, and other fiscal procedures.

In Fortaleza, the municipal benefits include simplified registration; exemption from the tax on services rendered (ISS, *Imposto Sobre Serviços*); a 50 percent reduction in operating permit fees; and the elimination of several bureaucratic procedures.

Microenterprise Registration in Ceará

Once it became possible to register as a microenterprise, in March 1985, many "clandestine" firms took advantage of the opportunity to register legally and to register as microenterprises whereas others held back in distrust of the government (believing that the government would suddenly change the rules and start charging taxes). However, a real jump in registration took place with the February 1986 *Plan Cruzado* economic package, when private citizens began to demand official receipts and many people opened new firms to take advantage of the price freeze and the apparently favorable economic conditions. Beginning in November 1986 and continuing in the following two years, economic decline led to fewer firms taking advantage of the statute's provisions and a number of firms losing their status as microenterprises. Table 5.1 shows the number of firms that registered with the *Junta Comercial* in Ceará between March 1985 and August 1988. No data are available on microenterprise bankruptcies.

Other information from the *Junta Comercial* shows that, of the firms registered from 1986 to 1988 as individual firms or as partnerships, roughly

Table 5.1 Microenterprise Registration in Ceará, Brazil, 1985–1988

	1985[a]	1986	1987	1988[b]
Newly registered firms qualified as microenterprises	2,570	9,871	8,934	4,659
Already registered firms qualified as microenterprises	6,790	3,151	2,916	906
Firms that lost microenterprise status	—	27	43	18
Year total	9,360	12,995	11,807	5,547
Cumulative total	9,360	22,355	34,162	39,709

Source: Junta Comercial do Estado do Ceará. Also published in *O Povo*, September 10, 1988, p. 12.
— = Data not available.
[a]March through December.
[b]January through August.

three-quarters registered as microenterprises. In addition, of the approximately 120,000 firms registered in Ceará at the end of August 1988, around one-third are microenterprises.[7] The following two sections of this chapter provide details on how registration and operation as a microenterprise are carried out, at least in ideal terms.

The Bureaucratic Procedure for Microenterprise Registration

The registration of a new microenterprise requires some or all of the following steps:[8]

1. The firm owners determine the type of firm they wish to register: an individual firm or a partnership. In addition, they determine the amount of capital investment (social capital) they wish to declare in their application.

2. The firm goes to the municipal government for approval of the location where it intends to operate. This step requires two documents: the application itself (*Consulta para Requerer Alvará de Funcionamento*) and a notarized (*autenticada*) copy of the last bill paid for local land taxes (IPTU, *Imposto Predial e Territorial Urbano*), which are assessed on all households and businesses in the city. The application fee is Cz$96.50 in 1988 (US$0.30 in September).[9] Following the submission of this application, a municipal inspector visits the firm to measure the space and to determine that the firm has not yet begun to function. If it has been functioning, a fine is assessed.

3. The *Junta Comercial* is consulted regarding whether there is another firm with the same name that the new firm plans to use. There is a special document for this step, the *Certidão de Busca Prévia*, with a fee of Cz$330 (US$1.03).

4. The individual firm declaration or the partnership contract is prepared. For individual firms there is a special form, and for partnerships a standard model exists, although it need not necessarily be followed exactly.

5. The firm registers with the local *Junta Comercial* and receives a national commercial registration number (NIRC, *Número de Inscrição no Registro do Comércio*), which grants the firm's legal existence. Simultaneously, the firm is registered with the internal revenue service and receives a number, CGC,[10] which is a fiscal requirement. In Ceará, which has an "instantaneous registration" procedure,[11] this registration can actually be done in one to two hours, if all of the paperwork is in order.

Two fees are collected for these registrations, with the actual values being readjusted on a regular basis. The first is for the NIRC, which requires a special form (*requerimento*), and the second is for the CGC, which is paid with the federal payment form (DARF, *Documento de Arrecadação de Receitas Federais*). Both can be paid in the *Junta Comercial* building when the other papers are submitted. The amount of the fee varies slightly, but the average in September 1988 for individual firms was Cz$4,010 for the NIRC and Cz$400 for the CGC (total, US$13.65). Partnerships paid, on average, Cz$8,660 and Cz$2,000 for the two respective fees (total, US$32.99). There is no fee for being qualified as a microenterprise because the status of microenterprise is independent of the condition of being a legally registered firm. In other words, if the firm ceases to qualify for microenterprise status, it need not go through the process of legally constituting the firm itself once again. It simply begins to operate as a normal enterprise.

6. The applicant obtains an operating permit (*Alvará de Funcionamento*) from the municipal government. This process normally takes one month and requires the following documents: the application form (*Solicitação de Alvará de Funcionamento*), a copy of the national registration number (CGC), a copy of the notarized copy of the last bill paid for local land taxes, and a notarized copy of the microenterprise declaration form. Microenterprises pay only 50 percent of the fee, which is based on the physical area of the firm.

7. The firm next registers in the state Internal Revenue Office (*Coletoria Estadual da Fazenda*, or *Coletoria Estadual*) to receive a CGF (*Cadastro Geral da Fazenda*) number that it will use to pay taxes on commercial transactions (ICM). In 1988 the fee was Cz$574.20 (US$1.78 in September). The fee can be paid in any agency of the state bank (*Banco do Estado do Ceará*) by using the special state payment document (DAR, *Documento de Arrecadação*). There is an inspector who personally visits the firm in order to verify (a) if it is a microenterprise, (b) if it has already been functioning, and (c) if the address is the same as the one submitted on the application.

8. Once the firm has the three registrations in steps 5, 6, and 7 completed, it usually seeks to print official ICM receipts. Authorized printing shops have the necessary authorization form (*Autorização de Impressão de Documentos Fiscais*), which they can supply only if the registration in the state (step 7) has been completed. The form costs Cz$600 (US$1.86).

After the authorization is granted, the printing of the official receipts is done by the printer, and the actual receipts are approved by the *Coletoria Estadual*, for which a fee of Cz$95.70 (US$0.30) is charged.

9. For those firms that render services, registration in the municipal government's finance office is required, so that tax on services rendered (ISS) can be paid. No fee is charged for this registration.

After the registration is completed, the firm requests authorization to print official ISS receipts, which requires the appropriate authorization application form, the legal name of the printer, and proof of registration with the municipal government (*Cartão de Inscrição*).

Once the receipts are made by the printer, they must be approved, which involves returning to the municipal finance office with the printer's official receipt for the application for authorization, and the printer's official receipt for the preparation of the receipts. A fee of Cz$193 (US$0.60) is charged and the receipts are legalized through perforation.

10. This step is optional. One further operating license may be necessary, although normally only in the case of firms that work with food. This is the municipal health department's operating permit, which generally takes 60 days to be processed.

CEAG Registration Service

Some of the firms interviewed for this report used the CEAG to register their firms; therefore, the discussion continues with a description of how the CEAG goes about dealing with the registration bureaucracy.

The *Centro de Apoio à Pequena e Média Empresa do Estado do Ceará* is one of the many similarly named private, nonprofit organizations that operates independently in each state of Brazil. The CEAGs, while legally independent entities, form part of a system that is headed by an umbrella organization, CEBRAE (*Centro Brasileiro de Apoio à Pequena e Média Empresa*), which is linked to the Ministry of Industry and Commerce. Funding for an individual CEAG normally comes from its state government, from CEBRAE, and from service contracts or consulting for individual firms.

One of the services offered by the CEAG, through its *Balcão do Empresário*,[12] is assistance with the registration of new firms. Although the fee the firms pay normally exceeds the fees paid on their behalf in the different government agencies, this is not always the case, and the CEAG may actually lose money in delivering the service. In any case, both CEAG staff members and other firm owners confirm that the price is less than that which would be charged by an accountant performing the same service. In early August 1988, CEAG charged Cz$8,000 (US$30.10) to register an individual firm, with the actual registration costs approximating Cz$6,000. Partnerships were charged Cz$15,000 (US$56.43), with fees and other costs running about Cz$13,000. Due to inflation, these prices are readjusted regularly. The *Balcão* staff also advises businessowners of all sizes on legal matters regarding the operation of their firms.

The steps in the registration procedure that the CEAG does not follow to the letter include those listed here.

a. In practice, the CEAG skips the prior approval of the operating location and does all of the paperwork with the municipal government in one visit (step 6).

b. In practical terms, prechecking the firm name is required only when the firm has a very common name. The process takes five working days and it is unusual, especially for individual firms, to have the same name. Also, the *Junta Comercial* has a special fee (Cz$133, or US$0.42) for changing only the name if the rest of the paperwork is in order, so turning in the papers for registration (step 5) without doing the name search first is quicker and less expensive than doing the formal search.

 c. Because large numbers of firms are registered at the same time, the CEAG office usually leaves the paperwork with the *Junta Comercial* one day and goes back the next day to pick up the registrations.

 d. Due to frequent strikes and general bureaucratic inefficiency, it is not unusual for a firm to operate for long periods without an actual municipal operating permit. When a firm pays the operating permit fee, it receives a paper that is sufficient proof should an inspector make a visit and request the actual permit. The CEAG has a staff person who goes regularly to the municipal government to see if any of the operating licenses they have applied for are ready.

 e. The CEAG staff is in frequent contact with the state and municipal government inspectors (see steps 6 and 7), so they are able to notify their clients as to when the inspector is likely to visit. Because most firms actually begin operation before going through the registration procedure, they must hide their merchandise or face a fine for the period during which they operated illegally. The CEAG notification reduces the amount of time that a firm actually has to keep things hidden and reduces the risk of a fine.

 f. The CEAG does not handle printing official receipts for the firms they help register, although they do have a list of printers with cheaper prices.

 g. The CEAG has begun to request the health permit for all of the firms it registers, even though the municipal government requires it only from firms that deal with foodstuffs. Apparently, if you request the permit without an inspector demanding it, no inspector visits the establishment.

Once registration is completed in the three government entities, the *Junta Comercial*, the *Coletoria Estadual*, and the municipal government, the firm is legal but lacks the accoutrements necessary for legal operation. The following section describes what a microenterprise must do to carry out its operations in a legal fashion.

Obligations and Rights of a Registered Microenterprise

As indicated above, microenterprise status implies obligations and rights at the three different levels of government—federal, state, and municipal. In addition, for those firms with employees, a series of labor requirements must be satisfied. These obligations and rights are presented below.

Federal

a. The firm is required to have an official-style federal rubber stamp with its CGC registration number, but no special authorization is required for this procedure. The September 1988 price was around Cz$700 (US$2.17).

b. Each firm must pay an annual tax, which is 8 percent of the capital invested, to the appropriate business owners' union.

c. Annually, each firm must submit an income tax declaration showing that the 10,000 OTN limit was not surpassed.

d. On an annual basis, each firm is required to submit a social report on each employee (RAIS, *Relação Anual de Informações Sociais*).

Firms are not required to have an accountant, nor to keep fiscal books for federal inspectors.

State

a. The firm is required to have an official-type state rubber stamp made with its CGF registration number. Again, there is no special authorization required, and the cost is the same as the cost for the federally required CGC stamp, approximately Cz$700 (US$2.17).

b. The firm is obliged to save all official receipts for purchases made (e.g., inputs or other supplies).[13] If the firm is apprehended with merchandise but no official receipt, a fine of 200 percent of the value of the merchandise can be assessed, and the firm will automatically lose its tax-exempt status as a microenterprise.

c. The firm is required to renew its microenterprise status annually, which requires a renovation form (*Renovação de Benefícios Fiscais da Microempresa*), an inventory listing, a registration form (*Ficha de Atualização Cadastral*, FAC-1; see step 7), and payment of the renovation fee (Cz$287.10, or US$0.89), using the special state payment document (DAR, *Documento de Arrecadação*).

With the microenterprise statute, firms are not required to keep fiscal books for state inspectors. The firm is also not required to provide an official receipt with its sales, unless the sale is going to a client in another state. However, clients may require an official receipt and if the firm cannot provide one, it may lose the sale. Apparently, once the firm begins to make sales using official receipts, it is required to make all sales using them.

Municipal

a. The firm must renew its operating permit on an annual basis, but it pays only 50 percent of the regular fee (see step 6).

b. Even though a firm with service activities is exempt from the tax on services rendered (ISS), it is required to use official receipts for services rendered in order to calculate whether or not the OTN limit allowed by municipal law has been surpassed. A simplified version of the official receipt is permitted.

Labor Obligations

Not all microenterprises have employees. However, those that do are required by law to follow specific guidelines in contracting their personnel. The presentation of these obligations is divided into three periods, each with its respective obligations. The periods are the moment personnel is hired, the period during which they are working, and the point at which they leave the firm. Upon admitting personnel, each firm must meet certain requirements.

a. The firm must register the employee in an employee registry, which is either a book or a set of individual cards. Microenterprises normally use a book, which has to be approved and the pages perforated by the local office of the Ministry of Labor. In addition, the firm must "sign" each employee's labor book.[14]

b. The firm is also required to have each employee sign a form declaring whether that employee wants a special fund for unemployment, FGTS.[15] If the firm has employees with the labor book signed, and if they want the FGTS, a special account must be opened in any bank. In order to open this account, the firm goes to the bank with a copy of its CGC and either the individual firm declaration or the partnership contract. Two forms are turned in at the bank: the list of employees (RE, *Relação de Empregados*) and the payment form (GR, *Guia de Recolhimento*). After the account is opened, the firm will make monthly deposits equal to 8 percent of the total payroll, which employees are entitled to receive upon leaving the firm or under other specific conditions, such as the purchase of a house.

c. The firm is also required to fill out a card with information on minor dependents of each employee in order to calculate the "family salary."[16]

d. In addition, the firm registers its employees in the social integration program (PIS), even though no payment is required for microenterprises.

e. Finally, the firm is required to send a form to the Ministry of Labor every time an employee is hired or fired (*Cadastro Geral de Empregados e Desempregados*).

The payment of regular legal employee benefits, or social welfare obligations,[17] involves deducting and paying the social security (IAPAS) at the lowest rate, which is 8.5 percent of the employee's total pay. In addition, the firm advances payment for the family salary, for which it is reimbursed through a deduction on what the firm pays for its employees. The firm itself also pays 23.8 percent on the total payroll to the IAPAS. This payment can be made in any bank using the special IAPAS payment form (DARP, *Documento de Arrecadação de Receitas Previdenciárias*). Other responsibilities include the advance payment of maternity leave,[18] for which the IAPAS reimburses the firm.

In addition to these IAPAS payments and the monthly FGTS deposit, the firm must make IAPAS payments for the employer/owner. This payment is separate from the IAPAS payment for the employees and the firm and is done with an individual payment booklet (*Carnê de Contribuinte Individual*). The monthly payment equals 18.7 percent of the national monthly minimum salary.[19]

In Brazil, employees are also entitled to a thirteenth salary (an official "Christmas bonus"), 50 percent of which must be paid by November 30 and the remainder by December 20. Once a year the firm is also obliged to deduct and pay the employee's obligatory union payment, equal to one day's work on the base salary (salary without any benefits).

One final benefit the firm is required to provide to its employees is the transport coupon (*vale transporte*). Each employee pays a maximum of 6 percent of the base salary and the firm pays the remainder and is repaid through an income tax deduction.[20]

Upon dismissing an employee, the firm is required to go to the regional office of the Ministry of Labor (or to the local labor union, if there is one that does this operation), to pay the employee his severance pay. However, if the employee has been with the firm for less than one year, the payment can take place at the firm itself. In addition, the firm must send the Ministry of Labor a form stating that someone left employment with the firm (*Comunicação de Dispensa*) and must give the employee the documents allowing him to use the money deposited in his unemployment fund (FGTS).

With regard to labor practices, microenterprise status exempts the firm from the following obligations: giving advance notice to the Ministry of Labor upon extending the work day, posting a list of employees and the work schedule in the workplace, noting vacations in the employee registry, requiring a medical examination before hiring a new employee, and keeping a labor inspection book.

Four Case Studies in Fortaleza, Ceará

The four firms described here, two individual firms and two partnerships, have gone through the legal registration process recently.[21] Dona Maria's Clothing is the only industrial activity described. The other three microenterprises, Zé's Cosmetics Products, The Sousa Brothers' Used Beauty

Parlor Furniture, and Roberto's Telephone Service, are all technically considered commercial firms, although Roberto's really belongs in the service sector. Of the other two, Zé's firm has nonfamily members working, whereas the Sousa brothers' shop is clearly a family business. The details of each firm's registration experience are introduced following a brief background on the firm and its owner.

Dona Maria's Clothing

Dona Maria, who is now fifty-seven years old, began sewing when she was twelve years old. She continued sewing for others as an adult, to bring in a little extra money, but because she had a job in the public sector she sewed only on evenings and weekends, always sewing tailor-made items on order. About six years ago, when she retired from her job, she hired a seamstress and opened a little "factory" in her own home. She was then able to sew larger quantities, even for boutiques. Approximately one year ago, she opened a little shop on a busy street in Fortaleza for her daughter to run, but her daughter was still in college and did not like having a shop, so Dona Maria sold it. Dona Maria now runs her small factory with three employees plus herself. Her daughter helps out with the paperwork. Dona Maria herself does all of the cutting (which is done manually) and quality control. Her firm has three industrial sewing machines, one overlock machine, and a small zigzag machine used to make buttonholes.

Dona Maria decided to register her firm for three reasons. First, she wanted to give greater security to the seamstress who has been working with her for four years. She had already tried giving her employee the money for her own IAPAS payments, but the seamstress did not pay—she kept the money instead. Dona Maria's second motive for registration was to protect herself on her individual income tax return. Because she and her husband are both retired public servants, they needed a way to explain where their belongings (properties, perhaps) were coming from. The third preoccupation was with unannounced inspectors' visits.

Dona Maria's hope is that with registration her firm will grow, but she has not yet made any changes in terms of divulging her new legal status, so no changes have yet taken place. Dona Maria currently sews mainly for middle-class clients, and with the registration she hopes to change her clientele from individuals to boutiques, to sell in larger quantities. Dona Maria has noticed no change in terms of suppliers, even though she now has to buy with an official receipt. She believes her suppliers are going to continue giving her the same discount as before. And even though she plans to ask for an official receipt, she will only ask them to write down the amount that she needs to show on the books, so that they will pay less in taxes and she will not surpass her OTN limit.

Dona Maria went to the CEAG to have her firm registered in June 1988 and paid Cz$4,000 (US$22.44) for the entire service. According to CEAG calculations, of the Cz$4,000 paid to them, registration costs represented Cz$2,395 and CEAG kept the remaining Cz$1,605 for its service. From the day she turned in the paperwork to the day she received her receipt for having paid for her municipal operating license, two months (forty-four working days) passed. The details of the procedure were as follows:

1. Dona Maria already knew she wanted to register as an individual firm and the capital investment declared in June 1988 was Cz$100,000 (US$560.95).
2. The CEAG did not do a formal check on the operating location before starting the registration process because they knew there would be no problem with her location.
3. The CEAG did not run a formal check on the firm name in the *Junta Comercial* because Dona Maria's firm name was not a common one.
4. The CEAG used the standard form for the individual firm declaration.
5. The CEAG left the registration papers at the *Junta Comercial* on June 6 and picked them up the next day.
6. Because of a strike, the CEAG was not able to turn the papers in to the municipal government until June 28, and an inspector came on August 3. Dona Maria operated with the receipt, which was sufficient as an operating license until the municipal government processed the actual license.
7. The CEAG turned her papers in to the *Coletoria Estadual* on June 8 and received them one or two days later.
8. Dona Maria's friend, who has a printer's shop, printed her official receipts. It took from September 6 until September 15, and she paid Cz$18,000 (US$55.70) for receipts for 125 sales.[22]
9. Even though Dona Maria still sews on order, sometimes even receiving fabric from her customers, she is not going to register her firm in the service sector and therefore did not register with the municipal government for the ISS receipts.
10. Dona Maria did not request the health permit from the municipal government.

After legalizing her firm with the federal, state, and municipal governments, Dona Maria made her owners' labor union payment in July 1988 in the amount of Cz$2,037 (US$9.57). Next, she paid Cz$3,100 (US$11.66) for her federal and state rubber stamps and bought the labor registry book for Cz$1,200 (US$4.51), both in August. Other requirements are being satisfied as Dona Maria's daughter gets to them.

In terms of labor obligations, of the three people working for Dona

Maria, only one has her labor book signed. Francisca has worked for Dona Maria for four years and was always paid on a piece rate. In August, the first month she earned a salary with the labor book signed, she received Cz$24,000 (US$90.29), but in her labor book she is listed as earning only one minimum salary, or Cz$15,552 (US$58.51).[23] Social welfare benefits paid on her behalf, based on her declared salary, included Cz$1,244 (US$4.68) for her unemployment fund (FGTS) and Cz$4,500 (including Cz$523, or US$1.97 for her family salary), which is equivalent to US$16.93 for social security (IAPAS). The second woman who works in Dona Maria's shop has not decided yet if she wants her labor book signed. (Dona Maria wants to sign the book, but the woman is not sure it is really in her interest to change from a piece rate to a flat salary.) Based on her production level, she earned Cz$20,000 (US$75.25) in August, with no other benefits. The third person who works for Dona Maria is a retired woman who works out of her own home. She earned Cz$12,000 in August (US$45.15), based on a piece rate. No consideration is being given to signing her labor book because she works out of her own home.

Zé's Cosmetics Products

Zé and his wife, Ana, have a small shop that sells products for making perfumes and cosmetics, homemade chocolate and other sweets made in molds, and handcrafted women's clothing accessories. In addition, the shop offers courses on how to make the items for which they sell the inputs. Technically, the couple has had two separate firms with identical activities. The first, Ana's, was registered as a microenterprise in March 1985 and operated in an upper-class neighborhood in Fortaleza. This firm was started as an experiment, and when it did well the couple decided to open another. The second firm was registered as an individual firm in Zé's name in June 1987 and operates in downtown Fortaleza, where low- and middle-income Fortaleza residents do their shopping. After opening their shop downtown, the couple decided to close the first shop because they saw that the clients of the new store actually made a living from the activities they learned whereas the women who took courses in the first shop enrolled only as a pastime and never bought much in the shop afterward. The first firm was kept open until February 1988, when it was declared legally closed.

The decision to register the first firm as a microenterprise was at least in part a result of the news coverage that took place following the passage of the Microenterprise Statute. Experience was the deciding force in the case of the second registration. The technical expertise for both firms comes from Ana, who teaches many of the courses that the store offers and goes to São Paulo to order nearly all of the products that they sell in the shop. Zé, who used to be a full-time employee of a bank in Fortaleza, is responsible for the business operations of the shop. Zé and Ana's firm has grown considerably and will probably not be able to continue as a microenterprise after next year. In fact, they are preparing to move soon to a new location in the heart of downtown Fortaleza, where Zé's father has some land.

Zé and Ana have a friend who knows about how to register firms, so he helped them register the second firm and advises them on all of the paperwork associated with the operation of the firm. Their total registration costs are estimated at US$43.45. From the day the first paperwork was delivered to the day they received their receipt for having paid for the municipal operating license, more than two months passed (thirty-one, nonconsecutive working days were involved). An additional twenty working days passed before Zé and Ana received the actual operating permit. The details of the ten-step procedure follow:

1. Zé and Ana had already decided to register the second firm as an individual firm. The capital investment was registered as Cz$50,000 (US$1,253.13).
2. The couple did not pay for a formal check on the operating location before starting the registration process because they knew there would be no problem with a commercial activity in downtown Fortaleza.
3. Because Zé's name is not common, they did not run a formal check on the firm name in the *Junta Comercial*.
4. The standard form was used for the individual firm declaration.
5. Their friend left the registration papers at the *Junta Comercial* on June 23, 1987, and picked them up two days later. They paid Cz$340 (US$8.52) for both the NIRC and the CGC.
6. The papers for their operating permit were turned in to the municipal government on July 30, an inspector came almost immediately, and they received their actual operating permit on September 1. The fee they paid was Cz$137 (US$3.05).
7. On June 26 they turned in their papers to the *Coletoria Estadual* and received them back on June 30. The registration fee totaled Cz$76.10 (US$1.91).
8. For their second set of official receipts, in August 1988, Zé and Ana paid Cz$500 for the authorization, Cz$3,000 for the printing, and Cz$95.70 for the authentication, or a total of US$13.53. They received receipts for fifty sales.
9. Even though one of the main activities is the teaching of courses, Zé and Ana did not register their firm in the service sector and therefore did not register with the municipal government for ISS receipts. If they were somehow caught by inspectors, Ana says they would offer the courses free of charge and start charging much higher prices for the materials they sell, which is what the larger stores do.

10. Ana insisted on having a health permit from the municipal government for the second shop because she had encountered difficulties in the first one. In the other shop, the inspectors kept making demands until she gave them a present, but with Zé's firm no inspector ever came.

After registering the firm, Zé and Ana wrote a letter requesting authorization of their labor registry in late August 1987. In January 1988, they paid the owners' union Cz$893 (US$11.51). In addition to the other obligations, they filed an income tax form for their 1987 operations. The value in their declaration was equivalent to 551 OTN but they were entitled to 5,000 OTN because they operated only from July to December. Ana thinks they will be able to maintain microenterprise status only for another year at most, because even by doing only a part of their business with official receipts, they are going to exceed the established limit. They also renewed their operating license in April for Cz$338 (US$2.70), but they have not received the permit itself. They are operating with their payment receipt.

Zé and Ana have four young women working for them, all earning the national minimum salary, or Cz$23,700 (US$89.16) in August 1988. Only one woman, who has been with the firm for six months, has her labor book signed, and she cost the firm an additional Cz$7,536 (US$28.35) for her social benefits (IAPAS and FGTS). For the woman who has her book signed, they deducted Cz$415 (US$1.56) from her salary in July for her union fees and paid them in August. In addition to the regular employees, the firm has teachers for the courses. The teachers have no formal relationship with the firm, but receive one-third (or sometimes one-half) of the registration fees received for the courses they give.

The Sousa Brothers' Used Beauty Parlor Furniture

The Sousa Brothers' Used Beauty Parlor Furniture shop is owned jointly by João and Fernando, but it is really João who runs things. Fernando has a full-time job in a bank and set up the firm in order to help out his family. He does not take an active part in the administration of the business. The brothers' mother, Dona Socorro, has been buying and selling used beauty parlor equipment since about 1978,[24] but they have been operating in the present location in downtown Fortaleza only since November 1987. The shop deals with used hair dryers, chairs, wash basins, and other beauty shop furniture, as well as beauty parlor products such as solutions for permanents, hair dyes, and the like, all of which is bought from closing beauty shops in the poorer neighborhoods of Fortaleza and nearby towns in the interior. In addition, the firm functions almost like a pawn shop, even buying portions of bottles of solutions from women who need quick cash. Besides João, the only other person working in the shop is his cousin, who helps with sales. Dona Socorro used to work regularly, but due to health reasons she has not been able to work. Many of the machines that João buys require repairs, which he has done by a person who always did these repairs for his mother, but this man is not an employee of the firm—he is paid individually for each repair he does.

The Sousa brothers decided to register their firm for two reasons. First, the clientele wanted some guarantee in buying their products, which the brothers felt they could provide only if they were registered, and second, they were concerned about inspectors giving them trouble because the shop is located downtown. Since registration, which was not complete on the day of the interview (September 16, 1988), no changes had taken place in the clientele or the suppliers of the firm. However, with time, João would like to expand his business. His dream is to be the representative for new beauty parlor products made by foreign firms.

João and Fernando went to the CEAG to prepare their registration papers on June 27, 1988, and paid Cz$15,000 (US$84.14) for the entire service. From the day the brothers turned in the paperwork to the day of the interview, almost three months (more than sixty working days) passed. Part of the delay was with obtaining the operating permit, but due to a series of illnesses in the family, João had not gone to the CEAG to pick up his papers. The step-by-step details of the procedure are as follows:

1. Before contacting the CEAG, the Sousa brothers already knew they wanted to register as a partnership for a declared capital investment value of Cz$200,000 (US$1,121.89).
2. Because the CEAG staff knew that there would be no problem with a commercial establishment in downtown Fortaleza, they did not do a formal check on the operating location before starting the registration process.
3. The CEAG did not run a formal check on the firm name in the *Junta Comercial* because the chosen name was not a common one.
4. The CEAG prepared the partnership contract based on the standard model.
5. The CEAG probably left the registration papers at the *Junta Comercial* just after June 25 and picked them up one day later.
6. The CEAG turned the papers in to the municipal government (probably in late June or early July), but an inspector did not come until September 6. Even so, she only came when Fernando brought her, because there were no cars available to bring her. The firm did not have a sign posted on the outside, so the approval was not given and the inspector will have to return to see the sign in place. In addition, the firm is being required to place signs reading, "Room 1" and "Room 2" on the wall because there is a wall-like division in

the shop. It is likely that this is being required so that the municipal government can charge a higher rate for the operating license. João decided to have electrically lighted signs made (although this is not a requirement) for Cz$4,000 (US$12.38).
7. Because they already submitted paperwork for the operating license, the CEAG had probably already turned their papers in to the *Coletoria Estadual* and received them back by the time of the interview.
8. The brothers had not yet gotten to the point of printing their official receipts.
9. Because they do not work with service delivery, João does not plan to register with the municipal government for the ISS receipts.
10. The Sousa brothers did not request the health permit from the municipal government.

Because the firm's registration was not complete at the time of the interview, none of the other maintenance procedures had been initiated.

At the time of the interview, João was earning Cz$8,000 per week (US$99.02 per month) and his cousin Cz$5,000 every two weeks (US$30.95 per month). Neither has a signed labor book because they have not yet submitted the paperwork, but they are interested in doing this so they will have the IAPAS health benefits.

Roberto's Telephone Service

Roberto's Telephone Service is registered to sell electrical equipment and telephone parts, but in fact it does mostly installations of telephone systems (e.g., PBX and key systems), closed circuit television, and automated gates (electric garage doors). Roberto is actually in a partnership with his mother and his sister. Roberto is the one who understands telephones because he used to work for a multinational firm and later was a partner in another similar firm, and his sister helps with the bookwork. Their mother does not take an active part in the firm's operations. Roberto listed her mainly to provide them with some security. The firm itself started operating in late November 1986, but the labor registration process with CEAG was begun only after Roberto had made several trips to the *Junta Comercial* in an attempt to do everything on his own.

Because of the type of institutions that buy his equipment, Roberto would not be able to expand beyond simply selling his services unless he had a registered firm. In fact, his firm sometimes "lost" business to him (as an individual) when he did not have official receipts with which to do the work. Roberto's decision to register as a microenterprise was a result of the encouragement of a friend who works in the CEAG. Eventually Roberto hopes to expand his business, but telephone equipment is expensive and he does not have the necessary working capital so he continues as a service operation and puts aside money so that he can eventually begin selling the equipment itself. At the time of the interview, the firm had already changed locations once because the first site was no longer large enough physically for the volume of work they were receiving. In terms of suppliers, once Roberto gets his official receipts for sales (ICM), he will be able to purchase equipment outside of Fortaleza for resale. At the time of the interview, he was buying everything on the retail market in Fortaleza in order not to call attention to himself and risk being fined for not having the official ICM receipts with which to sell the merchandise he bought.

Originally, Roberto tried to register his firm without any help. He started out by getting three "free and clear" declarations (*Declaração de Desimpedimento*) for himself, his mother, and his sister. He also typed a partnership contract himself, but after four of five trips to the *Junta Comercial*, in which he was always informed of another form that needed to be submitted, he lost patience and decided to go to the CEAG to have his firm registered. He paid the CEAG Cz$1,200 in December 1986 (US$82.30) but he was not very organized in going to sign forms, so he did not receive his registration back until February 19, 1987. From the day the first paperwork was delivered to the day he received his receipt for having paid for the municipal operating license, one and one-half months, or thirty-one working days, passed.

The details of Roberto's registration experience follow:

1. Roberto is the one who decided to register the firm as a partnership, in the interest of his family.
2. Roberto used to sell real estate and knew there would be no problem in the location he had selected for his firm, so he did not pay for a formal check on the operating location before starting the registration process.
3. According to Roberto, the CEAG actually carried out a formal name check for his firm.
4. Because Roberto had already organized all of the information for the partnership contract, all the CEAG did was revise a few things and type the contract in the conventional format.
5. The CEAG turned in the registration papers at the *Junta Comercial* on February 18, 1987, and picked them up the following day.
6. The papers for the operating permit were turned in to the municipal government in February, and an inspector came to the firm one to one and one-half months later. Roberto did not receive the actual operating permit until August. He operated with his payment receipt for that entire period.
7. The CEAG probably turned in Roberto's papers to the *Coletoria*

Estadual as soon as they received the materials back from the *Junta Comercial*.
8. Roberto had not sought official receipts for sales because he works primarily with service delivery. He was beginning this procedure at the time of the interview.
9. Roberto registered with the municipal government on May 29 and printed his ISS official receipts in June. For his receipts, he paid Cz$40 for the authorization and Cz$550 for the printing (total US$14.79) and received receipts for 150 service contracts.
10. Roberto did not request a health permit from the municipal government.

After receiving his three registrations, Roberto had his two stamps made for Cz$59 (US$1.11) in July 1987. He said he just recently had learned about the obligation to pay the owners' labor union and is getting the paperwork ready.

Four people work in this firm, and all of them are going to have their labor books signed once Roberto prepares the necessary paperwork. He currently pays them their salaries and gives them the money for the IAPAS health care, which they are to pay as self-employed workers. The firm also provides meals and transportation to its employees.

Cost and Benefits of Registration

Table 5.2 summarizes the key information presented for each of the four firms interviewed and allows for comparison to the official calculations. The five main sections correspond to the five concerns with the costs and benefits of registration set out at the beginning of this chapter. Two notes of caution are in order regarding the interpretation of the dollar values shown, especially in using them to compare the firms' actual values to the official values. First, with high monthly inflation rates and no readjustment in fees (by the *Coletoria Estadual* or the municipal government), values are highly dependent upon the month in which registration took place. Second, there is a trade-off between incomplete data for recently registered firms (that had not yet made a complete conversion to legal operation) and inaccurate information for firms registered less recently (that do not have exact values or dates for their transactions). As mentioned above, high inflation modifies converted dollar values quite considerably, and a one-month memory lapse has a significant impact on the dollar value calculated.

Notwithstanding these observations, Table 5.2 shows certain consistencies in the four firms' experiences. In terms of time required, it is clear that the municipal government is the controlling factor in delaying the completion of the registration process. Luck plays an important role here. Zé

Table 5.2 Costs and Benefits of Microenterprise Registration

	Official Version (Individual Firm)	Official Version (Partnerships)	Dona Maria (Individual Firm)	Zé and Anna (Individual Firm)	João (Partnership)	Roberto (Partnership)
Working days required for legalization						
Junta Comercial (NIRC and CGC)	0.5	0.5	1	1	1[a]	1
Coletoria Estadual (CGF)	2	2	1	2	2[a]	2[a]
Municipal Operating Permit (receipt)	20	20	28	3	Incomplete	25[a]
Total	23	23	44	31	>60	31
Fees and taxes (US$)						
CEAG			22.44		84.14	82.30
JUCEC	13.65	32.99		8.52		
Coletoria Estadual	1.78	1.78		1.91		
Municipal Operating Permit[b]	1.49	1.49		3.05		
Municipal Health Permit	0.60	0.60		0.60[a]		
Legal receipts[c]	17.15	17.15	55.70	13.53	—	14.79
Rubber stamps	4.33	4.33	11.66	4.33[a]	—	1.11
Business owners' labor union fee[d]	24.75	24.75	9.57	11.51	—	—
Total	63.75	83.09	99.37	44.12	84.14	98.20
Costs of operating modifications (US$)						
Labor book	1.98	1.98	4.51	1.98[a]	—	—
IAPAS for the firm 23.8% of the total payroll			16.93	21.22	—	68.48
FGTS for the employees 8% of the employee's salaries			4.68	7.13	—	—
INPS for employer/owner 18.5% of the national minimum salary			10.82	16.49	—	—
Transport coupons Amount exceeding 6% of employee's salary			—	—	—	Pays transport
Miscellaneous			—	—	12.38	—
Total			36.95	44.85	12.38	68.48

Benefits of legalization (US$)			
Decrease in fines or payoffs	0	0	0
Decreased costs or increased sales	0	Costs	Both
Benefits from partial legalization[e]	28.71	85.06	44.94
Total	28.71	85.06	44.94
Costs of illegal operation (US$)			
Fines or payoffs	0	0	0
Lost sales	0	0	Some losses
Total	0	0	0
Net benefits[f] (US$)	−107.61	−3.91	−51.67	−121.74

[a] Estimate only.
[b] Costs for official version based on smallest area (less than 30 square meters).
[c] Costs for official version include estimate of US$15.00 for actual printing, which varies widely.
[d] Costs for official version based on declared capital investment of Cz$100,000.
[e] Corresponding to the IAPAS and FGTS benefits that would be paid if employees had their labor book signed for one minimum salary.
[f] Equal to benefits minus fees, taxes, and costs.

and Ana, for example, had a case of mixed luck. Although they waited more than a month to register with the municipal government because of a strike, they had the good fortune for the inspector to come almost the same day that they submitted their papers, so the total time elapsed was not much different from the month estimated. In contrast to the municipal government, the *Junta Comercial* and the *Coletoria Estadual* seem to be predictable in terms of their processing time, whether or not the applicant is receiving outside assistance in the registration process.

With regard to fees and taxes, two variables have the greatest influence on final costs. First, as described above, the month of registration is important because of unadjusted values at the state and municipal levels. Due to inflation, the later in the year a firm registers, the less the real cost. However, the fee for registration with the federal government, which is readjusted frequently, is clearly the main cost as far as registration payments are concerned. Official receipt costs are the other significant registration cost. Besides the total number of receipts the firm chooses to have made, the selection of the printing shop that will prepare the official receipts and rubber stamps makes a significant difference. Zé and Ana commented that they saved some money the second time they printed receipts because they did comparison shopping. And even though Dona Maria printed a large number of receipts (compared to the other firms interviewed), her "friend" was clearly not the cheapest option available.

Costs associated with operating modifications represent basically labor costs and are clearly dependent upon the number of employees for which the firm signs the labor book. Because these are recurring costs, this must certainly be an important consideration in a firm's decision to register.

The benefits of legalization, if only true benefits such as decreases in fines or payoffs, decreased costs, or increased sales are considered, are essentially nonexistent in the opinion of the microenterprise owners interviewed. The exceptions would be Zé and Ana, who are able to buy their merchandise in São Paulo only because they are legally registered, and Roberto, who hopes to purchase goods in São Paulo in the future. In both cases, the large quantities of merchandise shipped to their firms on a regular basis would call the attention of inspectors, and their firms would either face a fine (and perhaps lose their microenterprise status) or lose the merchandise itself. The other "benefit" reported in the chart—the benefit from partial legalization from having a "mixed" operation—is a result of legalization to the extent that legal status provides a facade behind which less-than-legal operations can take place. Once again, the key variable is labor costs. The numbers reported here correspond to the money that the firm saves by either not paying social benefits on the salary actually paid to the employees (Dona Maria's case) or from having employees without a signed labor book or the associated social benefits (all four firms).

If we subtract the three cost categories (fees and taxes, costs of operating modifications, and costs of illegal operation) from the benefits, the final value (or net benefit) is negative in all of cases studied. In other words, none of the four interviewed firms has accrued net benefits from having its operations legalized, which is surprising.[25] Furthermore, none of the firms reported actual losses, such as fines or payoffs or lost sales, as a result of operating without legal registration. Not only are there no net benefits to registering a firm, there were no costs associated with not having the firm registered in the first place!

This unusual result has three plausible explanations. First, microenterprise owners are not rational economic actors. Second, microenterprise owners register their firms for noneconomic motives. Third, the research design was not able to pick up the benefits of registration that the firms actually receive.

The conclusion that the microenterprises visited are run by nonrational owners is plausible, but the great amount of research on the informal sector and on small farmers suggests that this is not the case. If risk calculation can be considered an indication of rational economic behavior, all of the owners considered the risks involved in illegal operation, so they behaved in a rational manner, economically speaking. Because none of them actually had been fined or threatened with a fine, this risk was a perceived one rather than a real one, but it was a risk nonetheless.

The possibility that firms are registered for noneconomic reasons is also possible. Ana, for example, initially registered her firm (in the upper-class neighborhood of Fortaleza) more as a pastime than as an economic activity. Only when it started showing results did Zé actually open a firm in his own name or give consideration to giving up his bank job. Dona Maria also does not depend on her firm for her livelihood, and in fact is under very little threat of being fined because she operates from her own home.[26] It appears that both firms were registered for the status involved in being a microenterprise owner, although the economic benefits were not disregarded entirely.

The most likely explanation for the "irrationality" of the cost-benefit results is that the research, which was carried out over a short period of time with recently registered firms, did not identify the benefits that result from registration. In their response to questions on what they hoped to gain as a result of registering their firms, each of the owners suggested that in the short term things would be worse, but that they had growth plans for the future. It appears clear from this study that firms do not benefit over the short run; to know whether they benefit from their registration over the long run would require a different research design. Only in this way would it be possible to measure whether the intent of the Microenterprise Statute to provide start-up support for new firms is actually realized.

To summarize, registration as a microenterprise is not, at least in the short term, of economic benefit to the firm involved, although future research may be able to clarify benefits accrued over the long run. Neither, it is clear, is microenterprise registration or maintenance a particularly simple procedure, in spite of the improvements that have taken place since the passage of the Microenterprise Statute. Even the literate people interviewed here find themselves turning regularly to the CEAG or knowledgeable friends to negotiate the paperwork involved. Microenterprises such as corner shops in the low-income periphery of Fortaleza, run by illiterate or semiliterate owners, although they do actually register as microenterprises, must certainly face enormous difficulties in dealing with the paperwork involved with operating in accordance with the law. The following section describes how it may be that firm owners, both literate and illiterate, face the complicated task of owning a legal enterprise in Brazil.

Real Versus Ideal and the Brazilian *Jeitinho*

Having described the legalization process for these four firms, it is useful to observe that not one of the firms, even though registered, is completely legal. Ideally, they should all have undergone registration and begun their legalized operations as described in the sections of this chapter preceding the case studies. In real life, however, each of the firms has either some missing document, an unregistered employee, a falsely declared salary, or some other less-than-perfectly-legal facet to its operations. In fact, the determination of the part of the CEAG that a firm is legal once it is registered with the federal, state, and municipal governments is largely arbitrary. Technically, a firm exists legally once it is registered with the *Junta Comercial*. However, it cannot operate legally without the other two government registrations. Even if it had these two registrations, though, the firm would not have the stamps and other documents necessary to function legally. The question that arises, then, is: When is a firm completely legal and how does it go about becoming so?

There is probably no correct answer to this question, but the fact is that in Brazil this may not even be the correct question! The existence of the Brazilian institutions of the *jeitinho* and the *despachante*, discussed below, suggests that a more adequate rendition of the concern with legal operation would be: What aspects of a business operation have to be carried out legally in order for the firm to operate in relative peace, without incurring unnecessary expenditures, and without losing clients, and what is the easiest way to register those activities?

For analytical purposes, Rosenn (1971, pp. 515–516) divides the *jeitinho* into five different behaviors:

1. When a public servant deviates from his legal obligations because of private pecuniary or status (friends, family, or clique) gains. . . .
2. When private citizens employ subterfuges to circumvent legal obligations which are sensible and just (in an objective sense). . . .

3. When the speed with which a public servant performs his legal obligations depends upon private pecuniary or status gains. . . .
4. When private citizens employ subterfuges to circumvent legal obligations which are unrealistic, unjust, or wasteful (in an objective sense). . . .
5. When a public servant deviates from his legal obligations because of his conviction that the formal norms are unrealistic, unjust, or wasteful.

Rosenn goes on to observe that the first two of these behaviors constitute the conventional conception of corruption, and that the third may also be considered corruption, although it is less morally offensive than the first two. The last two types "illustrate behavior in which public purposes are served by evading legal norms, that bear no stigma and have made the jeito into such a highly prized national institution" (Rosenn, 1971, p. 516). It is in this sense that the term *jeitinho* is being applied to the registration and operation of microenterprises discussed here.

In the case of microenterprise registration, the first *jeitinho* (of the last two types identified by Rosenn) may be invoked in declaring the value of the capital investment. Because this value is used on a percentage basis for calculating the fee paid to the business owners' union, it is in the firm's interest to declare a value lower than the actual value. However, the value cannot be so low as to attract attention. Usually, the firm declares some low, round number that sounds like it is "in the ballpark."

The Microenterprise Statute makes provisions for already existing firms to qualify for microenterprise exemptions and was designed, at least in part, to bring firms out of their clandestine operations. In practice, the statute operates on the fiction that all firms registering with the *Coletoria Estadual* or the municipal government are beginning their operations at the same time they are registering. A second *jeitinho* comes into play when dealing with the inspectors sent by these entities to see the "new" firm. The hiding of merchandise and personnel on the day of inspection is a fiction that both firms and inspectors accept while both parties pretend that the official story is the real story. Registering firms probably accept the practice as a necessary evil and inspectors, who must be aware of the practice because they often catch firms operating and assess a fine, may actually derive some personal monetary benefit from maintaining the fiction.[27]

A third registration *jeitinho* comes into play in the decision to register only some of the activities. For example, Dona Maria has not gotten ISS receipts for the tailor-made clothing she makes for her clients. Similarly, Zé and Ana do not plan to declare the courses they give as a service activity. In fact, they have already figured out a *jeitinho* for future operations should an inspector catch them!

The *jeitinho* and its accompanying calculations come into even heavier play when the firm begins to legalize its day-to-day operations. The first fiction is in the use of official receipts. First, most business transactions, at least in the case of microenterprises, are not carried out with the use of official receipts. When asked, Zé and Ana replied that probably less than half of their sales were being made using official receipts. João said that once he got his receipts, he expected that none of his transactions would be done with them. Roberto was the exception, in responding that all of his transactions were already being done with receipts. Another way of using receipts to the benefit of the microenterprise is underdeclaring the value of a sale, so as not to surpass the OTN ceiling for microenterprise status.

Underdeclaring the value of a purchase is another common trick because microenterprise purchases must be made with official receipts, and the risks are great if firms are caught buying inputs without a receipt. However, the fictitious value cannot be too low because an inspector may decide to be very rigorous. In this respect, Dona Maria's flexibility in her receipts for the purchase of fabric has already been mentioned. Besides this, Dona Maria said she would probably write down only half of the value of her sales whenever she used an official receipt. One final technique is the creation of official receipt values whether or not a sale takes place. This practice is frequently employed by accountants (or whoever is doing the bookwork) to make things balance out or look good at the time paperwork is being done. "You need a few receipts totaling this amount," is not an uncommon command.

The area of labor relations is by far the richest arena for operating by rules of the *jeitinho*. At least in the smaller firms in northeast Brazil, "employees" are considered to be only the people who have their labor book signed, and the only people with their labor book signed are the ones who have been working with the firm for some period of time—those who have earned the trust of the owner. Most small firms, then, will have one or more employees for which they do not sign the labor book. However, this decision also requires a bit of calculation. For firms not interested in the risk associated with no legal employment document whatsoever, there is the legal probation contract (contrato de experiência). With it, an employee is legal for a short period of time before a firm is required to sign the labor book. According to the law, if the person is suitable for the position when the period ends, the labor book is signed. However, this rule opens up another loophole in the labor area. People are hired with a probation contract but never transferred to the labor book. Once the probation period ends, another person is hired to replace the first. Ana said that a Ministry of Labor inspector once came to her first firm, where she had workers without either a probation contract or a signed labor book, and the inspector gave her seventy-two hours to get everything into order. She did so, at least for the employees she had at the time, and in the end no fine was assessed. In Ana's opinion, this leniency is extended to all microenterprises because "they can't be expected to operate just the way large businesses do."

A second *jeitinho* in labor relations is signing the card for the minimum acceptable value (the national minimum salary) but actually paying more. Although employers recognize that their employees merit more than the minimum salary, they are not interested in paying the higher IAPAS and FGTS fees associated with a higher salary. By signing the labor book for the minimum amount permitted, they provide unemployment and social security benefits but do so without paying higher fees. Their justification is that there is no difference in coverage provided to those for whom higher fees are paid, so there is no point in wasting their money. Another alternative, although probably more common in large firms, is declaring one value on the labor book and actually paying a lesser amount to the employee.

Although it is possible to get around many unpalatable bureaucratic procedures, the *jeitinho* is not a solution for all of the difficulties a new microenterprise will face. Some of the rigid bureaucratic requirements call for another approach, which will be described here.

Even though the Microenterprise Statute was designed to provide for simplified registration and operation, a quick glance at the documents in the appendix to this chapter attest to the complexity of becoming and functioning as a microenterprise—even under the privileged conditions they have been granted. With the exception of the instantaneous registration procedure in the *Junta Comercial*, the bureaucratic procedures faced are not unlike to what Rosenn (1971, p. 535) calls the "bureaucratic imbroglio":

> Bureaucratic practices could hardly be designed more appropriately to promote administrative inefficiency. Many departments are open but a few hours a day. A plethora of documents are required for any claim. Official documents usually require stamps, which must be purchased elsewhere than the agency processing the documents. Governmental forms must be purchased separately from commercial stationers; until recently, even income tax returns had to be purchased. Payments of processing fees generally must be made at commercial banks and the receipts presented to the processing agency. As a general rule, a person is compelled to run from place to place and endure the customary slow-moving lines many times before he has arranged all the necessary pieces of paper. Then he may be forced to wait weeks, months, or years while the process is sent up for "higher consideration."

In 1988, one might also add to the above list of complications continual strikes and lack of automobiles or gasoline for transporting inspectors to the site. Recall that all four firms described here had someone to help them with their registrations, with one doing so only after unsuccessfully attempting registration on his own. Even though the firms were chosen with the assistance of the CEAG, the experience of Roberto suggests that simplification is another fiction and that another Brazilian institution, the *despachante*, is essential for the Microenterprise Statute to be operable. Rosenn defines the *despachante* as "an intermediary who, in return for a commission or fee, purchases and fills out the multiplicity of legal forms, delivers them to the proper persons, and extracts the needed permission or document" (Rosenn, 1971, p. 536).

No data are available on the number of individuals who register their own firms, or on those who use *despachantes* such as accountants or the CEAG, so it is impossible to say with certainty whether the experience of the four firms above is typical. However, there is no question that using a service such as the CEAG shortens the registration time considerably. All of the CEAG shortcuts described for the ten-step registration procedure represent time, if not money, saved for the microenterprise owner, who is most likely more interested in staying with his firm than in standing in lines or deciphering government paperwork.

To conclude, the existence of the *jeitinho* and the *despachante* are aspects of Brazilian bureaucratic reality that make the Microenterprise Statute operable. Even though conditions improved considerably with the statute, all of the improvements intended by its authors did not completely eliminate the complexity of registering or operating a small firm legally. The result is that microenterprises make calculated risks as to the aspects of their operations for which they will follow the law to the letter. In the same way, owners decide which procedures they themselves will deal with and which they will contract out. Without a doubt, even though people will continue to be able to resort to the *jeitinho* and the *despachante*, procedures could be improved in Brazil, as is taking place with the *Junta Comercial* in Ceará. In countries where flexible bureaucratic norms are not the standard, however, a note of caution is in order for modeling microenterprise legislation of the Brazilian Microenterprise Statute.

Appendix:
Instantaneous Registration in the *Junta Comercial*

Since 1985 the *Junta Comercial* in Ceará has operated with an "instantaneous registration" procedure for individual firms—a system that is based on industrial assembly-line production models. In 1987 the system was introduced for partnerships. The system involves a *Junta* employee receiving the necessary papers from the firm registering, checking to see if everything is present, and turning the papers over immediately to one of the two bank teller's windows on either side of him. The bank receives the firm's payment and the paperwork goes into one of two slots in the wall, for individual firms or partnerships. On the other side of the wall are two tables with four staff members each. Each person carries out one step in the bureaucratic checking, analysis, and number assignment associated with the firm being legally registered. Finally, the paperwork comes out around the corner and is delivered to the applicant, all in approximately one hour. What is remarkable is that the paper travels only around fifteen or twenty meters, and that staff from two other government bureaucracies (the *Banco do Estado do Ceará* and the *Receita Federal*) work inside the *Junta Comercial*, all of which makes instantaneous registration logistically possible.

According to the General Secretary of the *Junta Comercial* in Fortaleza, the instantaneous registration system was developed in Ceará beginning around 1977. Until that date, firms had to go personally to the *Receita Federal* to get their CGC number. After "a lot of talking," the *Junta* managed to get a *Receita* staff person authorized to work in the *Junta* building to assign CGC numbers. This reduced the average registration time from ten to four days. Later, vertical movement of paper was replaced by horizontal movement. That is, rather than moving stacks of files from one floor to another, the registration process was carried out on one floor only. Finally, the physical distances were reduced as much as possible and the overnight stack of papers to be processed was eliminated, to the point where the one-hour average was attained. Currently, staff members process the papers that arrive at the beginning of the day and end the day with no papers on their desks, which has reportedly improved morale in the *Junta*.

In addition to the decrease in registration time, another improvement, from the perspective of the registrant, is the decrease in "tips" or payments to *Junta* staff for hurrying the bureaucratic procedure because the applicants know exactly how long the procedure is supposed to take. Although the Ceará model is used only for simple registration, it is considered a national model and is being adopted by *juntas* throughout Brazil.

One remaining problem in the legal registration process was identified by one of the firms that was interviewed. Even though the *Junta* has set aside a room, "the accountant's room," and has staffed it with someone to answer questions, applicants still find it difficult to know precisely which documents they need and how to fill them out.[28] Also, the "tips" for assistance are still common in this room—not for hurrying along the process, but for providing clarifications on filling out the paperwork.

Notes

The author is grateful to the CEAG office in Fortaleza for patient explanations of the procedures described here and for assistance in contacting micro enterprise owners who were in the process of registering their firms. Thanks are also due to Ruth Yabes for her comments on an earlier version of this chapter.

1. According to Rosenn (1971), *jeito*, or *jeitinho*, is "an untranslatable term that corresponds roughly to a 'knack', 'twist', or 'fix'." *Despachante* is translated as "expediter." The *jeitinho* will be discussed at greater length at the end of this chapter.

2. The legislation details further restrictions concerning which firms may not qualify as microenterprises. This information can be found either in the

legislation itself or in books such as that published by Ceará, *Governo do Estado, Secretaria da Fazenda, Coordenação da Tributação* (1985).

3. OTN (*Obrigações do Tesouro Nacional*, or Readjustable National Treasury Bonds) is a monetary index equivalent to approximately US$7.50–7.70. (Calculation made by dividing the OTN value by the average official dollar-cruzado exchange rate as published in the *Conjuntura Econômica*, July 1988, p. 59).

4. The *Junta Comercial* in Ceará is part of the national commercial registration system, which consists of the following hierarchy: *Ministério da Indústria e do Comércio* and *Departamento Nacional de Registro do Comércio*, both at the national level, and the *Secretaria de Indústria e Comércio* and the *Junta Comercial do Estado do Ceará*, both at the state level.

5. The PIS (*Programa de Integração Social*) is a system in which monthly payments are made to the employees from the profits of the firm where they work. FINSOCIAL (*Fundo de Investimento Social*) is a program whereby firms pay a proportion of their receipts to fund a program that aids small farmers with housing, health, education, and the like.

6. Fiscal books are those required by tax laws, particularly those related to ICM and IPI (*Imposto sobre Produtos Industrializados*). In these books, a firm (without microenterprise status) registers purchases, sales, ICM payments, IPI payments, inventory, use of fiscal receipts, and so forth from its legal receipts and payment stubs, all to facilitate the work of government inspectors.

7. The *Junta Comercial* in Ceará has been registering firms since 1877.

8. These ten steps represent my adaptation of the eight-step model described in materials handed out by the CEAG to microenterprises undergoing the registration procedure.

9. The municipal and state governments do not recalculate their prices during the calendar year, so inflation reduces the real values considerably as the year approaches its end. The September 16, 1988, official exchange rate of Cz$232.17 per US$1 was used for this and future September calculations. For other months, mid-month values or those published in the *Conjuntura Econômica* are employed. Note that the average January official exchange rate was Cz$77.59, which would make the same fee equal to US$1.25.

10. *Cadastro Geral de Contribuintes do Ministério da Fazenda*, CGC-MF, usually just CGC.

11. See Appendix at the end of this chapter.

12. "Businessman's Counter," an information and referral service.

13. Because microenterprises do not pay income tax, one objective of the microenterprise statute is to generate taxes indirectly. Thus, the firm is required to save its purchase receipts, and the OTN calculations for sales limits are made based on purchases rather than on sales.

14. The labor book (*Carteira Profissional do Empregado*) contains the following information: personal information, dependents, changes in identity, registration of regulated professions, description of previous labor books, labor contracts, labor union payments, changes in salary, holidays, information on the obligatory retirement fund, general observations, benefits received, and so forth.

15. *Fundo de Garantia por Tempo de Serviço*, a form that has become nearly a mere formality because almost everyone opts for the FGTS.

16. *Salário família*, a payment for each dependent child, equivalent to 5 percent of the national minimum salary. A firm pays the family salary and deducts it from what it owes to the IAPAS.

17. *Encargos sociais*, including payment to the IAPAS, FGTS, PIS, and FINSOCIAL.

18. *Salário maternidade*, payment for 84 days leave. With the new constitution, women will receive 120 days of maternity leave.

19. The *Piso Nacional de Salários* is the minimum monthly salary that an employee can legally receive. Since August 1987 there is also a *salário mínimo de referência*, which is used in the calculation of salaries that are multiples of a minimum salary. For example, a person can be hired for 5 minimum salaries per month, which would be calculated with the latter salary.

20. Because microenterprises do not pay income tax, this is not a just system from their perspective. Some lobbying is taking place to allow a deduction in other payments to the government.

21. The selection of firms was by no means random, although the four firms visited are believed to represent a range of experiences in registration because they are from the industry, commerce, and service sectors and involve either family or nonfamily labor. In addition, there are two individual firms and two partnerships. Willingness to cooperate with the research was the main criterion for selection. Pseudonyms are used for all of the owners.

22. This includes fifty receipts for small local sales, fifty for local sales of larger quantities, and twenty-five for sales outside of the state.

23. The purpose of this arrangement is explained in the final section of this chapter.

24. The dates and monetary values from this interview are not entirely reliable. Nevertheless, the firm was the smallest of the four firms visited and is included here for the contrast it provides.

25. This is not to say that the profits from the operations did not cover the expenses incurred in legalizing the firm's operation. What is being considered here is simply the incremental benefit associated with operating legally.

26. Fortaleza has a very high concentration of clandestine clothing factories, most with many more than two employees.

27. The CEAG staff told of one incident in which they warned the owner of the firm they were registering that an inspector would probably come in about a week and that they would let him know when to hide his goods. To everyone's surprise, the inspector went out the same day that the papers were turned in, found everything in full operation, and assessed a hefty fine for operating without a license. At this point, everybody started looking for another *jeitinho* to get the fine reduced to at least a reasonable amount. As a result of long discussions, the inspector was finally persuaded to reduce the fine to one-half the original amount.

28. A typical occurrence involves the applicant being told about another form that needs to be filled out, but never being informed of all the forms that need to be turned in.

6
The Costs of Becoming Legal for Informal Firms: The Case of Venezuela

Vanessa Cartaya

The objective of this chapter is to systematize the formalities involved in making microenterprises legal in Venezuela. First, the obligations that must be fulfilled in accordance with the various laws in force will be described. Some of these are necessary to register firms, that is, to commence activities, whereas others are necessary to continue to operate legally. To see how such obligations affect microenterprises, the implications of compliance with the law for the finances of enterprises as well as their operating conditions in general will be studied for two firms, one in the commerce sector and one in the industrial sector. In conclusion, some brief observations will be presented regarding the implications for such enterprises of complying with the legislation in force.

Three methods were used to collect information for the first stage. First, the registration offices were visited and information was requested on each of the permits necessary, as well as the time estimated by officials for completing formalities. Second, the relevant legislation was perused with a view to obtaining information on the fees and penalties because it was extremely difficult to obtain the information directly from the offices. Third, the valuable assistance of a lawyer, adviser to the Assistance Program for Economic Management Units (AUGE, *Programa de Asistencia a Unidades de Gestión Económica*), was used to verify the information obtained and to provide an overall perspective of how in practice this complex and confusing sector functions.

For the selection of case studies and systematization of information, the valuable collaboration of José Luis Colmenares Carías, an economist with AUGE, was used, and he also brought to this analysis his wide knowledge of the conditions of small enterprises in Venezuela.

Legalization of Microenterprises in Venezuela

There are very few specific regulations in Venezuela relating to microenterprises. In general, they have to comply with the legislation applicable to all businesses. This section describes the requirements to be fulfilled and, where appropriate, the exceptions contained in the various laws. In line with conventional classification, the formalities to be completed are presented in terms of the cost of access and the cost of continuing the activity.

The Cost of Legalization

For the owner of a microenterprise, access to legality implies a series of complex formalities related to compliance with trade, tax, and labor legislation that are not easy to understand because there is no information system for this purpose in the various offices to which the owner must go. The findings of this study show that several trips must be made to the appropriate offices to assemble all the information and that often contradictory information is given. The most difficult information to obtain concerns penalties for noncompliance and in the great majority of cases these are known only once the law has been broken.

Although in most cases the registration offices say that the owner can undertake the formalities, in practice "agents" often are used, thereby adding further costs to those payable under the law. The recruitment of an agent is a practice employed by the larger enterprises.

In each case studied in this chapter, the requirements to be fulfilled are shown first followed by the cost in time and money of fulfilling each formality. Next come the ancillary or indirect costs, which are of two types: (1) the cost in paper, photocopies, and other material costs such as the professional fees payable in certain cases; and (2) the cost of adapting the premises or acquiring the equipment needed to comply with some of the registration requirements. Lastly, the cost of noncompliance, for example, fines or loss of benefits and incentives paid by the state, will be shown.

Access to legality varies according to whether the enterprises are in the industrial or commercial sectors and whether they need a health permit (see Figure 6.1). A total of 310 days is needed to complete formalities in the most complex cases, and 170 in the simplest cases. Total costs for a private firm (excluding repairs to premises and fulfillment of obligations to employees) vary between Bs 28,749 and Bs 7,169 (see Table 6.1).

Figure 6.1 Permits Required for Access to Legality

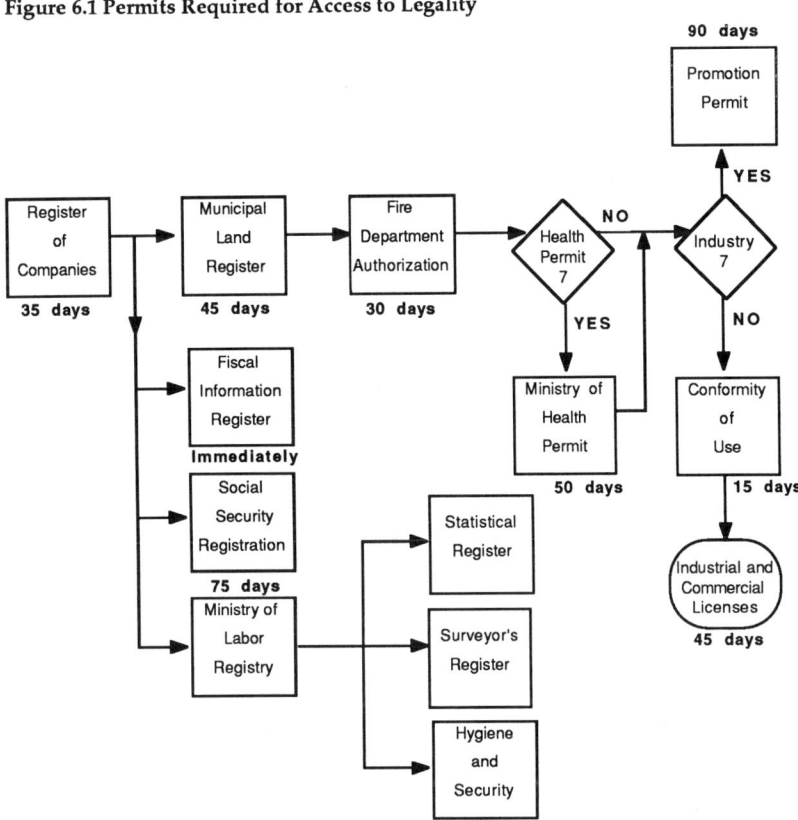

Commercial Legislation: Register of Companies

The first legal obligation for any business of whatever nature is registration in the Register of Companies, which is also necessary for any subsequent formality related to legalizing the enterprise or any future commercial transaction. The formalities vary according to the type of business. For the type of firm with which we are dealing, registration can be as a natural person or as a legal entity, in this case a limited liability company (SRL) corresponds to microenterprises.

The estimated time needed to complete registration is five weeks. At least eight visits to the Register of Companies are required, and a total payment estimated at Bs 4,544 for registration as a natural person or Bs 8,244 for a SRL.

If it is assumed that the owner-worker is the person who undertakes the formalities and that each visit implies the loss of half a day's work, the

Table 6.1 Breakdown of Costs of Legalization (in Bs)

Register	Charges	Stamps	Fees	Copies	Material	Travel	Other	Total
Register of Companies								
Private firm	980	60	2,000	24	1,200[a]	80	200[b]	
Limited liability company	1,080	60	5,000	24	1,800[a]	80	200[b]	
Municipal taxes	300	5	—	4	—	80	—	
Health permit	—	3	7,000	220	100[c]	100	—	
Promotion permit[i]	—	—	3,000	20	—	100	—	
Tax information	1	—	—	—	—	30	—	
Fire department	—	—	—	37	—	40	500[d]	
Conformity of use	—	—	—	10	—	30	—	
License								
Industry	750	5	1,000	55	5[e]	50	—	
Commerce	250	5	1,000	55	5	50	—	
Social security	—	—	—	10	—	40	—	
Labor inspection	—	—	—	10	100[f]	60	—	
Safety and Hygiene[i]	—	—	6,000	10	4,500[g]	30	—	
Industry[h]								
With health permit	2,031	73	19,000	400	5,905	640	700	28,749
Without health permit	2,031	73	12,000	180	5,805	540	700	21,329
Commerce[h]								
With health permit	1,531	73	10,000	370	1,405	510	700	14,589
Without health permit	1,531	73	3,000	150	1,305	410	700	7,169

[a]Accounts ledgers.
[b]Publication in the press.
[c]Plans.
[d]Cost of inspectors' visit.
[e]File.
[f]Hour card.
[g]Plans.
[h]For a private firm; for a limited liability company, add Bs 3,700 to total costs.
[i]Only applicable to industry.

equivalent of four days' earnings as well as transport costs must be added to the amounts mentioned above. The alternative is to employ an agent to carry out the formalities, whose fee would be a minimum of Bs 500.

The cost of noncompliance is basically the impossibility of fulfilling other obligations because registration is a mandatory requirement. A large number of stable microenterprises are therefore registered and use this to show the tax authorities that they have begun legalization procedures. This procedure, however, has no direct tax implications.

Tax Legislation

Tax legislation includes obligations under the law on profits tax as well as under more local laws regarding the use of sites and public services.

Register of Tax Information

Registration with the Register of Tax Information (RIF, *Registro de Información Fiscal*) is mandatory for all economic entities, even when, on the basis of their declarations, it is decided that they are exempt from payment of the relevant tax. Such registration functions as an economic identity card for an enterprise and is an indispensable requirement for carrying out any transaction that has to be registered legally, as well as for obtaining credit and any other benefits granted by the state, for which submission of a tax clearance certificate is required. Registration is free, the only costs involved being the loss of working hours (one and a half days) and the cost of transport.

Industrial or commercial license

The industrial or commercial license is granted by the Municipal Council. In the case of Caracas, there are two Municipal Councils: that of the Federal District, which covers all areas situated in the center and west of the city, and that of the Sucre District of Miranda State, which covers all enterprises situated in the east and south of the city. The requirements to be fulfilled are very similar. Obtaining this license involves an endless number of procedures subject to fees. Among these are copies of the registration with the Register of Companies, the lease on the premises, a Municipal Sanitation certificate, the latest balance sheet, and a declaration of the number of employees. In addition, special authorizations are required according to the branch of activity.

The minimum overall cost of this registration, not including intermediate authorizations, is Bs 755. Taking into account the five visits required, two and a half working days plus transport costs must be added.

*Special legislation on street vendors and
those with permanent stalls on the city streets*

Street vendors have to fill out an application and submit it to the Municipal Council's commission on small-scale retailers, street vendors, and similar occupations.

The estimated cost for this procedure is approximately Bs 200, not including a health permit. It involves the loss of approximately four working days.

Municipal taxes

To obtain a tax clearance certificate for property tax (*derecho de frente*), an entrepreneur must apply to the Payments Office (Land Register and Property).

Issuance of the certificate takes from twenty-five to forty-five days. The minimum cost is Bs 359, to which must be added the equivalent of two working days lost.

*Tax clearance certificate from the
Municipal Urban Sanitation Institute*

Buildings situated in the Caracas metropolitan area are obliged to pay charges for a tax clearance certificate twice a month. The charges vary according to the area and the use made of the premises.

The cost is equivalent to the quarterly sums due plus travel and is estimated at a minimum of Bs 100, assuming that there are no payments in arrears. It involves the loss of one and a half days' work.

Fire Department approval

The purpose of Fire Department approval is to ensure that the building complies with minimum safety requirements to prevent accidents and to allow evacuation. The person concerned must apply to the Fire Brigade nearest to his residence.

The procedure takes a minimum of one month. However, the major obstacle for microenterprises is the high cost of adapting the premises in order to obtain approval.

Conformity of use

The conformity of use requirement results from the need to ensure that the activity to be carried out on the premises is consistent with the uses authorized by the Municipal Urban Planning Office and with the building specifications prescribed by the Municipal Engineering Department.

Decrees No. 134/74 on Industrial Decentralization and No. 135/74 prohibit the installation of any new industries in the Caracas metropolitan area. Therefore, only commercial establishments can obtain conformity. Industries can be granted conformity under exceptional circumstances and in very specific areas, but this violates the regulations, and is very costly.

If there are no problems, a certificate of conformity can be obtained in fifteen days.

Ministry of Promotion permit

A Ministry of Promotion permit (license) is necessary for the installation of industrial activities. Registration of the business with the Ministry of Promotion involves registration of the project in the Register of Potential Industry as well as registration of the firm or invention in the Industrial Property Register.

Ministry of Health permit

A Ministry of Health permit is required for firms manufacturing food, cosmetics, and medicines, as well as for enterprises selling fruit and liquor and for hotels and guest houses.

The principal problem in this connection is that the regulations, which are aimed at safeguarding the health of consumers, are extremely strict. Those regulations most relevant to microenterprises include (1) regulations on the height of the roof and the materials used for its construction, the materials used for the surface of the walls, the slope of the floors, the existence of toilet facilities, sufficient and satisfactory water supplies, the size of work areas, ventilation, and lighting; (2) regulations on work clothing, for example, the use of uniforms, head gear, gloves, and so on; and (3) regulations on the wording of labels, type of packaging, and so forth, in addition to standards for laboratory analyses.

In general, fulfillment of these regulations makes it impossible for the great majority of microenterprises to operate legally, particularly in the food sector.

Issuance of health certificates

To obtain a health certificate, the owner of the premises and each of the employees must go to the nearest Health Unit to undergo a medical examination. This is absolutely free of charge and takes half a day. However, due to the large number of people waiting, one or two visits are necessary before being examined.

The certificate is given immediately.

Labor Requirements

Legalization of a business from the point of view of labor requirements necessitates registration with the Ministry of Labor (Statistical Register, Industrial Safety and Hygiene, and Labor Inspectorate), the Venezuelan Social Security Institute, and the National Educational Co-operation Institute (professional training institute).

Statistical register at the Ministry of Labor

The applicant must go to the Offices of the Department of Labor Statistics at the Ministry of Labor, where a copy of registration is given at once free of charge. Penalties for not fulfilling this requirement are set out in the Labor Law and involve a fine that is so low (Bs 50) that there is no real incentive to fulfill this obligation; therefore, hardly any microenterprises do so.

Registration in compliance with labor requirements

Registration with the Labor Inspectorate and compliance with safety and industrial hygiene standards guarantee the fulfillment by enterprises of the regulations contained in the Labor Law for the protection of employees.

Registration with the Venezuelan Social Security Institute

The Venezuelan Social Security Institute requires all businesses, whatever their size and activity, to be registered with their local Regional Fund. The procedure is free of charge. Penalties for nonfulfillment are fines that vary from Bs 100 to Bs 2,000.

Registration with the National Educational Co-operation Institute

Registration with the National Educational Co-operation Institute (INCE) does not apply to microenterprises because only establishments employing more than ten workers are obliged to fulfill this requirement.

Operating Costs

On the assumption that an enterprise has fulfilled all the requirements to make it legal, its continued legality implies the periodic fulfillment of a number of formalities related to renewing permits; payment of taxes, licenses, and contributions; and annual declarations. Each of these formalities involves different requirements in terms of cost, time for completion, and visits to various offices. Following the same order as in the previous section, this section delineates these operating costs.

Commercial Legislation: Register of Companies

Registration does not have to be renewed. The only reason for changing it during the lifetime of an enterprise would be a change in one of the enterprise's characteristics, for example, a change of owner or branch of activity. Nevertheless, enterprises must submit their balance sheets annually to the Register of Companies for the purpose of updating the information. This involves payment of fees for drawing up the balance sheet, estimated at a minimum of Bs 1,000 assuming that the enterprise keeps its accounts up to date, which implies a monthly expenditure of Bs 500, or Bs 6,000 annually.

Tax Legislation

Declaration and payment of profits tax

There are two types of obligation under the profits tax (1) enterprises are obliged to submit an annual declaration of profits, together with the necessary supporting documents, which vary according to the case; and (2) tax is deducted monthly from the salaries of the natural persons working in the enterprise, including the owner.

Renewal of the industrial or commercial license and other related formalities

Continued legality as far as industrial and commercial regulations are concerned involves (1) the obligation for the owner to obtain a new license whenever he moves, extends his branch of activity, or the firm or owners change; (2) an annual declaration of gross sales and profits tax for the previous year; and (3) payment of the annual tax. The exercise of economic activities involves an annual tax calculated as a percentage of gross sales and/or gross earnings for the fiscal year ending in September of the previous year.

Renewal of health permits

Where necessary, health permits have to be renewed annually, following the same procedures used to obtain the original permit. The establishment's health permit has to be renewed only if there have been changes.

Municipal taxes

Municipal taxes are paid only by the owners of premises and consist of the quarterly payment of the property tax (*derecho de frente*) and the bimonthly payment of the urban sanitation service, which in Venezuela is administered by the municipal authorities.

Labor Obligations

As far as the cost of legalization is concerned, the principal element is the issue of an industrial or commercial license, whereas the cost of continued legality has far-reaching consequences, especially with regard to labor obligations. In the case of enterprises with several employees, the cost is high.

Payment of salaries and legal compensation

The legal minimum wage in urban areas (as of September 1988) was Bs 2,010 a month. Other payments to employees in accordance with the law include compensatory bonuses, overtime, work on holidays and rest days, holidays, retirement pensions, payment of Christmas bonuses and profit sharing.

Payment of compulsory social security for the enterprises and employees

Social security contributions must be paid monthly to the appropriate regional fund. The sum is calculated as a percentage of the salary of each employee, in relation to the enterprise's risk level. Annual expenditures under social security vary between 7 percent and 9 percent of the cost of the job.

Maximum risk	Enterprise 9%	Employee 4%
Medium risk	Enterprise 8%	Employee 4%
Low risk	Enterprise 7%	Employee 4%

Other periodical obligations

Enterprises are obliged to submit an annual and quarterly list of the payroll to the Ministry of Labor (Schedules 305 and 357).

Case Studies

To show the practical advantages and disadvantages as well as the possibility of legalization for microenterprises, two case studies will be used: a plastic products industry and a cosmetics retailer. Both firms are situated in a working-class area in the west of Caracas in a zone covered by an assistance program for microenterprises, the AUGE Program (Assistance to Economic Management Units), administered by the People's Action Service Center (CESAP).[1] This facilitated access to microenterprises, which are generally reluctant to divulge information of the type sought, and also ensured the collaboration of the program's legal adviser to compare the data obtained from various official offices with the reality.

The units selected are stable microenterprises with a degree of dynamism, and which have encountered problems in becoming legal. In the commerce sector, a more general commerce (such as grocery or other type of small shop) would have been a better situation to study, but in the zone visited it was not possible to have access to economic data and information on legalization, which was relevant to the subject being studied.

The two enterprises studied desired legalization so as to present a more serious image to their customers and to avoid harassment by tax inspectors from various public bodies. Nevertheless, these enterprises were starting to realize that the obstacles of the legalization process outweighed the possible advantages.

This section gives a brief description of each of the enterprises and their financial situation. Second, the costs of legalization for each are shown as well as the effects on their finances and operations.

Plastic Products Factory

Activity

The plastic products factory manufactures large resistant plastic containers for cattle food, packaged cheese, and industrial use (for example, for paint). The process utilized is very simple but does not permit large-scale production.

The business started two and one-half years ago using a secondhand machine. It has built three more machines, introducing improvements that have made the process more efficient.

The molds, which were originally bought from another workshop, have been made on the spot for the past year following the installation on the same premises of a small toolshop. The machinery used in this shop is mainly secondhand. This has allowed the firm to lower manufacturing costs considerably and to offer better delivery times as a result of greater independence. The models were obtained from a larger firm through a former work colleague still employed there who also provides information on prices and markets. Some clients supply specifications for the containers they require.

Background

The plastics microenterprise started as a result of the concern of two friends, former fellow high school classmates (although they did not complete their studies). One of them had worked in a rival factory, where he obtained the basic knowledge. They started two and one-half years ago with capital of Bs 30,000. The first six months were occupied in setting themselves up, and they commenced production two years ago. Since then they have greatly increased activities as well as the volume and diversity of production. After many ups and downs, production has now been stabilized and they have acquired a vehicle for transport; they have also brought in a new partner, another former classmate with a higher level of formal education. These two facts, together with the decision to make the molds themselves, have enabled them to reach this year's level of profits and they hope to use their profits to diversify production further by starting to manufacture domestic water tanks for the local market.

Premises and assets

The factory operates in rented premises, which was formerly a house, with an area of 130 square meters. It does not therefore comply with the minimum requirements for an industrial workshop. In order to reduce costs, they sublet one of the five rooms to the brother of one of the partners, who has a carpentry workshop. The district mainly comprises housing, but there are also a number of small industrial workshops (manufacturing tools, clothing, and footwear), which are all illegal.

The enterprise's assets consist of four machines for processing plastic, two metal-bending machines, a welding machine, a cutter, and various small tools, estimated to be worth a total of Bs 123,831. There is also a vehicle, valued at Bs 114,738, on which Bs 72,440 is owed and paid off as income permits. There is a minimum of office equipment (desk and filing cabinet).

Organization of work and utilization of labor

There is no division of labor. All three partners carry out all the stages of the manufacturing process, as well as the marketing, purchasing of inputs, and other tasks.

The sister of one of the partners is employed to clean the premises once a week. In busy periods, temporary labor is recruited exclusively from among relatives and friends who are paid Bs 80–100 for a day's work. It is estimated that temporary help is needed 144 days a year.

The partners refuse to employ permanent salaried workers for two reasons: first, the return and profits are not the same and in this connection they have had negative experiences in the past; and second, they cannot afford to comply with the labor laws this would involve. For these reasons, they took on one of the temporary workers as a partner when there was a need to have another person on a permanent basis.

Table 6.2 shows the labor costs for this microenterprise. The original two partners each receive a monthly salary of Bs 6,000, which they deem sufficient to cover basic needs (equivalent to three minimum legal wages and the approximate cost of the average household budget). The partner who recently joined receives a slightly lower salary. No partner receives any of the benefits provided under the Labor Law.[2] They did consider the possibility of belonging to the social security system, but finally decided that "given the way it functions, it is not worth paying."

Markets

For the major part of its production, as mentioned above, this firm competes with a larger enterprise by fixing lower prices (10 or 20 percent lower). It is not possible to assess whether or not the quality is the same, but it would appear to be so. They have several regular customers, such as the Hippodrome, some cheese transporters, and a paint workshop. They also have temporary customers for whom they manufacture models on request, and these are found through an advertisement in the metro guide. They market some of their production through two salesmen who work on commission.

However, the greatest obstacle to expansion derives from the purchase of inputs and is due to the low level of working capital (made up of earnings from sales), which does not allow them to purchase supplies regularly or in large quantities. This results in two serious problems. First, the basic input, plastic pellets, is manufactured by a state enterprise, which exports and sells locally at a lower price as a result of regulations on the protection of domestic industry. There is thus a scarcity of the product on the domestic market. The state enterprise sells directly only to those who buy large quantities. Small-scale manufacturers have to buy the pellets through private distributors at a higher price. Not only do they have to buy at higher prices and for cash, but they are also limited by the quota imposed by the

Table 6.2 Plastic Products Factory Labor Costs (in Bs)
(September 1987–September 1988)

Employee	Monthly Wage	Benefits	Annual Cost
Employee 1	6,000	—	72,000
Employee 2	6,000	—	72,000
Employee 3	5,600	—	67,200
Cleaner	495	—	5,940
Temporary work[a]	1,200	—	14,400
Total	19,295	—	231,540

[a]On average, 12 days per month at Bs 100 per day.

seller, which is much lower than the amount needed for full-scale production. This has meant that two of the machines are at a standstill.

In addition, input is subject to continual increases in prices. Because the factory with which the microenterprise competes buys large quantities, it can maintain its selling price for a longer period, obliging the microenterprise to withdraw from the market until the larger factory has exhausted its stocks and raises prices. In recent months, the partners decided to do metalwork during the lulls in production, and they are thinking of extending this diversification strategy in the future and transforming it into a permanent production line.

Economic situation

The enterprise does not keep account records; therefore, the amounts shown in Table 6.3 are an estimate made with the help of the AUGE Program advisers and probably contain errors. These data show that for the past year the enterprise made a profit equivalent to 10 percent of total sales, despite having invested money (the most important investment being the purchase of a vehicle).

Problems of legalization

The microenterprise is interested in becoming legal. There are three basic reasons for this. First, the feeling that they are "transgressing the law" worries them. Second, they wish to present a serious image to their potential clients. And last but not least, not being legal implies financial costs due to the need to "neutralize" the tax inspectors so as to avoid closure of the

Table 6.3 Plastic Products Factory Profit and Loss Account (in Bs) (September 1987–September 1988)

Receipts	
Sales	1,041,666.66
Refunds	(19,957.33)
Net sales	1,030,709.33
Expenditures	928,073.33
Direct production costs	800,595.33
Raw materials	569,055.53
Labor	231,540.00
General expenditures	127,478.00
Supplies	40,939.00
Rent	30,000.00
Other general expenditures[a]	56,539.22
Profit	102,636.00

[a] Includes commission to salespeople.

enterprise. According to their estimates, this involves a minimum monthly sum of Bs 500.

Tables 6.4, 6.5, and 6.6 show the costs and formalities required to become legal and to remain legal, on the basis of the information collected from the various bodies and the economic data regarding the enterprise over the past year.

First, the enterprise is registered in the Register of Companies, although the cost does not appear in the profit and loss account (Table 6.3). The accounts ledgers required as one of the registration formalities have not been opened nor are the accounts kept in accordance with the Code of Commerce. The enterprise is also registered in the Tax Information Register. These two registration documents serve as protection vis-à-vis the authorities by showing the firm's intention to pursue the legalization procedure.

The next step is to obtain an Industrial and Commercial License, which, as Figure 6.1 shows, involves a number of prior formalities such as obtaining a certificate of Conformity of Use from the Municipal Engineering Department. According to a 1974 decree on Industrial Decentralization, the creation of new industries in Caracas is prohibited except in restricted zones and in exceptional cases. It is not therefore possible for the enterprise to obtain a conformity certificate legally and thus it cannot obtain an operating license.

This situation resulted in two options, which were considered by the partners. One option was to move away from Caracas. The other option was to obtain a license as a distributor of plastic products and hide the manufacturing activity by modifying the premises, situating the stock of finished products and a small office at the front. This was done using "influence" by paying Bs 12,000. This represented a considerable saving because avoiding inspection economized the cost of modifying the premises, but it also meant the enterprise is still illegal.

Even if a certificate of Conformity of Use as producers were obtained, the cost of modifying the premises to comply with the requirements incumbent upon an enterprise that works with materials that produce toxic emanations and gas (the heat source is obtained using gas) laid down by the Fire Brigade and the Safety and Industrial Hygiene regulations would prevent them becoming legal because, as can be seen from Tables 6.3 and 6.4, these modifications alone would absorb 181 percent of the profits for the previous year.

It can also be seen in Table 6.4 that payments related to formalities, excluding the modification of the premises and labor obligations, are relatively low (Bs 24,134), equivalent to 23 percent of profits. Breaking down this amount, it can be seen that the major part is composed of fees, and the taxes and charges payable to the state are insignificant.

It should also be mentioned that the cost of registration with the Safety and Industrial Hygiene Department could be eliminated because, according to

Table 6.4 Cost of Legalization for the Plastic Products Factory

Registration	Cost (in Bs)	Days Utilized
Register of Companies (SRL)	8,244.00	4.0
Tax Information Register	31.00	3.5
Conformity of Use	40.00[a]	1.5
Fire Brigade	577.00	2.0
Municipal tax clearance certificate	79.00	4.0
Industrial and Commercial License	1,415.00	2.5
Ministry of Promotion permits	3,040.00	1.5
Social security registration	44.00	2.0
Social security arrears (from commencement)	33,037.20	—
Ministry of Labor registration	164.00	3.0
Safety and Hygiene registration	10,500.00[b]	3.0
Accumulated arrears for employees[c]	52,491.36	—
Subtotal	109,662.56	27.0
Modifying premises as a result of legalization		
Repairs, electrical, and health installation (Fire Brigade and Safety and Hygiene)	30,000.00	
5 fire extinguishers (@ Bs 875)	4,375.00	
2 ventilators (@ Bs 10,068)	20,136.00	
3 drinking water fountains (@ Bs 350)	1,050.00	
Welding protection	800.00	
New roof (Bs 1,000 per m^2)	130,000.00	
Subtotal	186,361.00	30[d]
Days lost (calculated on the basis of one day's production per worker)		
27 days for formalities	19,821.30	
30 days building work for three persons	85,231.60	
Subtotal	105,052.90	
Total	401,076.46	

[a]Travel only (costs are paid by the owner because the premises are rented).
[b]This registration is not often complied with.
[c]See Table 6.5 (benefits of the labor law).
[d]Repairs will necessitate shutting down operations for one month.

Table 6.5 Cost of Fulfilling Labor Legislation for Plastic Products Factory Legalization (accumulated arrears)

Sector	Calculation	Bs
Social security	9% of the annual salaries of partners 1 and 2 and the cleaner for 2 years	26,989.20
	9% of the salary of partner 3 for 1 year	6,048.00
	Subtotal	33,037.20
Holidays	3 days' wages for partners 1 and 2 and the cleaner	1,249.50
	1 day's wages for partner 3	186.66
	Subtotal	1,436.16
Bonuses	30 days' wages for partners 1 and 2 and the cleaner	12,495.00
	15 days' wages for partner 3	2,800.00
	Subtotal	15,295.00
Benefits	70 days' wages for partners 1 and 2 and the cleaner	24,990.00
	30 days' wages for partner 3	5,600.00
	Interest (12% fund first year plus 12% fund second year)	5,170.00
Total		85,528.56

the information obtained, this is not required of this type of enterprise, despite the fact that the regulations do not specify any exceptions. This would allow a reduction in costs of Bs 10,500.

The most important expense, apart from the above-mentioned modifications, concerns the costs for labor obligations, which once again shows that this is a cost that enterprises try to reduce, sacrificing the welfare of the workers in order to continue operations. Updating the situation in this microenterprise, and giving their workers the remuneration they would receive as employees in the modern sector, would amount to 83.33 percent of profits.

Table 6.6 shows the cost of remaining legal. It includes the additional annual recurrent costs involved in fulfilling all the formalities. One important cost for microenterprises is the legal obligation to keep the accounts up to date. On the one hand, this means entering the accounts daily, which implies a level of organization that they are not currently in a position to bear. Furthermore, the cost of the professional services of accountants (equivalent to Bs 6,000 per annum) would constitute an additional burden for such enterprises. There are two ways of resolving this dilemma. One is currently being tried out by the microenterprise studied. The partners themselves keep the accounts, which uses up time that could be

Table 6.6 Plastic Products Factory Continued Legality: Formalities and Costs

Sector	Total Cost (in Bs)	Days Utilized
Fees for keeping the enterprise's accounts[a]	6,000.00	—
Register of Companies		
Annual submission of financial statement (fees)	1,000.00	0.5
Payment of license charge	1,000.00	2.0
Presentation of sworn statement	30.00	1.5
Profits tax[b]	—	—
Tax statement	31.00	1.5
Payment of social security	19,562.00	6.0
Labor obligations	42,932.00	
Bonuses	9,047.00	
Holidays	1,019.60	
Benefits reserve	20,365.40	
Overtime (200 hours annually)	12,500.00	
Subtotal	70,555.00	
Production lost for completion of formalities	15,857.40	
Total	86,412.40	

[a]Required for the Industrial and Commercial License, the Register of Companies, and the Tax Information Register.
[b]The cost of legalizing the enterprise and renewing its legalization mean that it incurs losses and there is therefore no profits tax.

devoted to other activities. Nevertheless, the cost is low compared to the alternative of having the accounts kept by a permanent employee specially recruited for the purpose, which would be much more costly and not justified in economic terms.

Another cost of remaining legal is related to labor obligations, which mean an increase in labor costs of 18.5 percent if one takes into account what is owed to workers, and 27 percent if one adds social security contributions.

To summarize, the total amount to be paid in order to remain legal represents 68.7 percent of the enterprise's profits. If one adds the production time lost, this sum rises to 84.1 percent of the profits.

Cosmetics Business

Activity

The cosmetics microenterprise studied markets a depilatory wax to be used cold, which is produced by the owner's family. The main work consists of visiting the final consumers in the area where the owner lives, for example, beauty salons and perfumeries.

Background

The owner of the enterprise was a traveling salesman for pharmaceutical and cosmetics companies but had little economic success. Members of his family then manufactured shampoo and other cosmetics and finally started to produce this wax, made at very low cost from natural products (basically glucose and citric acid). In principle, there is no difference between the production and marketing activities, but one year ago they decided to devote themselves more seriously to marketing as the only way of consolidating the product on the market.

Premises and assets

Because sales are essentially made outside, requirements as far as premises are concerned are minimal. The business basically occupies the entrepreneur's house, where he has a small stock of products and does his invoicing. However, so as to have legal cover and an office in which to receive customers, he also rents premises by the hour in a building in the city's business district. On payment of a monthly sum of Bs 1,000, he has access to the following facilities: use of a fully equipped office for three hours a week where he can receive customers; use of a business card that shows the name of the firm, the address of this office, telephone number, telex, and even fax; answering of telephone calls and enquiries during the week; and minor secretarial services. These premises have a valid operating permit in the name of their owner.

The microenterprise does not have any other assets, except for a small filing cabinet in the owner's home. The products are transported in hired vehicles such as taxis. In fact, the most important asset is the business card of the microenterprise.

Organization of work and utilization of labor

Sales are mainly the task of the owner (approximately 70 percent of his time), who also plans the work of the others, designs the advertising, and supervises the invoicing and receipt of payments.

The personnel consists of a salesman, who is the brother-in-law of the owner. Past experience with unknown salesmen was negative and the owner was swindled. There is a demonstrator who also sells but whose main task is to demonstrate the product in beauty salons and perfumeries.

The owner has a fixed monthly wage of Bs 4,000, plus Bs 3,000 for household expenses. The salesman has a monthly wage that is just above the legal minimum wage, and the demonstrator earns the legal minimum as a basic salary (see Table 6.7). The percentage they receive in commission is very different and is undoubtedly due to the fact that one of them is a family member. As in the previous case, benefits under the labor law are not paid and the microenterprise is not affiliated with the compulsory social security system. This is not perceived as a problem, neither by the owner nor his employees, in a relationship that depends above all on trust.

Markets

The microenterprise realizes that its product is aimed at the medium to upper class, a market that it has not yet managed to penetrate. The price shown on the packaging (Bs 96) was based on prices for rival products. The advertising and design of the packaging was recently changed to imitate the aesthetic models that dominate the market. Rival products are of two types: chemical depilatory products and waxes, which act on the same principle but have to be heated. Because it is applied cold, it is a unique product. The sales strategy therefore centers on highlighting the natural ingredients of the product, on the one hand, and its ease of use on the other.

The bulk of current sales is to perfumeries and pharmacies located in the center of the city, to whom the product is sold at half price and with credit of thirty days. Sales are also made to beauty salons. Direct sales to consumers in a busy commercial center west of the city have been tried out with a certain amount of success. All these sales are made with a discount of 50 percent.

The present strategy is to consolidate the more important customers because, in view of the high cost of transport, diversification is expensive. As a result of regulations imposed by the Ministry of Health, to obtain a health permit for manufacturing the product, the production process had to be moved to a laboratory outside the city in the eastern sector.

Table 6.7 Cosmetics Business Labor Costs (September 1987-September 1988)

Employee	Monthly Salary (in Bs)	Percentage of Sales	Annual Salary (in Bs)	Annual Commission (in Bs)	Total (in Bs)
Owner	7,000[a]	70	84,000	—	84,000
Salesman	2,500+ 20% on sales	20	30,000	25,920	55,920
Demonstrator	2,000+ 10% on sales	10	24,000	12,960	36,960
Total					176,880

[a]Bs 4,000 in wages plus Bs 3,000 taken for household expenses.

Economic situation

The microenterprise of this case study also does not keep accounts. The profit and loss account (Table 6.8) was calculated by studying invoices and estimating costs together with the microenterprise. As can be seen, during the past year the microenterprise made a profit equivalent to 20 percent of sales as a result of its special strategy. Nevertheless, for a commercial activity, this is not a large profit.

Problems of legalization

Undoubtedly, legalization formalities for an enterprise in the commerce sector are simpler and easier to fulfill. Only in the case of food or fruit sales is the procedure more complicated due to the need to obtain health permits. The main difference is that requirements regarding premises are less strict. Moreover, this type of activity is much easier to dissimulate and therefore noncompliance with requirements does not lead to the same problems with the authorities that manufacturing microenterprises have to face. The major difficulty faced by manufacturing microenterprises is conformity of use, which is easily obtained in the case of commerce.

The strategy with regard to premises has also given protection with regard to legalization. The owner's house, where the major part of his activity is carried on, is located in a marginal district where discovery would be difficult. Even if an inspector does visit the house, it will be very difficult to ascertain that any economic activity is taking place there. The premises rented by the hour possess all the necessary permits for the activity declared by the owner.

In addition, for cosmetics, the crucial authorizations concern their manufacture, and in this sphere the regulations are very strict. These were obtained by the manufacturers at a relatively high cost in time and money and

Table 6.8 Cosmetics Business Profit and Loss Account (in Bs) (September 1987–September 1988)

Receipts	648,000
Expenditures	522,880
Purchase of products	288,000
Personnel costs (including commission)	176,880
General costs	58,000
Rent and secretarial services	16,200
Transport	16,800
Advertising	7,000
Stationery (invoices, etc.)	6,000
Credit written off	12,000
Profit	125,120

while this procedure was taking place they pursued their activities using a false health registration lent by a friend.

This microenterprise is registered in the Register of Companies, but does not have all the accounts ledgers required under its provisions. It is interested in continuing with the legalization process, but gives priority to the purchase of a vehicle before any other expenditure. The only aspect in which it is not interested is compliance with labor obligations.

Tables 6.9, 6.10, and 6.11 show the cost of legalization. As can be seen, the legalization process costs the equivalent of 32 percent of the enterprise's profits. If one adds the days of production lost due to completion of formalities, the percentage rises to 46 percent. In addition, taking into account the need to rent its own premises, the cost would increase by Bs 24,000 in rent and approximately Bs 3,000 in equipment in order to comply with the regulations applicable to commercial premises.

Payment of labor obligations increases labor costs by 13.5 percent if one takes into account what is payable directly to employees, and by 18 percent if one adds the enterprise's contributions to social security. It is in the enterprise's favor that it has been operating for only a year so the accumulated arrears on behalf of the employees are not very high. Nevertheless, this is the most important heading.

Finally, it should be emphasized that for this microenterprise, it is much more costly to continue operating legally because the recurrent annual costs are more or less equivalent to half of the annual profits.

Table 6.9 Cost of Legalization for the Cosmetics Business

Registration	Cost (in Bs)	Days Utilized
Register of Companies (private firm)	4,574	4.0
Tax Information Register	31	3.5
Conformity of Use	40	1.5
Fire Brigade	577	2.0
Municipal tax clearance certificate	79	4.0
Industrial and Commercial License	1,665	2.5
Social security registration	44	2.0
Social security arrears	9,660	—
Ministry of Labor registration	164	3.0
Accumulated arrears for employees[a]	22,748.8	—
Subtotal	39,578.8	22.5
Days lost for completion of formalities	18,268.6	
Total	57,851.4	

[a]Costs equivalent to one year of operations.

Table 6.10 Arrears for Employees in Cosmetics Business

Sector	Calculation	Bs
Social security	7% of the annual salaries of the 3 employees, including commission	9,660.00
Holidays	1 day's wages for each employee	490.00
Bonuses	15 days' wages (not including commission) for each employee	5,750.00
Benefits	1 month's wages for each employee plus 12% interest	16,508.00
Total		32,408.80

Table 6.11 Cosmetics Business Continued Legality: Formalities and Costs

Sector	Total Cost (in Bs)
Fees for keeping the accounts	6,000.00
Register of Companies submission of financial statement	1,000.00
Payment of license charge (2.5% of profits)	3,168.00
Presentation of sworn statement	30.00
Payment of social security	9,720.00
Labor obligations	22,748.00
Subtotal	42,666.00
Profits tax[a]	9,862.00
Subtotal	52,528.00
Production lost for completion of formalities	9,121.80
Total	61,649.80

[a]Simplified calculation: profits minus (costs of legalization plus costs of continued legality) by 0.15.

Final Remarks

The data given here show that legalization for a microenterprise is a multifaceted problem, but is basically rooted in these units' precarious situation and not in the existence of suffocating regulations. The most costly aspects of compliance with the legalization process are related to fulfillment of safety and industrial hygiene requirements, consumer protection, and the social protection of workers. Even though formalities in these sectors could be simplified, it is difficult to suggest that they should be eliminated because these regulations—which microenterprises cannot fulfill because their situation in the market does not provide them with sufficient profits—guarantee the existence of "high quality" jobs (with respect to both remuneration and minimum working conditions).

The disadvantages suffered by microenterprises in comparison with larger enterprises are also highlighted in this study. First of all, the burden of wages in their overall structure is much higher, and therefore compliance with regulations on salaries affects them to a greater extent. Second, the existence of the same regulations for all enterprises has a proportionately greater effect on microenterprises. For example, compliance with most regulations means that microenterprises must keep their accounts up to date. For large enterprises, this is normal, but for microenterprises it means important changes in their day-to-day existence, and it cannot be done without outside help.

There are also significant differences in the burden of legalization in relation to the enterprise's activity. First, it is much easier to function legally for commercial enterprises than for industrial firms. The greatest difficulties are faced by industries that manufacture food or carry out other activities that require health permits, use dangerous products, or use machinery (for example, the plastics industry).

In an analysis of the cost of legalization, taxes paid directly to the state are not very important. The highest costs, apart from modification to premises required to protect workers and increases in jobs to comply with labor legislation, are those for professional fees.

Along the same lines, it is not so much the number of days required to obtain all the permits necessary for legalization but the number of days lost for completing the formalities that is important for microenterprises. As far as this aspect is concerned, in the case of the majority of permits, attestation that the proceedings have been initiated often protects the microenterprises from controls.

The most important conclusion of this analysis is the effect of compliance with the regulations on the operating conditions of the enterprises. Taking into account the specific manner of functioning of this type of economic unit, in which there is little division of labor and owners are also workers, the innumerable visits to various public departments and the need to keep the accounts up to date signifies lost production or obliges the owners to pay an administrator, with the attendant increase in costs. In addition, the proportion of costs for professional fees shows the disadvantage suffered by enterprises that do not have the qualified personnel to carry out this work, which is not the case for the larger enterprises.

Last, as can be inferred from the difficulties faced in the course of this research, information on the formalities to be fulfilled, but particularly on the penalties for noncompliance, are very difficult to obtain for owners of microenterprises.

These considerations show that the theory that has become common in Latin America recently that the elimination of governmental regulations would lead to the development of enterprises that had been suffocated by states is, to say the least, simplistic.

Notes

1. Centro al Servicio de la Acción Popular, an organization that, after several years' work in the area, initiated a program in support of economic activities.

2. Even though it is not explicitly stated in the law, jurisprudence has declared that working partners are not deemed to be solely owners but also employees, and as such can receive the benefits granted to employees. The partners in this case, however, do not consider that they can allow themselves this "luxury."

PART 4

REGULATION AND INFORMALITY

7
Protection for the Informal Sector in Latin America and the Caribbean by Social Security or Alternative Means

Carmelo Mesa-Lago

In this chapter, the term "social security" is used in its formal sense: a system of protection against social risks created by a modern state by means of legal instruments. ILO's broad concept, which includes within social security various programs such as social insurance, social assistance, national health schemes, and family allowances, will be followed. The concept of social insurance is, however, more restricted both in regard to the programs it includes and its coverage of the population. The term "informal social protection" as used in this study means protection against social risks that are not prescribed by the law but are provided by the family, community, district, occupation, tribe, and so on.

This study covers thirty-four countries in Latin America and the Caribbean. There is more detail concerning the former geographical area than the latter, although systematic information on the Bahamas, Barbados, and Jamaica is given. Technically, the majority of countries in the region have formal social insurance systems (which are called "Bismarckian" systems); only a few have more traditional social security systems. Available knowledge on informal social protection in this region is minimal, and one of the objectives of this study is to amplify this information.

This chapter is composed of four sections. The first, which consists of a summary of relevant texts on the informal sector, succinctly identifies the main categories of informal workers that should be protected, as well as the principal characteristics of informality, and it provides a summary of statistics on the size of the sector in countries in the region.

A review of the texts on social security in the region shows the enormous gap in cover of the informal sector. The objective of the second section of this chapter is to summarize the general studies available on social security in the region as they relate to coverage of the informal sector, completing the summaries wherever possible with new information. A short description of the legal and statistical coverage of informal workers in the thirty-four countries in the region is provided, and the reasons for the lack of coverage or its limitations are analyzed. Some examples of the extension of social security are discussed, and the overall cost of extension using the existing structure and services is estimated.

In the third and fourth sections, there are a number of policy recommendations based on four case studies carried out (for Costa Rica, Jamaica, Mexico, and Peru), which serve to provide guidelines and encourage debate on a subject that up until now has been virtually ignored.

Basic Concepts on the Informal Sector and Its Scope in the Region

The formal subject of this study is the protection of the informal sector by social security or alternative means. It is not intended to enter into an academic debate on the definition and characteristics of the informal sector. The chapter is limited to establishing a concept of work with the objective of identifying as concretely as possible the groups that should be the subject of protection.

Categories of Informal Workers and Characteristics of Informality

On the basis of a number of studies by PREALC and other experts, five categories of (urban) informal workers can be identified: (1) owners or employers (self-employed) in microenterprises with a small number of employees—for example, five; (2) self-employed or independent workers who do not receive wages but have an income; (3) paid workers in microenterprises, usually without contracts; (4) family workers, who work for the head of the family and are not paid or do not receive wages; and (5) paid domestic workers.[1]

Informal work is sometimes combined with formal work, and this has repercussions for our study because if the formal work is covered by social security, the problem of protection is resolved. However, because there is no detailed information on this at the regional level, for practical reasons it is assumed that this duality does not exist.

Other controversial definitions in texts on the subject have practical implications for this study—for example, those regarding the level of income of informal workers and their legality or clandestinity. Recent studies show that informality is not necessarily equivalent to poverty because some informal workers have high incomes (Castells and Portes, 1989; Fortuna and Prates, 1989). This is important because if the informal worker (i.e., a professional or the owner of a microenterprise) has sufficient income, he can cover himself against social risks such as illness or old age by paying private insurance or using other means.

Statistical information on several countries nevertheless shows that there is a close link between poverty and the informal sector. In 1980, the average income in the informal sector represented the following proportions of average income in the formal sector: 51.3 percent in Costa Rica, 46.6 percent in Mexico, 44.4 percent in Lima, and 36 percent in Chile (PREALC, 1982). In Brazil in 1983, 66 percent of those working in the informal sector had an income lower than the minimum wage; in Lima in 1980, 62 percent of the poor were in the informal sector; and in San Jose in 1982, half of the workers in microenterprises suffered from extreme poverty (Haan, 1985; ECLAC, 1986b; Tokman, 1987b).

A comparison among three countries (Costa Rica, Colombia, and Peru) regarding the differences in income among categories of workers shows that an informal owner receives the highest income, followed by the self-employed and persons employed in the informal sector, and that a domestic servant receives the lowest wage. The ratio between the highest and lowest wages fluctuated between 2.8 and 5.4; however, these differences decrease when, for example, one adds the cost of board and lodging to the wages of domestic workers and when owners' incomes are adjusted to take into account the incomes of family members (Tokman, 1987b).

Other characteristics of informality that are positively related to low income are lack of qualifications and capital, limited access to institutionalized credit, and the use of traditional or labor-intensive technologies. If there was precise information on the (apparently minority) high-income group, it could be subtracted and the study could concentrate on the protection of the rest of the informal sector, but unfortunately this distinction cannot be made a priori. Nevertheless, proof of the need for payment of social benefits can always be required.

The question of legality is also important from the point of view of social security because an informal worker is an underground or clandestine worker who cannot register to receive benefits. Tokman (1987a) maintains that there are differences between these two concepts, but that the majority of informal activity takes place outside the institutional framework. Therefore, it is impossible to fulfill the regulations in force, even though there may be the will to do so or coercion on the part of the government to impose the regulations.

The case of the informal owner of a microenterprise is more serious than that of an informal self-employed worker because the former's situation outside the social security network affects not only the owner but also that owner's informal workers. One question is whether, if given the choice, informal workers in microenterprises would join the system. Here again, information is scarce, although one source affirms that workers usually respond negatively because of the amount they would have to pay to enter the system (Weihert, 1986). Another reason that explains this negative attitude in some countries is the low quality or amount of social security benefits. In any event, by saving the cost of contributing to social security (or paying other taxes), an informal entrepreneur lowers production costs and advantageously competes with formal enterprises. This situation allegedly contributes to the deterioration (or disappearance) of formal employers. In times of economic crisis, it also allegedly encourages the transfer of personnel from the formal to the informal sector, which in turn decreases social security revenue and the number of workers (in the formal sector) covered by social security. On the other hand, obliging an informal employer to fulfill his social security obligations (assuming the ability to do so) would noticeably reduce his limited profits. It is therefore necessary to "reconcile the protection of [informal] workers and their families with the need to maintain this source of employment which, although precarious, is preferable to open unemployment" (Tokman, 1987b, p. 308; PREALC, 1988).

The Extent of Informality in the Region

The first part of Table 7.1 shows the distribution of the labor force in 1980 according to the PREALC classification in fourteen Latin American countries for which information is available. Until 1987, no figures were available for non-Latin Caribbean countries, although there were plans to collect statistics in Barbados and in Trinidad and Tobago (Witter, 1987). The percentage of the informal economically active population (EAP) varies considerably from 12.4 percent in Costa Rica to 23.8 percent in Peru and 25.4 percent in Ecuador. Although during the period 1950–1980 formal employment as a percentage of the EAP rose by 14.4 percentage points and informal employment by 5.8 points, due to the economic crisis in 1980–1985, formal employment decreased by 7.8 percent and informal employment rose by 3.8 percent; in other words, the rate of increase was four times higher (PREALC, 1981b, 1988). Another study gives an even higher figure (6.8 percent) for the increase in employment in the informal sector in 1980–1985. Separate information on nine countries for the period 1980–1985 (comparable to 1950–1980) also shows a significant increase in growth of the informal sector in almost all cases (PREALC, 1986; Tokman, 1987b; Rodríguez and Wurgaft, 1987). The important increase in the informal sector makes the need to protect it even more urgent.

The second part of Table 7.1 gives information from ILO, mainly from the beginning of the 1980s, on occupational categories similar to the five informal categories defined previously. Nevertheless, there are important differences: (1) the figures include the overall labor force, not just that in urban areas; (2) self-employed workers and employers are not distinguished and include independent professional people with high incomes as well as employers in large enterprises; (3) there is no distinction among employees according to the size of the enterprise; and (4) there are no separate figures for

Table 7.1 Percentage Breakdown of the Labor Force in Latin America, Circa 1980

Country	By sector[a]				By job category[b]		
	Urban		Rural			Self-employed and Employers	Unpaid Family Members
	Formal	Informal	Modern	Traditional	Employees		
Argentina	65.0	19.4	8.8	6.3	71.2	25.1	3.2
Bolivia	17.9	23.2	5.2	50.9	38.2	48.9	9.2
Brazil	45.2	16.9	9.8	27.6	65.3	27.0	5.1
Chile	54.1	20.1	14.0	8.8	66.7	25.3	3.6
Colombia	42.6	22.3	15.8	18.7	53.5	-42.5	—
Costa Rica	52.9	12.4	19.6	14.8	75.2	19.6	3.9
Cuba	n.a.	n.a.	n.a.	n.a.	88.8	5.4	0.3
Dominican Republic	n.a.	n.a.	n.a.	n.a.	51.3	36.5	3.3
Ecuador	22.7	25.4	13.7	37.9	47.6	37.3	5.8
El Salvador	28.6	18.9	22.3	30.1	59.2	28.2	10.9
Guatemala	26.7	17.8	22.3	33.1	46.9	42.2	6.7
Haiti	n.a.	n.a.	n.a.	n.a.	16.6	59.4	10.4
Honduras	n.a.	n.a.	n.a.	n.a.	45.4	33.3	14.6
Mexico	39.5	22.0	19.2	18.4	44.3[c]	27.0[c]	6.6[c]
Panama	45.3	20.9	9.1	24.6	63.3	23.2	3.6
Paraguay	n.a.	n.a.	n.a.	n.a.	36.7	41.2	11.6
Peru	35.0	23.8	8.0	32.0	45.1	49.1	5.8
Uruguay	63.3	19.0	9.5	8.0	69.4	23.8	2.0
Venezuela	62.6	16.4	4.4	15.1	64.1	26.5	3.1
Latin America[d]	44.6	13.8	12.5	22.8	n.a.	n.a.	n.a.

Sources: PREALC (1981a, 1982) and Mesa-Lago, based on ILO (1981–1986).
n.a.=not available
[a]Not including a very small percentage in mining.
[b]Not including unclassified workers. The years do not correspond to 1980 in the following cases: Bolivia (1976), Chile (1983), Cuba (1979), Ecuador (1982), Guatemala (1981), Haiti (1982), Honduras (1977), Paraguay (1982), Peru (1982), and Uruguay (1975).
[c]The results of the 1980 census are not reliable and give a much higher percentage (22%) of unclassified.
[d]Not including 5.6% in domestic service and 0.7% in mining.

domestic service workers. Table 7.1 does not therefore provide a precise estimate of the occupational categories of informal workers but it does at least give an idea of the size of the categories, and this will be useful for the subsequent analysis of cover. It should be pointed out that in the most developed countries in the region (Argentina, Brazil, Chile, Costa Rica, Cuba, Panama, Uruguay, and Venezuela) the proportion of non–wage-earners (which is the category most similar to the informal categories) fluctuates between 5.7 percent and 29.6 percent. In contrast, in the least developed countries, the figure varies between 39.1 percent and 69.8 percent. There is a positive correlation between the proportion of the formal sector, which is the more modern sector, and the proportion of the wage-earning labor force; and between the proportion of the informal sector, which is the traditional sector, and the proportion of the non–wage-earning labor force.

More precise figures concerning the distribution of the labor force among the five occupational categories in nine countries is given in Table 7.2. There are two significant differences in this table compared to Table 7.1: it is based on a survey of households (the labor force in the case of Jamaica), and, with the exception of four countries, its scope is limited to the metropolitan area of the most important cities. Table 7.2 shows a higher proportion of employees (except where the survey was at the national level) and lower percentages in the other categories. The advantage of Table 7.2 is that it is closer to the categories in the informal sector because it is restricted to urban areas (in the majority of countries) and shows figures for employers and domestic service (the latter in only two countries, although estimates of the national EAP are given). Nevertheless, Table 7.2 suffers from the same defect as Table 7.1 because it does not distinguish the high-income group among employees, employers, and self-employed. The percentage of employers varies between 1.6 percent and 4.3 percent; in the 1970 figures for eighteen countries, this percentage fluctuates between 0.5 percent and 6.5 percent, with an average of 3.3 percent for Latin America. The employer category shows the lowest figure and would be even smaller if employers in large enterprises were deducted. Next in order of importance comes the category of unpaid family workers, with a range of 1.1 percent to 9.8 percent; practically all of this group belongs to the informal sector. The next category in size is domestic service, which in two countries is around 6.6 percent; the 1980 figures for eighteen countries (six are shown in brackets in Table 7.2) give a figure that varies between 1 percent and 10.7 percent (PREALC, 1982); this category is almost wholly informal. The two major categories are the self-employed and employees; the percentage of the former varies between 13

Table 7.2 Percentage Breakdown of the Labor Force by Separate Occupational Category Selected, Latin American Countries, 1978–1980

Country	Scope of Survey	Employees	Employers	Self-employed	Family	Domestic[a]	Other[b]	Total
Brazil	4 regions	68.1	3.8	18.3	9.8	(6.2)	—	100.0
Chile	Santiago	73.7	2.6	19.1	1.6	(6.2)	3.0	100.0
Colombia	4 cities	63.2	4.2	23.9	1.9	6.7	0.1	100.0
Costa Rica	Nationwide	74.9	4.3	16.1	4.7	(5.3)	—	100.0
Jamaica[c]	Nationwide	53.5	41.2	—	4.3	1.0	0.3	100.0
Mexico[d]	D.F.	63.4	5.7	23.2	7.7	(3.7)	—	100.0
Panama	Nationwide	67.9	1.6	25.9	4.6	(8.8)	—	100.0
Peru	Lima	61.1	4.2	23.6	3.7	6.5	0.9	100.0
Uruguay	Montevideo	79.6	3.7	13.0	1.1	(6.0)	2.6	100.0

Source: PREALC (1982).
[a]The figures in brackets are independent estimates of the national EAP and should not be added to the total.
[b]Not specified or seeking a job for the first time.
[c]1985; refers to the employed labor force.
[d]1970; the figures in the 1980 census are not reliable.

percent and 41.1 percent, and the majority of those in this category are most likely informal workers. The range of the percentage of employees varies from 53.6 percent to 81.2 percent, and the majority are probably in the formal sector. Because the latter two categories are the most numerous, they represent the most serious problem with regard to social security coverage.

Current Social Security Coverage in the Informal Sector

Two Methods of Protection

In the beginning of this chapter, a distinction was made between formal social security and informal social protection. The two terms are used in order to avoid the terminological debate summarized below.

Some authors refer to formal or modern social security—which has developed over the past century in industrialized societies—and informal or traditional social security—which is found in precapitalist societies (mainly in rural areas) or in enclaves in industrialized societies. It is argued, however, that there are obsolete programs and informal elements within formal social security, just as there are innovative systems and formal elements within informal social security. The latter is a response by the family, village, or community that is not protected by the law against social risks, and it can be in an archaic or modern form, be relatively simple, or be quite complex. Another manner of distinguishing the two concepts is to use the state-legal dichotomy (in place of formal-modern) and non-state–solidarity (rather than informal-traditional). This approach is more appropriate because, first, the state concept includes not only the central government but also the provinces (states or departments), the municipalities, and other local government; and second, common or popular law regulating protection is included within the concept of solidarity (Bryde and Hirtz, 1988). A third alternative is to distinguish between internal and external solutions. The former operate in the vicinity of the problem (e.g., family, group, place of work); the latter are outside this area (e.g., social security provided by the state) (Zacher, 1988).

The development process involves a transformation that leads from archaic social conditions, in which there is traditional solidarity, to a modern, urban, industrial society with social security. Zacher (1988) states that social insurance is the instrument of social security that protects the labor force under "normal" conditions in a modern society, whereas social assistance is the mechanism that protects those who are in "subnormal" conditions. Nevertheless, social assistance can operate only when the subnormal conditions are exceptional (affect a minority) and temporary. The problem is that in developing countries, such as in Latin America, social insurance often covers a minority of the labor force whereas the majority exist in semipermanent subnormal conditions and cannot therefore be protected by social assistance.

Another problem is that the institution of reduced social security has a negative effect on informal social protection. For example, social security leaves uncovered the majority or a large part of the population, whose traditional methods of protection deteriorate (Bryde and Hirtz, 1988). It should therefore be realized that it is necessary to have pluralist social security in which both methods of protection complement each other, and that forms of solidarity should be strengthened while at the same time the progress of the subnormal sector to normal conditions is facilitated (Zacher, 1988). However, it is not easy to identify ways of strengthening traditional protection institutions through government action and harmonize them with social security systems (Midgley, 1984).

Concretely, formal social security—in accordance with the ILO concept—includes the following programs: social insurance (old-age, disability, and widows' pensions); cash benefits and medical and hospitalization insurance for sickness and maternity; insurance against accidents at work and work-related illnesses; unemployment benefits; family allowances; social assistance (noncontributory pensions for persons without incomes and not covered by social insurance); national health systems or public health programs; and so forth (ILO, 1984). Social insurance—which predominates in the region—has a more restricted scope (the four programs mentioned above) and covers less of the population. There also are other differences compared to social security related to the integration of risks and administration, the method of financing, the standardization of benefits, and so on (Mesa-Lago, 1985a).

Information available on informal social protection has been compiled mainly by anthropologists and sociologists (Witter, 1987) and generally refers to families, communities, or villages in rural areas in developing countries. In 1988, however, two international multidisciplinary meetings were held to review informal social protection and formal social security. The first was the International Symposium on Formal and Informal Security held in Tutzing, Germany, in June 1988. It studied mainly informal rural programs in ten developing countries in Africa (Tanzania, Ghana, and Botswana), Asia (Indonesia, Philippines, South Korea, Taiwan, and Sumatra), the Middle East (Egypt), and Latin America (Colombia). Work focused on the protection of families, fraternities, clans, and village communities through associations, cooperatives, or groups, which offer solidarity or mutual assistance in cases of death, illness, accident, disability, old age, or similar adversity. One program of particular interest (which we shall see later exists in Jamaica and Peru) consists of a weekly or monthly collection among a specific number of relatives or friends and rotates among each of the members of the group. The programs in urban areas studied at the Tutzing meeting concerned groups of African migrants in France and

Indonesian migrants in the Netherlands, which duplicated the situations existing in their rural areas of origin (von Benda-Beckmann et al., 1988). The only Latin American case studied was that of a peasant community in Boyacá, Colombia (Freiberg-Strauss and Jung, 1988).

The second meeting was the Social Security in Developing Countries Workshop, organized by the Suntory-Toyota International Centre for Economics and Related Disciplines, London School of Economics, in July 1988. Ten surveys were presented, analyzing prevention and insurance programs against hunger, agrarian reform, and credit and education programs. This workshop also presented microeconomic studies with an economic anthropological focus on precapitalist forms of protection, mainly in rural areas in developing countries: India, Bangladesh, Sri Lanka, China, and countries in southern and sub-Saharan Africa (Ahmad and Drèze, 1989). One of the studies was on traditional systems of protection, including "mutual insurance" in rural societies in the Third World, which consist of reciprocal networks for the exchange of goods or work on credit, so as to deal with various contingencies by combining risks within the village. The author concluded that these traditional systems had been effective in the past, but were being eroded or had proved inadequate to meet current insecurity, so governments should supplement them or replace them with formal programs (Platteau, 1988).

Without denying the importance of the aforementioned studies, they focus on rural areas (generally in countries with a lower level of development than those in Latin America and the Caribbean) and they therefore do not help in the study of informal social protection of the urban informal sector in this region. In the third section of this chapter, some similar systems are described, but the remainder of this section refers only to formal social security.

Legal Social Security Coverage

The relevant texts distinguish between "legal" and "statistical" population cover. The former is prescribed by the law, but not always applied, whereas the latter refers to estimates of the population actually covered. There is also the "real" coverage, but there is no precise comparative information at the regional level to be able to calculate effective access by the population to services.

Tables 7.3 and 7.4 show legal health and pensions coverage, respectively, in the thirty-four countries of the region studied; the costs of these two programs take up more than 80 percent of the social security costs.

Table 7.3 distinguishes between countries with social insurance and national health systems because, in the former, social insurance provides cash benefits as well as medical and hospital care, whereas in the latter the national health system provides medical and hospital care and social insurance provides the cash benefits. The table does not include public sector coverage (Ministry of Health) in countries where there is no national health system because there is not usually any "right" to benefits in such countries.

In the sixteen countries with national health systems (the non-Latin Caribbean countries plus Cuba and Nicaragua), all the inhabitants are covered for medical and hospital care, including the informal sector. In eleven of these countries, social insurance covers all employees for sickness benefits; in Bermuda, St. Vincent, and Suriname there are no cash benefits; and in St. Lucia, the law has not yet entered into force. Self-employed workers have legal coverage for cash benefits in only four of the countries, and coverage is voluntary in two other countries. Domestic workers have compulsory coverage in four countries and voluntary coverage in one other. None of the countries provides benefits for unpaid family workers, and at least four of them exclude temporary workers.

Of the seventeen countries with social insurance, according to Table 7.3, in eight the law provides cash benefits and medical and hospital care for all employees, although some countries exclude temporary workers and in two the geographical coverage is limited to the capital and urban areas. In the remaining nine countries, legal coverage is limited to employees; agricultural, domestic service, and temporary workers are generally excluded (in one country coverage is restricted to the capital and urban areas). In Haiti, the sickness-maternity law has not yet come into force. The law provides compulsory coverage for self-employed workers in only two countries and in a further nine there is voluntary coverage; domestic workers are in a better situation: ten countries provide compulsory coverage and two voluntary coverage. Dependents of those insured (usually the spouse and under-age children) are covered for medical and hospital care in all the countries except Ecuador; in five countries, there are restrictions (i.e., maternity care for the wife or only pediatric care for the children). The retired usually also are protected.

Table 7.4 shows the legal pension coverage in the thirty-four countries in the region studied. In twenty-one countries (the most developed, including almost all the non-Latin Caribbean), all employees are covered, and in the remaining thirteen countries, only some employees are covered (generally those in industry, commerce, the civil service, and transport, excluding agricultural and temporary workers). Self-employed workers have compulsory coverage in ten countries and voluntary coverage in eleven, whereas domestic workers have compulsory coverage in fifteen countries and voluntary coverage in two. None of the countries has coverage (at least mandatory coverage) for unpaid family workers. Nevertheless, six countries have noncontributory pensions (public assistance) for those who do not qualify for a social insurance pension, and in another two countries there are options for those not insured.

Table 7.3 Legal Coverage of Health Benefits Under National Health Systems and/or Social Insurance in Latin America and the Caribbean, 1985

Country	All Inhabitants	Wage-earning Employees All[a]	Wage-earning Employees Part[b]	Self employed	Domestic Service
Social Insurance					
Argentina		X		X[c]	X
Bolivia			X	X	
Brazil			X	X[c]	X
Chile		X		X[c]	X
Colombia			X	X[c]	X[c]
Costa Rica		X		X[c]	X
Dominican Republic			X	X	
Ecuador			X		X
El Salvador			X		
Guatemala			X[d]		
Haiti					
Honduras			X[d]	X[c]	
Mexico			X	X[c]	X[c]
Panama		X		X[c]	X
Paraguay		X		X[c]	X
Peru		X			X
Uruguay		X			X[e]
Venezuela		X[d]			X
National Health System					
Antigua-Barbuda	X	X		X	
Bahamas	X	X		X	X
Barbados	X	X		X[f]	X
Belize	X	X			
Bermuda	X				
Cuba	X	X			
Dominica	X	X			
Grenada	X	X		X	
Guyana	X	X			X
Jamaica	X			X	X[e]
Nicaragua	X	X		X[c]	
St. Kitts & Nevis	X	X			
St. Vincent	X				
St. Lucia	X				
Suriname	X				
Trinidad & Tobago	X	X			X

Sources: Compiled by the author on the basis of U.S. SSA (1986) and additional information from several countries.

Note: In the non-Latin Caribbean, Cuba, and Nicaragua there is a national health system (with the exception of Bermuda, where private hospital insurance is obligatory), and the coverage of all inhabitants shown in the table refers to medical and hospital care. In addition, these countries generally have a social insurance system that provides cash benefits, and these are shown in the table whether for employees, self-employed and/or domestic service. In the other countries, the coverage shown refers to social insurance, both medical-hospital care and cash benefits.

[a] Nearly all countries exclude unpaid family workers and eight countries also exclude temporary workers from this category.
[b] Normally this covers permanent employees in industry, commerce, mining, transport and communications, and civil and public service, and excludes those in agriculture and domestic service, as well as temporary workers, those who work at home, and unpaid family workers.
[c] Voluntary coverage: in Panama those affiliated to trade unions are obligatorily covered.
[d] Coverage limited geographically to the capital city and some urban areas.
[e] Only for maternity.
[f] Optional continuation when moving from the wage-earning employee category to the self-employed category.

Table 7.4 Legal Coverage of Old-Age, Disability, and Widows' (Pensions) Benefits Under Social Security in Latin America and the Caribbean, 1985

Country	Wage-earning Employees All	Wage-earning Employees Part	Self-employed	Domestic Service	Other
Antigua-Barbuda	X				
Argentina	X		X	X	X[a]
Bahamas	X		X	X	X[b]
Barbados	X		X	X	X[b]
Belize	X		X[c]		
Bermuda	X		X		
Bolivia		X	X[d]		
Brazil		X	X[e]	X	
Chile	X		X[d]	X	X[b]
Colombia		X	X[d]	X[d]	
Costa Rica	X		X[d]	X	X[b]
Cuba	X		X[d]		X[b]
Dominica	X				
Dominican Republic		X		X	
Ecuador		X	X[d]	X	
El Salvador		X			
Grenada	X				
Guatemala		X			
Guyana	X		X	X	
Haiti		X			
Honduras		X	X		
Jamaica	X		X	X	
Mexico		X	X[d]	X[d]	X[f]
Nicaragua		X			
Panama	X		X[d]	X	
Paraguay	X				
Peru	X		X[d]	X	
St. Kitts & Nevis	X		X[d]		
St. Vincent		X			
St. Lucia		X			
Suriname	X		X		
Trinidad & Tobago	X			X	
Uruguay	X		X	X	X[b]
Venezuela	X			X	

Sources: Compiled by the author on the basis of U.S. SSA (1986) and additional information from several countries.

[a]Those under fifty-five years of age who do not work can take out voluntary insurance.

[b]Assisted (noncontributory) pensions for those not insured, paid by social insurance; in Barbados and Uruguay, only for old-age pensions.

[c]Optional continuation when moving from the wage-earning employee category to the self-employed category.

[d]Voluntary: in Ecuador, it is compulsory for self-employed professionals; in Mexico, coverage is progressive; in Panama, it is compulsory for those belonging to trade unions.

[e]Only the urban sector.

[f]Those not insured can take out voluntary insurance.

Table 7.5 summarizes the legal coverage situation in the region for three categories of informal workers previously identified. Regarding cash benefits (health and pensions), approximately half the countries do not provide any legal coverage for self-employed and domestic workers. (The best situation is that of pensions for the self-employed in which only 38 percent of the countries do not provide coverage.) In 44 percent of the countries there is compulsory coverage for domestic workers, compared to 15–30 percent for self-employed workers; in approximately one-third of the countries there is voluntary coverage for the latter. No country provides coverage (at least compulsory coverage) for unpaid family workers. Almost one-quarter of the countries provide social assistance pensions or voluntary coverage for workers who are not already covered.

Table 7.5 shows that legal coverage for medical and hospital care is broader than that for cash benefits: 74 percent of the countries have compulsory coverage for domestic workers (6 percent have voluntary coverage), 65 percent for the self-employed (26 percent have optional coverage), and 47 percent for unpaid family workers, that is to say that countries with no coverage at all amount to 20 percent, 9 percent, and 53 percent, respectively, for each of the three groups. This is mainly due to the fact that national health systems in the non-Latin Caribbean (plus Cuba and Nicaragua) provide coverage for the total resident population and all of these groups are therefore included. On the other hand, the number of countries with social insurance that provides legal coverage for these benefits to the three groups (whether compulsory or voluntary) is much lower.

It should be noted that Ministries of Health legally cover the population not protected by social insurance, but their resources are not sufficient; for

Table 7.5 Percentage Distribution of Latin American and Caribbean Countries by Type of Legal Coverage Provided for Each Category of Informal Worker, 1985

Legal Coverage	Cash Benefits					Medical/Hospital Care Benefits		
	Self-employed		Domestic		Unpaid Family	Self-employed	Domestic	Unpaid Family
	Pensions	Health	Pensions	Health				
Compulsory	30	15	44	44	0	65[a]	74[a]	47[a]
Voluntary	32	35	6	6	0	26	6	0
None	38[b]	50	50[b]	50	100[b]	9[c]	20[c]	53[c]
Total	100	100	100	100	100	100	100	100

Source: Calculated by the author on the basis of Tables 7.2 and 7.4.
[a]The majority of countries with national health systems that legally cover all residents.
[b]18% of the countries provide assisted pensions to those not covered, and 6% give those not covered the option of voluntary insurance.
[c]Legally covered by the Ministry of Public Health.

example, in Colombia, the ministry covers 82 percent of the population protected by the public sector (i.e., ministry plus social insurance) and receives 38 percent of the public health revenue; in the Dominican Republic, the proportions are 91 percent and 53 percent, respectively; in Ecuador, 89 percent and 59 percent; and in Peru, 76 percent and 50 percent. In other Latin American countries with the percentage of social insurance coverage below 25 percent, the Ministry of Health is responsible for covering three-quarters or more of the population with minimum resources (Mesa-Lago, 1989).

Other social security programs in the region provide the three main groups in the informal sector with even more restricted coverage. The work-related accidents and illnesses program usually covers only salaried workers in the formal sector and is exclusively financed by the employer. In the vast majority of countries, self-employed, domestic, unpaid family, and temporary workers are specifically excluded. However, in three countries (Bahamas, Cuba, and Venezuela) this program obligatorily covers self-employed workers, and in four (Chile, Ecuador, Nicaragua, and Paraguay) coverage is optional or restricted. Regarding domestic workers, only Uruguay provides compulsory full-scale coverage, whereas two other countries (Belize and Ecuador) limit the group covered to benefits (U.S. SSA, 1985).

Unemployment insurance exists in only five countries in the region (Barbados, Brazil, Chile, Ecuador, and Uruguay) and, as in developed countries, it covers only workers in the formal sector to help them during periods of recession. The informal sector is excluded due to the difficulty of implementing systems to monitor compliance with labor legislation; it is nevertheless probable that some of those receiving unemployment benefits seek work during this period in the informal sector (IDB, 1987; Rodríguez and Wurgaft, 1987).

Lastly, a family allowance program operates in only six countries in the region and is compulsory for the domestic service sector solely in Uruguay (U.S. SSA, 1985).

Statistical Coverage and Trends Toward Extension

Table 7.6 shows that legal coverage does not apply in the majority of countries in the region. It should be noted that these statistics are often based on rough calculations and overestimate real coverage. The statistical coverage of social insurance for sickness and maternity is usually wider than for pensions, without taking into account Ministry of Health coverage, which is not shown in Table 7.6. The table does not include non-Latin Caribbean countries whose coverage for medical and hospital care (through national health systems) is deemed to be universal, and whose coverage in cash benefits for the EAP (through social insurance) is very high (e.g., 93 percent in Jamaica, 86 percent in the Bahamas, and 81 percent in Barbados) (Mesa-

Table 7.6 Percentage of Economically Active and Total Population Covered by Sickness and Maternity Insurance in Latin America 1960, 1970, 1980, and 1985

Country	Economically Active Population				Total Population	
	1960	1970	1980	1985	1980	1985
Argentina	55.2[a]	68.0[a]	69.1[a]	79.1[b]	78.9	74.3[b]
Bolivia	8.8[c]	9.0	18.5	n.a.	25.4	n.a.
Brazil	23.1	27.0	87.0	n.a.	96.3	n.a.
Chile	70.8	75.6	61.2	70.0	67.3	n.a.
Colombia	8.0	22.2	30.4	30.2	15.2	16.0
Costa Rica	25.3	38.4	67.4	68.2	81.5[d]	84.6[d]
Cuba	62.6[e]	88.7[f]	93.0[f,g]	n.a.	100.0[g]	n.a.
Dominican Republic	n.a.	8.9	n.a.	11.3	n.a.	5.9
Ecuador	11.0	15.8[h]	21.3	23.4[i]	9.4	11.1[i]
El Salvador	4.4	8.4	11.6	n.a.	6.2	n.a.
Guatemala	20.6	27.0	33.1	26.6	14.2	12.9
Honduras	3.7	4.2	14.4	12.8[b]	7.3	10.3[b]
Mexico	15.6	28.1	42.0	41.7[i]	53.4	59.7[i]
Nicaragua	5.9	14.8	18.9	31.5	9.1	37.5
Panama	20.6	33.4	52.3	56.4[b]	49.9	58.1[b]
Paraguay	8.0	10.7	14.0	n.a.	18.2	n.a.
Peru	24.8[c]	35.6[h]	37.4	38.0	16.6	18.6
Uruguay	109.0[a,j]	95.4[a,j]	81.2[a,j]	72.4[a,i]	68.5	67.0[i]
Venezuela	11.9	24.4	49.8	54.3	45.2	49.9[i]
Latin America	n.a.	n.a.	61.2	n.a.	61.2	n.a.
Latin America excluding Brazil	n.a.	n.a.	42.7	n.a.	42.7	n.a.

Source: Mesa-Lago (1989).
n.a.=not available
[a] Pension coverage.
[b] 1984.
[c] 1961.
[d] Including coverage of the poor.
[e] 1958.
[f] Estimate based on legal coverage and population census.
[g] 1981.
[h] 1969.
[i] 1983.
[j] Subcoverage as a result of multiple protection.

Lago, 1987b). In Latin America, coverage of the EAP extended rapidly in some countries between 1960 and 1980: to 400 percent in Brazil and Venezuela and 300 percent in Costa Rica, Mexico, and Panama. Although there is no precise figure for Cuba at the end of the 1950s (the figures in Table 7.6 show pension coverage), information shows that health coverage increased by 500 or 600 percent during this period. In the other countries, despite some progress, the EAP coverage in 1980 was only one-third or less.

Table 7.6 shows that in 1980, 61.2 percent of the total Latin American population was covered. If one excludes Brazil (which in 1980 had one-half of those insured in Latin America), this coverage falls to 42.7 percent, and in half of the countries it was less than 25 percent. There are significant differences in coverage among the countries: 75–100 percent were covered in Cuba, Brazil, Costa Rica, and Argentina; 50–74 percent in Uruguay, Chile, Mexico, Panama, and Venezuela; 25–49 percent in Bolivia; 10–24 percent in Paraguay, Peru, Colombia, and Guatemala; and 9 percent or less in Nicaragua, Ecuador, Honduras, El Salvador, and the Dominican Republic.

The scarce information available for 1985 shows that in Nicaragua extension of coverage increased; in some countries (Ecuador, Costa Rica, Panama, Peru, and Venezuela) coverage continued to extend at the same rhythm; and other countries (Chile) regained and exceeded the level of coverage they appeared to have lost (Mesa-Lago, 1987a, 1988d). In other countries (Argentina, Colombia, and Mexico), the trend is not obvious and there are contradictions between coverage of the EAP and that of the total population. Finally, there was a drop in the percentage of coverage in some countries (Guatemala and Uruguay, although in the latter case it could be the result of the elimination of dual coverage). The economic crisis during the decade led to a slower rhythm of extension of coverage and a decrease in coverage as a result of the increase of unemployment, evasion, and work in the informal sector.

In Latin America, the population with no social security coverage is principally made up of the informal sector, the unemployed, and agricultural workers, especially non–wage-earners (Mesa-Lago, 1985a). Studies carried out toward the end of the 1970s in two countries in the region confirm this. In Panama in 1978, the percentage distribution of the non-insured sector was 44.2 percent self-employed, 15.3 percent unemployed, 9.4 percent employed in small enterprises, 8 percent unpaid family workers, 2.9 percent employers, and 20.2 percent other temporary or part-time workers. For sickness and maternity insurance in Costa Rica in 1979, the distribution was 40.1 percent workers (mostly employed in small enterprises that evaded regulations and in agriculture), 17.9 percent unpaid family workers, 15.5 percent unemployed, 13.3 percent self-employed (the figure for pensions must be much higher), and 13.2 percent employers (Isuani and Mesa-Lago, 1981; Mesa-Lago, 1983a).

Table 7.7 shows the percentage of coverage of self-employed workers in nine countries in the region for which there are statistics. The highest coverage is in Costa Rica (93 percent for sickness and maternity), Bahamas (48.4 percent) and Barbados (24.8 percent); the rest are less than 20 percent, and in six countries (including the pensions program in Costa Rica) less than 10 percent. Compulsory coverage does not appear to lead to a higher percentage of coverage; for example, Jamaica has 4 percent (only 1 percent if one takes into account active contributors) with compulsory coverage and Costa Rica has 93 percent with voluntary coverage (sickness and maternity). The difference between the two coverages in Costa Rica is due to the fact that the rate of contributions for health is much lower than for pensions. It should be noted that coverage partly includes high-income professionals who do not

Table 7.7 Percentage of Coverage of Self-Employed Workers in Selected Latin American and Caribbean Countries, 1978–1987

Country	Year	Type of Coverage		Percentage of Coverage	
		Compulsory	Voluntary	Self-employed	EAP
Bahamas	1985	X		48.4	85.9
Barbados	1983	X		24.8	81.9
Chile	1986		X	11.9/17.5^a	72.8
Colombia	1984		X	0.6	30.4
Costa Rica	1985		X	2.0/93.0^b	69.0/85.0^b
Jamaica	1985	X		4.0^c	93.2
Mexico	1987		X	0.8	41.7
Panama	1978		X	1.5	44.9
Peru	1985–86		X	4.0	38.0

Sources: Isuani and Mesa-Lago (1981); Mesa-Lago (1985a, 1987b, 1988a, 1988d, 1989); Mesa-Lago and De Geyndt (1987), and Tables 7.3 and 7.4.
^{a}The lowest estimate corresponds to contributors and the highest to those registered.
^{b}The lowest figure corresponds to pensions and the highest to health; the last figure includes assistance for the population as a whole.
^{c}Registered; only 1% were active contributors.

belong to the informal sector. The countries in Table 7.7 (with the exception of Colombia) are those with the highest coverage in the region (together with Argentina, Cuba, and Venezuela for which figures regarding self-employed workers covered are not available). A comparison of the percentage of coverage in the last two columns of Table 7.7 shows that, with the exception of Costa Rica for health and the Bahamas for pensions, the self-employed have social security protection that varies between 1 percent and 30 percent of the overall coverage of the EAP.

There are virtually no statistics concerning coverage of domestic service workers. With regard to this group, PREALC (1981a, p. 315) reports that at the beginning of this decade there was "generalized non-compliance with the legal provisions on registration and payment for social security." Several countries in which there is compulsory coverage for domestic workers report that it is very low due to evasion by employers, for example, in Ecuador. On the other hand, Peru reports that 77 percent of domestic workers are covered, but it has not been possible to verify this figure (Mesa-Lago, 1984, 1988b).

There are no statistics either on the coverage of unpaid family workers, although it has been seen that this group is practically excluded under the legislation.

Causes of the Lack or Low Rate of Social Security Coverage in the Informal Sector

Before analyzing the lack or low rate of social security coverage in the informal sector, it is important to study the reasons for the low rate of coverage of the population in general in Latin America because the two aspects are linked. One explanation of the second phenomenon is that the Bismarckian model of social insurance has not been able to operate effectively in Latin America because in developed European countries the majority of the labor force was and still is in the urban wage-earning sector, whereas in many Latin American countries the majority of the EAP is self-employed or works without pay for a member of the family or in agriculture. The Bismarckian model is financed by contributions from the employer and the insured (and sometimes from the state) based on the salary of the person insured, whereas in Latin America a self-employed worker has to replace the employer's contribution, and an agricultural worker receives a very low wage, is isolated, and has little job stability. This partly explains why in many countries in the region the percentage of the population covered has continued to decrease for decades, is usually confined to urban areas, and excludes nonsalaried workers (Arroba, 1979; Isuani, 1986).

A comparison of Tables 7.1 and 7.6 shows that in the most developed countries in the region (Argentina, Brazil, Chile, Costa Rica, Panama, Uruguay, and Venezuela) a large percentage of the labor force is wage-earning (63–89 percent) and a low percentage are self-employed and family workers (6–32 percent), and there exists the highest rate of social security coverage (54–93 percent). In contrast, the least developed countries (Haiti, Paraguay, Bolivia, Honduras, Guatemala, Ecuador, and Peru) have a very low percentage of wage-earners in the labor force (17–47 percent), a very high percentage of non–wage-earning workers (43–70 percent), and low coverage of the EAP (1–38 percent).

A more detailed and systematic analysis of social insurance coverage indicators in Latin America was made by a research team from the University of Pittsburgh, who looked at four independent variables. Figures on the decline showed that the most important individual variable was the percentage of the wage-earning EAP, followed by the per capita gross domestic product (GDP), the degree of urbanization, and the percentage of non-agricultural GDP, in that order (Mesa-Lago, Cruz-Saco, and Zamalloa, 1988).

The reasons for the low coverage in the informal sector are (1) ineffective organization and political activity to oblige the state to provide better protection; (2) high cost of financing social insurance protection; (3) no income or low income in most of the sector; (4) difficulty of detecting, controlling, and inspecting microenterprises; and (5) unattractive quantity and quality of benefits.

Studies carried out in nine Latin American countries show social security coverage is highest in economic activities such as utilities (electricity, gas, and water), financial services, government, and manufacturing; it is lowest in personal services, agriculture, and (in some countries) certain commercial and construction activities. The geographical areas (provinces, states, departments) best covered are those that are most developed, trade unionized, and industrialized, with the highest per capita income, whereas those least covered are the least developed, most agricultural, least unionized, and with the lowest per capita income. This situation is in part the result of the diverse degree of power exercised by pressure groups, which, in the twentieth century, exerted pressure on the state to obtain social security concessions, progressively instituting a stratified system. Legislation was first obtained by the most powerful groups, which have the highest population coverage, receive the highest benefits in the most programs, and pay proportionately less for social insurance (receiving contributions from employers, the state, and consumers). Some categories in the informal sector (self-employed and domestic workers) were the last to be covered, and have no coverage or inadequate and costly coverage, due to their low level of organization and/or mobilization vis-à-vis the state (Mesa-Lago, 1978, 1985a).

Table 7.8 shows that even in countries where self-employed workers have legal compulsory or voluntary coverage, the cost of financing it is much higher than for wage-earners: between 1.0 and 1.9 times in three countries, twice as high in four countries, and three or more times as high in five countries. It is only in Chile that both groups show a similar rate of contribution. Table 7.8 also shows that in the majority of countries the wage-earner (who has a much higher average income than a worker in the informal sector) legally pays one-third or less of the total contribution and the remainder is paid by the employer and the state; but the self-employed do not have employers, and the state (with exceptions) does not supplement their contributions. The rate of contribution is so high for self-employed workers that even when they are affiliated with social insurance (whether compulsorily or voluntarily), only a small minority pay: in Jamaica, only one-quarter of the 4 percent registered contributed in 1985, and under the new system in Chile (there are no figures on the former system), less than half the 10.5 percent registered contributed in 1987 (Mesa-Lago, 1987b, 1988d).

As was seen in the first section of this chapter, workers in the informal sector generally have a very low income, and if they are employed within the family often they are not paid. Statistics for Brazil in 1983 show that as wages increase so does the percentage of wage-earners contributing to social security; for example, only 4.7 percent of those not earning a wage and 6.2 percent of those earning less than half the minimum salary make contributions, but the percentage rises sharply to 46.6 percent for those who earn between half and a full minimum wage and continues to increase up to 94 percent for those who receive more than ten minimum wages (ECLAC, 1986b). A survey of employers and workers in microenterprises in Cuenca, Ecuador, in mid-1988 revealed coverage of less than 5 percent of those surveyed. The reasons for this are twofold: (1) the workers declared that their wages were just enough to cover food and housing so they could not pay social security, and because they wished to receive their full wages, they did

Table 7.8 Comparison of the Rate of Social Security Contributions by Wage-earners and Independent Workers in Latin America and the Caribbean, 1985–1988

Country	Year	Rate of Contribution		
		Wage-earner (on wages)	Self-employed (on income)	Total[a]
Argentina	1985	14.0	18.0	49.8–52.6
Bahamas	1987	1.7–3.4	6.8–8.8	6.3–8.8
Barbados	1987	4.65–5.5	8.0	9.55–11.5
Brazil	1985	8.5–10.0	19.2	25.6–29.2
Chile[b]	1988	20.6–28.5	19.45–27.4	21.4–29.4
Colombia	1986	4.5–6.2	15.0–20.0	19.0–24.0
Costa Rica	1988	9.0	12.2–19.5	35.66
Cuba	1985	0	10.0	10.0
Ecuador	1985	9.4–11.4	14.0–16.0	19.2–21.2
Guyana	1985	4.9	10.5	12.3[c]
Jamaica	1987	2.5[d]	5.0[d]	5.0[d]
Mexico	1987	3.75	13.57	18.04
Peru	1987	3.0	9.0	9.0
Uruguay	1985	13.0–16.0	n.a.	32.0–40.0

Sources: Mesa–Lago (1985a, 1987b, 1988a, 1989); Mesa–Lago and De Geyndt (1987); U.S. SSA (1986).

n.a.=not available

[a] Including contributions by the employee, the employer, and the state (when fixed as a percentage of salary).

[b] Including old and new systems; the employee's contribution includes unemployment and excludes occupational hazards, whereas the opposite is true for the self-employed.

[c] The premium for occupational hazards must be added.

[d] A contribution of a fixed amount must be added.

not denounce their employer; and (2) employers stated that their profits were very low and they could not pay the contributions (Roche, 1988).

The problem of evasion is acute among employers in the informal sector because many of them are clandestine or have a small number of employees. Studies carried out in Colombia and Peru show that the fewer employees an enterprise has, the more difficult and costly it is to detect and inspect the firm and ensure payment of social insurance (Mesa-Lago and De Geyndt, 1987; Mesa-Lago, 1988b). In some cases, the cost of such an operation is higher than the sums collected. Furthermore, in countries such as Costa Rica and Chile, where there are assisted (noncontributory) health and pensions programs for the poor, informal employers put pressure on their workers to apply for these benefits, even though they are usually less in financial and benefits terms, in order to economize the cost of contributing. In the case of domestic workers, the head of the household is usually responsible for deducting contributions from the employee and adding his own contribution, but it is extremely difficult to verify wages, payments, and other pertinent figures.

Self-employed workers find it difficult to pay the contributions, which have to be made directly to the social security office. In some countries (Costa Rica, Mexico, and Panama) an attempt has been made to solve this problem by making associations and trade unions responsible for registering and collecting contributions from the self-employed. Jamaica is considering paying commissions to small shops used by the self-employed for the collection of contributions (Mesa-Lago, 1987b).

In surveys and interviews in a number of countries, informal workers stated that there was no advantage in joining the social security systems because the benefits were low or of poor quality. The little information available shows that average pensions paid to the self-employed or domestic workers are much lower than the average pension in general; for example, in Uruguay, these pensions were between approximately one-half and one-sixth of the pensions of the armed forces or bank employees, and this difference was not due only to the contributions paid (Mesa-Lago, 1985a; Dauriex, 1987).

The possibility of extending traditional social insurance coverage in the region has decreased during the present decade due to the fact that the formal sector has decreased, as explained above, whereas the informal sector has grown, reversing the trend from 1950 to 1980: "there is a consensus that even by the most optimistic estimates growth in coming years will not accelerate [except moderately; therefore, as a result] the possibility of reducing the extent of the informal sector . . . will also be less" (Tokman, 1987a, p. 298). In the middle of the 1980s, there was a brief recovery in some countries; in Uruguay, however, the 1986 recovery was accompanied by increased growth of the informal sector (Melgar, 1988).

Countries that Have Endeavored to Overcome Structural Obstacles to Extension

The foregoing analysis might give the false impression that social insurance coverage can be extended only parallel to development and that there is no way of overcoming the structural obstacles (such as salaried EAP) to the Bismarckian model. On the contrary, some studies (Rosenberg, 1980; Mesa-Lago, 1978; Malloy, 1979) show that the political will of governments has been crucial in a number of countries in the region in reforming the model and extending coverage beyond what was possible in accordance with the degree of development. The analysis of the decline discussed previously shows that the combination of two variables—the wage-earning EAP and the level of "political commitment"—best explains the degree of social insurance coverage in Latin America. "Political commitment" has been defined as the decisive role played by the government in extending coverage to a significant degree and, in some cases, achieving universal coverage; this is the case in Argentina, Brazil, Chile, Costa Rica, Cuba, and Uruguay. Tables 7.1 and 7.9 show that in Venezuela the percentage of wage-earners in the EAP and the formal urban sector is similar to that in the aforementioned countries, but the percentage of social insurance coverage is much lower. This situation is explained by the political decision in the former countries to accelerate the extension of coverage using nontraditional means of financing, as will be seen below.

In Costa Rica, social insurance covers the population without resources (the "poor") not eligible for contributory benefits, providing them with assisted health care and noncontributory assisted pensions, both financed by the state. The former system in Chile was financed by state subsidies and transfers from the covered sector. The new system has eliminated the solidarity aspect, but still has social assistance benefits (for health and pensions) financed by the state. The informal sector not covered can therefore at least receive these benefits in both countries, although the pensions are not very high. The same situation prevails in Uruguay, where there are social assistance pensions for all those who do not qualify under social insurance (Mesa-Lago, 1985a).

Regarding sickness and maternity, another model is the national health system as it functions in the non-Latin Caribbean, Cuba, and Nicaragua. In the majority of these countries, access to health services is free for persons with low incomes (which includes the majority of the informal sector), for certain age groups regardless of their income, and for some services. Proof of

Table 7.9 Percentage of Total Social Insurance Expenditure Over GDP Calculated on the Basis of Universal Coverage in Latin America, 1980

Country	Social Insurance Expenditure per GDP	Total Population Covered	Expenditure per GDP as a Percentage of Population Covered
Argentina	11.9	78.9	15.1
Bolivia	2.9	25.4	11.4
Brazil	5.2	96.3	5.4
Chile	11.0	67.3	16.3
Colombia	2.8	15.2	18.4
Costa Rica	7.5	81.5	9.2
Cuba	8.6	100.0[a]	8.6
Dominican Republic	0.7	5.9	11.9
Ecuador	3.7	9.4	39.9
El Salvador	1.3	6.2	21.0
Guatemala	1.6	14.2	11.3
Honduras	0.9	7.3	12.3
Mexico	2.9	53.4	5.4
Nicaragua	2.3	9.1	25.3
Panama	6.1	49.9	12.2
Paraguay	1.2	18.2	6.6
Peru	2.6	16.6	15.7
Uruguay	8.1	68.5	11.8
Venezuela	1.3	45.2	2.9

Source: Based on Mesa-Lago, Cruz-Saco, and Zamalloa (1988).
[a]Legal coverage; there are no statistics.

income is generally required for free access to benefits (except in Barbados and Cuba).

In the 1980s, some countries in the region introduced a system of payment of part of the costs by users of public health services, sometimes even including those with low incomes. When these payments do not involve large amounts, they do not have a negative effect on coverage (or rather they do not exclude the informal sector for reasons of cost) and they can limit unnecessary recourse to the services, but they do not contribute significantly to the financing of services. On the other hand, when the payments involve large amounts, they can constitute an important source of revenue and help to maintain and improve services (thereby benefiting the informal sector), but this leads to problems of exclusion and administration. To avoid exclusion, low-income groups should be exempt from payment; if not, such payments will have a regressive impact. It has been suggested that prevention and hygiene should be exempt from payment, whereas part of outpatient and hospital services, as well as medicines, should be subject to payment (Mesa-Lago, 1986d, 1987b).

In some Latin American countries, social insurance has extended primary health care to low-income rural areas: in Brazil, through the transfer of contributions from the urban sector, and in Mexico and Ecuador through state support, transfers from sectors covered (solidarity), and nominal support and/or community work by the peasants. Although these models do not at present cover the informal sector, they could do so in the future. Nevertheless, the current economic crisis has had a negative impact on these programs due to the decrease in state support or transfers under solidarity, thus leading to deficits in some cases, deterioration in services, and stagnation or regression of the extension process (COPLAMAR, 1983; McGreevey et al., 1984; Mesa-Lago, 1989).

The Cost and Feasibility of Extension

One common feature of some of the above-mentioned models of coverage applied or applicable to the informal sector is the existence of a duality of benefits: normal benefits for those insured, and another type of assistance, which is less costly or of lower quantity or quality or provides fewer services, for others. This situation, which is nevertheless discriminatory, has at least allowed those in need who previously received no care to receive some services at a much lower cost than that of normal social insurance benefits. In many countries in the region, social insurance is currently facing a crisis due to the imbalance between income and expenditure, which underlines its unsuitability as a vehicle for the extension of coverage.

Sickness-maternity programs for the social community have historically shown a deficit in Latin America; this has been true, for example, during thirty-seven of the forty-five years of operation of such a program in Mexico, eleven of the last twelve years in Peru, seven of the last eight years in Ecuador, and six of the last eight years in Uruguay. Even in countries with more solvent programs, the deficit can be considerable. For example, the deficit was US$44 million in Costa Rica during the period 1977–1981.

The causes of the deficit in income are threefold:

1. Contributions in some countries, even though they are high, are not sufficient to cover expenditure and the deficit has often been financed by transfers from the pension programs, thereby contributing to its capital depletion.
2. Evasion and arrears reach alarming proportions in some countries (65 percent in Peru, 42 percent in Brazil, 35 percent in Jamaica, US$135 million in Colombia), and with the increase in the informal sector and inflation this situation has deteriorated (interest and penalties for arrears are much lower than the rate of inflation so it is in the employer's interest to delay payment, deposit the money in a bank, and pay later, having made a profit).
3. The public debt has increased during the present decade (US$500 million in Ecuador in 1984), and the debt has been devalued as a result of inflation (it has been estimated that social insurance in Peru lost US$1,280 million in 1969–1988 due to this factor).

The reasons for the deficit in expenditure include (1) the predominance of costly curative medicine rather than preventive medicine; (2) the excessively generous benefits and conditions in some countries, at least for a privileged group (for example, travel and medical and hospital treatment abroad when treatment inside the country did not exist cost Peru US$8.7 million for 131 insured persons in 1982); (3) high administrative costs (in 1980, in fourteen out of twenty countries in the region, administrative costs as a percentage of total expenditures were 10–27 percent, compared to 2–3 percent in industrialized countries), mainly due to the surplus of staff and relatively high pay; (4) inefficiency in hospitals (low occupancy and long average periods of stay), partly due to bad planning and coordination among public health services; and (5) the increased costs of medicine and the tendency to overprescribe (ECLAC, 1986b; Mesa-Lago, 1989).

Social insurance pension programs are in a better financial situation than sickness-maternity programs due to the accumulation of reserves and their relatively recent introduction in some countries, but they are also facing an actuarial imbalance in the majority of countries and a liquidity crisis in the pioneering countries. As far as income is concerned, in addition to the causes described above, funds have been invested inefficiently—a situation that has been exacerbated by inflation over the past decade, resulting in a negative return in the majority of the countries. With regard to expenditure, the additional causes of the imbalance are (1) the early age of retirement in the pioneering countries, where there is the longest life expectancy (in Costa Rica, the age of early retirement dropped from 64 to 55/57 years in 1948–1984, whereas life expectancy rose to become one of the highest in the region); (2) long-service pensions, which allow people to retire after twenty to thirty years of service, no matter what age; (3) the retirement age for women is five years less than that for men, although they live on average three years longer; and (4) the generous indexing of pensions to cost of living (Feldman, Golbert, and Isuani, 1986; McGreevey, 1988; Diéguez and Giral-Bosca, 1988; Mesa-Lago, 1984, 1985a, 1987b, 1988a).

The state has come to the rescue of social insurance in a number of countries (Argentina, Chile, Colombia, and Uruguay) through transfers, subsidies, taxes, and the like, but this burden is becoming increasingly heavy, particularly in a context of prolonged economic crisis. In addition, in some countries, state support has been at the expense of resources for health care and other programs that protect the uninsured population. During the 1980s there was a substantial decrease in the public budget for health care in real terms in nearly all countries in the region (Musgrove, 1986).

The cost of extending coverage to the whole population under the present Bismarckian model of social insurance would not be economically feasible for many countries. Table 7.9 extrapolates the effect on GDP of total social insurance expenditure if all the population were covered. This is simply an exercise because it would mean a large increase in current expenditure. Three countries have universal coverage with a low percentage of GDP: Venezuela (2.9 percent), Mexico, and Brazil (each with 5.4 percent). In Venezuela and Mexico, the high level of income and GDP as a result of oil production reduces the relative cost of coverage; in addition, the rural extension programs in Brazil and Mexico have increased coverage at relatively low cost, which partly explains the low percentage calculated for these two countries. Cuba (8.6 percent) and Costa Rica (9.2 percent) have higher percentages and already cover almost the entire population. A group of countries that has almost universal coverage but high cost would see this cost rise significantly: Uruguay (11.8 percent), Argentina (15.1 percent) and Chile (16.3 percent). It should be noted, though, that these countries already have public health (or social insurance) programs for the poor with reasonable services at the regional level; therefore, the calculation exaggerates the cost (this remark also applies to Costa Rica). In some of the least developed countries in the region, the estimated cost of universal coverage is obviously too high: Ecuador (39.9 percent), Nicaragua (25.3 percent), El Salvador (21.0 percent), Colombia (18.4 percent), and Peru (15.7 percent).

A recent study carried out in Peru showed that the cost of covering the informal sector solely for sickness and maternity under the social insurance system would take up 88 percent of the present cost of covering the insured population. It should be noted that the sickness-maternity program in Peru is facing increasing deficits and that the income from contributions by the informal sector would be much lower than that from the population currently insured. The study also showed that if only the first level of services under social insurance were provided, the cost of incorporating the informal sector would fall to half the cost of full-scale services. If the Ministry of Health's health center model were followed, the cost would decrease to less than 1 percent of the current cost of social insurance coverage (Mesa-Lago, 1988b). Clearly, the services provided by the latter two programs are greatly inferior to those under the full-scale social insurance system. Nevertheless, the main point is that this group, currently without protection, would at least receive some services at a more feasible cost.

Conclusions of the Analysis of the Situation in Costa Rica, Jamaica, Mexico, and Peru

Although there are gaps in information and problems of whether statistics are comparable in this study, it can be stated that the largest informal sector is to be found in Peru, followed by Jamaica and Mexico (it is impossible to determine which of the two has the larger informal sector), and the smallest informal sector is in Costa Rica. Proportionately, the informal sector in Peru is three times that in Costa Rica. In principle, the feasibility of covering the informal sector by social security is greater the smaller the sector and vice versa because in the region the Bismarckian social insurance system elaborated for a formal wage-earning EAP prevails.

However, the countries studied—particularly Costa Rica and Jamaica rather than Mexico and Peru—have endeavored to adapt the Bismarckian model to the characteristics of their labor force so as to extend coverage to the informal sector through: (1) legal provisions prescribing the obligation to cover groups in this sector (i.e., Jamaica for all groups, and Costa Rica and Peru for domestic service workers) or giving the possibility of voluntary affiliation (i.e., Mexico for the self-employed and domestic workers, and Costa Rica and Peru for the self-employed); (2) universal coverage systems that do not discriminate among population groups (i.e. the national health systems in Jamaica) or discriminate between the insured and the poor but provide equal benefits (i.e., the sickness and maternity program in Costa Rica); and (3) social assistance systems that provide noncontributory services to the poor not eligible for contributory services (i.e., Costa Rica and Jamaica for pensions).

Statistics and other information on coverage show that both the national health system in Jamaica and the sickness-maternity program of the Costa Rican Social Insurance Fund (CCSS, Caja Costarricense de Seguro Social), which integrates and gives equal treatment to the poor, have managed to protect the informal sector. This achievement is particularly noteworthy in

Jamaica, where the informal sector is larger than that in Costa Rica, although the standard of service appears to be better in the latter. This study does not go into whether this achievement is due to the social security system or to the country's level of development. In any event, in both countries considerable state financing is needed—more so in Jamaica, where the system is directly financed by the state, than in Costa Rica, where the state reimburses (at least in theory) the social insurance for care given to the poor.

There is no significant difference in the statistical coverage of compulsory and voluntary legal pension systems for the self-employed: 2.4–5.3 percent are under a compulsory system in Jamaica, and the figures for voluntary systems are 4 percent in Peru (16 percent in Lima), 2.6 percent in Costa Rica, and around 1 percent in Mexico. A compulsory system could help to increase the coverage of pension programs for domestic workers, which is around the same as that for employees in Costa Rica and covers 31 percent in Lima as opposed to 0.1 percent in Mexico, where coverage for this category is voluntary. General coverage of the EAP in these countries does not appear to be a determining factor in these variations because it is similar in Mexico (43 percent) and Peru (39 percent). A lower rate of contribution by domestic workers compared to contributions by the self-employed (which have to include the employer's contribution) might explain the higher degree of coverage of domestic workers in Costa Rica and Peru (this will be discussed in greater detail below). Legal social insurance coverage for sickness and maternity is voluntary in the three countries that have such a system. Nevertheless, there are considerable differences in the statistical coverage of the self-employed: almost universal coverage in Costa Rica compared to 4 percent in Peru and 1 percent in Mexico. These differences probably result from a lower effective rate of contribution in Costa Rica, together with the greater efforts deployed by the social insurance administration to cover the self-employed and the assimilation (at the insistence of employers) of the self-employed and employees. To summarize, health coverage is much broader than pension coverage (and coverage for occupational hazards), and making a system compulsory does not in itself appear to increase the extent of coverage of the informal sector, particularly the self-employed.

Of the three informal job categories for which we have information on the cases studied, statistical coverage of the domestic service category approximates that of wage-earners in the formal sector (except in Mexico), whereas the self-employed have very much lower coverage (except in Costa Rica and Jamaica for health care), and unpaid family members have no coverage (except in Jamaica). There is no information on the statistical coverage of employees and employers in the informal sector. Not enough data are available to permit a comparison among the four countries regarding the proportions of these five groups in the informal labor force; however, the few figures available show that employees and the self-employed combined represent 67–76 percent of the total. In Mexico in 1976, employees represent

50 percent, the self-employed 26 percent, domestic workers 14 percent, and family workers 10 percent of the overall informal sector; in Lima in 1983, the self-employed represent 49 percent, employees 18 percent, domestic workers 16 percent, and family workers 8 percent. The lack of information on employees prevents an assessment of their coverage. In Costa Rica and Jamaica, 95–98 percent of the self-employed are not covered for contributory pensions (but are eligible for much lower social assistance pensions and only when the budget is sufficient), whereas 96–99 percent of the self-employed in Mexico and Peru have no coverage whatsoever for health and pensions and only very rarely are they covered for occupational hazards. In Peru and Mexico, between 69 percent and almost 100 percent of domestic workers have no coverage for health, pensions, or occupational hazards.

Analysis of the reasons for the low coverage of the informal sector shows that the high cost of contributions together with low incomes is a determinant in the four countries, although there are significant variations among them. The full rate of contribution to be paid by the self-employed for health and pensions compared to that paid by employees amounts to 3.6 times as much in Mexico, 3 times as much in Peru, 2 times as much in Jamaica (pensions only), and 1.6 times as much in Costa Rica. Furthermore, the highest rates of contribution by the self-employed are to be found in Peru (18 percent) and Mexico (13.6 percent). This partly explains the corresponding degree of coverage in the four countries.

The study revealed that the income of the self-employed was lower than that of the employed, so the burden of contributions is not only heavier in terms of percentages but also in terms of income. However, contributions by employees are usually based on a higher tax level than that of the self-employed because they take into account total remuneration, whereas the level for the self-employed is fixed on a minimum: 75 percent of the minimum agricultural wage in Costa Rica, a minimum guaranteed wage in Peru, and 1.6 times the minimum salary in the D.F. in Mexico. Unfortunately, information is available only in Mexico on the current average contribution by employees and the self-employed; therefore, it is not possible to pursue the analysis further. It was noted that the differences in contributions among programs have a noticeable effect on the respective degrees of coverage. For example, in Mexico and Peru, the ratio between the rate of contribution by the self-employed and the employed is equal for the pensions and sickness-maternity programs, although in Costa Rica the self-employed contribute 2.9 times as much for pensions and 1.1 times as much for sickness-maternity, which probably explains the greater affiliation and coverage for health in Costa Rica. Domestic workers have a lower income than the self-employed, but their contributions are also much lower. The rate of contribution for a domestic worker is equal to that of an employee, and is therefore much lower than that for a self-employed worker. Furthermore, in Peru, the salary base used is one-third of the minimum guaranteed wage, so the domestic worker pays an effective contribution of 33 percent or less of the effective contribution of an employee and 40 percent of that of a self-employed worker. This helps to explain why domestic workers have better coverage than the self-employed in all the countries studied except Mexico. In the latter, a domestic worker's voluntary affiliation depends on the employer, who has to pay 13.54 percent, so there are very few instances of domestic workers being affiliated voluntarily.

The second reason for the low coverage of the informal sector encountered in the four countries is the difficulty of detecting, registering, and monitoring the payment of contributions by informal microenterprises, the self-employed, and domestic workers. The bigger the size of the informal sector, the more complex and costly is the process; in the case of microenterprises in Peru, it was noted that the fewer the number of employees in an enterprise, the more difficult and costly was its control. In some countries, such as Jamaica, the body responsible for insurance is partly to blame for the problem due to the excessive "paperwork" required to register an enterprise.

In all the countries studied, the inspection units do not have the capacity to effect satisfactory controls. The result is very high levels of evasion and arrears; for example, in Peru, 35–40 percent of the contributions and 65 percent of the enterprises are in arrears or evading payment, and 36 percent of employees also evade payment; in Jamaica, 44 percent of the enterprises registered are in arrears. With regard to the self-employed, the compulsory regime in Jamaica has not solved the problem, and it is estimated that 330,000 workers in this sector are evading payment; therefore, identifying and controlling them would be even more difficult and costly than doing the same for microenterprises. Incentives such as a lower rate of contribution exacerbate the problem; for example, in Costa Rica, it is in an employer's interest to affiliate his employees as self-employed because he would save half the employer's contribution. Lastly, there is the problem of fraud, due to the difficulty of proving income in addition to political problems; in Costa Rica and Jamaica, there are a number of informal workers who receive social assistance pensions for the needy, although in fact they are not poor, thereby reducing the number of self-employed who should be affiliated in the contributory regime.

Not only is affiliation more costly for workers in the informal sector and more difficult for the administration to control, but also the services are poor, and thus the incentive to affiliate is even less. Proof of this was seen in Jamaica, where in 1986 the average pension was equivalent to one-fifth of the national per capita income, yet despite an increase in pensions in 1987, affiliation continued to be low. The formalities to be completed in order to obtain a meager pension are so complex and lengthy that only half of those who have the right bother to complete them. In Peru, groups of informal workers declared that they were not interested in becoming affiliated with social insurance because of the very low amount of the pensions, the poor quality of the health services, the time lost in waiting, and the long distances to services.

Another reason for low coverage is the weak or ineffective mobilization of the informal sector. In Costa Rica, Mexico, and Peru, the better organized, more powerful occupational pressure groups belong to the formal sector; they were the first to be affiliated with social security, have a higher percentage of coverage and enjoy greater benefits at relatively lower cost. Groups in the informal sector were the last to be affiliated, have much lower coverage (except in the case of health in Costa Rica), and receive fewer benefits at relatively higher cost (at least as far as the self-employed are concerned). In Jamaica, legal coverage of the informal sector began at the same time as that of the formal sector, but the real coverage for pensions in the informal group is much lower and, as in the other countries, the cost for the self-employed is relatively higher. Part of the problem is that persons employed in the informal sector are to a large extent clandestine workers to whom the labor law does not apply, so their ability to organize themselves and become mobilized to demand effective affiliation with the social security system is hampered. In the case of the self-employed, the analysis of Jamaica, but above all that of Peru, shows that the large group of street vendors is mobilized, but that its primary objectives are to guarantee the security of their stalls or improvement of the markets in which they function. The fragmentation among the numerous associations, the lack of any long-term plan with broader objectives, and the absence of consensus and sustained action have prevented the effective incorporation of street vendors into the social security system.

In terms of coverage of the informal sector and the quality of social security benefits available to this sector, Costa Rica clearly stands out as the most advanced of the four countries studied, followed by Jamaica, Mexico, and Peru, in that order. It should be noted that these four countries are relatively advanced for the region and that only a small group of countries (those of the Southern Cone, Brazil, Panama, and some in the non-Latin Caribbean) have more advanced or equivalent social security systems. The feasibility of social security effectively being extended to cover the informal sector in the four countries follows the same pattern, partly because Costa Rica and Jamaica have already made considerable progress, but also due to the relative financial solidity of their current programs.

The Costa Rican CCSS has the most solid system: its sickness-maternity program has a surplus and it is estimated that the pension program will achieve a balance in a few years (according to different calculations, some time between the early to mid-1990s). Nevertheless, the latter program requires a complicated in-depth reform in order to increase the balance before endeavoring to incorporate the informal sector: increases in contributions (which are already among the highest in the region), changes in the age of retirement and investment profitability, as well as fulfillment of official financial obligations and reduction of expenditure. A project to extend the sickness-maternity program to the self-employed makes coverage obligatory, fixes a uniform scale of contributions in relation to income subject to annual review, generalizes contributions by associations of the self-employed, and reserves the small state contribution for those who are not affiliated. These are positive measures and the sector to be incorporated is very small, but the greatest need is to extend the pension program. There is not yet any project on this, but the possibility of establishing a special fund for the self-employed is being discussed, financed by contributions lower than the present ones and benefits situated halfway between current contributory and social assistance pensions. Alternatives to social security in Costa Rica are very limited, partly due to its large-scale expansion. Social security is not one of the objectives of nongovernmental organizations (NGOs), and associations of informal workers and the insurance monopoly of the National Institute of Insurance (INS, Instituto Nacional de Seguros) and the CCSS have prevented the development of the private sector in this field. For the above reasons, social security appears to be the most effective channel for extending coverage in Costa Rica, subject to the reform of the pension program and a project to incorporate the self-employed that would reduce contributions and benefits.

Following a long period of financial stability, in 1987, the increase in National Insurance Scheme (NIS) benefits in Jamaica without a corresponding increase in contributions led to an imbalance, and it is estimated that the reserve fund will be exhausted in 1994. However, the NIS enjoys a better financial situation than the majority of countries in the region because it is not responsible for the health program, whose administrative costs are low, and the pension program was created only recently. A moderate increase in contributions (the lowest of the four countries), together with more efficient investment of the fund, could restore the balance. Once this problem has been resolved, the most serious obstacles to effective incorporation of the self-employed would be administrative problems. A system of commissions that would register the self-employed and receive contributions, once it has been tried out in practice, together with completion of computerization, a publicity campaign, and simplification of the application formalities for pensions, could increase coverage in the contributory regime. Jamaica's national health system covers the informal sector, but has suffered a deterioration over the decade due to a substantial cut in its budget. In 1988, the government decided that the quality of health services could be improved by generalizing charges for its use; promoting private prepaid programs, coordinating services within the Ministry of Health, the NIS, and social welfare; and eliminating abuse. As in Costa Rica, the development of social security in Jamaica has resulted in few alternatives of an informal nature (partner burial societies), and wherever NGOs are working in this sector they are not dealing with social security. Subject to the reforms described above, it appears possible to extend coverage to the informal sector in Jamaica.

The Mexican Social Insurance Institute (IMSS, Instituto Mexicano de Seguro Social), the social insurance institution legally responsible for extending social insurance coverage to the informal sector in Mexico, has suffered a persistent deficit in its sickness-maternity program and even though the pensions program has a surplus, it is showing a downward trend in income that will probably increase toward the end of the decade. In order to remedy this situation, the following measures should be taken: raise the rate of contribution for sickness-maternity so that the program becomes self-financing (thereby avoiding the need to transfer sums from the pension fund); increase rates of contribution for pensions (unchanged since the creation of the fund and relatively low at the regional level); improve investment profitability; and drastically reduce administrative costs. Due to the economic crisis, the high rate of inflation, and political pressure, such reform will not be easy to implement.

Because of these problems and the fact that 99 percent of those in the informal sector are not covered, it is doubtful whether the IMSS would be the effective instrument for achieving universal coverage of the informal sector. Each of the IMSS projects envisages extending coverage to the self-employed and domestic workers, but not for pensions, except as a result of the payment of large amounts for disability and widows' pensions (nothing for old age); coverage would continue to be voluntary for the self-employed, but they would pay only one-third of the current contribution (on a salary basis amounting to two-thirds of the current one), and the state would pay half the cost of the program; coverage of domestic workers would be made compulsory and the contributions would be divided equally between the insured and the employer (reducing the latter's contribution to half).

These projects deal with some of the problems mentioned above and increase the viability of extension by lowering contributions by the self-employed, making coverage compulsory for domestic workers, and providing a "package" of reduced but financially feasible benefits. Even though Mexico has more resources than Costa Rica and Jamaica and, through IMSS-COPLAMAR (General Coordination of the National Plan for Depressed Areas and Marginal Groups), has achieved significant extension of primary health care in the field, the accelerated growth of the urban sector and the recent transfer of IMSS-COPLAMAR users to the Secretary of Health (SS, Secretaría de Salud) reinforce the doubts expressed above. Incorporation of the informal sector into the IMSS sickness-maternity program would increase current coverage by 20 percent; because, as the authorities warn, the IMSS medical and hospital services are already saturated, and any extension will mean a decrease in other public and private services. Inasmuch as the public health sector has deteriorated significantly during the 1980s, participation by the private sector will become important, combined with effective integration of health services in the public sector and greater emphasis on primary health care.

Examples of protection using alternative methods are few in Mexico (although a more detailed study on this aspect is called for), but there are arrangements between groups in the informal sector and private clinics subject to the prepayment of a monthly contribution. To summarize, despite the extension of social security coverage in Mexico (in particular, to the rural sector), there are serious doubts as to whether the IMSS is the appropriate instrument for extending coverage to the informal sector as a whole. On the other hand, there do not appear to be any suitable alternative methods. Only successful conclusion of an in-depth reform of the IMSS, together with a well-thought-out integration program, could provide the bases for commencing progressive extension.

The financial situation of the Peruvian Social Security Institute (IPSS, Instituto Peruano de Seguridad Social) is the most unsuitable for extension. The sickness-maternity program has a permanent deficit covered by transfers from the pension program, which has thus suffered gradual capital depletion. The latter has generally had a surplus, but this is decreasing in comparison to income and, in 1988, the two programs faced a serious crisis. The 1988 emergency plan tried to restore the balance by increasing contributions to both programs, tightening control of evasion and arrears, improving investment profitability, complying with the state's obligations, and reducing staff costs. However, the serious economic crisis in 1988, a rate of inflation of around 2,000 percent, and the high rate of contribution (higher than Mexico's) jeopardized the success of this plan. The law on the extension of coverage to the informal sector, enacted at the end of 1987, was limited to the sickness-maternity program. The law's regulations—although not approved by the end of 1988—provide for a lower contribution rate by the self-employed, from 9 percent down to 4 percent (if they are members of an association, they would pay only 1.5 percent and the remaining 2.5 percent would be paid by the association), and the state would contribute to extension by paying 1 percent of total wages. Even though some aspects of the regulations are positive, incorporation of those in the informal sector and their dependent families would extend the current IPSS coverage by 150 percent although its medical and hospital infrastructure is already notoriously inadequate. Furthermore, the state did not contribute the 1 percent it should have paid in 1988, and extension to the informal sector would cost 88 percent of the current cost of those covered, which could obviously not be met by the sector incorporated. Contributions and incomes are lower for the informal than the formal sector, whose contributions already are insufficient to cover the costs of the program. Unlike the other countries described above, Peru has numerous informal protection mechanisms, such as *juntas* and collects; there are also NGO programs to provide family insurance at low cost, and the possibility of promoting cooperatives of physicians with credit and training is being explored. There is a consensus that the current social security model in Peru is not a viable channel for incorporating the informal sector and that only economic progress in this sector will allow it to be protected in the future, through either the market or the state or a combination of the two. In the meantime, the alternative methods appear to offer greater possibilities for protection and they should receive support from NGOs and international bodies.

General Policy Recommendations

The following policy recommendations are based on the analysis of the four cases as well as general reports by experts in the fields of social security and the informal sector (Mesa-Lago, 1985a, 1989; Tokman, 1987b). The problem should be approached through a long-term plan that brings together all the different aspects and promotes participation and discussion among the various sectors concerned, especially the informal sector, as well as social insurance, the Ministry of Health, NGOs, international agencies, the private sector and so on. Temporary or short-term programs promoted by governments, NGOs, or international agencies, which cannot be sustained in the long term nor ultimately be self-financed by the informal sector, should be avoided because they lead to frustration and cause relative deterioration.

The case studies highlight the differences that exist among countries (the present state of coverage, viability of social security as a model for extension, or alternatives) and the impossibility of providing a general recipe for making coverage comprehensive. This study also shows the enormous gaps in information on crucial aspects such as the size of the informal sector and the job categories it contains and its degree of coverage, among others. It is indispensable to identify and quantify these groups better and to define their characteristics; for example, age is vital for a pension program, the number of dependent family members for a sickness-maternity program, and the income of those in the informal sector in both cases. Even though some household and employment surveys have included questions on social security, almost none have focused on the informal sector. If they do contain information on this sector that could be cross-referenced with questions on social security, such cross-referencing has not been done. Statistics by social security institutions should include a breakdown of those insured by job category (self-employed, domestic workers, and so on) so as to provide information on income, contributions, and benefits received by these groups. The little information available on informal protection against social risks and on activities of this nature by NGOs also needs to be amplified.

Coverage of the informal sector cannot be considered in isolation but only in an integrated fashion. In the long term, the most effective ways of resolving the lack of protection are the creation of productive employment, legalization of informality, support for the sector in the form of credit and training, elimination of obstacles hindering the sector's development, and like measures. Such steps will, in the end, increase the income of those in the informal sector, thus allowing them to self-finance their coverage, whether through social security or other means. It is therefore necessary to combine social security policies with policies on credit, employment, education, and training. It is not advisable, however, to postpone the solution indefinitely; during the transitional period, reforms will have to be introduced to alleviate the situation of the informal sector.

Any plan to extend coverage, even in countries with greater resources and development of security, implies definition of priorities among programs, the risks to be covered, and the groups to be incorporated. Health care should receive priority because it is the most urgent need. It could be based on one of several models—for example, the national health system of Jamaica or the integrated social insurance system for sickness and maternity in Costa Rica. These programs would provide medical and hospital treatment for sickness and accidents, whether in general or work-related. A second priority would be a program of cash benefits for old age, disability, and death. This could be a contributory pension program combined with a social assistance pension program (as in Costa Rica and Jamaica); however, few countries have the necessary resources for such a program and they would have to implement much more modest (and less costly) programs based on high amounts when such risks occur. With regard to the groups to be covered, that of domestic workers is the easiest due to its smaller size and the fact that it involves an employer contribution, which is not the case for the self-employed. The most difficult group to incorporate is that of unpaid family members, not only because they do not have an income but also because it is extremely difficult to extract a contribution from the employer–head of family.

In the majority of countries, coverage of the informal sector would be impossible—at least in the short and medium terms—at the same level of benefits, quality of service, and technology currently available to the formal sector (in many countries, a minority of the labor force) under social insurance because the cost in terms of percentage of the GDP would be intolerable. The ideal system would be for social security to provide universal basic benefits (based on solidarity among income groups) and promote a complementary system of benefits (with a strict correlation between contributions and benefits), whether through social security, the private sector, or a combination of the two. The non-covered population without incomes would be eligible for social assistance benefits.

Under this model, the population as a whole would be protected and those who had resources would receive better benefits, although these would be financed through their own funds and not through public subsidies, as now occurs. When such an ideal model is not politically acceptable, there could be a dual system of protection, keeping the level of care already covered in the formal sector and providing coverage with a "package" of reduced benefits for the informal sector. This is the alternative chosen by those countries whose programs to extend health care to the rural sector emphasize primary health care (i.e., IMSS-COPLAMAR).

It is vital to undertake a study of each country (as has been done in this study) in order to determine the feasibility of extending coverage under social security or alternative means. If it is decided that the former solution is feasible (as in Costa Rica and Jamaica), it is indispensable first of all to introduce the necessary reforms to strengthen the financial situation of the general regime and, second, to estimate the cost of the various "packages" of benefits with corresponding contributions for each group. This calculation has been done in very few countries; one of these, as has been seen, is Peru. When fixing the amount of contributions by the self-employed, it is necessary to abandon the notion that these could compensate for the absence of any employer's contribution because this would result in a very high sum that is not feasible. It is preferable to fix an attainable contribution and to adapt the benefits to this. On the other hand, if the benefits are of very low quality or quantity, this will be a disincentive to affiliation; therefore, the informal sector must be consulted so that it understands what the viable alternatives are and can make its views known.

In an ideal model of basic benefits and social solidarity, benefits for the informal sector without resources or with very low incomes could be improved by transfers from the formal sector and/or groups with higher incomes. In the alternative model of dual systems, any state support should be used to improve the benefits for the informal sector with lower incomes.

Wherever those in the informal sector are grouped together in associations and have a satisfactory level of resources and organization, an effort could be made to obtain contributions from the association. However, it must be noted that such support usually comes directly from members so it will not be substantial and will be for redistribution. Last, forms of financing other than wage-based contributions should be studied because they could be more effective (for example, taxes on sales, income, capital, and so forth), although their adverse effects should always be assessed.

If it is decided that social security is not a feasible instrument for extension, and alternative means are preferred (as is the case for Peru), these other means need to be promoted and supported. In this connection, it is recommended that a meeting be held at the national level of organizations of informal workers, NGOs, and international bodies cooperating in this sector, together with representatives of private insurance companies, to discuss the mechanisms for extension. The topics to be discussed should include credit and training to promote mutual insurance associations between informal workers and cooperatives of physicians or contracts between an association of informal workers and a clinic, with fees accessible to the sector; encouragement of private insurance companies to offer collective insurance policies with a premium financed by members of associations of informal workers; integration of the medical and hospital services financed by foreign and national donors with public services, on the basis of a modest fee for use; and, through the use of advertising and standardization, promotion of *juntas*, partners, and other types of permanent or temporary collectives for the purpose of confronting social risks.

Legal provisions on extension of coverage should take into account the fact that the compulsory nature of coverage may have a positive result in groups such as domestic workers (provided that contributions are reasonable), but that it has no effect on other informal groups such as the self-employed. For the latter, fixing a reasonable rate of contribution and assuring an adequate level of benefits are more important incentives to affiliation, even when it is voluntary. Although in principle it is advisable to ensure greater efficiency of the mechanisms to detect, register, and control payment by those who legally should be insured (including small-scale employers and their employees, the self-employed, domestic workers with obligatory coverage, and so on), a cost-benefit exercise should be undertaken to see whether such control is viable and profitable. If it is not, it is preferable to promote voluntary affiliation using the incentives mentioned.

Institutions that cooperate in the informal sector should involve the various groups making up the sector to a greater extent and should reach agreement on long-term plans that include social security objectives, supported by sustained action on the part of leaders and members for the implementation of these objectives. Promoting awareness among these associations is important for effective mobilization. One concrete example of such action that could be followed is the effective use of sums collected by the municipal tax service (FOMA) in Peru to provide health services for street vendors.

Both for reasons of equity and for economic reasons, it is necessary to improve the system for verifying income declarations in those countries that have assisted health programs and/or pensions for the poor in order to eliminate abuse and redirect the resources to reach the truly needy informal population and improve the level of social assistance benefits.

In countries that have social security systems that provide compulsory or voluntary coverage for informal workers, the authorities should make an effort to reach these groups and make them aware of the advantages of affiliation, using explanatory leaflets and publicity campaigns. It is important to change the negative attitude in some administrations regarding these groups (e.g., with respect to street vendors). Lastly, the formalities for applying for benefits must be simplified, particularly when they concern low amounts.

Notes

1. A study by PREALC shows five categories (excluding self-employed workers with thirteen or more years of education), and another study (PREALC, 1981a) shows domestic service as a separate category in the formal and informal

sectors; Tokman (1987b) excludes unpaid family workers, but this is because he is making a comparison of income and the others are not; Haan (1985) excludes domestic service; and Aguirre and Méndez (1988) justify the inclusion of domestic service on the basis that workers in this sector do not receive the minimum urban wage, are in the lower income strata, and have no control over their working conditions. Other authors mention specific activities that are common in the informal sector, for example, street vendors, transporters, and small workshops, which can be classified in one or other of the five categories mentioned (Matos, 1986).

8

The Taxi Market in Chile: Regulation and Liberalization Policies, 1978–1987

Mariana Schkolnik

The main objective of this chapter is to analyze the effect on the taxi market of the changes implemented over the past decade in policies regulating the public transport sector. The study focuses on both the regular and the collective taxi services. Regarding the transformations that have occurred in the taxi market, the aim is basically to identify the changes in the operational methods of this market with regard to the manner of fixing fares, routes, and the entry and withdrawal of operators and vehicles. From the foregoing, it will be possible to analyze the effects these changes have had on the incomes and profits of drivers and owners, working conditions, the quality of service, and maintenance of the vehicles. Analysis of existing regulations in this market should include general aspects that limit or liberalize fares and entry and withdrawal of vehicles, as well as rules governing aspects such as the driver's ability and the quality of service (color of the vehicle, age, technical maintenance, and like factors).

The generally accepted belief is that when there are controls on entry, fares tend to increase above the level of equilibrium and a monopolistic position is adopted. In the case of the regular taxi service, it is clear that the policy on liberalization of entry implemented in 1978 was justified because it did not lead to excessive increases in fares over costs (Jeftanovic, 1987).

This assumption leads to the first question concerning how fares and costs have evolved since 1978. In 1981, a decree was adopted in Chile granting partial freedom to fix taxi fares. This system, which is still in force, was basically aimed at making the sector more competitive and inciting it to lower fares to benefit users. Nevertheless, as will be seen, there is in fact a single rate of fares.

Our conclusion in this respect is that even when there was free entry of new taxis, and fares—or rather the initial hiring charge—were no longer fixed by the authorities, which determined a range of rates, that in practice the trade union fixed the rate. This was due to two fundamental reasons: first, as will be seen below, there was no interest in competing by lowering fares, and second, taxi drivers perceived that demand was very elastic.

If, as pointed out by Jeftanovic (1987), it can be assumed that taxi fares have risen slightly over costs and that the number of taxis has increased, it is possible that the earnings of taxi drivers have decreased, together with the quality of service. Finally, an analysis will be made of the collective taxi market, where since 1984 there have been legal barriers to the entry of new vehicles and the establishment of new routes, although fares can be freely fixed. According to Jeftanovic's reasoning, this should have resulted in a considerable increase in fares owing to a monopoly. If this was not the case, the question is: What criteria govern the fares of collective taxis?

In addition to evaluating the impact of the changes in policies directly aimed at regulating public transport, it will also be necessary to assess the effect of some particularly relevant economic policy landmarks. One important event that must be taken into account is the international oil crisis, which led to a great increase in the cost of gasoline, the most important input in this sector. This undoubtedly had a far-reaching impact on the situation in the sector, which started to become more clear from then on. However, it will be constitute only an element of this study, which seeks to define the market's mode of functioning since 1978, the year in which liberalization commenced.

The "shock" policy implemented in 1974–75 subsequently led to a generalized fall in purchasing power at the national level in Chile. On the one hand, there was a reduction in the demand for taxis, but at the same time the increase in unemployment also had an effect on the sector. To this must be added the policy of cutting down employment in the public sector and the increase in facilities granted to those dismissed to become taxi operators.

The liberalization policy and the entry of taxis in 1978 therefore took place in a context of a recessionary market and fares fixed by the authorities. This accentuated competition to win passengers at a time when it may be assumed that demand had fallen and supply had increased.

Another key event in the sector was the rise in the value of the dollar in June 1982. This occurred just after a large number of taxi operators had contracted debts in dollars to pay for new vehicles, following a period of opening up of trade and issuing of special permits to import taxis. The revaluation of the dollar and its continued upward trend meant an increase not only in the debts in dollar terms but also in the cost of spare parts, which represent a large portion of expenditure. For the debtors, interest rates have also played an important role in recent years. Finally, the 1982 recession meant new restrictions on the demand for taxis, together with a considerable increase in open unemployment.

The study compares the importance of regulatory mechanisms in relation to general economic policy measures in determining the principal variables of the taxi market. Ultimately, the study considers that the determining factor in the fixing of rates is not the "free play" of supply and demand, even when there is freedom to fix fares and free access and withdrawal (as is the case for taxis), but that other more central variables are involved. These can be constituents of costs (for example, fuel), on the basis of whose price fares fluctuate, or the rate for another form of transport considered by taxi operators to be an alternative.

In addition to this type of variable, which enters into play in determining fares, given the characteristics of the taxi market itself, it is not possible for fares actually to be fixed at the halfway point between supply and demand because there is no such halfway point (see the next section of this chapter). When they are "free" to be set, taxi fares soon become harmonized because, as occurs in Chile, it is obviously not easy for a consumer to distinguish between an expensive taxi and a cheap one, and he will take the first taxi he sees.

The idea that this is monopolistic behavior resulting from governmental regulation is a question that no longer applies since the liberalization of entry in 1978 and of fares in 1981. This study endeavors to verify whether the current harmonization of fares in the taxi market is purely the result of trade union activity, which means monopolistic behavior, or is the product of the intrinsic nature of the market, which means that regulation is necessary, and whether taxi drivers benefit from this or not.

It remains to be determined whether, within this context, the sector earns large profits, whether minibuses and taxibuses are effective alternatives and whether there is "free play" of supply and demand.

The Taxi Market

Brief Summary of the Theories Concerning the Functioning of a Taxi Market

With regard to the functioning of the taxi market, there are basically two types of theoretical models proposed in the relevant texts. The first is the one put forward by Chanock Shreiber, originally in 1975 and then reformulated in 1977 and 1981, which proposed a model of equilibrium for an "unregulated market." Coffman (1977) then proposed a totally divergent model in response to the first one.

Both models are based on similar assumptions:

- The mode of operation for taxi drivers is to search for customers (as opposed to those who wait at a taxi stand).
- The cost of driving an empty taxi is the same as driving with passengers. Therefore, operating costs are related to the length of time the taxi functions.

- All taxis have the same cost structures and levels.
- Demand is constant in terms of time (homogeneous period).
- All taxis operate individually, competing with each other.

To provide an analysis of the market in taxi services, Shreiber (1981) uses an individual isoprofit curve (see Figure 8.1). This curve represents all possible combinations of price and number of effective trips (with passengers) by a taxi driver, which allows the driver to earn a balanced income. In other words, an income that allows him payment of all costs and includes the driver's wage. This curve does not show any profit for owners.

The point x_1 represents the maximum number of effective trips it is possible to make and assumes a rate of use of the taxi of 100 percent. With this number of trips and a p_1 fare, the operator would cover costs. With x_1 trips and fares lower than p_1, the operator would not cover his costs and would leave the market.

When the number of taxis functioning is very high, the rate of use and the number of trips with passengers or effective trips decreases, going down, for example, to x_2 In this case, it is not to the taxi operator's advantage to work for a fare less than p_2.

This shows that the lower the number of effective trips, the higher the price in order to be able to cover costs. The isoprofit curve shows the

Figure 8.1 Shreiber's (1981) Individual Isoprofit Curve

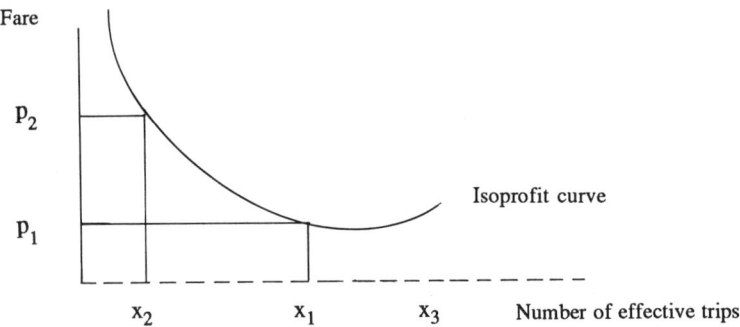

possible points of equilibrium in taxi operations when entry and withdrawal are free. When the fare, given a specific number of effective trips, is above the one shown by the curve, this means that additional profits are being earned. This will encourage new taxi operators to enter the market, thereby lowering the rate of use of taxis already operating, until the equilibrium shown by the curve is reached. The same occurs in the other sense. To put it in another way, entry into and withdrawal from the market will be the adjustment variable in comparison to a specific fare.

In 1981, Shreiber added to the analysis a supply curve, which represents all taxi operators (see Figure 8.2). This curve shows, for each fare level, the total supply of trips offered. However, its construction differs totally from traditional curves because it takes into account the demand curve. It is necessary to know the ratio of passengers to supply of trips in order to determine how many trips each taxi driver would have to make to in order to cover his costs.

In this curve, Shreiber endeavors to clarify one of what he considers to be the most relevant characteristics of the taxi market: the problem of the lack of synchronization between supply and demand. In other words, when there are suppliers seeking demanders and demanders seeking suppliers, they do not come together because of geographical variables. In this particular case, for demand to be met, supply must exceed the quantity demanded by a

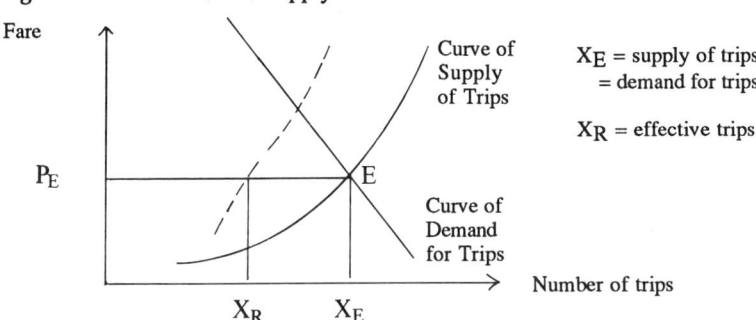

Figure 8.2 Shreiber's (1981) Supply Curve

X_E = supply of trips = demand for trips

X_R = effective trips

certain percentage, and vice versa, for the supply of taxis to be fully utilized there must be a higher percentage of demanders than suppliers. This percentage depends on the extent of the lack of synchronization.

The intersection between supply and demand does not constitute a point of balance, and even if in E the quantity demanded is equal to the quantity offered, the quantity of taxis effectively taken will be lower than the quantity demanded so that, within any time lapse, there will always be unsatisfied demand.

There is another aspect to this analysis, the concept of "waiting time," The rationale is the following: if the number of taxis increases, the rate of use declines and prices rise to make it possible to cover costs, while at the same time the waiting time for passengers decreases. This correlation is correct only if the number of taxis is so large that the waiting time is close to zero.

When waiting time is around zero, taxis compete by lowering prices. Nevertheless, fares will not descend below the level that allows costs to be covered. According to Shreiber, between the two extremes (floor and natural ceiling of prices), taxi operators face a demand curve that is highly inflexible.

Shreiber concludes that there is a natural trend for prices to stiffen when the supply of taxis increases and waiting time diminishes. This is due to the lack of competition, which encourages the lowering of prices, and the presence of forces that exert pressure for increases. This is because no taxi operator has any incentive to reduce fares individually because this will not increase the use of his taxi but it will lower his income.

Only operators who raise prices will increase earnings. There is therefore a natural tendency to increase fares, particularly if waiting time is long.

The rise in fares, which generates an increase in earnings, will lead to the entry of new taxis into the market and a reduction in waiting time for users and this trend will continue until a saturation point is reached, or what Shreiber calls "zero waiting time."

In fact, free competition in this market will not lead to a "satisfactory" price but a continued trend toward increases. There is, therefore, a need to regulate both fares and the number of taxis in operation.

The latter conclusion is strengthened if one takes into account Shreiber's view that the natural trend to increase the number of taxis gives rise to external negative factors such as traffic congestion and air and noise pollution, which imply a net social loss.

For Shreiber, the intrinsic characteristics of the taxi market that determine the need for regulation are succinctly the following:

- The trend toward increased prices means that the balance leads to a price-availability combination that is not the optimal solution from the social point of view.
- The low number of vehicles gives rise to negative external factors.

- Both supply and demand in this market fluctuate considerably according to economic cycles.
- The absence of any barriers to entry means that this job is the natural potential occupation of the unemployed, which creates instability and lack of professionalism.

If we accept the foregoing conclusions, other elements that can facilitate the subsequent analysis of the mode of operation of the taxi market are the following:

- It is a market that functions with a permanent lack of synchronization; in other words, a simultaneous situation of unsatisfied supply and demand.
- There are unsolvable problems of information and lack of transparency.

Both problems are particularly serious when taxis search for customers.

Assuming that taxis compete with each other by applying different fares, a user cannot benefit from the information on prices because he will most likely not use the same taxis. Unlike the market for goods, in this case there is no special place for carrying out the transaction. Even when there is publicity on different fares, it is not possible to have the information on a particular place in which a taxi is to be found at a specific moment.

The policy conclusion that results from the problem of the lack of synchronization is that in areas where there is a large demand for taxis, it would be more useful to have taxis waiting at stands rather than cruising for customers (Williams, 1980).

Other authors, unlike Shreiber, use perfect competition models to explain the functioning of the taxi market. Criticism against Shreiber consists of emphasizing that, even though the market does not operate perfectly, regulation could lead to even more inappropriate allocation of resources.

Coffman (1977) considers that it is possible to give better information using advertising in newspapers, magazines, television, and other media, if taxis decided to lower fares. He adds that highly visible announcements could be made on the vehicle itself showing the rate of fares. According to Coffman, in this way it is possible to halt the upward trend in fares, particularly if there is a relatively large number of taxis.

Another argument put forward is that a consumer will not necessarily always prefer a shorter waiting time, as Shreiber assumes, and will sometimes prefer to increase waiting time to pay a lower fare.

With regard to negative external factors, the authors who are in favor of deregulation (Coffman, 1977; Williams, 1980) state that it is not necessary to eliminate market mechanisms, but only that the external factors can be covered directly or indirectly through licenses, permits, tolls, and so forth.

Characteristics of the Taxi Market in Chile

The taxi market in Chile is composed of several different elements: regular taxis, tourist taxis, radiotaxis, and collective taxis.

The collective taxi component has existed since 1960 and was originally a service provided by taxi operators who functioned both as regular and collective taxis. According to former trade union leaders, this activity greatly decreased in 1972 and 1973 as a result of the increased profitability of the regular taxi service. The collective taxi service enjoyed a strong revival in 1978, first of all with 16 regular routes, and in 1986 it had 157 routes.

In 1970, the total number of taxis in the metropolitan region was 16,867, gradually decreasing to 9,961 in 1976 (see Table 8.1). Following liberalization of access to the taxi market, there was a large increase: in 1978, there were 16,021 taxis; and in 1982, there were 29,788. After the 1982 economic crisis, the number of taxis decreased and in 1986 it amounted to 16,031 vehicles in the metropolitan region. In the same year, the number of taxis in Chile reached a total of 35,584 (see Table 8.1).

Table 8.1 Trend in the Number of Taxis, Chile and the Metropolitan Region (1976–1987)

Year	Total Taxis, Chile (1)	Total Taxis, Metropolitan Region (2)	Regular Taxis, Metropolitan Region (3)	Collective Taxis, Metropolitan Region (4)	Number of Taxis per 1,000 Inhabitants. Chile (5)	Number of Taxis per 1,000 Inhabitants, Metropolitan Region (6)
1976	n.a.	9,961	9,951	10	n.a.	2.52
1977	17,573	11,380	n.a.	n.a.	1.65	2.84
1978	23,931	16,021	15,603	600	2.23	3.90
1979	34,296	22,646	21,272	800	3.20	5.43
1980	39,296	22,680	22,097	1,436	3.54	5.32
1981	53,913	28,809	26,813	2,073	4.77	6.59
1982	57,517	29,788	27,079	2,709	5.01	6.92
1983	53,920	26,094	22,749	3,345	4.60	5.71
1984	49,732	24,723	20,546	4,177	4.17	5.48
1985	39,964	18,258	13,186	5,072	3.30	3.83
1986	35,584	16,031	14,135	1,896	2.89	3.34

Sources: (1) Directory of Transport and Communications, INE. Statistical Yearbook of Overland Transport, Ministry of Transport and Telecommunications, 1985 and 1986; (2), (3), (4) Estimates, Paul (1982), and O'Ryan (1988); (5) and (6) National and Metropolitan Region Population, INE.
n.a.=not available

From an average of 1.65 taxis per 1,000 inhabitants in Chile in 1977, the average increased to five taxis for every 1,000 inhabitants in 1982, then decreased to 2.89 taxis per 1,000 in 1986. In the metropolitan region, there was an average of 6.92 taxis for every 1,000 inhabitants in 1982 and less than half that, 3.34 per 1,000 in 1986 (see Table 8.1).

These figures show that from the outset there has been a surplus supply of taxis because, according to the studies, an average of one taxi for every 800 or 1,000 inhabitants would be enough to meet the requirements of rapid and efficient transport.

The increase in the number of taxis over the past decade was contemporaneous with a large increase in the overall number of vehicles, particularly private cars. In 1978, private cars amounted to 146,807 and in 1983 reached a total of 251,749.

In addition, the operation and ownership of taxis is private and the overwhelming majority of taxi operators have only one taxi, although Ortega and Portales (1984) state that the average is two taxis per owner. There are small fleets of four, five, and up to ten taxis, which constitute small enterprises, but, according to data from the confederations, 70 percent of taxi operators own only one vehicle.

A study carried out in 1986 (O'Ryan, 1986) estimated that, as far as the whole transport system in the metropolitan region was concerned, 3.5 percent of all passengers traveled by regular taxi and 1.8 percent by collective taxi. In contrast, 39.3 percent used minibuses, 18.7 percent used taxibuses, and 31.2 percent used private cars. The underground transported 5.5 percent of all passengers. In 1983, according to the same study, taxis carried 69 million passengers, collective taxis 34 million, minibuses 773 million, and taxibuses 367 million.

This study also analyzed each form of transport's share of traffic congestion. The conclusion was that taxis were the most inefficient means from the point of view of utilization of road space by passenger carried. In 1983, regular and collective taxis, respectively, carried 440 million and 328 million passengers per kilometer covered, and minibuses and taxibuses carried 5,240 million and 2,491 million, respectively. Taxis take up 27.9 percent of streets in the center whereas minibuses and taxibuses use only 21.5 percent and 7 percent, respectively.

The study shows the surplus number of taxis, and also highlights their low rate of utilization. In 1983, the average daily rate of use (occupancy rate) was only 39 percent for regular taxis and slightly more (42 percent) for collective taxis. The same occurs with minibuses and private cars whose rates of utilization are 38 percent for each. The other means of transport— taxibuses and the underground—have higher daily usage rates, 57 percent and 50 percent, respectively (O'Ryan, 1986).

In another study carried out at the Catholic University by Paul (1982), a daily usage rate of 43.8 percent for taxis was estimated for 1982.

Another characteristic of taxis is that they use 15 percent of all the fuel used by urban means of transport; collective taxis use 2 percent, cars 52 percent, minibuses 19 percent, and taxibuses 11 percent. From this point of view as well, then, regular and collective taxis are the second most inefficient means of transport due to the high fuel consumption per passenger carried, after private cars.

From the point of view of employment, however, regular taxis are the form of transport that provides the most jobs (29,574 persons in 1983), compared to 11,873 persons for minibuses, 6,825 for taxibuses, 4,107 for collective taxis, and 1,507 for the underground (O'Ryan, 1986).

The methods of operation of regular and collective taxis are totally different. Collective taxis follow fixed routes, which generally intersect at different points in the city center, and have fixed pick-up and drop-off points. They can carry up to five passengers at a time at a fixed rate, even when the passenger travels only part of the route. Nevertheless, in certain places and at certain times, usually toward the end of the route and when the collective taxi has room, the rate can be negotiated, either to leave a passenger in front of his house or to pay a lower fare for the last stretch of the route.

Among regular taxis, which are those that provide an individual door-to-door service, there are two categories: "cruising" taxis, which constantly move and are the majority; and taxis at stands, a place where demand is stable and to which taxis return after each trip. The stand can be one legally established by the municipality or can emerge as a result of a decision by one or more individual taxi drivers.

A regular or collective taxi can be operated by up to three drivers: the owner and two persons who work under his orders and have to hand over to the owner a fixed daily amount. The owner is responsible for maintenance costs, repairs, licenses, and permits, and the driver must pay for the fuel, any fines he incurs, and sometimes oil or other minor costs. Those interviewed stated that collective taxis were often operated by two persons in order to derive the maximum benefit per vehicle.

General Economic Policies, Regulatory Policies, and Regulations That Affect the Taxi Market

Trend in Policies on Fare Regulation and the Entry of New Taxis into the Market

Before 1978, both the entry of new taxis and fares were determined by the state. The entry of taxis was regulated through the issue of licenses. The Ministry of Transport fixed a maximum quota of licenses for each community. In the same way, the price of the service was fixed by the ministry. From 1978, a policy of liberalization of the market was initiated as part of the neoliberal perspective of allowing the allocation of resources to be subject to the "free play" of supply and demand.

The transport sector is seen as one of the "most controlled and with obvious monopolistic characteristics . . . where freedom to work is hampered by numerous restrictions on the entry of new suppliers, thus leading to higher costs for users, through higher fares or poor service" (Jeftanovic, 1987). This is why, in 1978, entry into the taxi market and other forms of transport was liberalized. This was implemented through Resolution No. 873 of the Ministry of Transport and Telecommunications on July 17, 1978. Subsequently, on November 2, 1979, in a more formal manner, Decree No. 320 replaced all the legislation previously in force and granted total freedom for the incorporation of new vehicles for public transport and for the creation or extension of forms of public transport and their routes. During this period, regular taxi fares were still fixed by the government.

The same did not occur in the case of collective taxis, which reappeared in 1978. During the first phase, these operated freely without any official regulation of routes or fares. Moreover, regular taxis in practice operated as collective taxis when they found it convenient.

In 1981 in practice, and formally in 1984, controls on the circulation of collective taxis, buses, and taxibuses started to be imposed. On April 7, 1980, collective taxis were forbidden to enter the center of Santiago. In 1981, an administrative decision limited new routes and the incorporation of additional vehicles to the collective taxi routes. This was legally implemented in 1984 in Resolution No. 1 of the Ministry of Transport and Telecommunications (D.O. 1.2.1984).

Also in 1984, a decision provided for a clear division between regular and collective taxis. Taxi meters were no longer required in collective taxis, and more precise maps of routes had to be submitted. Applications had to be made to the Ministry of Transport and Telecommunications for permits or decisions on the incorporation of any new vehicle on a route. In practical terms, greater Santiago was declared to be a saturated zone. (Supreme Decree No. 163/84 contains the regulations governing all aspects of the operation of taxi services.)

Furthermore, in 1981, for regular taxis, a system of partial liberalization of fares, which until then had been wholly controlled, was established. This system of partial liberalization consisted of liberalizing the initial cost of hiring the taxi within a range of rates. However, the fares fixed by the ministry for every 200 meters or 30 minutes remained in force.

The entry of new taxis into the market, however, is still free. In addition to the general outlines for operation of this sector, there are a number of regulations that, even in the context of neoliberal policies, have not been eliminated.

Current Rules and Regulations Governing Taxis

Age of the vehicle. Article 93, DFL 279/60 and DL 557/74, of 1984 specify that road licenses for taxis will be granted only for vehicles that are not more than eight years old at the time of applying for the license for the first time.

Roadworthiness. Every two months, taxis must pass a roadworthiness test, unlike private cars, which are tested annually.

Meters. Meter use is compulsory for regular taxis, which have to undergo a biannual revision by the municipal authorities.

Driving license. The driver must have an A class license, like other collective means of transport, and at present this must be renewed annually; previously, it was valid for four years.

Insurance. Like private cars, taxis must have compulsory motor insurance. Since March 1988, collective means of transport are no longer obliged to contract this insurance with the State Insurance Institute. They can take out insurance with any insurance company, and collective taxis are exempt from issuing tickets (DFL 279/60; 557/74; Laws No. 18,679 and 18,681).

Appearance. Several decrees regulate the color of regular taxis (black with a yellow roof) and collective taxis (black). These regulations on color were first applied in 1969 when harmonization of taxis was imposed. In addition, regulations were adopted (Laws No. 18,059 and 18,290 of 1984) stipulating that public transport vehicles should be clean and their drivers have a neat personal appearance.

Environmental pollution. Law No. 18,563 provides for the withdrawal of taxis, and vehicles in general, that exceed the authorized levels of pollution.

Stands. In addition to general regulations on taxis, in recent years regulations on taxi stands authorized by municipal authorities have also been adopted. The municipal authorities rent out the relevant site and sometimes install a telephone, which must be paid for by the taxi operators. The municipal permit is subject to all taxis using the stand complying with its provisions.

It should be pointed out that, even though the above-mentioned regulations apply, the "Professional Driver's Statute" was rescinded in 1979, and compulsory trade union membership was eliminated in 1975 in Basic Charter No. 2.

Economic Policies Affecting the Taxi Market

In addition to the policies and regulations described above, the low exchange rate policy, which prevailed up to 1982, affected the taxi market. This significantly encouraged the import of taxis and was combined with the elimination between 1974 to 1978 of the existing provisions that prohibited the import of vehicles in general and public transport vehicles and taxis in particular.

Subsequently, the devaluation of the dollar in June 1982 meant that taxi operators who had bought imported vehicles and had contracted debts in dollars were seriously affected.

Tariff reductions occurred in 1976, and in 1979 tariffs were around 10 percent. However, the import of vehicles was subject to a tariff of 90 percent, which also applied to taxis.

On August 5, 1987, Law No. 18,634 was enacted, which allows taxi operators to pay customs duties in seven annual installments; the total of the installments must not be less than US$2,000 and the cost, insurance, and freight (CIF) value of the taxi must exceed US$3,800. Prior to that date, taxi operators paid customs duties of 90 percent of the CIF value to import their vehicles, the same rate as for private cars. Customs duties, together with payment of the value-added tax (VAT) decreed in 1979, increase the cost of vehicles in the following way: a 1979 Chevette, whose CIF value is US$3,296, has to pay US$2,966 customs duties plus US$1,252 VAT, or a total of US$7,514, of which taxes represent US$4,218.

There was also a credit policy favoring the purchase of new vehicles, promoted by the national banks and by the State Bank, which financed a number of operations:

- Between 1979 and 1981, 2,445 Peugeot vehicles were imported, with direct external credit endorsed to the State Bank.
- During the same period, 1,100 Chevette vehicles were imported, financed by the Credit and Investment Bank.
- During the same period, 2,000 Opals were imported, financed by the Credit and Investment Bank, the State Bank, the South American Bank, and the Bank of Brazil.
- In 1979, 160 Subaru cars were imported, financed by the Credit and Investment Bank.

These loans had the advantage of state guarantees. They had to be reimbursed in six-monthly installments over a period of five years. The loans were originally made in dollars plus interest. As a result of negotiations in recent years, they have been converted into readjustable units of promotion (UF, Unidades de Fomento) or pesos. Although they had state guarantees, many of the loans were granted against property mortgages. This situation particularly affected those taxi operators who had obtained consumer credits and used them to purchase taxis. The number of such taxi operators is difficult to determine; according to estimates by trade union leaders, they represent 10 percent of the total number who have debts.

Another aspect is the policy of redeploying the unemployed as taxi drivers, which started in 1975 with those dismissed from the public sector.

Last, reference must be made to the special fuel tax, which has been in effect since 1978 and represents 50 percent of the net cost of fuel. Like all private and public means of transport, taxi operators have to pay this tax in addition to the VAT, although the other means of public transport, such as buses, taxibuses, and lorries, are allowed to deduct the VAT. Therefore, if the cost of fuel is $2,809, 20 percent VAT, or $562 has to be added, plus the special tax of $1,629. The final cost of the fuel is therefore $5,000, and the treasury takes $2,191 in taxes.

Compliance with Legislation and Regulations

The research showed that, in general, there is a high degree of compliance with governmental regulations on the functioning of the taxi market. Those regulations that are violated do not usually present insuperable problems. On the contrary, our conclusion in this regard is that on the one hand, organizations of taxi operators are calling upon the government to extend or improve regulations applying to the sector, and, moreover, where there are no regulations, these are created by the organizations themselves—both grassroots organizations such as trade unions and intermediate or national organizations, federations, or confederations.

Compliance with regulations

One of the most serious violations of regulations concerns "pirate" collective taxis, which existed at one time but today have all been regularized. A vehicle can operate legally when it starts to work on a route while awaiting a ministerial decision. In such cases, the driver has formally joined the route and must pay to the association or trade union a membership fee, which can vary between 10,000 and 200,000 pesos. According to trade union leaders, in November 1987, 225 taxis were functioning without an official decision.

Another form of illegal operation is the existence of collective taxis from outside the metropolitan region operating on Santiago routes, for which permits are limited. Pirate taxis have also been detected in the airport taxi service. According to leaders in this sector, there is a large number of private cars that work as taxis without having the relevant authorization, and they function in collaboration with *vinchucas*, who are persons external to the airport who wait outside to attract passengers.

In this context, it is necessary to include the problem of collective taxis that carry six passengers, although they are allowed a maximum of only five. For this purpose, they set aside what is practically a fixed percentage of their earnings to pay fines or "shares" to the police.

Last, not all vehicles operating as individual or collective taxis fulfill the requirements on appearance and cleanliness described previously.

Demands by trade union organizations

As mentioned above, before the government liberalized the market, the trade unions in the sector themselves requested regularization of certain situations. Among the principal demands was the regularization of the division of taxis into regular and collective taxis in 1984, as the result of a demand by the taxi operators' federations to the government. This was in response to trade union concern to regularize the situation because until then regular taxis could function as collective taxis during rush hours. The trade union of collective taxi operators instigated this demand.

Recently, the National Federation of Taxi Operators of Chile (FENATACH, Federación Nacional de Taxistas de Chile) has made the following requests on regulations to the Ministry of Transport:

- Restoration of the Professional Driver's Statute, which would permit regulation of the activity from the professional point of view;
- A return to the system of licenses by commune;
- Fixing of fares by the ministry on the basis of a cost study;
- Compulsory membership of a trade union;
- An integral insurance system and health benefits;
- The possibility of insurance against accidents, robbery, and other misfortunes;
- Retirement after twenty-five years of work.

In addition, trade unions have made requests in a number of applications for:

- Elimination or subsidization of the special fuel tax. Alternatively, it is proposed that the fuel tax should finance comprehensive insurance, social security, a vehicle replacement fund, or assistance centers for taxi operators;
- Elimination of the additional tax on the import of taxis, subject to the commitment that the vehicle should remain in service for a specified number of years;
- A solution to the current debt problem;
- Readjustment of the rate for initial hiring and for every 200 meters.

The last of these requests was made in September 1987, calling for an increase in the range of the rate for initial hiring from 20–150 to 80–210 pesos, and in the rate for every 200 meters from 8–10 pesos. These rates were readjusted by the Ministry of Transport and Telecommunications in November, setting the rate for initial hiring at 20–250 pesos and the rate for every 200 meters at 10 pesos.

The collective taxi trade unions requested further permits for new routes and the incorporation of new vehicles. In a letter sent to the Ministry in November 1987, FENATACH proposed a draft decree aimed at "regulating and controlling the taxi operators' trade union in operating the various taxi services."

The text states the following: "The characteristic of this regulation is that, particularly as far as the regular taxi service is concerned, there should be taxi ranks, with or without a telephone, so as to avoid taxis driving around empty." The text added a series of general rules to enable legal differentiation of the various types of taxi service: regular, collective, tourism, and radiotaxis, as well as special regulations on the functioning and appearance of each category.

In its reply to the President of FENATACH, the Ministry of Transport and Telecommunications stated that: "Decree No. 163/84 regulates the operation of taxi services in all their forms." and that "it cannot accept a request to implement a system that would regulate the exercise of this professional activity since it has already been defined at government level that there should be no restriction on the freedom to work."

Internal regulations in the sector

As already mentioned, the taxi sector and the existing trade unions and professional organizations have themselves established a series of regulations covering various aspects. In the case of collective taxis, the issue is clear: the desire to fix stable and permanent routes spontaneously gives rise to the organization of associations and unions for each route. These associations create their own internal operational rules dealing with several aspects, including the fee or payment for joining; daily payment for maintaining the premises, cleaners, inspectors, and so forth; harmonization and sale of a sign to be put on top of the vehicle; and constitution of a mutual fund. Regular taxi operators, except those who belong to a trade union, are not obliged to comply with the internal rules of the trade union, but have to comply with the laws in force.

Despite the foregoing, there tends to be harmonization at different levels. For example, if a taxi stand is suddenly established, operators will quickly reach agreement on regulating the admission of new taxis to the stand or will initiate formalities for a municipal permit. As far as fares are concerned, because these are not currently fixed by the Ministry, taxi operators almost automatically agree upon them among themselves. It is rare to find a taxi that imposes fares below those imposed by other taxis. As taxi operators themselves declared when interviewed, when the trade union or a group of individual taxi operators finds it necessary to readjust fares, this happens almost simultaneously.

Collective taxis are free to fix their fares, which vary according to the route on which they work, its length, the degree of competition with other forms of transport, and similar considerations. However, once the fare for a route is set, all the collective taxis must apply it, according to their own internal rules.

The following section analyzes the factors on which changes in fares depend and the elements that are taken into account when modifying fares.

The Impact of Changes in Regulations and in the Economy on the Taxi Market

Analysis of How Fares Are Fixed and Why Taxis Enter and Leave the Market

The first aspect to be clarified in order to understand the way fares are fixed is the performance of taxi fares compared to other forms of transport.

Figure 8.3 shows that the most expensive journey is by regular taxi; its price reached 309 pesos per journey in 1987. In the same year, the average collective taxi fare was 118 pesos per journey, the minibus fare was 49 pesos, and the taxibus fare was 55 pesos (Table 8.2). The foregoing shows that regular taxis do not in any way replace minibuses and taxibuses.

The problem is more complex with regard to collective taxis because, using the average fare information just given, their rates are virtually twice those for minibuses and taxibuses (*liebres*). However, in the course of interviews with collective taxi drivers, they declared that in some sectors their fares were drawing equal and were currently identical to those of taxibuses. They also said that they would alter fares only when taxibuses did the same. On the basis of their statements, it could be determined that many of them were functioning as perfect substitutes for taxibuses, especially those operating in low-income areas.

Figure 8.3 shows regular taxi fares have their own momentum, whereas the fares of collective taxis, minibuses, and taxibuses show relatively parallel changes. This leads to a first conclusion: the fixing of regular taxi fares is relatively independent of that of other means of transport, but the same is not true for collective taxis, whose fares vary to a certain extent according to changes in fares for minibuses and taxibuses. This occurs despite the fact that, according to the INE, the average number of trips for collective taxis is higher than that for minibuses and taxibuses. In addition, although taxis are

Figure 8.3 Trend in Public Transport Fares (in pesos)

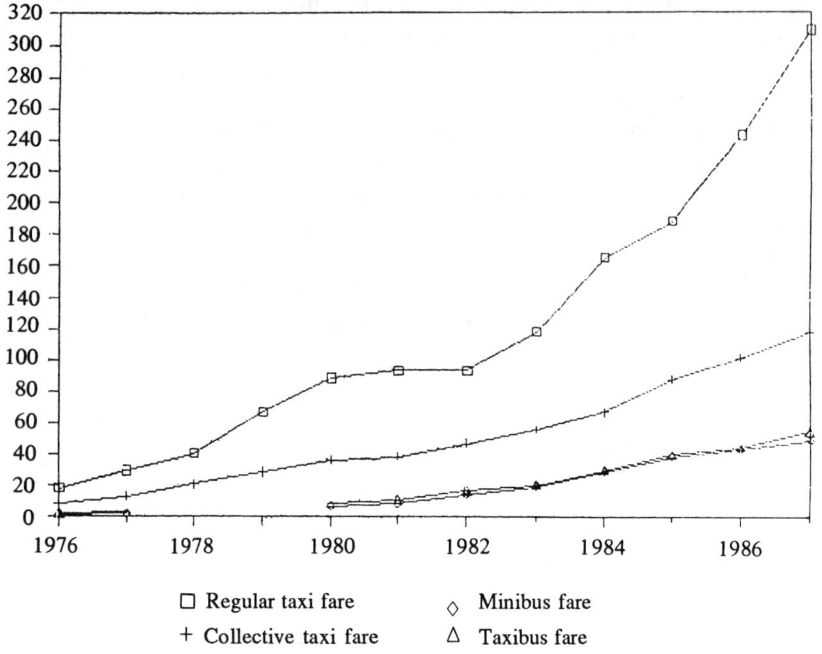

- □ Regular taxi fare
- ◇ Minibus fare
- + Collective taxi fare
- △ Taxibus fare

Table 8.2 Trend in Public Transport Fares, 1976–1987

	Fare (pesos)				Fare Ratio (1976=100)			
	Regular Taxi	Collective Taxi	Minibus	Taxibus[a]	Regular Taxi	Collective Taxi	Minibus	Taxibus[a]
December								
1976	18	8	1	2	100.00	100.00	100.00	100.00
1977	30	13	2	3	162.30	158.46	166.22	137.14
1978	41	21	n.a.	n.a.	221.48	250.06	n.a.	n.a.
1979	67	29	n.a.	n.a.	365.57	340.83	n.a.	n.a.
1980	88	36	7	9	482.51	429.59	466.22	375.51
1981	93	38	9	11	509.29	450.89	587.84	453.06
1982	93	47	14	18	509.29	550.30	959.46	714.29
1983	118	56	19	21	644.81	659.05	1,307.43	836.73
1984	165	67	29	30	901.64	792.90	1,961,49	1,223.67
1985	188	88	38	40	1,027.32	1,037.16	2,600.68	1,634.69
1986	243	101	43	45	1,327.87	1,195.27	2,906.08	1,824.08
1987	309	118	49	55	1,688.52	1,396.45	3,291.22	2,238.78

Source: Consumer Price Indexes, INE.
n.a.=not available
[a]Taxibus or *liebre*.

the most expensive means of transport, the readjustment of their fares has been much lower than that for other forms of transport.

Between 1976 and 1981, the trend in the fares of the different means of transport was very similar; subsequently, from 1981 on, the rate of readjustment of the fares became completely different. The cost of journeys on minibuses and taxibuses started to be readjusted much faster than that of regular and collective taxis, as can be seen in Figure 8.4. Therefore, since 1981, the factors determining the readjustment of fares for various forms of transport have differed.

One important feature seems to have been the semiliberalization of regular taxi fares in 1981. This cannot, however, be the only explanation because collective taxi fares followed a similar pattern, and they had been liberalized since 1978. Collective taxis cannot readjust fares above those of regular taxis and so they endeavor to attract passengers from the taxibus market.

Another factor that must be analyzed is the effect of cost fluctuations on the readjustment of fares. Figure 8.5 shows that, from 1976 to 1981, all fares rose in parallel with the increase in the price of fuel, but from 1981 onward only minibus fares rose in parallel with the cost of fuel. In contrast, fares for taxibuses, regular taxis, and collective taxis rose at a level lower than the increase in the price of fuel. In 1985, however, taxibus fares started to rise above the increase in the price of fuel.

The same effect occurs with regard to the price of tires, which constitutes one of the principal costs in this sector, together with the elements analyzed above. As Figure 8.6 shows, since 1981, minibuses and taxibuses have increased fares above the rise in the price of tires, and collective and regular taxis, whose readjustments were previously similar to those for tires, started to lose purchasing power.

It appears that from 1976 to 1981, readjustments of the fares for all public transport appeared to be interlinked and also related to the price of their two main inputs, namely, fuel and tires. The linkage ceased from 1981 onward, and regular and collective taxis started to show readjustments that were lower and did not cover the increase in their costs.

A study published by the University of Chile (Jeftanovic, 1987), shows that between 1978 and 1986, fares for buses and taxibuses were readjusted at a higher rate than costs. It also concludes that taxi fares were constantly lower than the rise in their costs. In the period 1978–1980, the difference between the fluctuations in fares and costs was very small, but it became much more noticeable subsequently. This confirms what is stated above. What are the causes of the variations in the fares for the various forms of public transport from 1981 onward and the different attitudes of each vis-à-vis their main inputs?

Changes in the policies regulating the sector should help to explain the different attitudes of the various forms of transport. First, it must be noted

Figure 8.4 Index of Public Transport Fares (1976 = 100)
(miles)

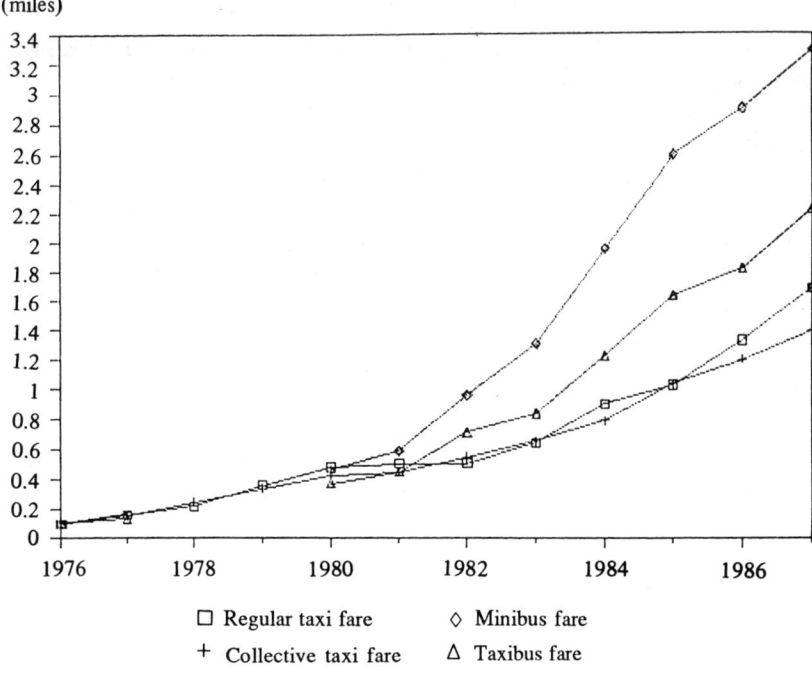

□ Regular taxi fare   ◇ Minibus fare
+ Collective taxi fare   △ Taxibus fare

Figure 8.5 Fares and Fuel Index (1976 = 100)
(miles)

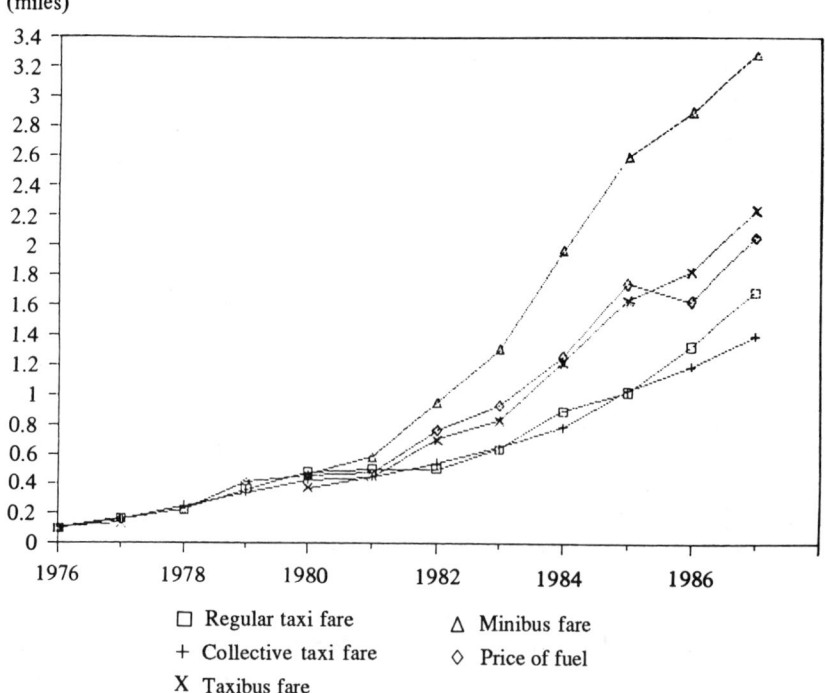

□ Regular taxi fare   △ Minibus fare
+ Collective taxi fare   ◇ Price of fuel
X Taxibus fare

Figure 8.6 Fares and Tire Price Index (1976 = 100)

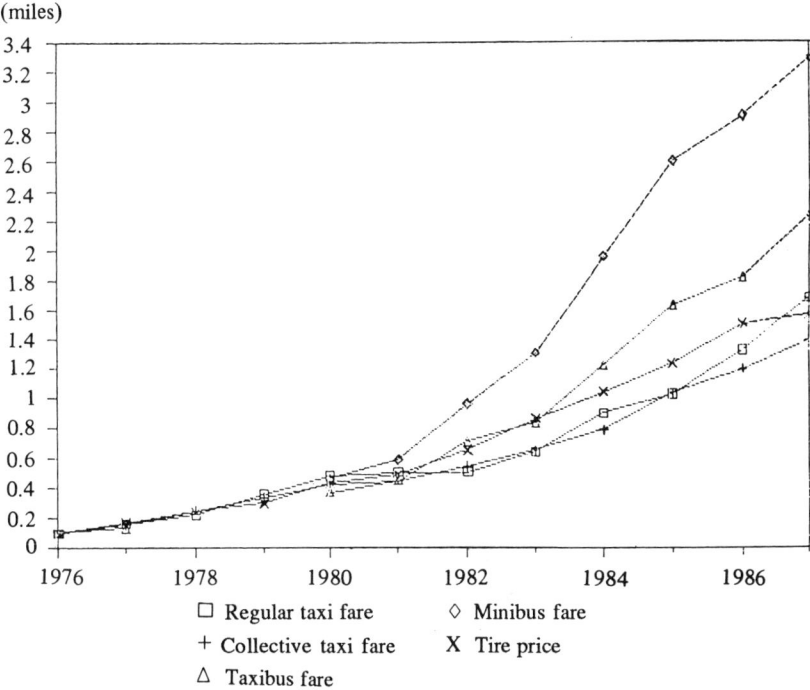

□ Regular taxi fare   ◇ Minibus fare
+ Collective taxi fare   X Tire price
△ Taxibus fare

that the liberalization policy on the entry of public transport vehicles in 1978 affected all forms of transport, and it should therefore have led to increased competition among them, which, according to neoliberal concepts, should have produced a diminution of fares.

In 1978, fares for various forms of public transport were liberalized, except taxis, which were partly liberalized in 1981. This means that in 1978 the fares for minibuses, taxibuses, and collective taxis should have decreased, but this did not happen. In the situation we are analyzing, collective taxi fares increased during the period 1978–1980 in the same way as regular taxi fares.

During this period not only could fares be fixed freely, but also the entry of new collective taxis was free. Any influence of "market" forces was to be seen in the readjustment of fares at a lower rate than the cost of inputs; therefore, the ratio of collective taxi fares to fuel prices suddenly decreased between 1978 and 1979 to a greater degree than in the case of regular taxis (see Figure 8.7).

It is worth mentioning that in the period 1980–1981, for which we have information on public transport fares, there was an increase in the fare-fuel price ratio in the case of minibuses and taxibuses; this occurred despite the freedom to set fares and free access to the market.

Figure 8.7 Fares/Fuel Index (1976 = 100)

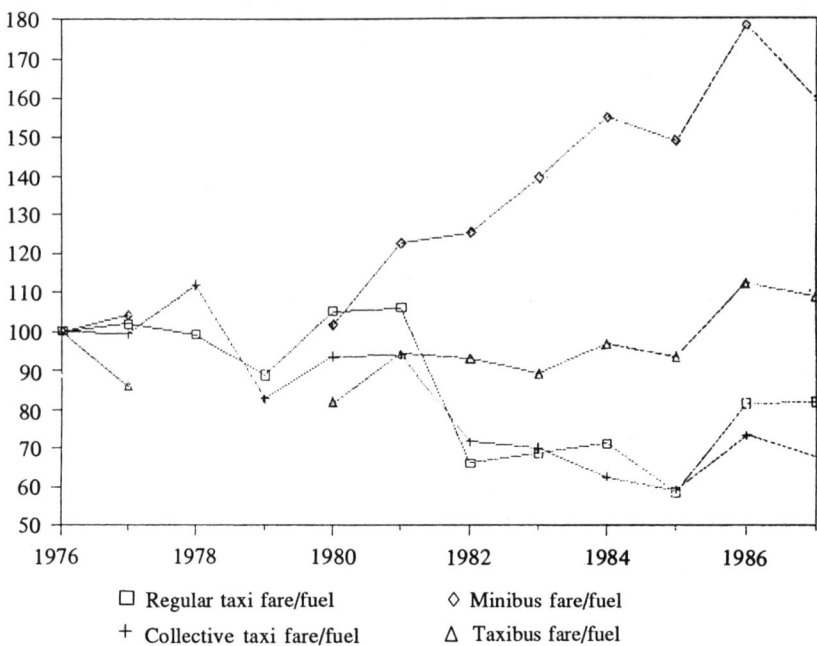

□ Regular taxi fare/fuel ◊ Minibus fare/fuel
+ Collective taxi fare/fuel △ Taxibus fare/fuel

Collective taxis, to which this liberalization also applied, first of all suffered a decrease in fares in terms of fuel prices, as explained above, and then a slight recovery up to 1981, when practical restrictions on the creation of new routes started to be imposed. Despite the fact that since then, and particularly since 1984, collective taxis could have adopted a monopolistic attitude as a result of the existence of barriers to access and freely set fares, this did not happen and the fare-fuel price ratio became even less important between 1981 and 1982, reaching its minimum level in 1985 (see Figure 8.7).

Moreover, regular taxis, for which access but not fares had been liberalized in 1978, also saw a decrease in the fare-fuel price ratio between 1978 and 1979, as a result of increased competition. However, as in the case of collective taxis, this ratio increased during the periods 1979–1980 to 1980–1981. Subsequently, from 1981 onward, when a semifree fare system operated, taxis experienced a considerable decrease (the same as for collective taxis with restricted access) of the fare-fuel price ratio, first of all very sharply between 1981–1982, with a slight recovery between 1982 and 1984, a drop between 1984–1985 and a subsequent increase.

In conclusion, in the case of regular and collective taxis, market liberalization policies have contrasting effects. On the one hand, collective taxis, which have had free fare structures and restricted entry since 1981, but more particularly since 1984 (and could therefore adopt a monopolistic attitude), have shown a greater tendency to increase their purchasing power than regular taxis. This can be seen both in the increased diminution of the fare-fuel price ratio and in lower fare increases. On the other hand, in the regular taxi market, with free entry and relatively free fare structures, competition should have led to a lowering of fares; however, decreases in fares compared to costs have been lower than in the case of collective taxis, and recovery has been greater.

It should be emphasized that, in comparison with other forms of transport (minibuses and taxibuses), the cost of a taxi trip has in fact decreased in relative terms, "market" mechanisms having functioned. This is one instance where free access has prevailed in comparison with other sectors in which new restrictions were imposed between 1981 and 1984.

Why have collective taxis not increased their fares further since there is restriction on access? To respond to this question, the points of view of those most directly involved should be mentioned. What has happened is that the collective taxis have gradually started to function as replacements for taxibuses. They have realized that the only way of attracting a larger number of passengers is to offer the same or similar fares as other forms of public transport. The increase in collective taxi fares has therefore been low because their point of departure charge was much higher than that of taxibus fares, so readjustments had to be smaller. As those interviewed stated, this assumes that the passengers who use collective taxis are potentially the same as those who use taxibuses, namely, consumers who are prepared to pay a slight difference in order to ride in a more comfortable vehicle. In fact, in various parts of the capital they have started to compete with vehicles that provide the underground-bus link.

The situation of regular taxis is radically different because their market has two extremes: on the one hand, there are passengers who take longer journeys and are necessarily people with high incomes, and on the other hand, there are passengers who take short journeys and are usually retailers, owners of small-scale enterprises, and so on. For regular taxi operators this fact is of vital importance, and they did not increase the initial hiring charge more because they realized that they would lose a large part of their clientele, particularly those who use taxis for short journeys. According to taxi owners, passengers taking short trips are less aware of an increase in the cost per kilometer than an increase in the initial hiring charge. They consider that the fare per kilometer should be increased, but this remains fixed by the authorities. Although there is freedom to readjust the initial hiring charge—within a fairly wide spectrum—the most important and ongoing demand of taxi operators to the state is readjustment of the cost per kilometer.

There is a situation of semiliberalization for the fixing of fares, although one element which, from the point of view of the trade union, is primordial in practice remains totally controlled, whereas, on the other hand, there is totally free access to the market for new vehicles. In the guise of a conclusion and synthesis regarding this aspect, it should be pointed out that the relative decrease in regular and collective taxi fares since 1981 to a stage where fares and costs fluctuate in relative harmony is attributable to different causes. On the one hand, as already pointed out, it is because both services are subject to contrasting regulations: regular taxis have semifixed fares and free access, whereas collective taxis have freely set fares and controlled access.

Collective taxis have not, in fact, been able to exercise a monopoly, despite obstacles to access, because in practice they have to compete with other forms of transport that have advantages in terms of cost, taxes, and other aspects that will be analyzed below. Regular taxis, on the other hand, are prevented from increasing fares for fear of losing passengers, particularly during periods of crisis or recession, and are not entitled to increase the cost per kilometer.

The last question that arises is why competition among taxis, as a result of the increased number of taxis in recent years, has not incited them to lower fares individually so as to carry a larger number of passengers and earn more, competing according to market forces? It has, in fact, resulted in a single price. Does this signify a monopoly despite an open market and mean that there is some form of trade union collusion?

The answer to these questions can be found in Shreiber's (1981) description of the functioning of the market. The taxi market has several distinct characteristics, such as lack of synchronization and information (discussed previously), which means that taxi operators who lower fares will only lower earnings and will not increase the number of passengers carried because a passenger will not be able to distinguish between an expensive taxi and an inexpensive one unless waiting time is increased.

If taxi fares have been harmonized, in general fairly rapidly, this is not due to the exercise of a monopoly because, as will be seen in the next section, it has not resulted in enormous profits, and earnings in recent years have not been enough for replenishment and capital formation. Harmonization of fares is fundamentally due to the fact that, because of the specific characteristics of this service, the preconditions for competition do not exist. This service does not operate like a transparent supply and demand market. If some taxis increase fares, those that do not follow will only reduce their earnings and will not increase the number of passengers. There is therefore a natural tendency to harmonize fares.

The second variable is the entry of new taxis into the market and their withdrawal. As already mentioned, before 1978 there was a law that limited the number of taxis in each commune. This was repealed in 1978, and the economic authorities have been made responsible for verifying the right of any person to operate a taxi. The trade union, for its part, defends the profession of taxi operator as a job that requires the fulfillment of specific requirements, such as the possibility of affording an acceptable standard of living to owners and drivers.

Another of the characteristics of the taxi market is that because there is free entry, it is affected by the fluctuations in economic cycles, becoming a potential source of employment for the unemployed. This is what has happened in Chile, particularly in the metropolitan region, where the number of taxis doubled in comparison with previous years between 1979 and 1984 (see Table 8.1), and the collective taxi sector saw strong growth.

According to the viewpoint of trade union leaders, collective taxis reappeared after some years of virtual absence, precisely at the time of liberalization of access. This to some extent compensated for the oversupply of taxis in relation to potential customers, making it possible to distinguish different markets and, in the case of collective taxis, to ensure a more stable income than that of regular taxi operators.

Figure 8.8 shows the trend in unemployment together with that in the total number of regular and collective taxis. It can be seen that during the period 1977–1979, as employment increased, the number of taxis also increased. This occurred before the government decreed free access to taxi services, which shows that, in practice, municipal authorities had already increased quotas during 1977. This could be the result of the "new entrepreneurs plan" implemented in 1975 with the objective of allowing civil servants dismissed from the public administration to set up small-scale enterprises, such as shops or taxi services.

Figure 8.8 Number of Taxis and Number of Unemployed (1977 = 100)

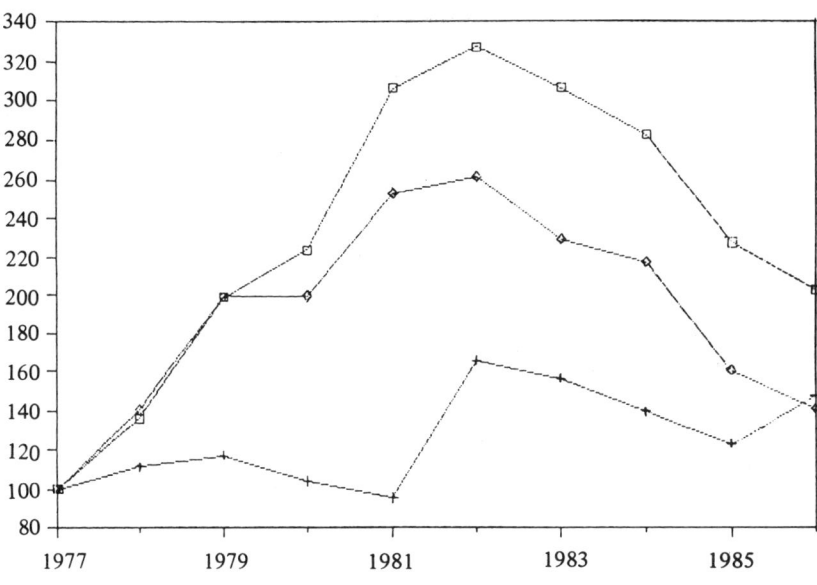

When access was liberalized in 1978, the increase in the number of taxis accelerated both in Chile as a whole and in the metropolitan region. Subsequently, unemployment started to fall and this process continued until 1981, although the number of taxis continued to increase, despite stagnation in the metropolitan region between 1979 and 1980.

On the basis of the trends noted, it is not possible to conclude definitely that the rate of unemployment has always had an impact on the number of taxis. It should be mentioned, however, that the trends are similar. In 1982, for example, when the rate of unemployment rose, so did the number of taxis. And simultaneously with the recovery in the employment situation, the number of taxis started to decrease at the national level and in the metropolitan region. Nevertheless, when unemployment rose again from 1985–1986, the number of taxis continued to decrease.

According to the taxi operators interviewed, this was due to the fact that the profitability of this activity fell below acceptable levels, and many taxi owners were forced to sell their vehicles and abandon the profession either because they could not repair their taxis or because their vehicles were auctioned off to reimburse their debts.

One indicator that gives an approximate overview of the profitability trend for taxi owners during those years is the fare-fuel price ratio because fuel is the main variable cost of operating a taxi.

In 1987, the regular taxi fare-fuel price ratio was 18 percent less than in 1976, and the collective taxi fare-fuel price ratio was 32 percent less (Table 8.3).

It is also interesting to note that between 1976 and 1981, a period during which there was considerable expansion in the number of taxis (Figure 8.9) profitability remained at approximately the 1976 level. The enormous growth in the number of vehicles was not due to a significant increase in earnings; just maintaining the level of earnings in a period of widespread unemployment was sufficient to cause the phenomenon of the oversupply of taxis. Between 1981 and 1982, profitability started to fall as the number of vehicles continued to increase. It can be assumed, therefore, that the considerable increase in unemployment during those years was a determinant factor.

In 1982, the average was five taxis per 1,000 inhabitants in the country as a whole and almost seven per 1,000 in the metropolitan region. Then the fare-fuel price ratio started to fall and this situation continued until 1985. Is it possible that from 1982 onward profitability fell due to the fact that a saturation point had been reached and taxis started to leave the market, according to the scenario described by Shreiber (1981)? In conditions of free entry and withdrawal, this functions as an adjustment variable in the face of changes in profits. When profits fall, taxis leave the market, whereupon rates of use increase and profits rise; taxis then enter the market, the rate of use declines, and so do profits.

Table 8.3 Trend in Taxi Fares and Fuel Prices, 1976–1987 (1976 = 100)

	Regular Taxi Fare/Fuel Price	Collective Taxi Fare/Fuel Price
1976	100.00	100.00
1977	101.86	99.45
1978	99.12	111.91
1979	88.84	82.83
1980	105.05	93.52
1981	105.91	93.77
1982	66.32	71.66
1983	68.76	70.28
1984	71.27	62.68
1985	58.71	59.27
1986	81.64	73.48
1987	82.03	67.84

Source: Consumer Price Index, INE.

Figure 8.9 Number of Taxis and Fare/Fuel Price (1976 = 100)

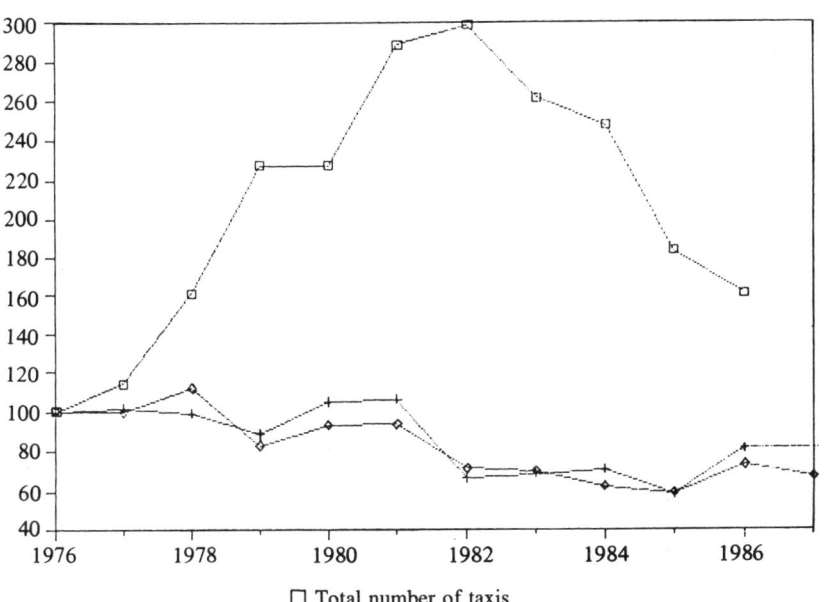

□ Total number of taxis
+ Regular taxi fare/fuel price
◊ Collective taxi fare/fuel price

Has the taxi market behaved in this manner?

In summary, during the period 1977–1982 there was an enormous increase in the number of taxis, despite the fact that there was no increase in profitability. Unemployment during this period was probably the determinant factor. During the period 1982–1985, however, there was a direct link between decreased profitability and the withdrawal of taxis from the market.

We can draw three conclusions from these trends. First, the increase in the number of taxis is related to the increase in unemployment in recent years because this sector absorbed the unemployed labor force. Second, before 1978 there was pressure to liberalize access to the taxi market. This can be seen in the fact that the number of permits granted in 1977 increased by approximately 40 percent, which was also the situation after liberalization and represented a much higher figure than in 1976 (14 percent) (see Table 8.1). Third, in the beginning, growth in the taxi sector was linked to a certain stability in profitability. Profitability started to decrease in 1981, when fares were semiliberalized, leading to the withdrawal of taxis from the market from then on, except during the period 1981–1982, when there was a large increase in unemployment.

There is one unknown factor for the 1985–1986 period, when unemployment increased and profitability increased (which apparently contradicts the views of the taxi operators), yet the number of taxis continued to decrease. One of the phenomena that might explain the withdrawal of taxis from the market at a time of increased unemployment is, as mentioned, the debt problem.

Other Effects of Changes in the Regulations

The effects of the changes in the regulations affecting the taxi market in terms of income and profits for owners and drivers, the quality of service, and working conditions is analyzed next. It should be noted that, despite an overall policy of liberalizing this market, there are still many specific standards and regulations in force regarding the age of the vehicle, technical maintenance, use of taxi meters, issue of drivers' licenses, compulsory car insurance, and so forth.

All these rules mean that, in practice, the market is not completely free. In fact, not anyone can become a taxi operator. The operator must have the capacity to contract debts or possess enough capital to purchase a vehicle, the taxi must not be older than eight years, and the driver must have a category A or professional driver's license.

In addition, there is an aspect that trade union leaders consider to be the central issue of the policies implemented in recent years. In 1978, and then again in 1981, the government liberalized the market, especially fares, but it kept direct or indirect control of the prices of the principal inputs and costs of taxis, thereby exercising control over profits in this sector.

The import of commercial vehicles is subject to the same additional import tax (90 percent) as private vehicles; there is also a special fuel tax, corresponding to 50 percent of value (since 1978), plus 20 percent VAT in both cases, and this cannot be deducted by taxi operators. As discussed previously, this means that the treasury takes 43.8 percent of the sum the taxi operator pays for fuel and 56.1 percent of the final cost of an imported vehicle.

To gain an impression of the importance of these measures for the taxi sector, as the interviews showed, it is necessary to take into account the fact that fuel constitutes the principal variable cost and it fluctuates between 40 and 60 percent of the total earnings of taxi operators. These figures are consistent with the cost structure shown by Jeftanovic (1987) and Sapag and Sapag (1987), in which 56 percent of total costs, including the driver's wages, was allocated for fuel.

Earnings and profits in the sector

Liberalization of entry into the market led to a surplus of taxis, reaching a level of almost seven vehicles per 1,000 inhabitants in the metropolitan region in 1982. Simultaneously with the increase in competition, the treasury imposed a tax on fuel, which increased its price by 88.8 percent in 1979.

As a result, between 1978 and 1979, taxi operators suffered not only a substantial increase in costs without being able to increase fares (which were still fixed by the authorities), but also increased competition from new taxis. The effects of this situation were seen in decreases in the regular and collective taxi fare-fuel price ratios (Figure 8.7).

Subsequently, a slow recovery took place until 1981, when a new crisis occurred as a result of the semiliberalization of fares. In 1982, the number of taxis reached the maximum level, as well as the number of unemployed. On the one hand, supply of this service increased to an unprecedented extent and, on the other, demand fell, probably due to the economic crisis that started in 1982. It was in this context of significant increase in supply and probable decrease in demand that fares were liberalized one year earlier. The result was a sharp drop in the fare-fuel price ratio between 1981 and 1982, without taxi operators being able to recover their purchasing power with respect to their main expenditure—fuel—until 1987.

The fare-fuel price indicator represents the income remaining to the taxi owner after having paid the cost of fuel. The costs of maintenance and spare parts, licenses, and amortization of the debt, in addition to other costs, in some cases have to be deducted. This gives the net income. The trend in the fare-fuel price ratio gives an approximation of the trend in taxi operators' incomes. The decline in this ratio from 1976 to 1986 shown in Figure 8.7 therefore reflects the drop in the incomes of taxi owners and drivers.

Not much information is available on taxi operators' incomes, but it is possible to throw some light on recent events. An interview with two taxi operators in 1981 showed that their incomes in real terms had systematically fallen since 1978. One operator had a monthly net income of approximately 40,000 pesos in 1978 and approximately 17,000 pesos in 1982 (in pesos at each year's rate). Another operator earned approximately 24,000 pesos a month in 1978, but earned only 9,500 pesos a month in 1988 (information provided by Taxi Operators' Trade Union No. 1 in Santiago).

According to a survey by the Catholic University of sixty-five taxi operators in Santiago in March and April 1982 (Paul, 1982), taxi owners earned a monthly average net income of 12,000 pesos. If the taxi was driven by a person who was not the owner, the driver had to pay the owner 658 pesos a day, approximately 16,450 pesos a month, with an average of 25 working days.

In the interviews carried out in April 1988 for the present study, there was a wide range in taxi operators' incomes, related to the mode of operation of the vehicle. A taxi driver who is also the owner of the vehicle can earn between 1,000 and 4,000 pesos a day, deducting the cost of fuel. Whether he earns the higher or lower amount is dependent on purely random factors.

In general, the majority of those interviewed declared that they earned an average of 2,000 pesos a day, deducting the cost of fuel. This corresponds to a monthly gross income of 50,000 pesos. From this must be deducted the costs of normal upkeep (adding or changing the oil, one tire every three months and so on), which amount to a minimum monthly average of 8,500 pesos. If the taxi operator has no debts and does not have to pay for a license, major repairs following an accident, or more complex repairs, his monthly net income will amount to 41,500 pesos. Some of those interviewed declared that their monthly net income was not more than 15,000 pesos because they had had to pay extra costs.

If taxis are not driven by their owners, the owners must be given a fixed sum of around 1,500 pesos a day. The owner therefore earns approximately 37,500 pesos a month with which he has to pay for maintenance, any repairs, licenses, and so on. After paying for fuel and giving the owner his share, the driver earns between 1,000 and 1,500 pesos a day, or between 20,000 and 37,500 pesos a month, without any other expenditure except for any fines.

The situation of a taxi operator who owns his vehicle and works for a radiotaxi company is different. The operator can make more than 60,000 pesos net a month, paying 30 percent of earnings to the enterprise (30,000 pesos a month) and meeting the costs of fuel and oil. If he has any other important costs, he must pay them himself. Due to the mode of operation of radiotaxis, the cost of fuel represents only 35 percent of earnings, which results in higher profits.

For taxi drivers working in collective taxis, the majority of whom were owners of their vehicles, monthly net earnings varied between 42,500 and 87,500 pesos, depending on the expenditure incurred during the month in question. Gross earnings, deducting fuel costs, showed less fluctuation and, according to the interviews, ranged between 75,000 and 115,000 pesos a month; but the costs of changing the oil, tires, spare parts, books of tickets, and fees for membership in the association have to be deducted in order to obtain net income. The situation was different for one taxi operator, who owned a Peugeot, for which he was still in debt: he had to pay a monthly sum of 65,000 pesos in reimbursement and interest on his debt, which meant that, without taking into account accidents or major breakdowns, his income dropped to 14,000 pesos a month and he therefore fell into arrears, with the risk that his car would be auctioned off.

Based on the analysis of the income situation, it can be concluded, first of all, that there has been a definite drop in the income of taxi operators in Chile since 1978, the year the market was liberalized, and that in 1982, the year of the economic crisis and after semiliberalization of fares, income was even lower than in 1978. In 1988, there was a slight recovery in comparison to 1982, but only in relation to the years prior to 1978.

Second, the net income of owners and drivers fluctuates greatly and, as the interviews revealed, ranges from 15,000 and 87,500 pesos a month. The income depends on the form of operation and random factors such as the sectors in which the taxi works, where it is at peak times, and the number of accidents and major breakdowns. Monthly income also depends on whether the owner of the taxi is in debt or not.

According to estimates by the trade union, there are currently between 6,000 and 7,000 debtors resulting from the various imports of vehicles. Many of them mortgaged their homes to guarantee their credit. This means that if they are unable to reimburse their debts they will not only lose their source of income but also see their homes auctioned off. And there is another problem: the debt was contracted in dollars and presently amounts to three or four times the current value of the vehicle.

Another of the problems faced in this sector is particularly serious for those in debt: no insurance company has agreed to insure vehicles that operate as taxis, so if they have a serious accident they will lose their unique source of income. Compulsory insurance covers only third parties, and the drivers and their passengers are not insured either.

As can be seen, the taxi operators' income does not permit the deduction of costs for maintaining the vehicle or compensation for accidents, nor does it allow them to save or set aside a reserve for depreciation and the possibility of purchasing a new vehicle.

Working conditions

A rapid glance at working conditions shows that, according to the taxi operators' own statements, the decline in their income, combined with the increase in competition, has obliged them to work the maximum possible number of hours and days. On average, operators of collective taxis work between 14 and 16 hours a day, and on Fridays and Saturdays they work up to 20 hours.

Owners of regular taxis work an average of 10 hours a day, except when the vehicle is operated in shifts which can be up to three a day. In shifts, the taxis are driven by family members (who may not possess the necessary license) or by hired drivers. In general, with the exception of large fleets of taxis, drivers do not have a contract, social security, holidays, or days off, and they have to hand over a fixed sum every day to the owner, after having paid for the fuel themselves. The owner's share has to be paid even if they have not carried any passengers.

Taxi operators, including owners, are not usually affiliated with any social insurance system. Following repeal of Law No. 15,722, which prescribed their affiliation to the special workers' fund, they have not generally joined any fund.

The foregoing leads to another important point, according to those interviewed: retirement is rare or nonexistent, so they are obliged to work the maximum possible number of years, without contemplating the idea of retiring at a particular age or when they have health problems.

Quality of service

From the discussion above, a number of points emerge that are relevant when analyzing the quality of service. The limited income of taxi operators means that there is no surplus to be used to maintain and repair the vehicle. In their own words, "we consume the vehicle," which means that of all their earnings are devoted to their living costs and those of their families. This is evident in the deterioration of the taxis operating, which have damaged coachwork and interiors and also often have mechanical problems and collision damage, yet are still operating.

Although there was, in fact, a renewal of the taxi stock following the imports in 1978, after ten years these taxis are still operating, and the majority of their owners have large debts and cannot afford to have them repaired. In addition, factors such as long working days and the stress of having to earn enough money every day in order to meet living costs, as well as the fact that older drivers continue to work, have a negative effect on the quality of service. Another very serious problem is that taxis do not carry any insurance for their passengers in case of accident. One aspect that has shown significant improvement in recent years, however, is the reduction in waiting time that has occurred since the number of taxis started to increase.

In the view of the trade union, the quality of service dropped from the moment when the Statute of Professional Driver of a Vehicle for Public Hire was repealed, thereby diminishing professionalism and the confidence that passengers could have in the abilities of the driver.

Synthesis and Conclusions

The main objective of this research was to determine what were the principal changes that occurred in the taxi market following the implementation of liberalization policies in Chile in 1978. The aim was also to define the impact of these policies on fares, entry into and withdrawal from the market, taxi operators' incomes, working conditions, and the quality of service. The hypothesis that served as a departure point was based on the various theoretical approaches used to analyze the situation in the taxi market: on the one hand, the neoliberal view, and on the other, the proregulation view.

The neoclassical theory predicts that, in any market, an increase in supply will lead to a reduction in price and consequently an increase in the consumption of the goods or services supplied. In this way, the increase in supply will benefit consumers as a result of the lowering of prices and will not prejudice the suppliers because their overall income (price x quantity) will remain the same.

Shreiber (1981), in his analysis of the operation of the taxi market, concludes that this market does not function like a "typical" market according to the neoliberal theory and that an increase in the supply of taxis, resulting, for example, from liberalization of access, will not lead to a lowering of fares. Fares are not likely to decrease in this market because of the existence of a geographical lack of synchronization that does not make it profitable to compete in this way. Any individual taxi operator realizes that if he lowers fares he will not be in greater demand than the other taxis because he is not able to inform the public of his lower fares and he cannot satisfy all potential users at the same time. This inflexibility with regard to the lowering of fares, together with an increase in supply, implies a reduction in the rate of effective use of taxis, or a curve of supply of effective trips that is less than the curve of total available trips.

What happens, therefore, is that there are more taxis, but as the number of effective trips does not increase because the price is the same, this larger number of taxis has to share the same amount of total income, and each taxi operator receives a smaller share. The increase in the supply of taxis does not lead to a decrease in fares and consequently does not benefit the consumer; it only reduces the rate of use of taxis and, as a result, the income of each individual operator.

Consequently, the adjustment variables are not fares but the entry of taxis into the market and their withdrawal from the market. According to

Shreiber (1981), the natural trend is toward a low rate of use together with a high fare. If free competition does not function according to the neoliberal theory, it will therefore be necessary to regulate fares as well as entry into and withdrawal from the market.

Summary of Trends in the Market, 1978–1987

Up to 1982, there was a large increase in the stock of taxis and subsequently a gradual reduction. The main events in the market for the period of 1978–1987 are the following:

- Unemployment increased, particularly from 1977 to 1979. Liberalization of entry into the taxi market in 1978 reinforced pressure by the unemployed to enter the market.
- Subsequently, in 1981, there was a vast increase in the stock of taxis. This was not due, however, to increases in profits but to the continuation of high rates of unemployment, which caused the problem of oversupply of taxis. This phenomenon became particularly acute between 1981 and 1982, when the profitability of the service was decreasing and the growth in unemployment led to an increase in the number of taxis.
- Both the level of unemployment and the number of taxis reached their maximum levels in 1982.
- Between 1982 and 1985, unemployment and profitability started to decline. Likewise, the number of vehicles also declined.
- What happened between 1985 and 1986, however, is difficult to interpret: unemployment and profitability increased, yet the number of taxis continued to decrease.

One of the reasons that could explain what happened between 1985 and 1986 is the series of problems that obliged taxi operators in debt to withdraw from the market and sell their vehicles or auction them off, which affected the sector. It is also necessary to take into account the fact that during this period, unlike the situation from 1978 to 1981, the dollar was high and no special measures were taken to promote the import of taxis. It was therefore not as easy to increase the stock of taxis as it had been in the beginning.

The policies implemented from 1978 onward led to an oversupply of taxis, and this had a negative effect on traffic. Taxis are, in fact, the most inefficient means of transport, from the point of view of both the use of road space and consumption of fuel per passenger. In 1982, in the metropolitan region, there were almost seven taxis per 1,000 inhabitants, at a time when, according to estimates, an average of one taxi per 800 or 1,000 inhabitants would have been sufficient to meet needs.

Paul (1982) concluded that, in Chile, this liberalization and greater access to the market had two positive effects resulting from the need to compete: one was the reduction in waiting time for users and the other was an improvement in the quality of service.

Although the reduction in waiting time is beneficial to consumers, greater competition did not lead to an improvement in service. This might have been the case in the beginning, when policies encouraged imports and renewal of the stock of taxis, but the information from this study, especially that on earnings, showed that taxi owners rarely had the necessary resources to maintain their taxis correctly, buy the spare parts required, or carry out repairs when they had major breakdowns or accidents. Moreover, the elimination of the Professional Driver's Statute gives users fewer guarantees concerning the ability and professional experience of the driver.

Together with the increase in the supply of taxis, an important degree of underutilization can be noted. The percentage of occupancy in 1982 and 1983 was 43.8 and 39 percent, respectively. This had an impact on the incomes of taxi operators and on fares, which had been semiliberalized in 1981. Increases in fares in this sector during the period analyzed were much lower than the increases in minibus and taxibus fares. This is because collective taxis, which have freely set fares, started to compete with these other means of mass transport, which in 1978 had much lower fares.

Taxis face very flexible demand, particularly on the part of passengers taking short trips, and it is therefore not feasible to make any substantial increase in the initial hiring charge (the fare per kilometer is fixed by the authorities), due to the possibility that this might reduce still further the rate of use. The fare-fuel price ratio is decreasing, thereby limiting the margin of potential earnings for taxi operators.

From the foregoing, it is not possible to conclude that the relative reduction in the fares of regular and collective taxis was due to increased competition following liberalization, as is the assumption of neoliberal thinking. This could be true to a certain extent for regular taxis, but it does not allow them to maintain their incomes because the rate of use is decreasing. Collective taxis also lowered fares, even though the access of new vehicles was controlled. The question to be asked is whether in 1982 —the year when there was market saturation of taxis and an economic crisis—if controls on access to the market had been reimposed, fares would have risen or would have behaved as they did in a situation of free access.

In our view, the problem is not simply the existence of restrictions and controls on access versus liberalization. It is necessary to analyze when these measures are adopted. In 1982, even though there were restrictions on access, taxi operators could not "monopolistically" increase fares because the point of saturation had been reached in the market and at the same time there was a decrease in purchasing power and national consumption. (A monopoly that wants to encourage an increase in the price of goods can create an artificial situation of scarcity. This is not possible in the case of taxis.)

One interesting element is that, within the public transport framework, taxis are the sector that provides the largest number of jobs.

Another important fact was that, despite liberalization of the market, the state continues to control directly or indirectly the prices of the principal inputs. This is particularly true for the price of fuel, the exchange rate of the dollar, and, as a result, the cost of all imported inputs. The state also imposes heavy duties on fuel and the import of vehicles. In the opinion of taxi operators, this is tantamount to almost total control over the sector's earnings.

Last, the study revealed that when regulations and standards for the market's operation are eliminated, taxi operators tend to create their own rules or ask the authorities to reimpose the previous regulations. This raises doubts regarding the feasibility of applying free market policies when there exists a social group that maintains relatively high levels of organization, constantly seeks to legalize and legitimize its activities through official implementation of standards and regulations, and establishes self-regulatory guidelines.

After analyzing the various aspects highlighted in this study, it can be concluded that during recent years there has been a surplus in the stock of taxis as a result of liberalization of the market, but that this has gone hand-in-hand with low fares, not high fares as predicted by Shreiber (1981). This is not due to the fact that taxi operators have competed among themselves by lowering fares, but rather because readjustments have not been sufficient compared with the higher costs of inputs and the fares of other forms of transport.

Taxi operators have raised fares slowly without competing among themselves and have rapidly reached agreement. This did not take place in a monopoly situation because they would not derive any great benefit from this. Taxi operators' incomes are scarcely sufficient for their needs; they do not even allow them to save nor set aside money to maintain their vehicle correctly or carry out repairs following an accident.

The result of the functioning of the free market has led to underutilization of taxis, but not to a tendency to increase fares, because taxi operators in Chile have faced situations that were not taken into account by Shreiber (1981). These took the form of two serious recessions and the consequent fall in purchasing power, which made taxi operators realize that they could not raise fares excessively.

In fact, a free market has not meant a lowering of fares but a relative reduction, which has to a certain extent benefited users of public transport. However, there is a range within which users of minibuses will not take taxis, however much they lower fares, unless these fares become the same as minibus fares.

The increase in the number of taxis has not benefited taxi operators, and semiliberalized fares have not allowed all the costs entailed in the service to be met. What, then, is the best option for this market: regulation or liberalization?

We consider that there are two types of factors that influence a decision on this question. On the one hand, it is necessary to identify priorities among combating unemployment, environmental pollution, and traffic congestion; benefiting users of taxis; or improving the incomes and working conditions of taxi operators.

Another series of elements to be taken into consideration are those that define the economic situation: high rates of unemployment, scarcity or saturation of taxis, decreases or increases in consumption, high or low costs of imported inputs, and so forth.

Taking into account these options and the different circumstances, there are three possible types of regulation, with a number of permutations. First is control of the entry of new taxis into the market; second, the fixing or liberalization of fares; and last, the adoption of specific regulations, which govern other aspects of the taxi market.

The first conclusion to be drawn is that it is not advisable to eliminate the special regulations that govern taxi service, such as the age of the vehicle, use of taxi meters, and professional driver's licenses, among others. In practice, even during the latest period of liberalization, these standards have not been abolished and they do at least ensure a minimum level of professionalism, quality, and safety of service.

A second conclusion to be drawn from the empirical analysis is that it is not advisable to implement a liberalization policy for entry while at the same time keeping a fixed or semifixed fare rate. This is because, in addition to possible underutilization and external factors (pollution and traffic congestion) resulting from free access, there is also a problem of insufficient earnings for taxi operators. This will jeopardize their standards of living and the quality of service.

The last conclusion contends that a policy of free access must be linked to a *totally freely set fare* (initial hiring charge and fare per kilometer). If some control of the market is desired, this should be done through regulating access. Once the question of access of new taxis has been solved, the state can fix fares, taking into account a realistic cost structure, if it considers that there is a relative scarcity of taxis and they could exercise a monopoly with regard to prices. In the opposite case, if free access is abolished, when the saturation point has been reached then fares can be liberalized. If there are no controls on access and this leads to increased competition, by leaving fare setting free, the taxi operators themselves should be allowed to determine the level of fares and, consequently, their earnings.

If priority is to reduce unemployment, when there is a scarcity of taxis, the solution of liberalizing access to the market will be extremely positive. However, if at the same time as supply increases, the country is going through an economic recession, fixing fares and imposing taxes on fuel, as has occurred, would undoubtedly mean that taxi operators would suffer a reduction in their earnings. Consequently, it is obvious that the operators themselves should determine fare levels, particularly if there is free access. We know that they will not adopt a monopolistic position because the demand for taxis is highly flexible and variable in accordance with economic cycles. Furthermore, when the saturation point is almost reached, taxi owners realize that the market is difficult and they cannot increase fares arbitrarily.

From the point of view of users, the increase in the stock of taxis resulting from liberalization has a positive effect because it reduces waiting time and fares increase less than for other forms of transport. Nevertheless, if fare readjustments are so low that they are not sufficient to pay for the satisfactory maintenance of vehicles, this will start to have a negative effect on the quality of service, which is another reason for liberalizing fares.

Once the saturation point has been reached, if it is perceived that taxis are creating problems of traffic congestion and environmental pollution, it becomes necessary to reimpose measures to control access, at least for a specified period.

At a more specific level, there are a number of proposals on improving the functioning of the taxi market that are of particular interest:

- Trade unions are calling for elimination of the tax on fuel, or for this tax to be used to finance insurance, health care, and similar benefits. At the same time, they ask for the reestablishment of measures to control the entry of new taxis and regulations on the sector.
- Other authors suggest that the problems of lack of synchronization and taxis cruising while empty could be avoided or limited by increasing the number of taxi stands with telephones in large areas where there is little demand, and increasing the number of taxi stands alone in small areas with high demand (Paul, 1982).
- The number of taxi stands should be increased to avoid taxis driving around empty, which would reduce the vehicle's operating costs, pollution, and congestion.
- O'Ryan (1986) points out that, from the point of view of efficacy of this means of transport, it is possible to reduce fuel consumption considerably by maintaining the vehicle properly. Also, its impact on the environment can be reduced if restriction measures are imposed on access, traffic is coordinated, restricted access zones are defined, and taxis are allowed to function only by half-days. This latter measure would be controversial, taking into account the already low levels of taxi operators' earnings.

Together with the above-mentioned measures, there could also be measures on:

- Renegotiating debts;
- The possibility of deducting VAT, as is done for other forms of collective transport; and
- Credit for the maintenance of vehicles.

9

Consequences of the Legal and Regulatory Framework in Peru's Taxi Market

Eliana Chávez

In this chapter an attempt is made to analyze the changes in the functioning of the taxi market in Peru as a result of the urban transport legislation in force and the macroeconomic variables that affect this activity. The analysis commences with a brief description of urban transport in the city of Lima, where the taxi service plays a special role.

The second section explains the current functioning of the taxi service and its different forms of operation, based on a description of the operators, the characteristics of the vehicle stock, the cost structure (both fixed and variable costs), the determinants of fares, and the working conditions of taxi operators, as well as the characteristics of the users.

The third section deals with the effect of the various regulations on the market, from the point of view of both supply and demand. An analysis of the series of regulations that have conditioned market trends since 1968 will be made for this purpose.

Because economic factors also affect the functioning of operators in this market, the fourth section of this chapter analyzes whether economic factors have been the main determinants governing access to and withdrawal from the market.

The final section consists of a series of conclusions on the growth of the taxi market in metropolitan Lima, which center on the hypothesis that, in the case of Peru, the free market, at least as far as taxis are concerned, does not guarantee satisfactory service and it is therefore indispensable to elaborate control measures that will provide a minimum of security, for both the driver and the user.

Description of the Urban Transport Service and its Implications for the Taxi Market

The transport system in Lima is chaotic. The demand for transport in the city is constituted by six million person-trips per day; 74 percent of these are by public transport and 26 percent by private car. However, the total number of private cars amounts to 72 percent (250,000 vehicles), whereas public transport vehicles represent only 3 percent (11,000 vehicles).

Regarding supply in relation to distribution of the total stock of vehicles for public transport of passengers in metropolitan Lima, in 1984 the formal supply was made up of forty-two bus routes, whose relative importance in meeting demand was 5 percent; illegal supply consisted of minibuses, collective taxis, and regular taxis, which represented more than 90 percent of the total stock (Table 9.1).

The analysis undertaken shows that there are five main problems concerning the transport service in Lima.

Unsatisfied Demand

Regarding the supply-demand relationship, the increasingly rapid decrease in the stock of vehicles, on the one hand, and the high rate of growth of demand, on the other, meant that in 1984 unsatisfied demand amounted to 4,000 trips per day. If the same conditions of reduced supply continued unsatisfied demand would amount to 6,000 trips per day in 1990.

Lack of Planning

The Lima public transport service does not respond to any rational criterion due to lack of adequate planning of the system, which means that distribution of the service over the whole urban area is unsatisfactory. There are contradictions between the horizontal growth of the city, the large pockets of population to be served, and a public transport system that does not

Table 9.1 Distribution of Total Stock of Vehicles Available for Public Transport of Passengers in Metropolitan Lima

	Stock of Vehicles	Relative Importance (percentage)
Formal supply	1,391	5.2
Illegal supply	25,099	94.8
Minibuses	12,464	
Collective taxis	2,373	
Regular taxis and vehicles		
For hire[a]	10,262	
Total	26,490	100

Source: Urban Transport Directorate and Metropolitan Urban Transport Office. Ministry of Transport and Communications. Taken from the Institute for Liberty and Democracy, 1988.
[a]Associations, private, and pirate vehicles.

correspond to the quantitative characteristics. In a city with six million inhabitants, there is no mass transport that serves as an axis for the system.

Inappropriate Legislation

For at least the last thirty years there have been no satisfactory regulations on the transport service. The regulations that existed have been only partial and in many cases have not been complied with, particularly by buses, minibuses, and taxis. This is due to a large extent to lack of control and the adoption of regulations that are in many cases inoperative.

Lack of Technical Criteria in the Fixing of Fares

For the last fifteen years, fares have not allowed the real cost of transport—between six and eight centavos per kilometer—to be defrayed. Combined with other factors, this has resulted in an obsolete stock of vehicles that lack the minimum technical specifications to operate, and an increased degree of risk for users. Fares have been the result of urban transport subsidies rather than technical studies due to the low salaries and the pressure exerted by the population with regard to increases in mass transport fares.

Limited State Participation

The state has always played a limited role in establishing "conditions of security," fixing the numbers of imported vehicles and spare parts, granting concessions on routes, and fixing the fares for buses and minibuses. Even though the fare in centavos is low, it remains constant as a result of regulation. The state share of the mass transport supply is only 11 percent.

Description of the Taxi Market and Modes of Functioning

The functioning of the taxi market is not exempt from the reference framework described above. Of the public transport vehicles registered in the metropolitan area, 7 percent are taxis, of which 90 percent are not registered with the Ministry of Transport and Communications. The Lima taxi market functions in total freedom, and this has been particularly true for the past ten years. There are no restrictions on the entry of new operators, and the service is chaotic, obsolete, and unsafe.

The change from a policy of relative control (in 1968–1975) to one of unplanned deregulation (in 1975–1988) has had the following effects:

- A number of operators whose vehicles do not fulfill the minimum safety requirements for transport vehicles have access to the market. This is reflected in the deterioration of the stock of vehicles, whose average age in 1973 was four years and in 1988 was twelve years.
- The number of pirate operators, who know nothing about the profession of taxi driver has increased significantly. The proportion of taxi "comités" (associations), as well as independent drivers who represent organized operators, in the market has fallen year by year.
- Drivers are uneducated regarding operating costs: fares are fixed in accordance with the driver's need for a personal income rather than technical criteria, except for the price of fuel which, as will be seen later, is the only item in the cost structure taken into account by drivers when fixing the price of a trip, defined as one journey by taxi.
- The trade union organization has disintegrated.
- Quality and safety in the service are nonexistent.
- The status of taxi drivers as a job category has deteriorated.
- The quality of life and earnings of taxi operators has decreased. This is due to a number of reasons, which are linked to the effects changes in entry barriers have had on their incomes and other variables resulting from economic crises.

The economic crises, inflation, increases in fuel prices, the scarcity of spare parts, and the higher cost of vehicles, as well as the deterioration of the population's income in real terms and the increase in unemployment and underemployment, are economic and social factors that play important roles in explaining the changes that have taken place in this market's functioning.

Trend in the Number of Taxis

The first problem faced when analyzing the taxi market in Peru is the difficulty of obtaining information on the volume of supply, due to the lack of an appropriate register, the change in the institutions responsible for regulating the system, and the high percentage of unregistered operators.

As Table 9.2 shows, during the period 1970–1975, the number of operators grew slowly. The first reason for this was the barriers imposed by the competent authorities on access to the market; the second reason was the pressure exerted by the drivers' organization against the entry of new operators; and the third, probably the relative economic stability of earnings and employment that characterized this period, which meant that the taxi market did not constitute an activity that was attractive to newcomers.

Since 1975, the stock of taxis and consequently the number of operators started to increase year by year; 1978 and the period 1983–1984 showed the

Table 9.2 Evolution of the Number of Taxis in Metropolitan Lima, 1970–1986

Years	Number of Taxis	Rate of Growth (in percent)
1970	2,800	
1971	3,240	
1972	3,320	
1973	3,427	
1974	3,521	
1975	4,000	
1976	4,300	7.5
1977	4,447	3.4
1978	6,300	41.7
1979	6,520	3.5
1980	6,781	4.0
1981	7,869	16.0
1982	7,510	4.6
1983	8,837	17.7
1984	10,260	16.1
1985	10,400	1.4
1986	10,530	1.3

Source: Ministry of Labor (1970–1980); Ministry of Transport and Communications (1981–1984); and Lima Municipal Authority (1985, 1986).

highest rate of increase, coinciding with the periods of the greatest economic crises.

Characteristics of the Stock of Vehicles

If one looks at the composition of the stock by type of vehicle, one can see the significant changes that have taken place over the past twenty years, which are related not only to the type of vehicle but also to the wear and tear caused by long use and the state of maintenance of the vehicles. The main problem is the length of time during which vehicles in the taxi service are used. During the period 1968–1975, the owners of the vehicles themselves provided the service and they therefore had an interest in ensuring good maintenance and in replacing vehicles after periods considered the optimum for good functioning (two or three years). However, since the mid-1970s (when the market was fully liberalized), the new operators, with their own forms of internal organization, lost interest in the efficient functioning of the service and exclusively concerned themselves with immediate interests in order to satisfy minimum needs. This was expressed in the purchase of secondhand vehicles and in behavior that had a greater emphasis on obtaining economic profits, even when it meant sacrificing good maintenance.

It should also be pointed out that these changes took place within the framework of far-reaching qualitative changes in economic policy, which meant adjustments in the prices of key elements for the functioning of the taxi market, such as the price of fuel, vehicles, and spare parts, as well as a process of deterioration of the population's income in real terms.

Methods of Operation

Taxi drivers in Peru operate mainly according to two methods, which can be defined as "organized" and "unorganized."

Organized taxi operators

The number of taxi operators who can be defined as organized has decreased in recent years, partly as a result of greater competition, but also because of the limited incentives to renew the stock of vehicles that have been noted since 1980, when the policy of exemption or special benefits for this sector of activity was modified. This service functions in various zones of the city and is the safest for users. It is made up of professional drivers with many years of service, who are the only ones to charge fares they have fixed themselves on the basis of technical criteria that include as a minimum variables that explain the cost structure. In other words, they do not only take into account the free play of supply and demand.

The method of operation of organized taxi drivers includes membership in taxi associations. Each association has a common fund from which it pays parking fees, health and insurance funds, and other benefits. Each member pays monthly dues to the fund. There is a common taxi stand with a telephone, and this is the departure point from which they cover the entire metropolitan Lima. Their fares are on average 50 percent above those of independent drivers. There are currently thirty associations, almost 50 percent fewer than in 1978.

Remisse is a service for hotels and the airport, which has modern cars up to about three years old. The rates are in dollars and are on average 300 percent higher than those of independent drivers. In 1980, independent drivers with an official license numbered more than taxi drivers belonging to an association. Both constitute a minority of the total number of taxis in the city. The majority of these belong to the drivers' federation, and this service is their main activity.

Unorganized taxi operators

Taxi drivers designated as unorganized or pirates, make up the largest number, and this number has grown rapidly in the last ten years. Among pirate taxi drivers, there are various forms, namely, *palancas*, those with no official licenses who work full time as independent drivers with their own cars, and independent pirate taxi drivers.

A *palanca* taxi driver works for a taxi company whose owner is not legally registered. The owner usually hires out very old and badly maintained cars to the *palanca* for a fixed daily sum and for a predetermined number of hours of work. The driver has to pay for fuel, but maintenance of the vehicle is the responsibility of the owner. The work of the *palanca* is very difficult and stressful because he has to pay the owner's share and also earn enough to pay his family's daily needs. Naturally, when a *palanca* is unable to work, either because the car has broken down or he is ill, he earns nothing. The fixing of fares responds more to the need to earn an income to meet needs than to other technical criteria. Apparently, it is this type of driver who distorts fares and causes instability in the market. In addition, the owner of the enterprise has no interest in training his *palancas* with the aim of providing better service because his sole objective is to exploit the vehicle to the maximum in order to obtain higher profits. According to *palanca* drivers, a car hired for 12 hours costs the drivers 1,600 intis a day (US$12), which must be handed over on the same day; the rest of the money earned constitutes the driver's income.

A second type of unorganized taxi operator is a taxi driver who works full time as an independent driver with his own car but does not have an official license. In the majority of cases, such a driver has no car insurance and no common support fund for cases of emergency.

A third very common group is that of independent pirate taxi drivers, whose main occupation is as an employee, generally for the state, and who uses his car as an additional source of income in his spare time. As a result of the depreciation of real income (as an employee), the money he makes as a taxi driver can be greater than that he receives from his main job. These drivers do not, however, leave their main job because the income and social protection it provides are a secure element of family income. Their incorporation in the taxi market is a permanent feature, but only during peak hours (6:00–9:00 A.M.) and at night; these hours do not interfere with their work as civil servants, but they do affect productivity.

Lastly, it should be emphasized that although there is not apparently any great degree of rivalry or aggressiveness between illegal taxis and those who have obtained their licenses, the professional operators do complain that the pirates debase the profession.

Costs

An analysis of the cost structure is fundamental for determining fares and consequently for the possibility of replacing vehicles. The belief concerning the functioning of the taxi service in a free market is that fares are far above the real costs of the service. According to the present study, taxi drivers in Peru do not use criteria related to real costs when fixing fares; their parameters are more linked to social variables (related to the satisfaction of basic needs). This latter aspect determines the existence of wide-ranging variations among fares for the same journey and implies a pattern of supply and demand through negotiating the fare with the user. As will be seen later, this has negative effects for both the taxi driver and the user.

In analyzing costs, it is necessary to differentiate between those that are fixed and variable, using the following parameters: technical specifications of the vehicle; characteristics of the service; payment of the labor force; consumption and fuel yield, tires, and oil; general expenditures; and application of different fares.

Fixed costs

The labor force. To calculate the cost of the labor force, the information obtained from the survey of taxi drivers and from the Ministry of Labor has been used. The wage level of taxi drivers is similar to that of short-distance lorry drivers and bus drivers, and almost 40 percent less than that of long-distance lorry drivers (Table 9.3). The daily wage of taxi drivers and the general wages of workers not benefiting from collective negotiation are similar. But compared to total average wages, taxi drivers earn less (Table 9.4). The wages do not include social benefits, bonuses, or gratuities.

Contrary to the prevalent view that taxi drivers are a privileged category, the incomes of taxi drivers have greatly decreased as a result of their inability to control factors related to real costs when fixing fares and their lack of control over continually rising prices, which have a direct effect on costs.

A large number of civil servants have joined the taxi market in order to earn an extra income over and above their main job. They are not concerned with fixing viable fares because this is only a temporary job compared to their principal activity. This explains the irrationality of fares and the pressure exerted when there are proposals to fix fares.

Depreciation. The cost of depreciation is a very important variable for taxis. However, the taxi operators interviewed declared that they did not take this criterion into consideration when fixing fares nor did they economize to replace the vehicle. When the car has finished its useful life, whose average length in real terms is fourteen years, these operators face considerable difficulty in replacing it.

On the basis of a calculation made by technicians from the Ministry of Transport and Communications to estimate the value of depreciation, hourly depreciation was 3.50 intis (in 1986) in the case of a new vehicle. The fact

Table 9.3 Wage by Job Category (February 1986)

Category	Type of Service	Monthly Wage	
		Intis	US$
B-2	Car (taxi)	1,136.30	81.46
C[a]	Lorry	1,197.89	85.47
D	Bus	1,262.87	90.53
E[b]	Lorry	1,838.21	131.77

Source: Commission on the Regulation of Transport Fares, 1986.
[a]Short distance service with a trailer of less than 750 kilograms.
[b]Long-distance service with a trailer of more than 750 kilograms.

Table 9.4 Comparative Wages (June 1985–February 1986)

Period	Daily Wage Taxis		General Wages Without Collective Bargaining		Total General Wages	
	US$	Intis	US$	Intis	US$	Intis
June 1985	2.20	23.69	n.a.	n.a.	n.a.	n.a.
July 1985	2.09	24.83	n.a.	n.a.	n.a.	n.a.
August 1985	2.15	30.05	2.43	33.87	2.98	41.58
October 1985	2.20	30.65	2.35	32.78	3.32	46.45
February 1986	2.72	37.88	2.61	36.37	3.82	53.27
Correlation coefficient			0.92		0.94	

Source: Commission on the Regulation of Transport Fares, 1986.
n.a.=not available

that this sum is not taken into account when drivers fix fares affects replenishment of the stock of vehicles.

Profits. Taxi operators do not estimate their profits; the amount they earn is considered to be gross income, from which daily costs (particularly food and fuel) have to be deducted and the remainder used to meet their needs. Very few taxi drivers said they economized, even to meet such important variable costs as spare parts and oil.

The Commission on the Regulation of Transport Fares estimated that the profit of a taxi operator using a new Volkswagen in 1986 was 7,452.80 intis (US$534.25) annually and hourly costs were 2.70 intis.

Variable costs

Variable costs include fuel, oil, tires, spare parts, and repairs. Their amount is estimated as shown on Table 9.5. On average, total costs are 54,504 intis per hour, 31,788 intis per hour representing variable costs, and 22,716 intis per hour representing fixed costs. The most important items are fuel (~25 percent), spare parts (~28 percent) and labor (~15 percent).

Fixing Fares

In the functioning of the taxi market, fixing the amount of fares is of primary importance, for both users and taxi operators. For the user, the possibility of access depends on the price of the journey; for the taxi operator, the fare is his pay—the means to meet family needs and to pursue this activity.

In Peru, two basic elements have characterized the fixing of fares: (1) the state has not intervened in any way in the fixing of fares; and (2) contrary to the belief that free competition among taxis will lead to an acceptable price, with a tendency to higher fares, the Peruvian situation has shown that the interaction of supply and demand appears to indicate a trend toward lowering of fares and unsatisfactory prices (especially in the long term).

As far as the actual fixing of fares is concerned, it corresponds to the

Table 9.5 Structure of Costs for Taxis, 1986

Item	Cost per Hour		Cost per Kilometer		Percentage of Total Cost
	Intis	US$	Intis	US$	
Fuel	13,638	0.98	0.544	0.04	25.02
Oil and filters	1,930	0.14	0.077	0.01	3.54
Tires and inner tubes	1,103	0.08	0.044	0.01	2.02
Spare parts and repairs	15,117	1.08	0.603	0.04	27.74
Subtotal	31,788	2.28	1.268	0.10	58.32
Labor	8,390	0.60	0.335	0.02	15.39
General expenditure	2,680	0.19	0.107	0.01	4.92
Depreciation	4,169	0.30	0.166	0.01	7.65
Financing	478	0.03	0.019	0.00	0.88
Insurance	4,289	0.31	0.171	0.01	7.87
Profit	2,710	0.19	0.108	0.01	4.97
Subtotal	22,716	1.62	0.906	0.06	41.68
Total cost	54,504	3.90	2.174	0.16	100.00

Source: Commission on the Regulation of Transport Fares, 1986.

characteristics of the different forms of operation. There is no general pattern that can serve as a reference for the fixing of fares.

In determining the amount of fares, drivers organized in associations use technical criteria, including operational costs and the expenditures entailed by their organization (common fund, telephone, insurance, and so on). This is why their prices are more than 50 percent greater than the prices fixed by pirate taxis.

Drivers working in the *Remisse* system fix their fares in accordance with international rates and the dollar exchange rate. As already mentioned, their rates are 300 percent higher than average.

Palanca taxi drivers fix their prices by adding the price of fuel, as a basic criterion, and the amount they have to pay to the owner every day. The need to earn a minimum wage incites them to utilize other criteria in fixing fares. This often means lowering fares in order to make more trips and spend less time empty, or fixing the fare according to the customer.

Independent taxi drivers who pursue this activity as a second job fix prices in accordance with the price of fuel plus a percentage for personal income. For example, for a short trip (two kilometers) the fixed price is the cost of a gallon of fuel plus 50 percent for other costs and to cover the driver's needs. This form of fixing prices covers only 75 percent of costs in accordance with the cost structure shown in Table 9.5, which in the long term means the withdrawal of operators from the market, deterioration of the stock of vehicles, and a decline in the quality of service due to the difficulties of replacement. Nevertheless, in the long term, the withdrawal of operators from the market is determined by trends toward increases in real wages because it is not the fare that increases supply but rather the need for supplementary income in order not to see a decline in the standard of living.

When journeys are longer, other criteria govern the fixing of fares: time, traffic congestion, distance, the possibility of finding a return fare, and knowledge of the area, among other factors.

Very few of the unorganized taxi drivers refer to the cost of spare parts, oil, tires, or other costs when determining prices. The cost analysis shows that these are determinant elements, but drivers include them only marginally.

Depreciation is not a factor taken into account by drivers when determining prices either. Their concerns are usually focused on short-term problems.

On the basis of the fare analysis, it can be concluded that taxi operators do not utilize technico-economic criteria when determining the fare for the journeys they make. The effects of this situation are negative for the taxi operator, whose income in real terms has declined over a period, and for the user, who sees a decline in the quality of service because, to a significant extent, the vehicles do not fulfill the minimum conditions necessary to function at an adequate level of safety.

As far as users are concerned, free fixing of fares by taxi operators has a negative effect because they are not able to verify whether the price is correct. To check the price, they would have to obtain and compare prices for two or three taxis. This would involve other variables such as the cost of the possibility of finding another taxi and the waiting time this implies. Also, it turns out that if the user does not ask the price before taking the taxi, the fare will usually increase by at least 30 percent.

Trade Union Organization

Trade unions have played a very important direct role in obtaining exemptions or benefits and an indirect role in ensuring a better quality of service. The drivers' organization to which the taxi drivers' trade union belongs was established following the problems in the 1960s, which affected the functioning of the transport system in general.

In the 1970s, the union gained considerable strength and became the spokesman for transporters vis-à-vis the government. Its demands on behalf of the taxi sector mainly focus on the possibility of obtaining exemption from taxes on spare parts and vehicles.

As a result of trade union activity, fares are more equitable and respond to technical criteria.

Drivers belonging to the federation (in the case of taxis) provide a better service because they know the routes, offer more stable prices on the basis of more technical criteria, know their customers better, and respect traffic rules. They attend training courses on highway safety and so provide a better service.

For political and economic reasons, the drivers' organization started to deteriorate in the 1980s, particularly for taxis. The growth in the illegal supply of taxis was one of the factors that led to the decrease in the organization's strength and in its ability to serve as a reference point for the functioning of the system.

Working Conditions

With the exception of drivers in the *Remisse* service, who constitute less than 10 percent of the total, working conditions have greatly worsened. Social protection is at a minimum and occupational hazards are at a maximum.

The level of social security registration is very low for the following reasons: (1) the service provided by social insurance is increasingly inefficient; (2) registration means loss of time waiting to be attended to; (3) registration implies a cost deemed to be high in comparison to income; and (4) for cultural reasons, drivers feel safer going to healers rather than medical services, although in many cases the cost is the same or even higher.

In addition, there is an increasing risk of work-related accidents due to the fact that vehicles are generally poorly maintained; road signs are deficient; streets are in a bad state of repair (studies carried out by the Municipal Authority show that there are more than 15,000 potholes in Lima); no safety regulations exist for the driver; spare parts are increasingly difficult to obtain; drivers often travel without spare tires, indicators, hazard lights, or windscreens due to lack of control and high prices; and assaults are increasingly frequent. In Peru, being a driver is considered to be a high-risk activity.

Users

According to users, the taxi service has serious deficiencies and is unsafe. The most important problems cited include the following:

- The vehicles are unsafe and do not carry proper identification. The only identification is a colored plastic notice on the windscreen reading "TAXI," which can be taken down at any moment. The vehicles are not of any special color that allows them to be identified and ensures security for those who use them. Many taxis (the majority pirate taxis) have no headlights, damaged doors, no rearview mirrors, and tires in bad condition with no spare.
- Taxi drivers do not habitually state the price of a journey. If the user does not ask prior to the trip, it is likely that the taxi driver will ask for a much higher fare. The cost of trips varies from taxi to taxi.
- Taxi drivers do not carry out their jobs properly. In many cases, they do not have small change; if the user does not have the exact amount, the driver will stop at a fuel pump or street stall to change money, resulting in a waste of time for driver and passenger.
- Taxi drivers do not know their way around the city and in many cases do not have maps or plans, so they waste time looking for a destination. There are areas of the city where taxi drivers do not want to go.
- There are no professional training programs. Drivers do not take proper care of their customers.
- Because there is no alternative mass transport system or an efficient control system, drivers neglect service and users have to accept it.
- The user is constantly in danger, not only because of the traffic problems mentioned above, which also affect the driver, but because

drivers go at high speeds in order to save time and make more trips, and they violate traffic rules.
- Association taxis are the safest on the market, but they are not sufficient to meet demand and their market is an exclusive one because the cost of a trip is more than 50 percent above that for pirate taxis (according to the Committee on the Regulation of Transport Fares, 1986).

Effect of Legislation on the Performance of the Taxi Market

The analysis of the performance of operators in the taxi market given above provides the necessary elements to explain the effects of changes in the legal framework for access and withdrawal of operators, fares, and the quality of service.

The Legal Framework, its Regulations and its Effects on the Taxi Market During the Period 1968–1987

Institutions

The institutions responsible for laying down standards for the functioning of the taxi service are the Ministry of Finance and Trade up to 1969, when the Ministry of Transport and Communications was created; the Ministry of Transport and Communications up to 1979, when the new Constitution of the Republic stipulated that regulations on overland transport should be the responsibility of the Municipal Authorities; and the Lima Municipal Authority, in effect since 1984.

Classification of Regulations

The overland transport legislation applicable to the taxi service is composed of three types of regulations: (1) permanent regulations, whose objective is to regulate and control the entry of operators into the system; (2) transitional regulations and fiscal exemptions whose objective is to improve the quality of service; and (3) proposals on restructuring of the service which are aimed at greater security for the user and improvement of quality.

Basic legislation

The regulations termed basic legislation are made up of a series of minimum requirements whose objective is to control the entry of new operators into the market. These requirements have not been modified for more than thirty years and are not always met by operators in the system. The regulations require registration as transporters with the Ministry of Transport and Communications. Only association, *Remisse*, or independent taxi operators whose main and unique activity is the taxi service register with the ministry. These represent approximately 10 percent of the total supply in the taxi market.

Despite the fact that the following measures are practically indispensable for entering the market, they have not functioned as adjustment mechanisms due to the lack of effective control.

- Use of the transporter's plaque. Only about 10 percent of the taxi market uses this special plaque.
- Professional driver's license. Only 50 percent of the operators apply for this license; the others have only a private driver's license and it is likely that some drivers have no license at all.
- Regulations on violations. Controls for the payment of violations occur only when the police decide to round up cars or when, after an accident, the driver has to go to the police station.

  Since 1985, within the framework of a strategy on global restructuring of the system, the regulation and control of violations has become more efficient. The cost of violations has increased sharply and a new system has emerged (to prevent bribery) whereby the police receive 30 percent of the amount of a fine. The fine must be paid within twenty-four hours to avoid an additional 20 percent penalty.

  The mechanism implemented has slowed down violations and has provided the Municipal Transport Secretariat with increased revenue. It has also improved the service in terms of road safety. The increase in the cost of fines has not affected the rate of fares because drivers do not include it as a variable price indicator;

- Regulations on roadworthiness tests. The objective of these tests is to control the general state of vehicles that use the roads so as to improve the road safety system. Since 1970 these tests have been carried out by private concessionaires on the basis of standards laid down by the state.

  The carrying out of roadworthiness tests (twice a year for taxis) was controlled very strictly by the authorities. However, for the last two or three years and most likely due to the scarcity of spare parts on the market, a new informal and unlawful activity has grown up around the centers where the tests take place: the hiring out of spare parts (tires, headlights, rearview mirrors, and so on) solely for the purpose of passing the test. As a result, this regulation no longer fulfills the purpose for which it was created, namely, to guarantee a better transport service in the city.

At the same time, transporters complain that, due to the lack of spare parts, they are not in a position to take the test[1]. In 1986, the Lima Municipal Authority decided to suspend the tests following pressure by transporters. The lack of interest on the part of the Municipal Urban Transport Secretariat in structuring and regulating this service also played an important role in this decision.

Regulations on exemptions and the fiscal regime affecting the taxi service

For a better understanding of the effects of tax legislation on the taxi market, it is necessary to distinguish four periods, corresponding to important qualitative changes in terms of economic policy and fiscal legislation.

1968–1975. Between 1968 and 1975, a serious attempt was made in the legislative field to regulate and improve the overland transport service, particularly taxi service. This involved a series of measures: (1) the Ministry of Transport and Communications was set up in 1969; (2) an effort was made to improve the stock of vehicles, which was facing a considerable crisis as a result of the rise in the price of vehicles and spare parts; and (3) an attempt was made to strengthen the transporters' trade union within the framework of a policy on strengthening trade union participation.

In 1968, for example, faced with the difficult situation of transporters in public services as a result of the rise in operating costs, a Transport Front (Frente Unico de Transporte) was created to find a solution to the problem, in collaboration with the government. This was followed by the adoption of a number of regulations on fiscal exemptions, which can be summarized as follows:

- For public transporters and their trade unions, exemption from payment of fiscal debts contracted with the government for taxes, transfers of vehicles, and vehicle tax (S.D. No. 260-68 HC);
- Exemption from minor levies;
- Reduction of 15 percent in import duties on motors, spare parts, and car accessories (S.D. 260-68);
- Exemption from taxes on the purchase of spare parts by cooperative associations and transport trade unions (1968);
- A two year period, exempt from all levies, for the purchase of vehicles assembled in Peru by cooperatives and/or associations and/or transporters' trade unions (1970);
- An authorization for a period of two years to associations, cooperatives, and trade unions to import, on behalf of their members, free from all duty, complete vehicles or parts needed to carry on their activities, provided that similar vehicles or parts are not produced in

Peru or that they do not compete with those produced domestically (1971); and
- Exemption from payment of property tax for the purchase and sale of property acquired by public transport enterprises, trade unions, or associations for garages, workshops, terminals, or similar enterprises.

This policy of support for the improvement of the stock of vehicles continued up to 1975 through decree laws, which extended the concessions granted mainly between 1968 and 1971. The policy had a number of effects on the taxi market. First, it strengthened the organization of transporters because it was possible to benefit from the laws only through these organizations. In the case of taxi operators, this was the period in which the secretariat was strongest. According to information given by the Drivers' Federation, during this period the number of transporters in the taxi service increased from 800 to more than 3,000 members.

The supply of operators did not grow at such a high rate as in subsequent periods. The laws on fiscal exemptions, linked to the suspension of authorizations for the functioning of new operators, limited the market.

The supply of this service by transporters belonging to the Federation of Transporters and registered with the Committee on the Regulation of Transport Fares constituted 70 percent of the total, according to the drivers. During this period, the volume of illegal supply was less, compared to the number of registered drivers; transporters complied with the order to attach proof of registration on the car, which was already a guarantee of greater safety in this service.

With regard to fares, the state did not intervene in the fixing of fares, which were subject to the free play of supply and demand. However, operators who largely belonged to the Drivers' Federation fixed fares in accordance with criteria previously discussed within the organization. These fares then constituted the reference for all the operators.

As far as quality of service was concerned, the effect of the policy of fiscal exemptions and the role played by the drivers' organization as the coordinating axis for operators in the system had positive results, which were expressed in modernization of the stock of vehicles, compliance with basic standards, safety for the user, and stable prices.

1975–1980. During the period from 1975 to 1980, the legal framework and economic policy were directed at reversing the trend toward support for the transport sector in the form of exemptions. This also meant that the participation and promotion of organizations in the development of the sector was also attenuated.

During this period, only two provisions affected the taxi market:

- The creation of a transporters' register, a provision that had no impact on the market because it was not part of a global development plan for the system and there were no effective controls;
- Approval of the constitution in 1979, which made the Lima Municipal Authority responsible for regulating public transport, traffic, and transit.

As a consequence of this policy of deregulating the market and eliminating exemptions, the supply of pirate taxis and illegal enterprises not linked to the organization of transporters grew; there was a sharp decline in the quality of service; and fares rose and became diversified with the breakup of the fare structure informally imposed by the drivers' organization. The macroeconomic context in which these policies were implemented was that of a liberal policy characterized by the application of price adjustment policies, which affected incomes and the population's living standards.

It is therefore not easy to determine whether the legal framework or the effects of the economic policy, or both, were the variables that determined the changes noted in the market in fares and quality of service. As shall be discussed later, it is likely that in Peru the variables that play the major role in determining the market's performance are economic variables.

1980–1985. In 1980, legislation on urban transport and the taxi system centered on two areas: (1) adoption of Decree Law No. 23,172 on fiscal exemptions and tariff reductions for the acquisition of vehicles for transport, including taxis, for a period of one year; and (2) obligation to use taxi meters so as to control the taxi system, reduce the number of illegal taxis, and improve service, as well as guaranteeing controlled fares to users.

Neither measure had the expected effects. In the case of fiscal exemptions, these affected a large number of transporters belonging to the Drivers' Federation, but had little weight in terms of the total number of transporters so they had no visible impact on supply. The obligation to use a taxi meter was a measure that, because of its control capacity, was accepted by many drivers (more than 2,000 taxis used a meter), but it did not have the anticipated effects because the taxi meters imported did not last for more than six months, there was no import system for spare parts, and the taxi operators felt they had been cheated.

During this period, the number of taxis grew at the highest rate since 1970. Here again, it is not possible to determine whether the deregulation policy or the economic crisis that affected Peru in 1982–1983 were the variables that best explain the growth in the illegal supply, the variations in fares, and the deterioration in the quality of service.

At the beginning of 1985,[2] the Municipal Authority established the Municipal Urban Transport Secretariat and, as part of a program to develop the public transport service, decided to regulate the taxi service. Following Order No. 003 in 1985, the following measures were adopted:

- Reregistration of all drivers of public transport vehicles, including drivers without vehicles;
- The obligation to be a professional driver in order to drive a public service vehicle;
- Compulsory use of a taxi meter;
- The obligation to pass a roadworthiness test twice a year; and
- The obligation to exhibit the transporters' registration on the vehicle.

This order came into force and started to be implemented in the middle of 1985.

The first measure—reregistration—was relatively successful. The next measure—use of the taxi meter—gave rise to animated discussion among taxi operators and users. As was expected, professional taxi operators and members of associations—in other words, those whose work as a driver was their main job—accepted use of the taxi meter as well as other measures to control growth in the informal supply. Drivers not registered with the municipal transport register, supported by one sector of transporters, did not agree to use of the taxi meter. After a heated discussion, the Municipal Authority imposed use of the meter and proposed to facilitate its purchase through staggered payments.[3] The new regulations, combined with global measures, did not have the expected effects due to changes in municipal administration which, as will be seen next, led to a total reversal of the approach to the problem.

1986–1988. From 1986 onward, with the new Municipal Authority, a policy of full-scale deregulation was initiated, suspending the previous authority's efforts to restructure the market. The deregulation policy affects the market, fares, and quality of service. Regarding the market, the following effects occur:

- The entry of part-time drivers is encouraged. Part-time drivers are the most inefficient, do not know the streets and traffic rules, and represent unsafe service.
- The inexistence of entry barriers means that the cost of entering the market is close to zero. The purchase of a plastic card with the word "TAXI" is the only requirement for those who wish to join the system, because not even the basic rules regarding safety measures are controlled.
- There is saturation of vehicles during peak traffic periods, which also coincides with peak hours for taxis and in turn leads to even greater congestion.

- The trade union organization is losing authority and has practically disappeared.

By opening up new opportunities for access to the different forms of the system, the deregulation policy has resulted in a greater fare differential for the same journey. In view of the great difference in price, the consumer will prefer to pay a lower price, even though this means a longer waiting time, particularly in Peru where there is no alternative (*liebres* collective or rapid means of transport), unlike other countries.

The only criterion used by drivers to calculate fares is the price of fuel. However, this can have negative effects in the long term because of the high cost of spare parts and replacing the vehicle, whose cost is not included in the fare, and this can end in withdrawal from the market.

It should be emphasized that it is difficult to imagine a similar service in other countries due to its deplorable conditions. In recent years, it has become increasingly common to see taxis that do not fulfill even the minimum safety requirements regarding spare tires, windscreens, unbroken windows, and rearview mirrors, and taxis that are not registered.

Together with the lack of control, this problem is exacerbated by the scarcity of spare parts, which has brought to a standstill almost 20 percent of the stock of vehicles, thereby seriously affecting the urban transport service (buses, minibuses, and taxis) in Peru.

Economic and Social Policies and the Taxi Market

In this section, a study is made of the effect of various economic policy measures on the performance of operators in the system with regard to access to and withdrawal from the market and the fixing of fares. These constitute important elements, which together determine operation of the market, although in many cases independently of the regulatory system. The trend in the economic cycle, the fluctuations in the price of fuel, the tariff policy, and the employment situation are considered.

Economic Cycles and the Taxi Market[4]

Between 1970 and 1975, the secondary sector developed without the support of the primary sector. Production grew at an annual average rate of 6.4 percent, whereas exports grew at −4.0 percent. Measures such as subsidies on imported foodstuffs, price control of basic foodstuffs and the maintenance of a fixed exchange rate led to both internal and external imbalances. The earnings and incomes of independent workers recovered during these years, and aggregate demand increased.

This led to inflation with temporary growth and indebtedness to increase national reserves due to lack of foreign currency. This economic environment created the need for higher incomes to meet the increased cost of living. The population working in the taxi sector increased slowly as a result of the effects of these factors.

During the 1975–1978 recession, exports rose rapidly; however, import of inputs by the private sector also grew, thus exacerbating the imbalance in the balance of payments. Between 1976 and 1978, an effort was made to readjust the balance of payments through devaluation, and floating exchange rates were abandoned. In addition, the private sector lacked credit because it was monopolized by the public sector, and this led to a recession in the economy. These factors caused increases in the rates of underemployment and unemployment, which in turn resulted in an increase in the number of persons working in the taxi sector.

During this period, wages decreased in real terms, making it necessary to undertake another activity, whether complementary or not, in order to maintain or earn an income that would allow continuation of a decent standard of living. In 1978, the number of taxis increased by more than 40 percent compared with the previous year.

From 1979 to 1982, a crisis occurred as a result of the opening of the domestic market, which followed a significant increase in Peruvian exports. In 1979, the maximum tariff was lowered from 355 percent to 155 percent and the average tariff from 66 percent to 40 percent. In 1980 and 1981, the reduction continued and reached an average tariff level of 32 percent.

During this period of growth, the GDP fluctuated only slightly and imports replaced new industrial products, especially cars and household appliances. This had a very adverse effect on industries manufacturing components as well as assembly industries, whose production in 1982 fell by approximately 70 percent compared with 1981. The entry of new operators into the taxi system, however, affected not only operators belonging to the Drivers' Federation but also operators working in other ways, in many cases as a way of paying for their vehicles. The opening of markets was prejudicial to increased growth in production because imports were mainly consumer goods and not inputs.

In 1983, two major natural disasters occurred—floods in the north and drought in the south. The effects of these crises were reflected in the number of taxi operators, which increased by approximately 1,500 in 1983 and 1984. This situation was also caused by the economic recession during these two years, which led to a fall in domestic demand.

With the change in government in 1985, there was a recovery in the economy; greater use was made of existing production capacity, wages and salaries were increased in real terms, payment of the debt was reduced, and inflation was brought under control to some extent, thus giving the population and investors renewed confidence in the formal sector. The trend continued in 1986 and was reflected in minor changes in the rate of the growth in the taxi market during these years of between 1 and 1.5 percent.

The Price of Fuel

Fuel is one of the most important items in the cost structure; its price therefore has a noticeable effect on operating costs and the use of taxis in the market. Any increase in fuel prices should discourage the entry of new operators into the market and at the same time cause the withdrawal of others due to the increase in operating costs. However, in Peru this did not occur and the empirical evidence even appears to show the contrary; a comparison of the rate of increase of fuel prices and the increase in the number of taxis shows similar trends (Figure 9.1). In 1975, although the price of fuel rose sharply, there was a small increase in the number of taxi operators. Since 1977, as fuel prices increased, there was not only an increase in the number of taxis but it exceeded those in previous years. For example, in 1978, the rate of increase in fuel prices was 83.30 percent and in the number of taxis was 41.70 percent. In 1979, the rate of increase of fuel prices was lower (63.6 percent), and the rate of increase in the number of taxis also fell (3.5 percent).

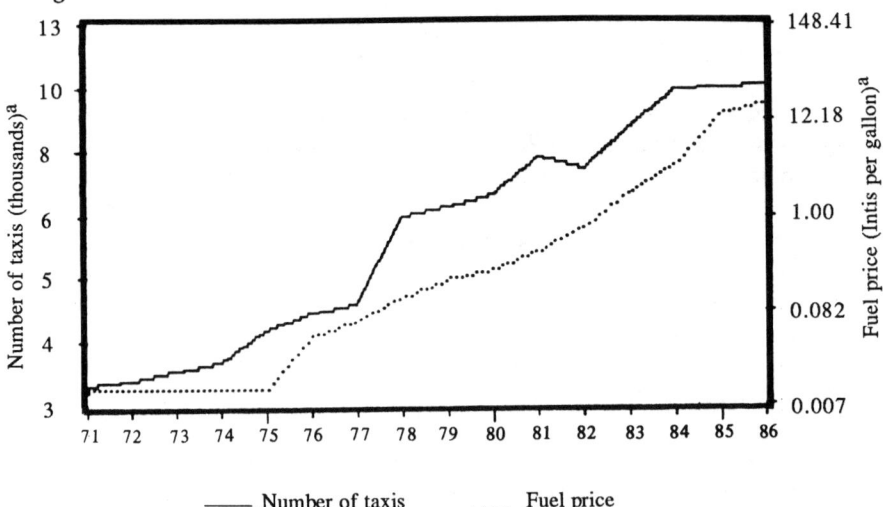

Figure 9.1 Number of Taxis and Fuel Prices

Source: Center of Studies for the Development and the Participation (of Peru) (CEDEP)
[a]Expressed in natural logarithms.

During the period 1975–1977, the increase in the price of fuel did not correspond to a similar increase in the entry of new operators into the taxi market, because the population had a level of income similar to the period 1970–1975. But from 1980 onward, the price of fuel showed more constant variations than in the 1970s. The rate of increase in the number of taxis was 16 percent, and the rate of increase in fuel prices was 60.9 percent. The fluctuations in prices, which did not lead to greater rates of growth in comparison with the prices fixed during the second half of the 1970s, appear to have encouraged the entry of new taxis into the market.

In 1982, the price of fuel started to rise sharply and there was a reduction in the number of taxis and a decrease in the rate of growth (–4.6 percent). However, in 1983, when the rate of increase in fuel prices was 149.3 percent, the number of taxis grew by 17.7 percent, and in 1984 by 16.1 percent.

It can therefore be affirmed that the policy adopted by the government regarding fuel prices directly affects the number of taxis in the market.

With the change of government in 1985, a new price policy was implemented in which the price of fuel was fixed until March 1987. In 1985, the rate of increase in the price of fuel was 265.2 percent and the effect of fixing prices (pursuant to the change in policy) did not appear to affect the taxi market because their number increased by only 1.4 percent and in 1986 by 1.3 percent. In these two years (1985 and 1986), there was an increase in wages in real terms as a result of the economic measures implemented by the government in July 1985. The increase in wages in real terms was the main reason for the decrease in the rate of the growth in the number of taxis because living standards improved and there was less need to seek additional economic resources in order to maintain salaries in real terms.

Fuel prices and the number of taxis thus appear to be directly related. This means that the substitution effect, which leads to greater demand for the service, would appear to negate the cost effect, which would reduce the profitability of the activity, making it less attractive. But what is perhaps the most important element is that increases in fuel prices coincide with general price increases, which affect wages in real terms, exerting supply pressure by new taxi operators joining the market. We shall return to this aspect at the end of this chapter.

Tariff Policies

Between 1968 and 1975, the car market opened up as a result of the liberalizing of imports and/or the lowering of tariffs on the purchase of vehicles assembled in Peru and on spare parts. These measures, which might have encouraged new taxi operators to join the market, did not have this effect because the state simultaneously decreed the temporary suspension of registration of new operators with the aims of maintaining a balance between supply and demand and improving the quality of service by replacing the stock of vehicles. During this period, as will be seen below, the illegal supply did not exert pressure on the market, not only because of better control but also because employment and wages maintained their real level.

From 1975 to 1980, the open policy for imports suffered restrictions and tariff rates rose sharply. Despite this, the number of taxis grew at a much higher rate than in the previous period due to the access of independent operators who entered the market ignoring existing regulations and controls and due to the trade union organization. This period was also one of high inflation and a fall in incomes in real terms, which obliged some sectors of the population to use their vehicles as a means of work, albeit a secondary means, in order to complement their incomes.

In 1980, the purchase of vehicles by transporters belonging to the Drivers' Federation was liberalized and such purchases were exempt from duty. The impact of this liberalization, which continued until 1981, was felt in the entry of new operators into the market, which increased by 16 percent.

From 1982 onward, the policy supporting imports of vehicles for the urban transport system was terminated, together with the fiscal exemptions for transporters. This affected the quality of service because it became difficult to replace vehicles, but it did not limit the growth in supply nor the access of new operators to the market. On the contrary, the period 1981–1985 saw the highest increases in the number of taxis, particularly pirate taxis.

In conclusion, as far as the impact of the liberalized imports and reduced tariffs variables on trends in the number of vehicles is concerned, the first variable does not affect the size of the market as much as the quality of service.

Employment Situation

The theory put forward in this section is that the growth in underemployment and unemployment have encouraged the access of new operators to the market, in different forms, as a response to the need to compensate for deterioration in wages and the lack of any other better-paid jobs. Because the taxi market has very few legal barriers on entry, it is not difficult to imagine that it is a popular activity to be taken up by employees when deterioration in their incomes affects their standards of living.

As stated by the pirate taxi operators interviewed in this study, the decision to enter the taxi market was of a temporary nature and only destined to bridge the gap resulting from the wage adjustments implemented toward the end of the 1970s. However, the deterioration of wages in real terms and the resulting imbalance between nominal and real incomes has been a constant feature over at least the last ten years. Therefore, not only are new operators entering the market, but for those already there it is becoming a permanent second activity.

In an analysis of the correlation, a positive relationship between the increase in underemployment and the number of taxis can be seen (Figure 9.2). An analysis of the years 1970–1976 shows that the levels of underemployment and the number of taxi operators rose very moderately. In 1977, as a result of the adjustment policies to restabilize the fiscal deficit, underemployment increased sharply and led to growth of 41.6 percent in the taxi market in 1978, due to the effect of the weakness and belated response on the part of the operators in the face of their needs. From 1980 until 1986, growth trends for both factors were similar. And from mid-1985 until the end of 1986, in response to the change in economic policy, growth rates for both variables decreased significantly.

The relationship between unemployment and the taxi market is positive; particularly in the period 1981–1984, when unemployment levels reached alarming levels and this corresponded to growth rates of 17 percent (in 1983 and 1984) in the number of taxis.

If, as stated above, the growth in underemployment and unemployment is accompanied by noticeable increases in the number of taxis, some relevant questions arise: Does this increase in number lead to imbalances in the market? What is the trend in demand? How is the fixing of fares affected by

Figure 9.2 Number of Taxis and Underemployment

―― Number of taxis · · · · Underemployment

Source: Center of Studies for the Development and the Participation (of Peru) (CEDEP)
[a]Expressed in natural logarithms.

the entry of new types of operator as a result of changes in the standard of living?

Although there is no empirical evidence that allows a detailed answer to be given to these questions, it can be stated that the growth in underemployment, together with the deterioration in wages, could have restricted demand and therefore caused imbalances in the market due to the simultaneous increase in supply. However, supply and demand have reached an equilibrium because operators, in fixing their prices, take into account the level of income in real terms of the population who demand their service. It is also necessary to take into account the existence of a chaotic public transport system that determines the use of taxis because there are no alternative transportation means (expresses, *liebres*, and so forth). The cost of fares has also decreased due to the operators' inability to fix the fares for journeys in the light of similar technical criteria. Independent taxi operators frequently take into account variables of a social character (earning a minimum income to meet needs, reimbursing debts, and so on) when fixing fares, ignoring the cost structure.

Tentative Conclusions

1. Urban transport in metropolitan Lima lacks any system of planning that would allow proper distribution of the service in order to respond to the population growth, which is one of the highest in Latin America. The number of vehicles does not grow at the same rate as demand and the number of operators has diminished, which meant that in 1984 the number of unsatisfied demands reached 4,000 trips per day. Organizational problems due to the lack of vehicles and spare parts exacerbates this situation. The same situation occurs with regard to the infrastructure, replacement of equipment, and quality and safety of the service—its deterioration is manifest. Legislation on the transport system has not been translated into precise and coherent provisions that would allow equitable regulations and promote an adequate and efficient service.

2. As far as the taxi system is concerned, operating in a free market does not lead to efficient functioning. In Peru, the effects have been negative both for the operators of the system and for users. The market liberalization process has had a negative impact on fixing the amount of fares, the quality and number of operators in the trade union organization, and the quality of service.

Regarding the fixing of fares and the new operators who have entered the market in recent years, the absence of technical criteria when establishing prices has led to a wide range of prices for the same journey. There are such different fares that the user does not know the average fare and has to wait for three or four taxis in order to get an idea of the price and, on that basis, negotiate a fare with the driver.

In connection with the quality and number of operators, free access to the market has resulted in a multiplicity of types of operator, all lacking any form of organization, who do not know the job and use vehicles that do not comply with the minimum safety regulations. This affects the quality and safety of the service and has consequences that are felt not only by the user but by the population as a whole due to the accidents and traffic congestion they cause.

The crisis in the taxi system is not, however, solely due to the fact that it operates in a free market system. There are, in fact, other reasons that have also contributed to its decline: inappropriate, partial, and inefficient legislation; lack of controls; economic crises; deterioration in the urban population's living standards; among others

3. The regulations and measures formulated over the past twenty years to restructure and regulate the system have been extremely partial and have not promoted an efficient and safe system. To this must be added the absence of any control over the system's operators on the part of those responsible for maintaining order.

Isolated and partial attempts to impose order have not had positive results. Moreover, in many cases, those drivers who have complied with the rules as well as users have felt cheated and are reluctant to accept new regulatory systems. There are no links between the proposed regulations, those responsible for control, and the operators.

Legislation affecting the taxi system principally covers two areas: (a) minimum safety measures for the vehicle and user; and (b) laws on fiscal exemptions for the purchase of new vehicles so as to improve the stock of vehicles and provide greater security. Such important areas as controlling the access of new operators and fixing fares have not been the subject of any regulations whatsoever.

During the past twenty years, there has not been any political will to formulate and implement more comprehensive regulations for this market so as to meet the demands of operators and users with regard to prices and personal and road safety.

4. It appears that economic measures closely linked to certain variables have had the greatest effect on the taxi market, particularly regarding the entry of new operators into the system. At the same time, social problems have had a noticeable impact on the chaotic situation in which the market currently operates.

Fuel prices, the tariff policy, and social variables have been chosen for further discussion because of their effects on the entry of new operators into the market, the amount of fares, and the quality of service.

Fuel prices. Because fuel is an essential element in the cost structure, when commencing this study, the theory that there was an inverse ratio between increases in fuel prices and the entry of new operators was put forward; in other words, it was thought that the higher the price of fuel, the lower the rate of growth in the number of vehicles. The empirical evidence obtained from the ratio between the increase in the number of vehicles and the price of fuel shows that for the past twenty years there has been a positive ratio between both of these variables and that when the price of fuel increases, it can be expected that the number of operators will also increase.

This phenomenon cannot be isolated from overall economic policy, because this trend can be explained by the fact that increases in the price of fuel and other commodities corresponded to measures taken to solve balance-of-payments problems. These had a direct impact on incomes in real terms, particularly for the middle- and lower-income sectors and employees. In response to this situation and in order to maintain existing living standards, some middle-income sectors of the population use their own vehicles as a means of work, supported by a legal framework in which there is almost no control on the entry of operators into the system.

Tariff policy. The principal effect of the lowering of tariffs on the purchase of vehicles assembled in Peru and the liberalization of imports of taxis was to improve the stock of vehicles as well as to raise safety levels for users. Their impact was not so important on increases in supply because the period 1970–1972, when this transport policy measure was implemented, coincided with relative economic stability and salaries that rose in real terms.

Social variables. Social variables related to living standards have led to a deterioration in the taxi system, expressed in the increased number of illegal operators, lack of professionalism among drivers, aging of the stock of vehicles, fares that are fixed without taking into account technical criteria and are completely arbitrary for the same journey, an increase in traffic accidents, and a high level of insecurity for users.

The decline in employment levels (a proxy variable used to measure living standards), especially the increase in underemployment, has meant the entry of few organized operators into the system. Employees whose incomes have been affected view markets that are easy to enter, such as the taxi market, as a good opportunity to supplement their incomes. This situation results in operators who have no organization, who lack professionalism, and whose activity is often a second job; this has been a major contributing factor to the deterioration of the taxi market.

For the period studied, the ratios show a positive relation between increases in the level of underemployment and increases in the number of vehicles.

In situations such as those described, the negative effects of the increase in the number of vehicles are not justified by the shorter waiting time and the possible decrease in fares, which could have positive effects for the user.

5. The performance of the drivers' trade union during the period studied showed that the union could constitute the most important catalytic element in the system, as it had done in the 1970s, as a spokesman vis-à-vis the government for fixing fares, regulating vehicles, or improving safety. The drivers' trade union could constitute the most appropriate channel in the future for the formulation and promotion of measures to make the service more efficient.

6. In conclusion, it is important to emphasize that in the rest of Peru, in medium-sized urban areas, the taxi system is more efficient. The Municipal Authority of each area is responsible for regulating and organizing the service. In some cities in the interior of Peru (Arequipa, Cuzco, Chiclayo, Huancayo, and Trujillo), a fare system has been imposed by dividing the cities into zones and establishing a fare that is acceptable to operators and users. Drivers must be registered and show the rates of fares and the municipal registration in the vehicle. In general terms, in more controlled markets such as those in cities in the interior of Peru, the service is safer and more efficient.

Notes

1. In 1988, 1,000 vehicles (minibuses and buses) were at a standstill due to the lack of spare parts. Because scarcity of spare parts represents a serious threat for the stock of cars, the prices of spare parts on the black market rose by more than 100 percent over the official price. For example, a Volkswagen nonradial tire, whose official price was 2,500 intis (US$15) sold on the black market at 20,000 intis (US$120).

2. Reference is specifically made to 1985 because this was when the Municipal Urban Transport Secretariat implemented an overall program to improve urban transport, which included special measures for taxis.

3. Around 20 percent of the registered drivers who paid the first installment for the meter were not able, as of 1988, to recover the amount of these installments due to problems related to the change of Municipal Authority. As a result, transporters in the taxi market have no interest in proposals to regulate the market through the use of meters.

4. The information in this subsection is taken from Iguiñiz (1986), and Jiménez and Nell (1986).

Bibliography

Acuña, J. A. 1988. *Propuesta de reforma al Reglamento de Trabajadores Independientes* (San Jose).
Aguirre, R., and Méndez, E. 1988. "El trabajo informal urbano en Uruguay." *Suma* (Montevideo: Centro de Investigaciones Económicas), April.
Ahmad, E., and Drèze, J. (eds.). 1989. *Social security in developing countries* (London: London School of Economics, WIDER).
Anderson, P., et. al. 1985. *Minibus ride: A journey through the informal sector of Kingston's mass transport system* (Mona: UWI, Institute of Social and Economic Research).
Arroba, G. 1979. "La financiación de la seguridad social en los países en desarrollo." *Estudios de la Seguridad Social*, 29.
Barrig, M., and Fort, A. 1987. *La ciudad de las mujeres: Pobladores y servicios. El caso de El Agustino* (Lima: draft).
Bolaños, V. 1988. "Protección social de grupos marginados urbanos en Costa Rica." Memoria de la Reunión sobre la Protección Social a los Grupos Marginados Urbanos (Mexico, Instituto Mexicano de Seguro Social-AISS).
Bromley, R. 1980. "Who are the Casual Poor?" In *Casual work in Third World cities* (Chichester: Wiley and Sons).
Bryde, O., and Hirtz, F. 1988. "Introduction: Between kinship and the State." In F. von Benda-Beckmann et al. (ed.), *Between kinship and the State* (Dordrecht: Foris Publications).
CANAPI (Cámara Nacional de Artesanía y Pequeña Industria). 1986. *Guía de asociados* (San Jose: CANAPI).
Carbonetto, D. 1985. "La medición del empleo en Lima." In D. Carbonetto et al. (ed.), *El sector informal urbano en los países andinos* (Quito: ILDIS/CEPESIU).
Carbonetto, D., and Chávez, E. 1984. "Sector informal urbano: Heterogeneidad del capital y excedente bruto de trabajo." *Socialismo y Participación*, 26 (Lima, Ediciones Socialismo y Participación).
Caro, B., and Acevedo, J. 1986. *Análisis de la problemática de legalización de la microempresa* (Bogota: Instituto SER de Investigación).
Casanovas, R. 1986. *El impacto de la Nueva Política Económica en el sector informal urbano en Bolivia* (La Paz: CEDLA/FLACSO/ILDIS).
Casanovas, R., and Escobar de Pabón, S. 1984. *Migración y mercado de trabajo en la ciudad de La Paz. El caso de los trabajadores por cuenta propia* (La Paz: CEDLA).

Casanovas, R., Escobar de Pabón, S., and Ormachea, E. 1982. *Migración y empleo en la ciudad de Santa Cruz* (La Paz: Proyecto OIT/UNFPA/Ministerio de Trabajo y Desarrollo Laboral).
Castellanos, J. 1988. "La atención de salud en áreas urbanas." Memoria de la Reunión sobre la Protección Social a los Grupos Marginados Urbanos (Mexico, Instituto Mexicano de Seguro Social-AISS).
Castells, M., and Portes, A. 1989. "World underneath: The origins, dynamics and effects of the informal economy." In A. Portes, M. Castells, and L. Benton (eds.), *The informal economy*, (Baltimore, Md.: Johns Hopkins University Press).
CCSS (Caja Costarricence de Seguro Social). 1983. *Memoria 1983* (San Jose: CCSS).
———. 1988. *Informe que estudia el aseguramiento obligatorio de los trabajadores independientes y temporarios* (San Jose: CCSS).
———. Various years. *Anuario Estadístico* (San Jose: CCSS), various numbers.
Ceará, Governo do Estado, Secretaria da Fazenda, Coordenação da Tributação. 1985. *Manual de orientação á microempresa* (Fortaleza: Imprensa Oficial do Estado do Ceará).
Chen-Young, P., and Aramovic, D. 1986. *Social effects of the economic crisis in Jamaica* (Lima: ECLAC).
CIPI (Comisión Institucional para la Pequeña Industria). 1987. *Guía de servicios de apoyo a la pequeña industria en Costa Rica* (San Jose: CIPI).
Coffman, R. 1977. "The economic reasons for price and entry regulation of taxicabs: A comment." *Journal of Transports Economics and Policy* (London, School of Economics and Political Science), September.
Conjuntura Economica. 1988. (Río de Janeiro, Fundação Getulio Vargas), July.
COPLAMAR. 1983. *Necesidades esenciales en México: Situación actual y perspectivas al año 2000. Salud* (Mexico: Editorial Siglo XXI).
Cortés, F. 1988. *La informalidad del sector informal extralegal* (Mexico: draft).
CRTT (Comisión Reguladora de Tarifas de Transportes). 1986. *Estudio tarifario del servicio público de taxis en Lima Metropolitana* (Lima: CRTT).
CUAVES. 1986. *Plan Unico de Salud* (Villa El Salvador: CUAVES).
Dauriex, H. 1987. "Papel de los gastos públicos en el Uruguay (1955–1984)." *Estudios CINVE*, 9 (Montevideo, Centro de Investigaciones Económicas).
Dávila, A. 1988. *Proyecciones financieras del seguro de vejez, invalidez y muerte para el año 2000* (San Jose: CCSS).
De Soto, H. 1986. *El otro sendero* (Lima: Editorial El Barranco).
De Wit, H. 1981. "El transporte público en Lima Metropolitana." *Cuadernos de Coyuntura* (Lima, Centro de Investigaciones de la Universidad del Pacífico).
Diéguez, H. 1986. *Social consequences of the economic crisis: Mexico: The facts* (Washington, D.C.: World Bank, draft).
Diéguez, H., and Giral-Bosca, J. 1988. *Uruguay, inquiry into social security: Its evolution, current problems and prospects* (Washington, D.C.: World Bank).
Durán, V. 1988. *Estudio y propuesta de una readecuación de contribuciones a los seguros sociales* (San Jose: CCSS).
ECLAC (Economic Commission for Latin America and the Caribbean). 1986a. *Balance preliminar de la economía latinoamericana* (Santiago: ECLAC).
———. 1986b. *Os impactos sociais da crise económica, políticas sociais e transição democrática* (Brasilia, ECLAC).
———. 1987. *Anuario Estadístico de América Latina y el Caribe, 1986* (Santiago, ECLAC).
———. 1988. *Balance preliminar de la economía latinoamericana* (Santiago: ECLAC).

Elizondo, N. 1990. "Costos de legalización de empresas informales en México." In PREALC, *Más allá de la regulación: El sector informal en América Latina* (Santiago: PREALC).

Equipo Técnico de la Municipalidad Villa El Salvador. 1988. *Villa El Salvador y su proyecto popular de desarrollo integral* (Villa El Salvador).

Escobar de Pabón, S. 1990. "Los establecimientos informales bolivianos ante la ley." In PREALC, *Más allá de la regulación. El sector informal en América Latina* (Santiago: PREALC).

Feldman, J., Golbert, L., and Isuani, E. 1986. "Maduración y crisis del sistema previsional argentino." *Boletín Informativo Techint*, 240 (Buenos Aires, Compañía Técnica Internacional).

FENATACH. 1987. *El taxista*, 1, 2, and 3 (Santiago, FENATACH).

Fernández, S., et al. (n.d.) *Proyección de la población económicamente activa para la República Mexicana: 1970–1985* (Mexico City: Centro Nacional de Información y Estadísticas del Trabajo).

Ferrari, C. 1986. *Desarrollo social y pobreza en Perú: Factores estructurales de la crisis externa, las políticas adoptadas para lograr el desarrollo económico y social* (Lima: ECLAC).

Fields, G. 1985. *Employment and economic growth in Costa Rica* (Washington, D.C.: USAID).

Fortuna, J. C., and Prates, S. 1989. "Informal sector versus informalized labor relations in Uruguay." In A. Portes, M. Castells, and L. Benton (eds.), *The informal economy* (Baltimore, Md.: Johns Hopkins University Press).

Freiberg-Strauss, J., and Jung, D. 1988. "Social security in the peasant society of Boyacá (Colombia)." In F. von Benda-Beckmann et al. (ed.), *Between kinship and the State* (Dordrecht, Foris Publications).

Galván, A. 1987. "Extensión del régimen del seguro social en los años recientes." *Cuestión Social*, 8 (Mexico, D.F.).

———. 1988. *Mecanismos innovadores de acceso a la seguridad social* (Mexico: draft).

García, A. 1988. "Mensaje a la Nación del Presidente . . ." *La Crónica*, July 29 (Lima).

García, H. C. 1987. *Extensión del régimen en el seguro social (IMSS)* (Mexico: IMSS, draft).

Giner de los Ríos, F. 1986. *Very small enterprises in Mexico: Stagnation, disappearance and growth (A typology of producers)*, doctoral thesis, University of Sussex.

Gómez, A., and Quijada, M. 1977. *Algunos aspectos de diseño en el sistema de transporte de la locomoción colectiva de Santiago* (Santiago: Universidad Católica de Chile, Departamento de Transporte; Mimeo).

Gordon, D., Edwards, R., and Reich, R. 1983. *Segmented work, divided workers: The historical transformation of labor in the United States* (Cambridge: Cambridge University Press).

Grompone, R. 1987. *Las políticas y programas para el mejoramiento de las condiciones de trabajo y bienestar de los trabajadores del SIU: El caso de Lima* (Lima: ILO).

———. 1988. *Iniciativas populares en Lima* (Lima: Instituto de Estudios Peruanos, draft).

Haan, H. 1985. *El sector informal en Centroamérica*. Series Investigaciones sobre Empleo/27 (Santiago, PREALC).

Hart, K. 1972. *Employment, income and inequality: A strategy for increasing productive employment in Kenya* (Geneva: ILO).

IDB (Inter American Development Bank). 1987. *Progreso económico y social en América Latina* (Washington, D.C., IDB).
Iguiñiz, J. 1986. "La crisis peruana actual: Esquema para una interpretación." In H. Bonilla (ed.), *Las crisis económicas en la historia del Perú* (Lima: Editorial Acuario).
ILO (International Labour Organisation). 1981–1987. *Anuario Estadísticas del Trabajo* (Geneva: ILO).
———. 1984. *Introduction to social security* (Geneva: ILO).
IMSS (Instituto Mexicano de Seguro Social). 1987a. *Memoria estadística 1986* (Mexico: IMSS).
———. 1987b. *Informe mensual de la población derechohabiente* (Mexico, IMSS), December, May.
———. 1987c. *Proyecto de decreto para incorporación voluntaria al régimen obligatorio del seguro social a los trabajadores independientes* (Mexico: IMSS, draft).
———. 1987d. *Ley de Seguro Social* (Mexico: IMSS).
IMSS, Asociación Internacional de Seguridad Social. 1988. *Reunión sobre la Protección Social a los Grupos Marginados Urbanos* (Mexico: IMSS-AISS).
INE (Instituto Nacional de Estadísticas). 1976. *Censo Nacional de Población y Vivienda* (La Paz: INE).
———. 1983. *Directorio Nacional de Establecimientos Económicos* (La Paz: INE).
———. 1987. *Encuesta Permanente de Hogares* (La Paz: INE).
———. 1988a. *Encuesta nacional de hogares sobre medición de niveles de vida, 1985–1986* (Lima: INE).
———. 1988b. *Perú: Compendio estadístico 1988* (Lima: INE).
INEGI (Instituto Nacional de Estadística, Geografía e Informática). 1987. *Agenda estadística 1986* (Mexico: Secretaría de Planificación y Presupuesto).
Instituto Libertad y Democracia. 1986. *Compendio técnico y estadístico de "El otro sendero"* (Lima, Instituto Libertad y Democracia), November.
IPSS (Instituto Peruano de Seguridad Social). 1988. *Estimados de la Dirección de Estadística* (Lima: IPSS).
Isuani, E. A. 1986. "Seguridad social y asistencia pública." In C. Mesa-Lago (ed.), *La crisis de la seguridad social y la salud: Experiencias y lecciones latinoamericanas* (Mexico City: Fondo de Cultura Económica).
Isuani, E. A., and Mesa-Lago, C. 1981. *La seguridad social en Panamá: Avances y problemas* (Santiago: ILPES).
Jeftanovic, P. 1987. "La locomoción colectiva: De la liberalización al control 1978–1986." *Revista de Economía y Administración* (Santiago, Universidad de Chile, Facultad de Ciencias Económicas y Administrativas), July.
Jiménez, F., and Nell, E. 1986. "La economía política de la deuda externa y el plan Baker: El caso peruano." *Socialismo y Participación* (Lima, Centro de Estudios para el Desarrollo y la Participación), June.
Larrazabal, H. 1989. "Legalidad ¿condición del exito económico en el sector informal urbano?" In *Informalidad e ilegalidad: Una falsa identidad* (La Paz, CEDLA), pp. 179 and following.
Le Frank, E. 1987. "Petty trading and labour mobility: Higglers in the Kingston Metropolitan area of Jamaica." Caribbean Studies Association Meetings (Belize).
Le Frank, E., McFarlane-Gregory, D., and Taylor, A. 1985. *The informal distribution network in the Kingston Metropolitan area* (Mona: UWI-Institute of Social and Economic Research).

López, L. 1988. *Estimación del costo financiero del subsidio en dinero para trabajadores independientes* (San Jose).
Maguiña, C. 1988. *Programa casa de la salud: Plan de trabajo y objetivos* (Lima).
Mallet, A. 1988. "Problemas contemporáneos de la seguridad social." In *Problemas contemporáneos de la seguridad social* (Mexico City: CIESS).
Malloy, J. 1979. *The politics of social security in Brazil* (Pittsburgh, Pa.: University of Pittsburgh Press).
Matos, J. 1986. *Los interlocutores sociales y el proceso peruano de la concertación* (Lima).
McGreevey, W. P. 1988. "Temas actuales en la seguridad social brasileña." In *Problemas contemporáneos de la seguridad social* (Mexico City: CIESS).
McGreevey, W. P., et al. 1984. *Política e financiamento do sistema de saúde brasileiro: Uma perspectiva internacional* (Brasilia: IPEA).
Melgar, A. 1988. "El mercado de trabajo en la coyuntura." *Suma* (Montevideo, Centro de Investigaciones Económicas), April.
Mesa-Lago, C. 1978. *Social security in Latin America: Pressure groups. Stratification and inequality* (Pittsburgh, Pa.: University of Pittsburgh Press). [Abridged Spanish version 1977. *Modelos de seguridad social en América Latina: Estudio comparativo* (Buenos Aires: Asociación Interamericana de Planificación).]
———. 1983a. *Financing health care in Latin America and the Caribbean with a special study of Costa Rica* (Washington, D.C.: World Bank).
———. 1983b. "Social security and extreme poverty in Latin America." *Journal of Development Economics* (Amsterdam, North-Holland Publishing), February-April.
———. 1984. *Social security in Ecuador* (Washington, D.C.: World Bank).
———. 1985a. "El desarrollo de la seguridad social en América Latina." Serie Estudios e Informes de la CEPAL, 43 (Santiago, ECLAC).
———. 1985b. *La reforma de la seguridad social: Análisis comparativo del Perú dentro del contexto latinoamericano* (Lima: Universidad del Pacífico-Fundación Friedrich Ebert).
———. 1986a. *La crisis de la seguridad social y la salud: Experiencias y lecciones latinoamericanas* (Mexico City: Fondo de Cultura Económica).
———. 1986b. "Estudio comparativo del desarrollo de la seguridad social en América Latina." In *Revista Internacional de la Seguridad Social* (Geneva: Agencia Internacional de Seguridad Social).
———. 1986c. *Financiamiento de los programas de salud del Instituto Peruano de Seguridad Social* (Lima: ANSSA).
———. 1986d. *Exploratory visit to the Dominican Republic to review the field and identify health financing studies* (Stony Brook, N.Y.: State University of New York at Stony Brook).
———. 1987a. "Atención de salud en Costa Rica: Auge y crisis." *Boletín de la Oficina Sanitaria Panamericana* (Washington, Oficina Sanitaria Panamericana, OPS/OMS).
———. 1987b. *Social security in Bahamas, Barbados and Jamaica* (Geneva: ILO).
———. 1988a. *Análisis económico de los sistemas de pensiones en Costa Rica y recomendaciones para su reforma* (Washington, D.C.: Development Technologies, Inc.).
———. 1988b. "Informe económico sobre la extensión de la cobertura poblacional del programa de enfermedad-maternidad del IPSS." Convenio IPSS-USAID (State University of New York at Stony Brook).

———. 1988c. "Medical care under social security: Costs, coverage and financing." In D. K. Zschock (ed.), *Health care in Peru: Resources and policy* (Boulder, Colo.: Westview Press).

———. 1988d. *Review of Chile SAL III conditions: Pension systems* (Washington, D.C.: World Bank).

———. 1988e. "Social insurance: The experience of three countries in the English-speaking Caribbean." *International Labour Review*, 127, 4 (Geneva, ILO).

———. 1989. *Financiamiento de la atención de la salud en América Latina y el Caribe con focalización en el seguro social* (Washington, D.C.: World Bank, Instituto de Desarrollo Económico).

Mesa-Lago, C., and De Geyndt, W. 1987. *Colombia: Social security review* (Washington, D.C.: World Bank, HRD).

Mesa-Lago, C., Cruz-Saco, M. A., and Zamalloa, L. 1988. *Determinants of social insurance/security cost and coverage: An international comparison with a focus on Latin America* (Pittsburgh, Pa.: University of Pittsburgh). [Abridged Spanish version, 1988. "Factores que determinan los costos y la cobertura del seguro social en América Latina y políticas para controlar el gasto," in *Problemas contemporáneos de la seguridad social* (Mexico: CIESS), pp. 119–138.]

Midgley, J. 1984. *Social security, inequality and the Third World* (New York: John Wiley and Sons).

Ministerio de Transporte y Telecomunicaciones. 1985, 1986. *Anuario Estadístico de Transporte Terrestre* (Santiago: Ministerio de Transporte y Telecomunicaciones).

Ministry of Health. 1986. *Annual report of the Chief Medical Officer, 1984* (Kingston: Ministry of Health).

Montaño, J. 1985. "Barreras institucionales de entrada al sector informal en Ciudad de México." Series Working papers/258 (Santiago, PREALC).

Montes, R. 1988. "Privatización y obligatoriedad del seguro social." *Análisis Laboral*, 134.

Morales, J. A. 1987. "Estabilización y Nueva Política Económica en Bolivia." *El Trimestre Económico* (Mexico, Fondo de Cultura Económica), September, special issue.

MSSCA (Ministry of Social Security and Consumer Affairs). 1988. *Information for prime minister's budget speech, 1988/89* (Kingston, MSSCA), May 16.

MTPS-DGE (Ministerio del Trabajo y Promoción Social, Dirección General de Empleo). 1979. *Cuestionario de la "Encuesta Nacional de Empleo y Seguridad Social"* (Lima: MTPS-DGE).

———. 1986. *Cuestionario de la "Encuesta de Niveles de Empleo"* (Lima: MTPS-DGE).

Musgrove, P. 1986. *The economic crisis and its impact on health care in Latin America and the Caribbean* (Washington, D.C., OPS), January.

NIS (National Insurance Scheme). 1978–1987. *Annual reports* (Kingston: NIS).

National Savings Committee. 1974. "Report on the partner study." Series Working paper, 14 (Kingston).

O'Ryan, R. 1986. "Energía y transporte de pasajeros en Santiago: Impactos de una gestión integrada." *Planificación energética para el desarrollo: Un enfoque alternativo, 4* (Santiago, Universidad de Chile, PRIEN/Facultad de Ciencias Físicas y Matemáticas).

Ortega, E., and Portales, F. 1984. *El pequeño empresario de clase media* (Santiago: Instituto de Estudios Humanísticos, preliminary document).

Palamara, J. 1987. "Economía de la contaminación atmosférica." *Revista de Economía y Administración* (Santiago, Universidad de Chile, Facultad de Ciencias Económicas y Administrativas), September.

Parra, E. 1985. *Microempresa y desarrollo* (Bogota: UNICEF/SENA).

Paul, L. 1982. *Análisis del comportamiento del mercado de taxis* (Santiago: Universidad Católica de Chile; Memoria de Ingeniería del Transporte).

Pinilla, S. 1986. *Concepción, características y promoción del sector informal urbano* (Lima: Instituto de Desarrollo del Sector Informal-IDESI).

———. 1987. *La mujer y el sector informal* (Lima: Instituto de Desarrollo del Sector Informal-IDESI).

PIOJ (Planning Institute of Jamaica). 1980–1987. *Economic and social survey Jamaica 1979 to 1986* (Kingston: PIOJ).

Piore, M., and Sabel, C. 1987. *The second industrial divide* (New York: Basic Books Inc.).

Placencia, M. M. 1990. "Costos de legalización de las empresas informales en Ecuador." In PREALC, *Más allá de la regulación. El sector informal en América Latina* (Santiago: PREALC).

Platteau, J. P. 1988. *Traditional systems of social security and hunger insurance: Lessons for the evidence pertaining to Third World village societies* (Namur: draft).

Pollack, M., and Uthoff, A. 1985. "Costa Rica: Evolución macroeconómica 1976–1983." Series Monografías sobre empleo/50 (Santiago, PREALC).

Portes, A. 1984. "Latin America class structures: Their composition and change during the last decades." Series Occasional paper, 3 (Baltimore, Md.: Johns Hopkins University Press).

Portes, A., Castells, M., and Benton, L. 1989. *The informal economy* (Baltimore, Md.: Johns Hopkins University Press).

PREALC. 1978. "Comercio informal en una comuna de Santiago." Series Investigaciones sobre empleo/11 (Santiago, PREALC).

———. 1981a. "Dinámica del subempleo en América Latina." Series Estudios e Informes de la CEPAL, 10 (Santiago, ECLAC).

———. 1981b. *Sector informal: Funcionamiento y políticas* (Santiago: PREALC).

———. 1982. *Mercado de trabajo en cifras, 1950–1980* (Santiago: PREALC).

———. 1985. *Más allá de la crisis* (Santiago: PREALC).

———. 1986. "The urban informal sector and labour market informations systems." Series Working Paper/283 (Santiago, PREALC).

———. 1987. *Ajuste y deuda social* (Santiago: PREALC).

———. 1988a. *Deuda social. ¿Qué es, cuánto es, cómo se paga?* (Santiago: PREALC).

———. 1988b. *Más allá de la regulación. El sector informal en América Latina* (Santiago: PREALC).

Quijano, J., and Antía, F. 1990. "Costos de legalización de microempresas del sector informal en Uruguay." In PREALC, *Más allá de la regulación. El sector informal en América Latina* (Santiago: PREALC).

Quiroz, R. 1987. *Síntesis de la labor de la comisión que estudia el aseguramiento de trabajadores independientes y temporales* (San José), September.

Raczynski, D. 1977. "El sector informal urbano: Interrogantes y controversias." Series Investigaciones sobre empleo/3 (Santiago, Convenio PREALC-CIEPLAN).

Roche, A. 1988. *The microenterprise in Cuenca, Ecuador. A case study in the informal sector* (Pittsburgh, Pa.: University of Pittsburgh, draft).

Rodríguez, J., and Wurgaft, J. 1987. "La protección social a los desocupados en

América Latina." Series Investigaciones sobre empleo/28 (Santiago, PREALC).
Rosenberg, M. 1980. *Las luchas por el seguro social en Costa Rica* (San Jose: Editorial Costa Rica).
Rosenn, K. S. 1971. "The jeito, Brazil's institutional bypass of the formal legal system and its developmental implications." *The American Journal of Comparative Law*, 19.
Rossini, R., Thomas, J., and Equipo Económico del ILD. 1987. *Los fundamentos estadísticos de "El otro sendero": Debate sobre el sector informal en el Perú* (Lima: Fundación Friedrich Ebert).
Rovira, J. 1988. *Costa Rica en los años 80* (San Jose: FLACSO-Editorial Porvenir).
Sáenz, L. F. 1990. "Costos de legalización del sector informal urbano en Guatemala." In PREALC, *Más allá de la regulación: El sector informal en América Latina* (Santiago: PREALC).
Salcedo, F., and Zamalloa, E. 1980. *Consideraciones sobre el sector informal urbano en la economía peruana* (Lima: Universidad del Pacífico).
Samaniego, N. 1986. *Los efectos de la crisis de 1982-1986 en las condiciones de vida de la población en México* (Lima: CEPAL).
Sánchez, C., and Pereyra, J. C. 1988. *La pequeña y mediana empresa industrial en Bolivia: Un diagnóstico y recomendaciones de política* (La Paz: UDAPE/HIID).
Sánchez León et al. 1988. *Paradero final. El Transporte público en Lima Metropolitana* (Lima: DESCO).
Sapag, N., and Sapag, R. 1987. "Algunas consideraciones en torno al IPC y la locomoción colectiva." Series *Coyuntura*, 5 (Santiago, Universidad de Chile, Departamento de Administración).
Schteingart, M., and Garza, S. 1984. "Ciudad de México: Desarrollo industrial y estructura del espacio en una metrópoli semiperiférica." *Demografía y Economía*, 4 (Mexico, El Colegio de México), p. 60.
Secretaría de Salud-SS. 1986a. *Anuario estadístico 1986* (Mexico City: Secretaría de Salud).
———. 1986b. *Población abierta 1985* (Mexico City: Secretaría de Salud).
———. 1988. *Estadística trimestral de la prestación de servicios: Acumulado anual 1987* (Mexico City: Secretaría de Salud).
Shreiber, C. 1981. "The economic reasons for price and entry regulation of taxicabs: A rejoinder." In *Journal of Transports Economics and Policy* (London, School of Economics and Political Science), January.
STPS (Secretaría de Trabajo y Previsión Social). 1985. *Características de la ocupación informal urbana* (Mexico City: STPS).
STPS; PNUD-OIT. 1979. *La ocupación informal en áreas urbanas 1976: Encuesta complementaria a la encuesta continua sobre ocupación* (Mexico City: STPS-PNUD-OIT).
"The Hospital (Public) Act." 1984. *The Jamaica Gazette*, November 19.
Tokman, V. E. 1978. "An exploration into the nature of informal-formal sector relationships." *World Development* (Oxford, Pergamon Press Ltd.), September–October.
———. 1979. "Dinámica del mercado de trabajo urbano: El sector informal urbano en América Latina." In R. Kaztman and C. Reyna (eds.): *Fuerza de trabajo y movimientos laborales en América Latina* (Mexico City: El Colegio de México).
———. 1987a. "El imperativo de actuar. El sector informal hoy." *Nueva Sociedad* (Caracas, Nueva Sociedad Ltda.), July–August.

———. 1987b. "El sector informal: Quince años después." *El Trimestre Económico* (Mexico, Fondo de Cultura Económica), July–September.
———. 1988. "The informal sector: A policy proposal." In K. Haq and U. Kirdar (eds.), *Managing human development* (Islamabad: North-South Roundtable Publications).
———. 1989a. "Economic development and labor market segmentation in the Latin America periphery." *Journal of Inter-American Studies and World Affairs* (Gainesville, University of Florida, School of Inter-American Studies), Spring–Summer.
———. 1989b. "Policies for a heterogeneous informal sector in Latin America." *World Development* (Oxford, Pergamon Press Ltd.), July.
Uceda, P. 1976. *La legislación de transporte terrestre en el Perú*, Vol. I (Lima: Editorial Minerva).
———. 1978. *La legislación de transporte terrestre en el Perú*, Vol. II (Lima: Editorial Minerva).
U.S. SSA (United States Social Security Administration). 1986. *Social security programs throughout the world* (Washington, D.C.: DHHS).
Universidad Católica de Chile. 1978. *Estructuración de la red de transporte colectivo de Santiago* (Santiago: Universidad Católica de Chile, Departamento de Ingeniería del Transporte).
Vedova, M. 1986. *Economic recession and the consequences on the poor* (Washington, D.C.: World Bank).
Velásquez, M. 1990. "Los costos de legalización del sector informal urbano: Chile, estudio de casos." In PREALC, *Más allá de la regulación. El sector informal en América Latina* (Santiago: PREALC).
Vereda, A. 1988. *Alternativas a la economía informal* (Lima: draft).
von Benda-Beckmann, F., et al. (eds.). 1988. *Between kinship and the State: Social security and law in developing countries* (Dordrecht: Foris Publications).
Weihert, U. 1986. "La microempresa en la rama de la confección. Estudios de casos en la ciudad de Lima." Series Working Papers/295 (Santiago, PREALC).
Wilkie, J. W. 1988. *Social security and health programs in Mexico to 1988* (Washington, D.C.: World Bank, draft).
Williams, D. 1980. "The economic reasons for price and entry regulation of taxicabs: A comment." *Journal of Transports Economics and Policy* (London, School of Economics and Political Science), January.
Witter, M. 1987. *Research issues on the informal economy* (Mona: UWI-Institute of Social and Economic Research, draft).
———. 1988. "The role of higglers/sidewalk, vendors/informal commercial traders in the development of the Jamaican economy." Symposium Higglers/Sidewalk Vendors/Informal Commercial Traders (Mona, UWI-Institute of Social and Economic Research, draft).
World Bank. 1988a. *World Development Report 1988* (Washington, D.C.: World Bank).
———. 1988b. *Progreso económico y social en América Latina* (Washington, D.C.: World Bank).
Zacher, H. 1988. "Traditional solidarity and modern social security: Harmony or conflict." In F. von Benda-Beckmann et al. (eds.), *Between kinship and the State: Social security and law in developing countries* (Dordrecht: Foris Publications).
Zschock, D. K. (ed.). 1988. *Health care in Peru: Resources and policy* (Boulder, Colo.: Westview Press).

Index

Activities: commercial, 6, 8; in developing countries, 4; home-based, 6; informal, 4, 23, 30*tab*; itinerant, 39; taxes on small-scale, 53
Administration: organization, 11; requirements in legalization, 11
Antigua-Barbuda: health system, 179*tab*; social security, 180*tab*
Apprenticeship, 14, 27
Argentina: health system, 179*tab*; informal sector, 173; insurance coverage, 183*tab*, 184; labor force, 173*tab*; social security, 180*tab*, 186, 188*tab*, 189, 190*tab*, 192
Assets, estimating, 58

Bahamas: health system, 179*tab*, 182; insurance coverage, 184, 185*tab*; social security, 180*tab*, 188*tab*
Banking, development, 25
Barbados: health system, 179*tab*, 182; insurance coverage, 184, 185*tab*; social security, 180*tab*, 188*tab*
Belize: health system, 179*tab*, 182; social security, 180*tab*
Benefits, 117; access to, 8; bonuses, 103, 118, 150; bypassing, 65; capacity to absorb, 69–77; holidays, 103, 138*n14*, 150; hours, 5, 19; housing fund, 70; indemnities, 13; leave, 5; minimum wage, 19; overtime, 150; percent of salary, 53; profit sharing, 70, 150; social welfare, 121; unemployment, 135, 176; vacation, 13, 19

Bermuda: health system, 179*tab*; social security, 180*tab*
Bolivia: costs of legality, 11, 47–51, 87, 105; General Labor Law, 26; health system, 179*tab*; informal sector, 23–54; insurance coverage, 183*tab*, 184; Integrated Tax System, 31; labor force, 173*tab*; microenterprises, 89*tab*; National Register of Commerce, 36–37; National Register of Small-Scale and Crafts Industries, 37–39, 92; New Economic Policy, 23, 24–25, 28–31; permanency costs, 13, 104; promotion of crafts, 37; public sector, 28; registration, 9*tab*, 90, 91*tab*, 92, 97, 98; rental contracts, 45–46, 46*tab*; Simplified Tax Regime, 31, 32*tab*, 33, 34*tab*, 40–47; social security, 26, 180*tab*, 186, 190*tab*; taxpayer registry, 6, 31, 33*tab*, 39–40, 99*tab*; tax reform, 11–12, 31, 40–47, 95
Brazil: CEAG registration service, 114–115; cost of registration, 9*tab*; costs of legality, 11, 87, 105; health system, 179*tab*, 182, 191; incentives law, 12; incomes, 171; informal sector, 173; inspection standards, 95; insurance coverage, 183*tab*, 184; *jeitinho*, 109–136; labor force, 173*tab*; location regulation, 93, 94*tab*; microenterprises, 89*tab*, 109–136; Microenterprise Statute, 96, 121, 131, 132, 133, 135; occupational

categories, 174*tab*; registration, 91*tab*, 92, 93, 97; social security, 180*tab*, 186, 187, 188*tab*, 189, 190*tab*, 192; taxpayer registry, 99*tab*; tax reform, 95; temporary licenses, 90
Bribery, 54, 78, 81
Bureaucracy: centralized, 97; decentralized, 97; inefficiency, 4, 11, 127; interference, 19; in microenterprise registration, 112–118, 127; relation to administrative costs, 106

Capital: access to, 4; fixed, 57; initial, 7; investment, 66, 112, 120, 133; underdeclaration, 7; working, 153
Cartaya, Vanessa, 7, 141–165
Casanovas, Roberto, 6, 23–54
Case studies: benefits of legality, 150–163; microenterprise registration, 118–127
Chile: cost of registration, 9*tab*; costs of legality, 11, 87, 105; health system, 179*tab*, 182; incomes, 171; informal sector, 173; inspection standards, 95; insurance coverage, 183*tab*, 184, 185*tab*; labor force, 173*tab*; location regulations, 93, 94*tab*, 101*tab*; microenterprises, 89*tab*; occupational categories, 174*tab*; permanency costs, 103–104; registration, 91*tab*, 93, 97; social security, 180*tab*, 186, 187, 188*tab*, 189, 190, 190*tab*, 192; taxi industry, 16–18, 207–245; taxpayer registry, 99*tab*; tax reform, 95
Colmenares Carías, José Luis, 141
Colombia: health system, 179*tab*, 182; incomes, 171; insurance coverage, 183*tab*, 184, 185*tab*; labor force, 173*tab*; occupational categories, 174*tab*; permanency costs, 13; social security, 180*tab*, 188*tab*, 190*tab*, 192
Commerce: activities, 6, 8; costs of legality, 10; development, 25; employment trends, 25; registered activities, 36
Competition, 13; with formal sector, 153, 172; with imports, 30; increased, 3; informal sector, 29, 153, 172; international, 3; surplus labor in, 4, 11; taxi industry, 212–213
Conflict, public/private interests, 10, 17
Contracts: labor, 13, 103, 138*n14*; partnership, 93; probationary, 7, 134; rental, 45–46, 46*tab*
Corruption, 133
Costa Rica: economically active population, 172; health system, 179*tab*; incomes, 171; informal sector, 173, 194–202; insurance coverage, 183*tab*, 184, 185*tab*; labor force, 173*tab*; occupational categories, 174*tab*; social security, 14, 15, 16, 180*tab*, 186, 188*tab*, 189, 190, 190*tab*, 192, 194–202
Costs: administrative, 65, 79, 106, 192; assessment, 72; of being legal, 8–14, 9*tab*, 47–51, 69, 70, 77, 80, 87–106, 141–165, 144*tab*, 156*tab*; indirect, 54, 142; input, 64–65, 153, 154; labor, 3, 12, 13, 49–51, 50*tab*, 69, 70*tab*, 72*tab*, 73*tab*, 75, 75*tab*, 80, 153*tab*, 160*tab*; location modification, 101*tab*; of noncompliance, 142, 145; operating, 49, 88, 148–150; as percent of profits, 71*tab*; of permanency, 13, 102–104; production, 53, 172; reduction, 3; registration, 8, 127–132; relation to profits, 10; social security, 49–51, 170, 191–194; tax, 49; taxi industry, 209–210, 253–256
Craft workshops, Bolivian, 30, 37–39
Credit: access to, 66; for microenterprises, 110; need for registration, 8; obtaining, 54, 145; programs, 177; special lines, 110
Cuba: health system, 179*tab*, 182; informal sector, 173; insurance coverage, 183*tab*, 184; labor force, 173*tab*; social security, 180*tab*, 188*tab*, 189, 190*tab*, 192

Decisionmaking, entrepreneurial, 56, 64–66
Depreciation, 254–255
Deregulation, taxi market, 11
de Soto, Hernando, 69, 104

Despachante (Brazil), 109, 132, 135–136
Devaluation, 219, 267
Domestic work: decrease in recession, 26, 28; health benefits, 179*tab*; incomes, 171; insurance coverage, 185; social security, 15, 170, 180*tab*, 181, 194, 195, 196, 197, 200
Dominica: health system, 179*tab*; social security, 180*tab*
Dominican Republic: health system, 179*tab*, 182; insurance coverage, 183*tab*, 184; labor force, 173*tab*; social security, 180*tab*, 190*tab*

Economic: crises, 73–74; dynamism, 55; independence, 68; recession, 80, 81, 267; stagnation, 75
Economic units: family, 26, 31, 47, 56; informal, 33, 35*tab*, 41, 48*tab*; in microenterprises, 88; single-person, 26; taxes, 50*tab*
Economy: market forces, 29; regulated, 5; stabilization, 28; stagnation, 24
Ecuador: costs of legality, 11, 87, 105; health system, 179*tab*, 182, 191; incentives law, 12; inspection standards, 95; insurance coverage, 183*tab*, 184; labor force, 173*tab*; location modification, 101*tab*; microenterprises, 89*tab*; registration, 9*tab*, 91*tab*, 92, 96, 97; social security, 180*tab*, 186, 188*tab*, 190*tab*, 192; taxpayer registry, 99*tab*
Elizondo, Néstor, 5, 55–82
El Salvador: health system, 179*tab*; insurance coverage, 183*tab*, 184; labor force, 173*tab*; social security, 180*tab*, 190*tab*, 192
Employees: categories, 170; domestic, 15, 26, 28, 170; effect on regulatory compliance, 66; family, 8, 14, 26, 31, 47, 56, 66, 79, 170, 178; informal, 170–172; labor rights, 96; salaried, 27, 78, 152; temporary, 152, 153; turnover, 8, 62; underdeclaration, 7; unregistered, 132
Employment: alternative, 68–69, 81; Bolivian, 23–54; by branch of activity, 25*tab*; instability, 14, 27, 62; lay-offs, 29; low productivity, 24; sectoral composition, 24, 25; security, 19; stability, 4; in taxi industry, 270–272; transitory, 14; of women, 26, 27. *See also* Taxi industry
Entrepreneurs: decisionmaking, 56, 64–66; informal, 64–66
Exchange: floating rates, 267; foreign, 17; rates, 17, 18, 219

Finance, employment trends, 25

Giner de los Ríos, Francisco, 57
Goods, reduction in demand for, 30
Government: centralization, 11, 74, 97; compliance control, 63, 81; decentralization, 11, 97; efficiency, 11; inspectional capacity, 8, 188, 197; intervention, 18, 52, 55, 62; role in social security coverage, 20, 189, 193
Grenada: health system, 179*tab*; social security, 180*tab*
Growth: negative rates, 24; and tax evasion, 73
Guatemala: costs of legality, 11, 87, 105; health system, 179*tab*; inspection standards, 95; insurance coverage, 183*tab*, 184; labor force, 173*tab*; microenterprises, 89*tab*; permanency costs, 104; registration, 9*tab*, 91*tab*, 96, 97; social security, 180*tab*, 186, 190*tab*; taxpayer registry, 99*tab*
Guyana: health system, 179*tab*; social security, 180*tab*, 188*tab*

Haiti: health system, 179*tab*; labor force, 173*tab*; social security, 180*tab*, 186
Health inspections, 5, 95, 147, 149
Health services; 95; certificates, 147; coverage, 15; deficits, 15; national, 14, 169, 176, 178, 179*tab*, 181, 190, 194; permits, 149; preventive, 191; quality, 16. *See also* Social Security
Honduras: health system, 179*tab*; insurance coverage, 183*tab*, 184; labor force, 173*tab*; social security, 180*tab*, 186, 190*tab*
Hyperinflation, 28; Bolivian, 24

Illegality: advantages, 51–53; and alternative employment, 68; complexity, 58; criteria, 61; disadvantages, 53–54; generalized, 62, 66, 78; levels, 63; restricted, 6n, 62, 78; vs. informality, 4, 23–54

Imports: competition, 30; duties, 262; input, 267; liberalization, 269; vehicle, 219, 221, 235, 242

Income: ad hoc arrangements, 13; alternatives, 60; average, 7; decreasing, 4, 11; levels in taxi industry, 17; loss of, 19; minimum, 20, 52, 79; operating, 17; redistribution, 20; reduction, 30; relation to legality, 80; in retail trade, 36; underdeclaration, 7. *See also* Wages

Inflation, 114, 127, 130, 192, 267

Informality: characteristics, 57, 170–172; extent, 172–175; relation to regulatory barriers, 105; vs. illegality, 4, 23–54

Inspections: capacity for, 8, 52, 188, 197; health, 5, 95, 147, 149; registration, 8, 93; risk of, 124, 133, 154–155; safety, 95

Insurance: accident, 176; Bismarckian, 169, 186, 193, 202; health, 176; maternity, 176, 183*tab*, 190, 191, 197–198; mutual, 177; private, 170, 204; unemployment, 182; vehicle, 218, 221, 237, 238. *See also* Social Security

Interest rates, 17, 18

International Labour Office, 55, 169, 172, 176

International Symposium on Formal and Informal Security, 176

Intervention, government, 52, 55, 62; Bolivian, 28; diminishing, 18

Investment, capital, 66, 112, 120, 133

Jamaica: health system, 179*tab*, 199, 203; informal sector, 194–202; insurance coverage, 184, 185*tab*; occupational categories, 174*tab*; social security, 14, 15, 16, 180*tab*, 187, 188*tab*, 189, 194–202

Jeitinho (Brazil), 7, 109–136; definition, 137*n1*

Labor: contracts, 103, 138*n14*; costs, 3, 8, 12, 13, 49–51, 50*tab*, 51, 69, 70*tab*, 71*tab*, 72*tab*, 73*tab*, 75, 75*tab*, 80, 153*tab*, 160*tab*; division, 27, 57, 66, 152, 159–160, 164; free hiring, 26; law, 7; legality, 19; legislation, 65, 157*tab*; markets, 74; obligations, 69–77; organized, 105; protection laws, 8; registration, 96; regulations, 19, 63; relations, 13, 27, 47, 62; rights, 96; strikes, 115, 135; surplus, 4, 11, 13; unpaid, 70

Lagos, Ricardo, 87–106

Laws: evasion, 19; incentive, 12; labor, 7; promotional, 18, 19. *See also* Legislation

Legality: barriers, 8–12, 87–106; benefits, 154–155; in billing, 8; cost-lowering activities, 7; costs, 8–14, 9*tab*, 47–51, 62, 69, 74, 87–106, 141–165, 144*tab*, 156*tab*; criteria, 61; degrees, 63*tab*, 64*tab*, 72*tab*, 73*tab*, 75*tab*; effect on profits, 67*tab*, 67–68; entry, 88–102; generalized, 62, 65, 66, 78, 80; indirect costs, 142; labor, 19; labor requirements, 148; need for invoicing, 60, 72; operational, 5; partial, 8; permanency, 158*tab*; relation to economic independence, 68; relation to productivity, 76; relation to profits, 79–80; restricted, 6n, 7, 63, 66, 74, 78, 80; stages, 5; taxes in, 6

Legislation: commercial, 143*tab*, 149; compliance, 142; effect on taxi industry, 220–223, 260–266; inadequate, 4; labor, 65, 81, 157*tab*; microenterprise, 109–136; tax, 145–148, 149; transport services, 249

Liberalization: Bolivian, 29; import, 269; in taxi industry, 208, 249–250, 264, 265

Licenses: commercial, 145; industrial, 145; obtaining, 39; operating, 40*tab*, 44, 123; renewal, 149; tax on, 44; temporary, 90

Location, enterprise, 58–60, 89, 93–102, 94*tab*, 155, 159; activity concealment, 94; conformity of use,

146; local resident participation, 94; modification, 142
Looye, Johanna, 7, 109–136

Manufacturing: costs of legality, 10; employment trends, 25; home-production activities, 46; job creation, 24; registration, 36
Markets: access to, 4, 8, 13, 53; exposure to, 72; forces, 29; integration, 63; labor, 74; open entry, 11; taxi industry, 209–217, 249–260; unregulated, 3
Maternity: insurance, 176, 183*tab*, 190, 191, 197–198; leave, 118, 139*n18*
Mesa-Lago, Carmelo, 14, 169–205
Mexico: costs of legality, 87, 105; economic crisis, 73–74; government intervention, 62; health system, 179*tab*, 191; incomes, 171; informal sector, 55–82, 194–202; insurance coverage, 183*tab*, 184, 185*tab*; labor force, 173*tab*; legality status, 6*tab*; location regulations, 93, 94*tab*; microenterprises, 89*tab*; occupational categories, 174*tab*; permanency costs, 104; registration, 9*tab*, 91*tab*, 92, 93, 97; social security, 14, 15, 16, 180*tab*, 188*tab*, 190*tab*, 192, 194–202; Special Statute for the Promotion of Microenterprises, 96; taxpayer registry, 99*tab*
Microenterprises: benefits, 110, 128–129*tab*; commercial, 59*tab*, 89*tab*; definition, 82*n6*, 110; exemptions, 110–111; incentives, 110–111; industrial, 59*tab*; investment, 87; legalization, 142–165; legislation, 109–136; manufacturing, 89*tab*; obligations, 115–118; priorities, 61–62; qualifying for, 110, 137*n2*; registration, 109–136, 111*tab*, 128–129*tab*; relations with formal sector, 60; rights, 115–118; service, 59*tab*, 89*tab*; Venezuelan, 142–165
Mobility, 56

Nationalization, 29
Nicaragua: health system, 179*tab*, 182; insurance coverage, 183*tab*, 184; social security, 180*tab*, 190*tab*, 192

Panama: health system, 179*tab*; informal sector, 173; insurance coverage, 183*tab*, 184, 185*tab*; labor force, 173*tab*; occupational categories, 174*tab*; social security, 180*tab*, 186, 190*tab*
Paraguay: health system, 182; insurance coverage, 183*tab*, 184; labor force, 173*tab*; social security, 186, 190*tab*
Paternalism, 14
Pensions. *See* Social Security
Peru: costs of legality, 11; economically active population, 172; health system, 179*tab*, 182; incomes, 171; informal sector, 194–202; insurance coverage, 183*tab*, 184, 185*tab*; labor force, 173*tab*; occupational categories, 174*tab*; social security, 14, 15, 180*tab*, 186, 188*tab*, 190*tab*, 192, 194–202; street vendors, 197–198; taxi industry, 16–18, 247–275
Population, economically active: branch of activity, 25*tab*; informal, 172; insurance coverage, 183, 183*tab*; by job category, 26*tab*; by sector, 28*tab*
Premises, types, 64*tab*
Prices: fuel, 18, 216, 225, 228, 273–274; input, 242. *See also* Costs
Production: costs, 53, 172; decentralization, 3, 4, 8; diminished, 24; family units, 47; means of, 27; organization, 26–27, 47; reorganization, 3, 24; resources, 39, 53; scales, 72; structural change, 24; units, 19
Productivity: employee, 81; in illegal enterprises, 68; indicators, 76; informal enterprise, 76; levels, 57, 77*tab*; relation to legality, 76
Profitability: in family enterprise, 66; in illegal enterprises, 68; in taxi industry, 234
Profit margins, increasing, 3
Profits: calculation, 82*n11*; impact of taxes, 80; operating, 82*n11*; reduction of worker protection, 4;

tax, 149; taxi industry, 235–238, 255; volume, 67*tab*, 67–68
Protection: for informal sector, 169–205; reduction in favor of profit, 4, 105

Recession, 80, 81, 182, 267
Reform: agrarian, 177; tax, 11, 12, 31, 40–47, 95
Registration, 5; access to markets, 8; administrative requirements, 12*tab*; benefits, 38, 92, 127–132, 130; commercial, 36; compulsory, 36; costs, 8, 127–132; craft enterprises, 38*tab*; fiscal, 78; incentives, 90; initial, 89–93; inspection, 93; instantaneous, 136–137; labor, 96; mandatory, 90, 92; microenterprise, 109–136, 111*tab*; minimum, 62; noncompliance, 19, 38, 52, 64, 72, 81, 97, 148, 164; obligations, 115–118; tax, 89, 95–96; taxpayer, 6, 31, 33*tab*, 44
Registro Unico de Contribuyentes (Bolivia), 6
Regulation, 3, 4; compliance in taxi industry, 220–223; evasion, 64, 72; hiring, 19, 20; inadequate, 4, 11; inspection in, 8; labor, 8, 19, 63; necessity, 10–11; noncompliance, 3, 19, 52, 64, 72, 73, 81, 97, 145; taxi industry, 16–18, 216–223, 259–260
Reinvestment, 56, 65, 79
Resources: access to, 4, 13; availability, 4; limited, 8; production, 53
Revaluation, 208
Risk: entrepreneurial, 66; of inspection, 124, 133, 154–155; in partial registration, 8

Safety: inspections, 95; regulations, 145
St. Kitts & Nevis: health system, 179*tab*; social security, 180*tab*
St. Lucia: health system, 179*tab*; social security, 180*tab*
St. Vincent: health system, 179*tab*; social security, 180*tab*
Salary, family, 117, 138*n16*
Schkolnik, Mariana, 207–245
Sector, commercial: legality in, 75, 79, 142; legislation, 149; licensing, 145; need for registration, 64
Sector, industrial: illegality in, 63, 75–76, 79; legality in, 142; licensing, 145; registration in, 6
Sector, informal: barriers to legality, 87–106; competition in, 29; complexity, 58; definition, 4; in economic crises, 60; fiscal contribution, 6; "formalizing," 87; generation, 4; goods and services, 30; growth, 172; illegality, 55–82; markets in, 4; poverty in, 171; profit levels, 67–68; protection for, 169–205; regulatory barriers, 4, 8–12; social security, 14–16, 169–205, 186, 189, 194–202; wages, 170, 171; work process, 8
Sector, private: increase in employment, 28
Sector, public: decentralization, 28; employment reduction, 28; job creation, 24; restructuring, 28
Sector, semienterprise, 27, 28; registration 36–37. *See also* Microenterprises
Sector, service: employment trends, 25; invoicing, 60; legality in, 76, 79
Self-employment, 19; health benefits, 179*tab*; increase, 26; insurance coverage, 185*tab*; social security, 15, 180*tab*, 181, 188, 194, 195, 196, 198, 200
Sentaje (Bolivia), 39, 46*tab*, 46–47, 51, 53
Smuggling, 39
Social assistance, 175
Social protection, 169; informal, 175–177
Social security, 14–16, 70; access, 15, 19, 96, 171; alternatives, 199–202; compulsory, 181*tab*, 185*tab*, 195; contributions, 5, 13, 150, 172, 188; costs, 15, 49–51; coverage, 15, 169–205, 176; deficits, 15, 192; for domestic workers, 15, 170, 180*tab*, 194, 195, 196, 197, 200; employer contributions, 82*n11*, 103, 117, 186, 188; expenditures, 190*tab*; extension, 170, 182–185, 189–194; government contribution, 20;

insurance, 169; legal coverage, 177–182; minimum rates, 110; obstacles to extension, 189–191; quality, 15, 171–172, 186, 189, 197–198, 204; registration, 148; reserve accumulation, 192, 199; for self-employed, 15, 19, 188; statistical coverage, 182–185; taxi industry, 258–259; undercapitalization, 15–16; underdeclaration, 7; universal, 14; variables in coverage, 185–189; voluntary, 178, 181*tab*, 185*tab*, 194, 195
Social Security in Developing Countries Workshop, 177
Stability, employment, 4
Subsidies: elimination, 29, 30; new venture, 7
Suriname: health system, 179*tab*; social security, 180*tab*
Synchronization, in taxi industry, 17–18

Tariffs, 11; effect on taxi industry, 17, 269–270, 274; reduction, 219, 264
Tax(es), 5; annual, 116; capacity to absorb, 69–77; on cars, 44; daily, 39, 46–47, 51, 53; economic units, 50*tab*; evasion, 8, 52, 73, 81, 97; exemption, 110, 111; fuel, 220, 244; impact on profits, 80; import, 221, 262; income, 102, 103, 110, 118, 123, 138*n13*; legislation, 145–148, 149; municipal, 43–45, 146, 150; operating license, 39; profits, 78, 103, 149; property, 39, 43, 150, 263; reform, 11; services rendered, 113, 117; small-scale activity, 53; on transactions, 31; value-added, 13, 31, 78, 102, 103, 245
Taxi industry: Chilean, 16–18, 207–245; competition, 212–213; consumers, 259–260; costs, 209–210, 253–256, 256*tab*; economic policies, 219–220, 266–272; effect of economic changes, 223–234; effect of fuel prices, 268–269; effect of tariffs, 269–270; entry, 216–217, 223–234; exemptions, 262–266; external diseconomies, 17; fare regulation, 209, 216–217, 223–234, 241, 242, 256–258; insurance, 218, 221, 237, 238; market function, 209–216, 249–260; operational methods, 252; organized, 252; Peruvian, 16–18, 247–275; pirates, 220, 250, 264; profits, 235–238, 255; quality of service, 207; regulation, 243, 259–260; regulatory changes, 223–234; service quality, 238–239; social security, 258–259; trade unions, 221–222, 258; unorganized, 252–253; use of meters, 217, 218, 264, 265, 275*n3*; vehicle maintenance, 207, 218, 241; vehicle stock, 248*tab*, 249, 250–252; vehicle types, 214*tab*, 215, 223, 229, 230, 248; waiting time, 212, 213, 241; working conditions, 238, 258–259
Taxpayers, 41*tab*; rate of payment, 42*tab*; registry, 6, 31, 33*tab*; urban concentration, 41
Technology, changing, 4
Time, for registration. *See* Costs
Tokman, Víctor E., 3–20, 88
Trade: clandestine, 59; foreign, 26, 29; retail, 44
Transport services: bureaucratic planning, 248–249, 272; demand, 248; fare regulation, 249; legislation, 249
Trinidad & Tobago: health system, 179*tab*; social security, 180*tab*

Unemployment: benefits, 135, 176; Bolivian, 24; effect on taxi industry, 231–232, 234, 240, 244, 267, 270, 271; insurance, 182; open, 24, 29, 208
Unions, trade, 3, 120; lack of, 14; membership, 62; payments, 138*n14*; retail, 36; in taxi industry, 221–222, 258, 275
Units, economic, registration, 6
Uruguay: costs of legality, 87, 105; health system, 179*tab*, 182; informal sector, 173; inspection standards, 95; insurance coverage, 183*tab*, 184; labor force, 173*tab*; location regulations, 93, 94*tab*, 101*tab*; microenterprises, 89*tab*; occupational categories, 174*tab*; registration, 9*tab*, 91*tab*, 92, 93, 96, 97; social security, 180*tab*,

186, 188*tab*, 189, 190, 190*tab*, 192; taxpayer registry, 99*tab*

Venezuela: costs of legality, 87, 105, 141–165; health system, 179*tab*, 182; informal sector, 173; inspection standards, 95; insurance coverage, 183*tab*, 184; labor force, 173*tab*; location regulations, 93, 94*tab*, 101*tab*; microenterprises, 89*tab*; permanency costs, 104; registration, 9*tab*, 91*tab*, 92, 93, 96, 97; social security, 148, 180*tab*, 186, 189, 190*tab*; street vendors, 146; tax legislation, 145–148; taxpayer registry, 99*tab*; temporary licenses, 90

Wage(s): deterioration, 29; freeze, 26, 29; minimum, 19, 52, 82*n12*, 96, 123, 135, 150; real, 18; severance, 118; taxi industry, 255*tab*

Workers. *See* Employees

Work process: family units, 8, 14; organization, 13, 159–160

About the Book and the Editor

There has been much discussion in recent years about the legal and institutional obstacles for "formalizing" the informal economies of Latin American countries, and it has been strongly maintained that government intervention through extreme regulation and bureaucratic constraints imposes high financial costs on the activities of informal producers. The authors of this book contest conventional wisdom, arguing, on the basis of extensive research, that the costs imposed by the existing legal and regulatory framework are not nearly as great as often claimed.

Among the findings of the study are that there are semilegal (or semi-illegal) activities in both the formal and informal sectors; that time and financial costs to the informal sector vary widely among countries, with no clear relationship to the legal/regulatory context; and that, while it is true that certain costs are caused by inadequate or useless formalities or regulations, others are legitimate and essential.

Víctor E. Tokman is director of the Regional Employment Programme for Latin America and the Caribbean (PREALC) in Santiago, Chile.